Viking Empires

Viking Empires is a definitive new history of five hundred years of
Viking civilisation and the first study of the global implications
of the expansion, integration and re-orientation of the Viking
world. Offering an assessment of Scandinavian society before
the 790s, the book traces the political, military, cultural and
religious history of the Viking Age from Iceland to the Baltic
states. The authors show that it is not possible to understand
the history of the Norman Conquest, the successes of David I
of Scotland or the relationship between the Holy Roman
Empire and the papacy without considering the impact of the
history of Scandinavia. The book concludes with a new
account of the end of the Viking era, arguing that there was no
sudden decline but the gradual absorption of the Scandinavian
kingdoms into the project of the crusades and a refocusing of
imperial ambitions on the Baltic and eastern Europe.

ANGELO FORTE is Professor of Commercial Law at the
University of Aberdeen and a specialist in maritime law.

RICHARD ORAM is Senior Lecturer in Scottish Medieval
History and Environmental History at the University of
Stirling. He has published widely on aspects of Scottish
medieval history and archaeology.

FREDERIK PEDERSEN is Lecturer in History at the
University of Aberdeen. He is the author of *Marriage Disputes in
Medieval England* (2000).

Viking Empires

ANGELO FORTE,
RICHARD ORAM AND
FREDERIK PEDERSEN

CAMBRIDGE
UNIVERSITY PRESS

CAMBRIDGE UNIVERSITY PRESS
Cambridge, New York, Melbourne, Madrid, Cape Town, Singapore, São Paulo

CAMBRIDGE UNIVERSITY PRESS
The Edinburgh Building, Cambridge CB2 2RU, UK

Published in the United States of America by Cambridge University Press, New York

www.cambridge.org
Information on this title: www.cambridge.org/9780521829922

First published 2005

Printed in the United Kingdom at the University Press, Cambridge

Typeface Quadratt (Vendor) 11/14pt   *System* Advent 3B2 8.07 [PND]

A catalogue record for this book is available from the British Library

Library of Congress Cataloguing in Publication data

Forte, Angelo.
    Viking empires/Angelo Forte, Richard Oram, Frederik Pedersen.
      p. cm.
    Includes bibliographical references and index.
    ISBN 0-521-82992-5
      1. Vikings. 2. Civilization, Viking. 3. Europe – History – 476-1492. I. Oram, Richard D.
    II. Pedersen, Frederik. III. Title.

ISBN-13 978-0-521-82992-2 hardback
ISBN-10 0-521-82992-5 hardback

To our children: Alasdair, Lauren, Lucy, Nikolas Asger and Thomas Jakob.
And to Pía and Sarah for their inspiration and support.

Contents

Figures

Maps

Acknowledgements

We have received valuable assistance and inspiration from a number of people. Ole Crumlin-Pedersen answered many questions, and Anton Englert gave up an entire day to guide us around the Marine-Archaeological Centre and the town of Roskilde. Poul Heide skippered the crew of the *Helge Ask* and provided a memorable experience of sailing (and rowing!) a reconstruction Viking Age military ship in Roskilde Fjord. Kaare Johannesen, director of the museum *Vikingeborgen Trelleborg*, shared his knowledge of the latest archaeology of Trelleborg with us. We thank our students at the Universities of Aberdeen and Stirling for exploring with us some of the ideas expressed in the book. We would also like to thank the Scottish Society for Northern Studies for sponsoring a conference dedicated to the theme of this book, and the scholars present there, whose questions provided the stimulus for further refinement to our work. Syddansk Universitet provided the framework for an ERASMUS visit that allowed us to put our ideas to a Scandinavian audience in Odense. We would also like to thank Kurt Villads Jensen, Tore Nyberg and their students at Syddansk Universitet whose questions made us refine our ideas. Thanks are also due to Graham and Anna Ritchie for their enthusiasm, hospitality and generous assistance in securing illustrations. Captain Ian Giddings of the Nautical Institute, London, and Bent Larsen in Copenhagen discussed and shared their knowledge of navigation in northern waters with us. In Copenhagen we also had many discussions with Tove Rasmussen and Bodil Heiede Jensen concerning the role of Vikings in Scandinavian history. Among our colleagues we would like to thank Dr Jane Stevenson, University Reader at Aberdeen, who provided valuable feedback, particularly on aspects of Roman imperial history, and Dr David Ditchburn for his support and many discussions both of the subject of this book and its wider implications. Allan Macinnes, Burnett-Fletcher

Professor of History at the University of Aberdeen, first put us together to teach a course on 'Vikings, Gaels and Normans, c. 800–1200' which provided the impetus for this book. We also thank Dr Michael Wood of the Geography Department of the University of Aberdeen for discussing with us mental mapping and ocean voyaging, Professor Colm O'Boyle for his insight into Irish poetry and the Scandinavians, and W. D. H. Sellar, University of Edinburgh. Pia Dewar provided useful guidance on Gaelic orthography and cast a sceptical eye on the use of sagas as sources. Jenny Jochens and John W. Baldwin of Towson College and Johns Hopkins University, Baltimore, discussed the project with us and provided valuable inspiration during their stay in Aberdeen. Our thanks are also due to our colleagues in the College of Arts and Social Sciences at Aberdeen and the Department of History at the University of Stirling who indulged our passion for all things Viking. During the writing of this book no fewer than two hard disks failed us; thanks to Barbara McGillivray the lost work was retyped, and thanks to David Keith at DACOLL a previously dead hard disk spun into life for a last hurrah, which allowed us to recover the almost completed manuscript and waste only one day instead of a month. Michael Watson, our editor at Cambridge University Press, provided valuable feedback on early drafts, and his enthusiastic support has been a source of encouragement at all times. Thanks also to Concetta Allan, who drew the illustrations for Chapter 5. Finally, the authors wish to express their gratitude to Dr Sarah Pedersen, who read several drafts of the book. Without her editing skills, her knowledge of the outline history of the period and her penetrating questions the book would have taken even longer to complete.

CHAPTER 1

Viking raiders, Scandinavian kingdoms and the wider world

This book begins and ends with the Scandinavian kingdoms reacting to a Roman Empire. We take as our starting point the way in which the Roman defeat at Teutoburg in AD 9 encouraged the formation of states and royal dynasties in Scandinavia. We end with the manner in which these Scandinavian dynasties and states became the thirteenth-century champions of Christianity in northern Europe. The Scandinavian kingdoms thus effectively bypassed the Holy Roman Emperor and established a direct line of communication with the Roman papacy. This book is the first study in English to take the discussion of the origins of the Scandinavian states back to the first century AD. It combines the approach of the archaeologist with that of the documents-based historian. The latest archaeological studies of Scandinavia (most recently in connection with the construction of a pipe-line across Denmark, which effectively put an 800-kilometre test trench through the country) and recent technological advances (such as earth radar, which allows the identification of submerged defensive structures) have caused a revolution in our understanding of the early history of Scandinavia. The sudden appearance of Scandinavian raiders in the written sources can now be shown to be the logical extension of political, cultural and economic contacts established in the pre-Viking Age.

A key feature of this book is the historical narrative which it provides for the whole of the Scandinavian westward colonisation. This narrative forms a spine upon which the analytical and discursive sections of the book are built. Past studies have focussed on comparatively short time-spans, mainly the so-called First or Second Viking Ages, or on geographically discrete or specialist subject-oriented studies, such as Viking Orkney or

Viking Age art. Here, however, we offer a structured overview which traces the over-arching continuities in the histories of the Scandinavian diaspora and its impact on western mainland Europe, the British Isles and the other North Atlantic islands through thirteen centuries. This central narrative places the Viking Age firmly into its wider historical context and enables its origins, development and end to be viewed as part of a single process, freed from the artificial constraints of modern geographical or chronological parameters. No previous modern study has attempted such an ambitious chronological range.

The argument advanced is that Scandinavia saw an early centralisation of power around the first and second centuries AD which allowed its magnates to wage war at a level of intensity and sophistication previously unknown. They did this by employing Roman military technology and strategy (which some may have learned while serving as members of the Roman army). As a consequence, a professional class of warriors had developed by the third century. The third to the sixth centuries saw an increasing concentration of authority, which is demonstrated by the fortifications and arsenals found in connection with wars waged in this period. The emergent aristocracy of Scandinavia made and broke alliances from northern Norway to the Black Sea. The seventh and eighth centuries witnessed a simultaneous professionalisation of the military and a decreased military activity which is evidenced by the lack of social stratification in sixth- to ninth-century graves in Denmark. The relative peacefulness safeguarded by the successful fortification of southern Scandinavia, combined with the improvements in the design of ships, allowed the Scandinavians to re-focus their attention overseas and become what we now call 'Vikings'.

That period of European history traditionally called 'the Viking Age' (most generally taken to run from c. AD 800 to c. 1050) saw the formation of the outlines of the political map of the Europe with which we are now familiar. At the beginning of this period it is only possible to recover the names of kings and construct an outline history of Scandinavia. However, it is not possible to talk about Scandinavian kingdoms with well-defined borders until the Christianisation of the north around 950, which we have therefore taken to be a convenient breaking point in our narrative. When we resume the story of the Scandinavians and Europe we argue that although the new religion preached that it was the duty of every Christian to maintain the peace, the Danes and Norwegians still continued hostilities. These conflicts adversely affected the Scandinavian response to the conquest of England by William of Normandy and necessitated a restructuring of Scandinavian empire-building which saw them concentrate more on crusading in the Baltic. The integration of the Scandinavians into the wider community of Christendom and their enthusiastic embrace of the ideology of crusading and Christian reform made them less of a threat to their neighbours to the west and south-west, and these two factors mark the passing of the era of the Vikings.

The 'Vikings' are imbued with the romance of sea travel and land conquest. One can hardly find anyone in the northern hemisphere who has not heard of and does not admit to a degree of admiration for the exploits of the Vikings. The discovery and settlement of the North Atlantic archipelago launched from the Scandinavian homelands and bases abroad – itself a feat only made possible by a highly developed maritime technology far in advance of that found in other contemporary northern European societies – is one lasting consequence of the era of the Viking Empires. The stirring tales associated with their voyages and the dangers that they faced as they braved the waters of the North Atlantic have left an indelible mark on the European psyche. From the badges of British cars to the Germanic operas of Richard Wagner, from the Holywood epics of the 1950s to the personal history of Anya, the ex-vengeance demon in *Buffy the Vampire-Slayer*, the image of the Viking and his love of freedom, individualism and predisposition towards violence have become an integral part of Western consciousness and culture.

The term 'Viking' is of course problematical. The *Oxford English Dictionary* dates its first appearance in the English language to 1807 and its second appearance to 1827. It is not until the 1840s that it gains widespread currency.[1] This does not mean that the term cannot be found in contemporary sources. Indeed, it is used *before* the Viking Age, in the late seventh-century Old English poem *Widsið*, where it refers to a Germanic tribe, the 'Viking

[1] *Oxford Dictionary of English*, ed. C. Soanes, A. Stevenson, J. Pearsall and P. Hanks. Oxford: Oxford University Press, 2003. s.v. *Viking*.

kin *Heoþobeardan*'.[2] Tenth-century glosses on Ælfric's work also refer to 'pirata, uel piraticus, uel … wicing' and to 'archipirata: yldest wicing'.[3] Although the term is commonly found in Norwegian and Icelandic sources, and more rarely in Danish and Swedish writings, the phrase was evidently used throughout the Viking Empires, and it even survives in Frisian law codes regulating trade and maritime activity in the eleventh century. In this book we use the term in recognition of the fact that the word has such common currency. However, when we use the word it should be understood as referring to a Scandinavian who participated in the settlement – peaceful or violent – of northern Europe and the Atlantic Islands during the period outlined above. Throughout this book we do not lose sight of the fact that the sea-faring capability of the Scandinavians was transmitted to the peoples native to the areas where they settled. Thus they extended an invitation to those peoples and their descendants to participate in the North Atlantic adventure.

This book also considers the end of a 'Viking Age'. There are many dates given for this event: English historians put it around the time of the Norman Conquest in 1066, Danish historians prefer 1085, when King Canute IV assembled an invasion fleet of 'a thousand ships' off the coast of Jylland (Jutland). In Scotland, Scandinavian earls continued to rule the islands and some of the mainland for hundreds of years. They were driven from the mainland in the mid-twelfth century but remained in the Northern Isles for another 300 years. Scottish historians date its demise to the Battle of Largs in 1263 and the subsequent Treaty of Perth in 1266. Historians' accounts therefore have one thing in common: they focus on a single military event which is taken as the convenient breaking-off point for their narrative of the Scandinavian domination of northern Europe. This book puts forward the argument that there is no such conveniently dramatic end to the Viking Age. Instead, it is our contention that its end came about as a slow process of acculturation and integration of the Scandinavian kingdoms into the wider body politic of

---

[2] *Wícinga cynn*. A modern English translation of the entire poem can be found in S. A. J. Bradley, *Anglo-Saxon Poetry*. London: Dent, 1982 (http://www.wwnorton.com/nael/middleages/topic_4/widsith.htm).

[3] F. Hødnebo, Viking. In *Kulturhistorisk leksikon for nordisk middelalder*, ed. O. Olsen, P. Skautrup, N. Skyum-Nielsen and A. Steensberg. Copenhagen: Rosenkilde og Bagger, 1959–77.

European Christendom. The Christianisation of Scandinavia in the tenth century brought the area to the attention of the Western Church and the Holy Roman Empire. The Scandinavian kingdoms were subject to the archdiocese of Hamburg-Bremen from the time of the earliest missions in the early ninth century. Therefore, tenth- and eleventh-century Scandinavian kings traditionally regarded as Vikings, such as Svein Forkbeard and his son Canute, both kings of England and Denmark/Norway, were major players in European politics and clearly saw themselves as such. They were not aware of themselves as Scandinavians; nor did they seek to impose specifically Scandinavian customs or institutions on the peoples they conquered. Indeed, they used the reform of the national Scandinavian churches to assert their independence from their old enemy, the Holy Roman Empire. They did so by means of English appointments to ecclesiastical offices in Scandinavia in contravention of the privileges of the archdiocese of Hamburg-Bremen, which had become a major player in imperial politics.

From its inception it was the purpose of this book to trace the history of Viking expansion both in the east and in the west. With the recent fall of the Iron Curtain there is a need for a re-evaluation of Scandinavian influence across eastern Europe, in particular in terms of the Scandinavian contribution to the region's military, commercial and dynastic development. However, this in itself would require a monograph, and early on in our work we decided that the time was not yet right to embark upon such a venture. Consequently, this book is westward-looking in its orientation. We cover the impact of the Viking Empires in their Scandinavian homelands, Francia, Scotland, Ireland, England and the islands of the North Atlantic archipelago – the Northern and Western Isles of Scotland (Orkney, Shetland and the Hebrides), the Faroes, Iceland, Greenland – and Vinland.

It has been our intention throughout the book to demonstrate that what is commonly called 'the Viking Age' was a truly international phenomenon and that what happened in one area of Viking hegemony could and did influence events in other regions. For the early period up to the mid-tenth century this is a difficult task, owing to the scarcity of reliable sources. It is easier to do for the eleventh and twelfth centuries, which provide much more information both in terms of quantity and quality – from the information about Danish history supplied to Adam of Bremen by the Danish King Svein Estridsøn, through the diplomas of King Canute IV, to the papal letters of Alexander III and the political histories that can be recovered from the saints' lives of the period. However, this analysis must be done with circumspection. Despite the increased volume of evidence, the later period is not without its pitfalls. Indeed, the twelfth century saw the composition of two of the truly great pieces of medieval literature masquerading as history: the *Gesta Danorum* or the *Deeds of the Danes* by the Danish cleric Saxo Grammaticus, and *Heimskringla* by the Icelandic scholar Snorri Sturluson, both of which formed the basis of much of the early scholarship on Vikings, but whose value as historical reporting has now been thoroughly undermined.

CHAPTER 2

The beginnings

For two centuries after the great era of Germanic migration across the North Sea in the late fifth and sixth centuries the waters around Britain held few horrors for the inhabitants of those islands. The sea was regarded, it would seem, with varying degrees of neutrality or indifference by the Anglo-Saxons, whose sea-faring ambitions appear to have largely withered away as they settled down as farmers in southern and eastern England. Amongst the Celtic peoples in Ireland and what was to become Scotland, there was a vibrant maritime tradition, although their sea-faring skills were not matched by their ship-building technology. For the Irish, Picts and Scots, ship-building technique appears to have developed little beyond the level attained in the late prehistoric era. Likewise on the continent, in the Frankish Empire built up by Charlemagne, there was little interest in the seas to the north and west. To the Franks, this was a secure frontier, unlike their long and exposed land borders to the south with Muslim Spain and to the east with the Slavs. It was only traders, missionaries or pilgrims who came across the unpredictable waters. There was, then, no awareness that these same waters would soon become the means of delivery of a cataclysmic storm that would tear apart the fabric of northern European society.

The shape of things to come was expressed in two brief annals: the first dated generally to the reign of King Beorhtric of Wessex (789–802), which recorded an incident at Portland; and one for 793, which recorded an assault on the holiest sanctuary of Northumbria, located on an island that had seemed immune to attack throughout its history.

[789–802] In this year king Beorhtric married Eadburh, daughter of Offa. And in his days for the first time three ships came [to Portland in Dorset]: and then the reeve rode there and attempted to make them go to the royal manor, since he did not know what they were, and they killed him. These were the first Danish ships to come to England.

[793] In this year terrible portents appeared over Northumbria, and miserably frightened the inhabitants: these were exceptional flashes of lightning, and fiery dragons were seen flying in the air. A great famine soon followed these signs; and a little after that in the same year in January the harrying of the heathen miserably destroyed God's church in Lindisfarne by rapine and slaughter.[1]

The killing of the West Saxon royal reeve, Beaduheard, who mistook a force of Danish raiders for merchants and attempted to make them go to nearby Dorchester to present themselves for inspection, is almost certainly not the first instance of a Viking raid on the British mainland. Recorded only in the late ninth century in the Anglo-Saxon Chronicle, it is an account that needs to be treated with some care, for the chronicle is a highly propagandistic work and there may be a strong element of 'spin'. Quite simply, it may have been inserted in that place to emphasise the idea that Wessex was, and always had been, both first victim and principal defender of the Anglo-Saxons against the heathen onslaught. We are, however, on surer ground with the second annal, which records a raid by a war-band from Hordaland in western Norway. It is a powerful record and one that still resonates after twelve hundred years.

The attack on Lindisfarne, the spiritual and intellectual heart of Northumbria, was a truly shocking event for the English at home and abroad. Founded in 634 by St Aidan, it was the centre from which the conversion of the pagan Angles of Northumbria had been achieved in the seventh century. Under the patronage of the kings of Northumbria it had grown rich, making it an attractive target. Later Durham tradition expands on the laconic words of the Anglo-Saxon Chronicle, telling how the raiders failed to find the jewelled shrine of St Cuthbert and the community's most valuable treasures, but describing how the buildings were plundered and burned, altars desecrated and some lesser relics destroyed. Some of the monks were killed, but, establishing a trend that was to become common in the future, others were carried off as slaves or as captives for ransoming. The incident sent a shockwave through Christian Europe. The Northumbrian scholar Alcuin, who lived in Aachen at the court of the Frankish ruler, Charlemagne, embarked on a veritable campaign of moral support for the English from 793

---

[1] *The Anglo-Saxon Chronicles*, ed. and trans. M. J. Swanton. London: Phoenix, 2000.

to 797: he sent letters of consolation to Lindisfarne, Wearmouth and Jarrow, and exhortations to bear the devastation of the Norse as a punishment from God to the archbishops of Canterbury and York, to the Kings Æðelred of Northumbria and Offa of Mercia, and to the people of Kent. He saw the failure of God or the saints of Northumbria to protect the region as a sign of divine displeasure at the sins of the people, and urged penitence and spiritual reform:

The pagans have contaminated God's shrines and spilt the blood of saints in the passage around the altar, they have laid waste the house of our consolation and in the temple of God they have trampled underfoot the bodies of the saints like shit in the street.[2]

And in another letter from the same year, this time to King Æðelred, he interpreted the attack as a punishment from God:

Behold the almost 350 years that we and our ancestors were inhabitants of this fair land, and never before has such a dreadful deed come to pass in Britannia as the one we now have been exposed to in the hands of a pagan people, nor was it thought possible that such a voyage could be made...Can it not be thought that these punishments of blood came upon the people from Northern lands?[3]

However, although it has grabbed the attention of generations of historians, the attack on Lindisfarne was not the first example of a Viking raid (Figure 1). The Vikings did not just appear out of thin air: they had a history of raiding before their appearance in their fearsome ships off the coast of northern Britain in 793.[4] This is hinted at by a charter of 792 in which – 'at the insistence of Æðelheard, the archbishop of Canterbury, in the thirty-fifth year of his reign (792)'– King Offa of Mercia confirmed the privileges of the churches of Kent at the synod of Clovesho. As they had been under previous kings, the churches and their tenants were to be

[2] Pagani contaminaverunt sanctuaria Dei et fuderunt sanguinem sanctorum in circuitu altaris, vastaverunt domum spei nostri, calcaverunt corpora sanctorum in templo Dei quasi sterquilinium in platea. J.-P. Migne, *Patrologiae Cursus Completus Series Latina*. Vol. CL, *Opera Alcuini*. Paris: Garnier, 1844–1905. p. 9.

[3] Ecce trecentis et quinquaginta ferme annis, quod nos nostrique patres huius pulcherrime patrie incole fuimus, et numquam talis terror prius apparuit in Britannia, veluti modo a pagana gente perpessi sumus, nec eiusmodi navigium fieri posse putabatur...Nonne potest putari a borealibus poenas sanguinis venire super populum? (The 'punishments of blood' may be a reference to Isaiah 26:21.) C. Christensen and H. Nielsen, eds. *Diplomatarium danicum*, 1. Række, Vol. I, *Diplomatarium danicum: Regester 789–1052*, Det danske sprog og litteraturselskab. Copenhagen: C. A. Reitzels Forlag, 1975. p. 4. Extracts from the other letters mentioned above are printed in ibid., pp. 1–6.

[4] A. Johannson, Die erste Westrwiking. *Acta Philologica Scandinavica*, 1934, pp. 1–67; G. Ward, The Vikings came to Thanet. *Archaeologiæ Cantiana*, 1950, pp. 57–62.

Figure 1
Lindisfarne
Priory,
Northumberland.
Ruins of the
twelfth-century
priory on the site
of St Cuthbert's
monastery, first
plundered by
Viking raiders in
793.

exempt from royal levies except in the case of providing military support against 'marauding heathens in roving ships'.[5] The wording of Offa's privilege makes it clear that Kent had been the target of attacks for generations before 792. The record of the privileges mentions that Offa was confirming privileges already given by Kings Æðelbald (716–57) and þyhtred (possibly a mistransliteration for Cenred (709–16)).[6] Therefore, this chapter explains who the Vikings were and what we know about how the society that spawned the Viking Age in Scandinavia developed.

[5] Christensen and Nielsen, *Diplomatarium danicum*, p. 1.
[6] W. d. G. Birch, ed. *Cartularium Saxonicum: A Collection of Charters Relating to Anglo-Saxon History*. Vol. I, A.D. 430–839. London: Whiting & Company, 1885. pp. ix–x.

The land

The raiders who attacked the British Isles and France in the eighth century came from what are now three countries in Scandinavia: Denmark, Norway and Sweden. The sixth-century historian Jordanes, who wrote a *Historia Getica* around 551 (and who seems to have been well informed about contemporary Scandinavian political geography), gave the names of twenty-nine Scandinavian tribes, each of which had their own homeland. Although one must be wary of the exact number of tribes listed in his *Historia* (the number twenty-nine corresponds to the number of Roman legions throughout the Empire), the Scandinavian political landscape was clearly much more complex and diverse than that of today.[7] Borders were different and alliances between petty kings and chieftains were formed and broken, waves of armies marched through the Scandinavian homelands and sailed over the Baltic Sea, conquering and being conquered. However, for the purposes of description for a modern reader it makes sense to use the modern names for the Scandinavian countries (see Map 1).

The northernmost of the three Scandinavian countries is Norway. Norway is an extremely mountainous land, nearly one-third of which lies north of the Arctic Circle. The country has a very long coastline intersected by fjords, which, in proportion to its area, is longer than the coastline of any other major country in the world. The relatively warm waters of an extension of the Gulf Stream flow along the Atlantic coast of Norway, where they have a pronounced effect on the climate. A maritime climate prevails over most of the coastal islands and lowlands. Winters, then as now, were mild and summers were normally cool. The country rises into mountains almost at once and, though well suited for pasture, the inner highland is not suited for cereal-based agriculture. However, the country is rich in fish, fur-bearing animals and minerals, and we must conclude that the Norwegians did not suffer hardship. Like the other Scandinavian countries Norway could clearly support a military

---

[7] *Iordanis Romana et Getica*, ed. T. Mommsen. Gesellschaft für Ältere Deutsche Geschichtskunde. Berlin: Weidmann, 1882. English translation in *The Gothic History of Jordanes in English Version*, trans. C. C. Mierow. Cambridge and New York: Barnes & Noble, 1960.

Map 1
Scandinavia.

class that was able to extract enough surplus from the land to invest in sophisticated arms, maintain central armories, train large armies and develop a sophisticated hierarchical society as early as the third century AD.[8]

---

[8] J. Ilkjær, Fjender og forbundsfæller i romertidens Nordeuropa. In *Fiender og forbundsfeller: regional kontakt gjennom historien*, Karmøyseminaret, 1999 (http:// www.illerup.dk/documents/illerup_78.pdf); J. Ilkjær and C. v. Carnap-Bornheim, Import af romersk militærudstyr til Norge i yngre romertid. In *I et hus med mange rum: Vennebok til Bjørn Myhre på 60-årsdagen*, ed. I. Fuglestvedt, T. Gansum and A. Opedal, Bind A, AmSrapport 11A, 2001 (http://www.illerup.dk/documents/ illerup_80.pdf). See the analysis of the Illerup Ådal finds, below, pp. 32–39.

Present-day Sweden is varied in its physical features. Like Norway, the northern part of the country reaches up to the Arctic Circle, while the southern part includes the central Dalar region and the former Danish possessions of Skåne, Halland and Blekinge. Sweden and Norway were covered mostly with pine forests, in contrast to Denmark, which had large woodlands dominated by beech. The Swedish climate is comparatively moderate, considering that Sweden is located so far north. The main moderating influences are again the Gulf Stream and the prevailing westerly winds which blow in from the relatively warm North Atlantic. In winter the influence of the warm waters is offset by cold air that sweeps in from Siberia. The climate of present-day northern Sweden is considerably more severe than that of the southern counties of Skåne, Halland and Blekinge (which during the later Viking Age were all part of the Danish kingdom) because it has higher altitudes and because the mountains cut off the moderating influence of the sea. In the north-west section are extensions of the Kjølen Mountains, which form part of the boundary with Norway. To the east of the mountains is a long plateau which slopes east to a coastal plain bordering the Gulf of Bothnia. Within the mountains of northern Sweden lie the sources of many rivers that flow south-east to the Gulf of Bothnia. These rivers often have elongated lakes and a number of falls and rapids, which may explain why Swedish Vikings mainly sought their fortune taking the overland route to Russia and Byzantium in the east, while the Norwegians and the Danes turned towards the British Isles, Ireland and the Atlantic archipelago to the west. South-central Sweden is made up of low-lying land with many lakes, including the largest lakes in the country, Lake Vänern and Lake Vättern. An upland region known as Småland is located south of the lowland. The plains of Skåne occupy the south-east tip of the Scandinavian peninsula and have traditionally provided the population with much high-quality agricultural land.

Sweden and Norway are separated from the continent by the North Sea and the Baltic, but southern Scandinavia, particularly the present-day country of Denmark (including Skåne, Halland and Blekinge), has always been the region's buffer against the continent. The country consists of the Jylland (Jutland) peninsula, which shares a small border with the continent, and hundreds of islands within easy reach of each other. The surface of the Danish mainland is generally low; the average elevation is about 30 metres above sea-level, and today the highest points in the country are the man-made pylons of the bridge between the islands of Sjælland (Zealand) and Fyn. The parts of the country that were not farmed were covered with beech forests and bogs. However, the Roman Iron Age saw a marked increase in the proportion of the country that was under the plough. This sustained extensive farming, particularly during the late Viking Age c. 900–1100, when (pollen analyses confirm) the country saw a substantial expansion of cultivated land. The chronicler Adam of Bremen, writing in the eleventh century, went so far as to say that the areas of Sjælland, Skåne, Halland and Blekinge were the most fertile agricultural regions in northern Europe.[9] Furthermore, the south-west part of the peninsula of Jylland contained large surface deposits of iron ore which could be smelted into good weapons and tools with relative ease using technology available as early as the second century AD. Jylland also benefited from extensive forests – a major advantage, as the smelting of bog iron required large quantities of fuel.

The earliest written and archaeological sources

The Viking raids on Portland and Lindisfarne reported by the Anglo-Saxon Chronicle and by Alcuin heralded the beginning of a long period of Scandinavian dominance in northern Europe. Over a period of some two hundred and fifty years the Scandinavians were in the ascendancy. These successes were followed by a period of slow integration into the larger European community of Christians. But although nineteenth- and twentieth-century writers have tended to regard the 'Viking Age' as a distinct period of history, it is arguable that the Viking raids were only the culmination of a much longer period of empire-building among the Germanic tribes that inhabited the Scandinavian peninsula, a process that found its beginnings at the start of the first millennium in what is now known as the Roman Iron Age. The

---

[9] Adamus Bremensis, *History of the Archbishops of Hamburg-Bremen*, trans. F. J. Tschan. Records of Civilization: Sources and Studies. New York: Columbia University Press, 1959.

beginning of this process was the re-alignment of military strategy that took place in the Roman Empire as a consequence of the Battle of Teutoburg Forest in AD 9.

There are few written sources that deal specifically with Scandinavia before this battle, and only a few authors throw light on developments in the area. Most of what has been preserved shows Scandinavia to be a source of fantastic stories for the inhabitants of the classical world, and can be dealt with quickly. The earliest narrative we have about Scandinavia was written by the late fourth-century BC Greek writer Pytheas from the Roman colony of Massilia (Marseilles).[10] He described a journey to a land of astonishing natural phenomena: the midnight sun, the late sunsets, frozen seas, tidal waters, and amber lying freely available on the beaches. His fantastic travellers' tales would hardly have convinced a sophisticated Roman audience (although later generations might have been familiar with Pliny's story of a Roman trading expedition to the north which was mounted to purchase amber for the decoration of a theatre in Rome), and Scandinavia was so far from the Roman Empire that it hardly mattered to them anyway.

The next Mediterranean observer of Scandinavia wrote around the time of the birth of Christ. In AD 5 the Emperor Augustus equipped a fleet under the command of his foster son, Tiberius, that set out from the Rhine. The emperor included this expedition in his autobiography, which was inscribed in bronze columns surrounding his tomb in Rome. This mausoleum is now lost, but his words are preserved in a copy inscription in Ankara in present-day Turkey, known as the *Monumentum Ancyranum*:

I extended the borders of all the provinces of the Roman citizens at whose borders were peoples who did not obey our command. I restored peace to the provinces of Gaul and Spain, likewise Germany, which includes the ocean from Cadiz to the mouth of the river Elbe. From the region which lies near the Adriatic Sea to Tuscany, I made the Alps be peaceful. I brought no unjust war against any nation. My fleet sailed on the ocean from the mouth of the Rhine to the region of the rising sun up to the borders of the Cimbri, where no Roman had gone before that time by land or sea.

Approximately a century earlier, the Cimbrians, a tribe from Jylland, had threatened the very existence of the Roman Empire,

---

[10] Pytheas, *Pytheas of Massilia on the Ocean*, trans. C. H. Roseman. Chicago: Ares, 1994.

and Augustus may have wanted to ascertain the military resistance he was likely to encounter to his plan to extend the Roman border from the Rhine to the Elbe. He indicates as much in the *Monumentum Ancyranum*:

And through their envoys, the Cimbri and the Charudes and the Semnones and the other Germanic peoples of the same territory sought the friendship of me and of the Roman people.[11]

Tacitus, writing his *Germania* some three generations later in about AD 98, confirmed the massive impact the Cimbrians had on the Roman collective memory:

Now they are just a small tribe, but great in renown. Many are the traces of their ancient fame, large camps on both sides of the river [Rhine] bear witness to the size of their migration.[12]

To Tacitus, and to the average educated Roman, the world was a system of concentric rings: at its centre was the apex of civilisation, Rome. At its northern borders were the now battle-weary Celts who had been severely weakened by their encounter with the superior Roman culture, and at the very ends of the earth were the barbarian Germanic tribes. The northern peoples' social institutions were also seen to be of decreasing complexity: the nearest Celts and barbarians were farmers who lived off the land. Next to them lived the nomadic tribes of the Germans, and beyond them, even further from Rome, were the hunter-gatherers of the far north. Tacitus described contemporary Germanic peoples whose social and military organisations were (to his mind) just and efficient, but he related their history from the comfortable position of a Roman aristocrat who was simultaneously

---

[11] Omnium provinciarum populi Romani, quibus finitimae fuerunt gentes quae non parerent imperio nostro, fines auxi. Gallias et Hispanias provincias, item Germaniam qua includit Oceanus a Gadibus ad ostium Albis fluminis pacavi. Alpes a regione ea, quae proxima est Hadriano mari, ad Tuscum pacari feci. Nulli genti bello per iniuriam inlato. Classis mea per Oceanum ab ostio Rheni ad solis orientis regionem usque ad fines Cimbrorum navigavit, quo neque terra neque mari quisquam Romanus ante id tempus adit, Cimbrique et Charydes et Semnones et eiusdem tractus alli Germanorum populi per legatos amicitiam meam et populi Romani petierunt. Augustus Res gestae divi Augusti. Ankara (Online) (http://www.csun.edu/~hcfll004/resgest.html), paragraph 26.

[12] . . . parva nunc civitas, sed gloria ingens. Veterisque famae lata vestigia manent, utraque ripa castra ac spatia, quorum ambitu nunc quoque metiaris molem manusque gentis et tam magni exitus fidem. *Die 'Germania' des Tacitus*, 3rd ed., ed. W. Lange, in collaboration with H. Jankuhn, paragraph 37 (Original work ed. and trans. R. Much (1937) (1967); Tacitus, *Germania*, ed. and trans. N. W. Bruun and A. A. Lund. Vols. I–II. Århus: Wormanium, 1974.

certain of the manifest destiny of the Roman Empire and upset at contemporary developments in Roman society. It is unlikely that he actually went far enough north to meet the Scandinavians face to face, and his descriptions of their mores and institutions were more part of an on-going political polemic about Rome than a reliable ethnographic report.[13] We must therefore be critical of his and other Romans' descriptions of the Germanic tribes and of their democratic societies. Although the Roman written sources peter out after the time of Tacitus, ample archaeological evidence confirms that not only did the Romans continue to trade with Scandinavian chieftains, but that the area was of crucial importance for imperial attempts to control the barbarians threatening the Roman Empire.[14] The Roman interest in Scandinavia was due to one cataclysmic event in Roman history: the destruction of three of the twenty-nine legions of the Roman army – the 17th, 18th and 19th – under the leadership of Publius Quinctilius Varus, in the Battle of Teutoburg Forest in AD 9.

Publius Quinctilius Varus had been the Roman governor of Judea and had put down a large popular rising there four years earlier, in AD 5. Varus might have been successful in Palestine, but he was unprepared for the guerrilla tactics of the tribes he faced on the northern border of the Empire, and his army was annihilated in the Battle of Teutoburg Forest. The defeat was so complete that it took another six years before the Roman commander Germanicus penetrated far enough into Germanic territory to bury the dead and raise a mound in their honour.[15] Tacitus' description of what they found is still powerful today and evokes the shock and horror of Germanicus' men:

In the middle of the field lay the whitening bones of men, as they had fled or stood their ground, strewn everywhere or piled in heaps. Nearby lay fragments of weapons and limbs of horses, as well as human heads,

[13] L. Hedeager, *Danmarkshistorien*. Vol. II, *Danernes land: fra ca. 200 f.kr. til ca. 700 e.kr.*, 2. ed., exec. ed. O. Olsen. Copenhagen: Gyldendal & Politiken, 2002 [1988]. p. 20; Lange, *Die 'Germania'*.

[14] P. Ørsted, *Danmark før Danmark: Romerne og os*. Copenhagen: Samleren, 1999; L. Hedeager and H. Tvarnø, *Tusen års europahistorie: Romere, germanere og nordboere*. Oslo: Pax, 2001.

[15] A. J. Church and W. J. Brodribb, trans. *The Annals*. London: W. Heinemann, 1925 (http://classics.mit.edu//Tacitus/annals.html); B. B. Rasmussen, The soldiers of the Roman Empire and the Roman army. In *The Spoils of Victory: The North in the Shadow of the Roman Empire*, ed. L. B. Jørgensen, B. Storgaard and L. G. Thomsen. Copenhagen: Nationalmuseet, 2003. p. 149.

prominently nailed to the trunks of trees. In the adjacent groves were the barbarous altars on which they had immolated tribunes and first-rank centurions. Some survivors of the disaster, who had escaped from the battle or from captivity, described how this was was the spot where the officers fell, how yonder the eagles were captured, where Varus was pierced by his first wound, where too by the stroke of his own ill-starred hand he found for himself death. They pointed out too the raised ground from which Arminius had harangued his army, the number of gibbets for the captives, the pits for the living, and how in his exultation he insulted the standards and eagles.[16]

Out of respect, the three legions were never reconstituted. The crushing defeat at Teutoburg forced subsequent Roman emperors to focus their efforts on keeping the Germanic tribes on the borders of the Empire under control. They did so by encouraging alliances with tribes, kings and chieftains in the lands beyond those of the Germanic tribes on the Roman border. Thus, the Scandinavians – the southern Scandinavians in particular – began to play a larger role in Roman politics and received diplomatic gifts and special Roman attention.

Trade links between the Empire and Scandinavia had existed for a long time. Less exalted Roman goods had been coming into Scandinavia for centuries. Roman pottery, glass beads, jewellery and – as time went by – Roman weapons were exchanged for Scandinavian luxury goods such as amber and fur. It is also likely that many Scandinavians, in particular Danes and Norwegians, served in the imperial Roman army, where they would have learned Roman military tactics and military craft.[17] Certainly, as we shall see, as early as the third century the Scandinavian peoples could not only muster and transport large armies of more than a thousand men over sea and land to fight pitched battles against each other, but they also bought military hardware from the Romans which was used in such internal Scandinavian warfare.[18]

The paucity of written sources means that the history of Scandinavia in the Iron Age must be written mainly without

[16] Church and Brodribb, *Annals*.
[17] B. Storgaard, Cosmopolitan aristocrats. In *Spoils of Victory*, see note 15 above, pp. 106–25; L. Hedeager, Vol. II, pp. 140–45.
[18] See below, pp. 36–37.

such help, and for the most part without being able to put names or even dates to events. We have to make do with placing events in their centuries and analysing artifacts to show the ebb and flow of cultural and dynastic interests. We also need to rely on the haphazard discovery of Iron Age sites, a technique that does not guarantee that we have found everything relevant to enable us to flesh out our narrative of the history of Scandinavia. However, the archaeology of the Iron Age *does* supply us with a fascinating and crucial outline of what Scandinavian society was like. The implication of the archaeological evidence is that although Scandinavia produced no written records and was too far from the Roman Empire to merit the serious attention of its writers, its peoples served an important role in outflanking Rome's Germanic enemies. After the fall of the Roman Empire in the late fifth century, and as far as the end of the Iron Age in the eighth century, the Scandinavians metamorphosed into sometimes the enemy, sometimes the ally, of the great successors to the Roman Empire, the Merovingians and the Carolingians.

The people

The Romans recognised several tribes that inhabited Scandinavia during the Roman Iron Age. The eastern half of the Scandinavian peninsula was said to be inhabited by two tribes of the Germanic peoples, and in the second century AD Ptolemy described several other tribes in southern Scandinavia: the Finnoi and Goutai in what he called Scandia (present-day Skåne, Halland and Blekinge), the Kimbroi and Charudes on the Cimbrian peninsula (present-day Jylland), and the Teutones in the southern part of the Baltic. Tacitus tells us that these tribes, although united in religious beliefs, were generally at war with each other. Early chroniclers, such as Jordanes (writing in the sixth century), add another tribe to the ethnic mix in the area: the Heruli, a warlike Teutonic tribe expelled from Scandinavia before the middle of the third century but returning again in the sixth century after two hundred years of roaming Europe. Around AD 260 the Heruli were allies of the Goths in their marauding expeditions around the coasts of the Black and Aegean Seas, but their luck and drive seem to have died out in the succeeding centuries. In the sixth century Procopius describes how the army of the Heruli King Rodulph was vanquished by the Lombards. Some of these warriors then returned to their Scandinavian homelands.[19] The archaeological record partly substantiates this story by showing clear indications of new burial customs in sixth-century Denmark. However, while we have little evidence of how such tribes lived, such a brief outline of the early history of the area can be fleshed out by an analysis of a selection of archaeological sites from southern Scandinavia.

The Iron Age chieftains of the Scandinavian tribes were professional warriors, but they could dedicate themselves to the art of war only because their wealth was based on the high productivity of their land. The Scandinavians seem to have re-organised agriculture to produce a surplus for the Roman market rather than just grow their crops for subsistence. The social differentiation that is necessary for a high agricultural yield is reflected in the differentiation of the houses that have left an archaeological record. Many different sizes of houses, workshops and byres have been excavated. These indicate more than differences in the size of the household stock of animals around the first and second centuries AD: they also indicate a change in the structure of animal husbandry, in particular in the efficiency with which manure was collected, and the intensity of labour and the size of the labour force on the farms. For the intensive gathering of manure indicated by the practice of keeping animals indoors and operating an in-field and out-field system of agriculture, you need more labourers on the farm to produce the same amount of cereal. On the other hand, the more intensive collection of manure that is part of keeping milk cattle indoors meant that cereal and hay productivity increased. Villages also grew in size and developed increasingly specialised buildings, while individual farms were fenced in to signify individual ownership. The small Roman Iron Age fields surrounded by low dykes all disappeared and vegetation patterns changed: in some areas forests

[19] R. Wenskus, *Stammesbildung und Verfassung*. Cologne: Böhlau, 1961; K. Hald, Daner. In *Kulturhistorisk leksikon for nordisk middelalder*, ed. O. Olsen, P. Skautrup, N. Skyum-Nielsen and A. Steensberg. Copenhagen: Rosenkilde og Bagger, 1959–77.

became more extensive, in others moors and open land became more dominant.

A colder and more hostile environment also led to new methods of cultivation. The pollen evidence shows how the increasingly poor soils of Scandinavia began to support different vegetation and how the dominant forests in Denmark changed from oak to beech forest combined with a spread of bogs and moors.[20] Such a change called for a re-organisation of the way crops were cultivated, and these changes took place in the first and second centuries AD. The re-organisation of production from one based around smallholdings, either in individual settlements or in small enclosed villages with limited fields and livestock holdings, to production based around a stratified village settlement is apparent in such villages as Vorbasse in Jylland.[21] This village was excavated between 1974 and 1987, and the results of the excavation were later confirmed by other excavations in Nørre Snede and Stavad. The Vorbasse excavations cover an area of around 2.6 square kilometres and document more than 1,200 years of habitation.[22] The earliest settlement of the area, dating from around the birth of Christ, was one of three separate settlements consisting of nine long houses and seven smaller buildings. The nature of the buildings, but not the settlement as such, was transient. All the houses appear to have been moved and rebuilt at intervals of about one hundred years. Around AD 200–400 the houses developed in size and complexity. The floor areas became larger and the side walls thicker, and the houses increased in length from 20 to 30 metres. The roof constructions were changed to take account of the heavier roofs that were a consequence of the larger floor areas. The interior layout also changed to take account of the larger floor

[20] J. Iversen, The development of Denmark's nature since the last glacial. In *Danmarks geologiske undersøgelse, V. Række*, No. 7-C, 1973; K. Randsborg, *The Viking Age in Denmark: The Formation of a State*, New York: St Martin's Press, 1980. p. 51.

[21] Storgaard, Cosmopolitan aristocrats. In *Spoils of Victory*, see note 15 above, pp. 108–9.

[22] Hedeager, *Danmarkshistorien*, Vol. II, pp. 186–89.; S. Hvass, Vorbasse. The Viking-Age settlement at Vorbasse, central Jutland. *Acta Archaeologica*, Vol. 50 (for 1979), 1980, pp. 137–72; S. Hvass, Årtusinders landsby. *Skalk*, 3, 1984, pp. 20–30; S. Hvass, Vorbasse. The development of a settlement through the first millennium A.D. *Journal of Danish Archaeology*, 2, 1992, pp. 137–72. The excavation reports are published on the Internet in Danish with an English summary by the Danish Kulturarvsstyrelse: S. Hvass, Vorbasse, 190604–295. Kulturarvsstyrelsen (Website), 2003 (http://udgravningsarkiver.ancher.kulturhotel.dk/vorbasse.htm); S. Hvass, Vorbasse, 190604–295. Digitale udgravningsarkiver, 2003.

space: the older houses were divided into two sections, one for cattle and one for human inhabitants, while the new houses further subdivided the human habitation into three or more rooms in the western end of each house. The eastern part of the houses was used to accommodate between twenty and thirty cattle. The younger settlement also saw the development of a new kind of house type: a partially submerged hut with a pitched roof supported by posts in the middle of the gable, which was used for storage or as a workshop (one such hut was definitely used as a smithy). The village houses in both settlement types were surrounded by fences, whereas one large fence had encircled the original village. The fact that by the fourth century the village had lost its communal area shows that the villagers began to conceive of their land as belonging to them individually. This increased stratification was partly a function of the introduction of livestock: the herding of cattle and the collection of manure was menial work, which was performed by serfs or slaves.

The new village at Vorbasse had one, very large farmstead: it encircled a square of almost 4,000 square metres and incorporated one large dwelling-house 45 metres in length and three smaller sheds. The new, larger, individual spaces also differentiated between the types of gate they employed: all of them had two gates, but one was narrow and thus designed for people, while the other was broad and allowed the entry of carts, which had obviously become common around this time, presumably for the transport of manure from the outfields.[23] Finally, the layout of the village had changed: whereas it used to be laid out around a central square and was enclosed by one large fence, the village now consisted of farms that were individually enclosed, indicating that they were run independently of each other.

The pattern that thus emerges is one of a transition to a more efficient mode of agricultural production. The later Vorbasse village is consistent with a change from an extensive, moderate-yield system of farming that required extended periods for the fields to lie fallow, to a system of intensive farming based on a mixed yield from animal husbandry and cereal production, with an infield/outfield system where cereals were grown on the infields while animals grazed on the outfields. The manure was

[23] Hvass, Årtusinders landsby, pp. 22–24.

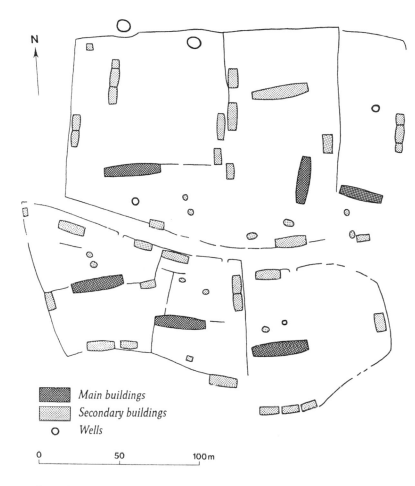

N

Figure 2 Plan of Vorbasse village (Jylland, Denmark) c. 900. The six fenced farms with gates opening onto a central track or street indicate that the village was organised into individual farm holdings. The fences were a new development of the sixth or seventh century.

Main buildings
Secondary buildings
○ Wells

0   50   100 m

gathered to act as fertiliser and transported to the infields on carts.[24] The differences in house size demonstrate that the villages saw an increased social stratification and that a rural lower class, consisting of landless farm workers, was in the making (Figure 2).

EARLY MAGNATES

The Emperor Augustus' boast to have equipped a fleet to sail north and east of the borders of the Roman Empire in AD 5 is the first indication that the rest of the civilised world was developing an interest in Scandinavia. It may have been the increased concentration of wealth that is evident in the changing settlement patterns that made southern Scandinavia in particular so interesting to the

---

[24] Storgaard, Cosmopolitan aristocrats. In *Spoils of Victory*, see note 15 above, p. 109.

Romans, since the period from around the birth of Christ to the sixth century saw the Scandinavians play an increasing role in the political development of Europe. This is seen particularly in the development of dynasties of rulers in the region. We do not know the names of the rulers, as they do not appear in the written Roman sources, but their development can be illustrated and to a certain extent described with the help of a selection of Iron Age excavations, the earliest of which concerns the complex around Hoby on Lolland, one of the larger islands in the Danish archipelago.[25] Some time during the first century AD a magnate was buried there. His grave was excavated at the beginning of the twentieth century and was found to contain the body of a middle-aged male. He had been interred with a number of personal belongings, including a belt buckle of bronze, two golden rings, a knife and – most importantly – a set of tableware, mostly of Roman origin, manufactured in Capua by Greek silversmiths, and of outstanding quality. The tableware makes up an almost complete Roman banqueting set, consisting of two exquisite silver drinking cups, bronze trays, decanters, saucers and a bucket, possibly a spittoon. The buckles for two drinking horns, a Scandinavian tradition, were also present. The only item missing from the standard Roman banqueting set was a wine crater, a ceramic bucket with a spigot mounted on a tripod for serving wine. In addition to the Roman items, the excavation discovered that the man had been interred with a couple of ordinary Scandinavian pottery vessels and a leg of ham. The magnate was thus embarking on his final journey expecting not to starve and also possibly to have to entertain in the next world. He had been clothed in his finery as well: his clothes were held together by seven fibulas, five of them made of silver and gold, two made of bronze. Around his waist he had a belt with an articulated buckle made of bronze; he wore two bronze rings on his fingers and a bronze dagger on his belt; and he had a bone needle and various buckles of iron and bronze.[26]

The most significant part of this grave is the Roman banqueting set, the only (almost) complete set found outside the borders of

[25] K. F. Johansen, *Nordiske fortidsminder*. Vol. II.3, *Hoby-Fundet*. Copenhagen: Gyldendalske Boghandel, 1923; U. L. Hansen, Hobyfundet. In *Arkæologileksikon*, ed. L. Hedeager and K. Kristiansen. Copenhagen: Politiken, 1986. pp. 125–26; Hedeager, *Danmarkshistorien*, Vol. II, pp. 140–45.
[26] Johansen, *Fortidsminder*, Vol. II.3; Hansen, *Arkæologileksikon*, pp. 125–26.

the Roman Empire. The cups and the bronze tray in particular allow us to speculate about the magnate's life and training. They are unique both in terms of their origins and their quality. Stylistically they are typical examples of the silversmith's art at the beginning of the first century AD. They are embossed with the Greek maker's mark ('Cheirisophos made it'), and their bottoms are engraved with their exact weight and the name *Silius*. We know that the Roman military commander of north Germania between AD 14 and 21 was called Silius. In contrast to much Roman metalware that reached Scandinavia from silversmiths on the borders of the Empire, this banqueting set was made near Capua in Italy. The cups are exquisitely fashioned, and their iconographic content is entirely classical. One would ordinarily have expected some Celtic elements in the iconography by this time and in this region of the world. Both silver cups depict incidents from Homer's Iliad: one shows the story of King Priam's secret plea to Achilles for the return of the body of Priam's son, Hector; the other shows the exploits of Philoctetes. The bronze trays are nearly the equal of the cups in quality. One tray continues the classical themes by depicting Venus, naked, surrounded by flying cupids who hold her mirror, while the bronze pitcher is of exquisite quality: made in Capua and stamped *Cn. Trebillius Romanus*, it displays unusually well-formed handles and fittings.

The Hoby find is not just interesting as an example of Roman artifacts (Figure 3). Although the find is unique in its quality and value, it is its state of preservation that raises important questions. The banqueting set appears to be complete. The only item that we can say for certain is missing from this fine tableware is the wine crater, although it is possible that two silver cups were replaced by Scandinavian drinking horns. The set shows no influence from a Celtic style of decoration, and it carries the name of the Roman military commander of north Germania AD 14–21. The interpretation of the decoration requires a detailed knowledge of classical culture and, with its depictions of Roman deities and events from classical literature, cannot in any way have served a religious function in a Celtic society. Furthermore, it shows no signs of having been acquired as a result of raiding: apart from (presumably) two cups – which have been substituted with two drinking horns – no pieces are missing and none of the surviving pieces have been damaged in transfer. The fact that the

Figure 3 The Hoby find. A selection of items from the Hoby find (Lolland, Denmark, c. AD 80). The find is the only known surviving Roman banqueting set outside the Roman Empire. If he were to have understood the iconography of the set, the magnate who owned it must have been familiar with classical literature. The two silver cups are stamped with the name *Silius*, which is the name of the Roman supreme military commander for the Roman province of Lower Germania AD 14–21.

banqueting set is devoid of any Celtic style of decoration indicates that it was made for a Roman or someone who had been educated in the Empire, and we can speculate that the chieftain who was buried at Hoby was regarded as important by the Roman commander Silius. In fact he was so important that Silius decided, for whatever specific motive, to make a gift of his own personal banqueting set (see page 27).[27]

---

[27] In our interpretation of this find – in particular, in regard to the literacy of the magnate – we are accepting Lotte Hedeager's analysis in *Danmarkshistorien*, Vol. II, pp. 180–82. The find is further put in its context in Storgaard, Cosmopolitan aristocrats. In *Spoils of Victory*, see note 15 above, pp. 111–12.

It is difficult not to see this burial as a reflection of the declared policy of the Roman Empire after the defeat at Teutoburg. Like the Americans in the twentieth century, who tried to encircle the Soviet Union through a series of military alliances with and financial aid to allied countries, the Romans aimed to form alliances with the tribes beyond the borders of the Empire in order to catch the Germanic tribes in a pincer movement. In order to do this, the Romans exploited an already existing power structure, for it is clear that the Hoby magnate was not the first magnate from his area. Not only does an earlier grave in the same area contain a double-edged sword and a bronze bucket in an Italian style, but not far from the graves is an Iron Age village large enough to have housed the magnate's retinue.[28] Thus all the indicators suggest that the man buried at Hoby was an ally of the Romans, perhaps someone who had served in the Roman army and acquired a good enough knowledge of classical culture for his decorated banqueting set to make sense to him. He was the latest ruler in an established dynasty in Lolland and, as mentioned above, he was important enough to the Roman Empire and its northern commander Silius to receive a gift of Silius' own personal banqueting set, perhaps in order to secure his support in the future or to reward him for past feats.

DYNASTIC POLICIES

Intriguingly, the mounts for a Roman wine crater made in a Greek style, possibly the very vessel that is missing from the banqueting set in Hoby, was found in a woman's burial from about a generation later at Bendstrup near Randers in Jylland, some 150 kilometres from Hoby. The circumstances surrounding the find were far from ideal. The grave was excavated in 1869 and the wine crater itself is now missing – possibly destroyed during the excavation by farm-hands. Roman wine craters are extremely rare, and although the ceramic bowl is missing, this one was the only example of such a wine crater to be found outside Italy. It is therefore possible that the banqueting set from Hoby was broken up and that parts of it followed a woman associated with the Hoby magnate to her new home in another part of southern Scandinavia.

[28] Storgaard, ibid., p. 112.

The suggestion that the Bendstrup woman was married to a magnate as part of a larger dynastic policy gains extra weight from the fact that her grave also contained a pair of gilded fibulas (most probably made south of the Danube), a large piece of amber and two pairs of unusual, small items: a pair of mussel shells and two ammonite shells. It appears that the Bendstrup woman started a fashion in the area around Randers: her unusual gilded fibulas were imitated in that area for the next century. A small, but significant, number of interments of wealthy women in the same area include jewellery that imitates the two fibulas found in the Bendstrup find. And these fibulas are found in only a few other places in southern Scandinavia. In addition, small and seemingly valueless objects such as sea-urchins, mussel shells or small amber pendants were also included in the graves of these women, making it clear that the later interments were intended to signify that the dead women were in some way politically or dynastically linked to the woman from Bendstrup. These wealthy women were all interred with the same, little, worthless items as the ones in Jylland – the mussel shells, the amber and the ammonite shells – but not the fibulas or the Roman drinking vessels. In other words, we must conclude that these women were signalling that they belonged to a particular group, whose members created and perpetuated military and familial associations through marriage.[29]

Further evidence of alliance-making and the gradual emergence of an hereditary noble class can be found in another group of first- and second-century female graves, and some male graves that were empty of weapons, near Hoby and Juellinge and scattered around the island of Fyn.[30] All of the female graves contained the same small items within them: the fossilised sea-urchins, the amber and the ammonites. But these graves from the Danish islands also share the fact that such small items were found only in rich graves and that the items were therefore clearly intended to set these women apart from their less fortunate sisters. The natural conclusion from these finds is that these women intended to signify their noble status through

---

[29] L. Hedeager and K. Kristiansen, Bendstrup: en fyrstegrav fra den romerske jernalder, dens sociale og historiske miljø. KUML, 1981, pp. 81–149.
[30] *Inter alia* Blidegn, Espe, and Nørre Broby on Fyn.

their grave goods, and that a national aristocracy was emerging, amongst other things, through intermarriage.[31]

Early kings and European involvement

The Hoby find is not the only indication of southern Scandinavian dynasties in the archaeology. The excavations in Himlingøje on Sjælland demonstrate that this area had a long-lasting dynasty of international importance. The site includes thirteen graves rich in Roman imports and aristocratic insignia, such as golden arm- and finger-rings. The magnates in Himlingøje were buried between AD 150 and 320.[32] Two empty cenotaphs and the presence of a young man whose dismembered bones were transported home to be buried in the family burial place make it clear that the graves commemorate the members of a ruling dynasty. The site has been connected to a further two sites on Sjælland, at Varpelev and Valløby. These also contain the rich remains of members of the aristocracy. Both the latter sites also suggest a significant aristocratic settlement: in Strøbylille, south-east of Valløby, a large building 47 metres long and 10 metres wide has been found, and finds close by at Østervang in Ejby suggest a rich settlement in the area.[33]

Such aristocratic dynasties were also of international significance. Two female graves – one in Nørre Rør in southern Norway and the other in Tuna in central Sweden – contain the bodies of two aristocratic women from Sjælland who were married off to male rulers in Norway and Sweden.[34] The additional evidence of

[31] Hedeager, Danmarkshistorien, Vol. II, pp. 166–68.
[32] U. L. Hansen, V. Alexandersen and T. Hatting, eds. Himlingøje, Seeland, Europa: ein Gräberfeld der jüngeren römischen Kaiserzeit auf Seeland, seine Bedeutung und internationalen Beziehungen. Serie B. Bd. XIII. Nordiske fortidsminder. Copenhagen: Kongelige Nordiske Oldskriftselskab, 1995.
[33] Storgaard, Cosmopolitan aristocrats. In Spoils of Victory, see note 15 above, p. 113.
[34] B. Magnus, En liten gylden ring. In Drik – og du vil leve skønt: Festskrift til Ulla Lund Hansen på 60-årsdagen 18 august 2002, ed. J. Pind, A. N. Jørgensen, B. Storgaard, P. Rindel and J. Ilkjær. Vol. VII. Publications from the National Museum, Studies in archaeology and history. Copenhagen: Nationalmuseet, 2002. pp. 255–62; U. L. Hansen et al., Himlingøje, Serie B. Bd. XIII; E. Straume, The grave from Nordre Rør, Rygge, Østfold: The burial of a Danish woman from the 3rd century AD? In Trade and Exchange in Prehistory. Studies in Honour of Berta Stjernquist. Acta archaeologica lundensia. Lund: Lunds Universitets Historiske Museum, 1988. pp. 167–76.

graves from the Limfjord area make it clear that the Himlingøje
dynasty was a major player in the politics of Scandinavia in the
early Roman Iron Age.[35] In fact it was a player on a European scale:
its influence can be traced in third-century graves as far away as the
Ukraine and the Black Sea.[36] The depiction of a second-century
Roman sword on a silver cup made by Scandinavian silversmiths
some time in the second century AD along with the Kolbenarmring
(a torc ring) from another grave in the Himlingøje complex show
that the Himlingøje dynasty participated as Roman mercenaries in
the Marcomannic wars AD 166–80.[37]

TO PROTECT AND TO SERVE

Dynastic policies during the Roman Iron Age were mirrored by
increased activity in road-building and fortification that would
have granted a small group of magnates increased political control over southern Scandinavia. Segments of roads made mainly
out of wood and dating from as early as the second century AD
have been found across the region. We have no means of knowing the extent of the Iron Age road network, as the wood used is
only preserved under narrowly defined circumstances.[38]
However, it is clear that such roads would have allowed magnates
to control the land by restricting access to their areas by means of
wooden ramparts that allowed them to impose customs and
duties. The study of these kinds of ramparts and their socio-
economic impact is still in its infancy, but Neumann's survey of
Jylland, which identified twenty-eight such structures (most of
which are still awaiting investigation), and Jørgensen's argument

[35] Storgaard, Cosmopolitan aristocrats. In *Spoils of Victory*, see note 15 above, p. 114.
[36] A. Kokowski, Ein sogenanntes 'Fürstengrab' von Rudka in Wolhynien. Seine
Bedeutung für die Rekonstruktion des Bildes der germanischen Eliten im späten
Altertum. In *Military Aspects of the Aristocracy in Barbaricum in the Roman and Early
Migration Period. Papers presented at an international research seminar at the Danish
National Museum, Copenhagen, 10–11 December 1999. Studies in archaeology and
history*, ed. B. Storgaard. Vol. V. Copenhagen: The National Museum, 2001.
pp. 41–53; B. Storgaard, The Årslev grave and connections between Funen and the
continent at the end of the later Roman Iron Age. In *The Archaeology of Gudme and
Lundeborg. Papers presented at a conference at Svendborg, October 1991. Arkæologiske
Studier*, ed. P. O. Nielsen and K. Randsborg. Vol. X. Copenhagen: Akademisk
Forlag, 1994. pp. 160–68.
[37] Storgaard, Cosmopolitan aristocrats. In *Spoils of Victory*, see note 15 above, p. 116.
[38] A. N. Jørgensen, Fortifications and the control of land and sea traffic in the pre-
Roman and Roman Iron Age. In *Spoils of Victory*, see note 15 above, p. 202.

for a total number of around eighty ramparts in the area of present-day Denmark demonstrate that this is a field that will yield significant results in the future. Three ramparts have so far been described in the literature: the best known is the 12-kilometre fortification known as Olgerdiget, which was probably established around 150. It has been calculated to have required the felling of more than ninety thousand oak trees in southern Jylland, more than ten times the number required for the famous ring fort, Trelleborg, which dates from the 980s.[39] Fifteen kilometres north of Olgerdiget is Æ vold, dated by dendrochronology[40] to around 278, and a further 50 kilometres north lies Kolding Fjord, where the contemporary Trældiget stretched over a distance of 12 kilometres. These ramparts were too weak to have been intended as a military defence; instead, they allowed magnates to control commercial traffic in the area – and thus to impose customs and duties on the traders passing through.[41] The relatively high number of identified ramparts in southern Scandinavia shows that restricting trade and access to major roads was a common way of raising revenue for Iron Age magnates.[42]

Such land fortifications were therefore about control of the countryside, but the emerging dynasties in southern Scandinavia also focussed on defence against maritime attack. New technological advances in archaeology mean that we must revise our interpretation of these features as more are identified. Before 1996 three defensive barriers in Danish fjords had been identified. These were located on the south-east coast of Jylland: two in

[39] H. Neumann, *Olgerdiget, et bidrag til Danmarks tidligste historie*. Skrifter fra museumsrådet for Sønderjyllands Amt. Haderslev: Haderslev Museum, 1982. p. 84; Hedeager, *Danmarkshistorien*, Vol. II, pp. 171–73.
[40] Dendrochronology is the science of dating wooden artifacts by analysing the clustering of year-rings in wood: as a tree grows, it puts on a new growth- or tree-ring every year, just under the bark. This growth varies according to the weather: a favourable year produces a wider ring, and an unfavourable year produces a narrower one. Over a long period of time there will be a pattern of wider and narrower rings which reflects droughts, cold summers, etc. Thus, the span of years during which a tree has lived will be represented by a unique sequence of tree-rings that can show not only when the wood was felled, but also where it grew.
[41] Jørgensen, Fortifications. In *Spoils of Victory*, see note 15 above, p. 205.
[42] Neumann, *Olgerdiget*, p. 49; M. S. Jørgensen, Vej, vejstrøg og vejspærringer: jernalderens landfærdsel. In *Fra stamme til stat i Danmark*. Vol. I, *Jernalderens stammesamfund*, ed. P. Mortensen and B. Rasmussen, Århus: Jysk Arkæologisk Selskab i Kommission hos Aarhus Universitetsforlag, 1988. pp. 106–7; Jørgensen, Fortifications. In *Spoils of Victory*, see note 15 above, pp. 204–6.

Haderslev Fjord (Margretes Bro and Æ'lei) and one in Kolding
Fjord. But since then a further three have been identified in Fyn
and Sjælland. All six exhibit the same construction details and can
be dated to the period from the mid-third century to the early fifth
century. Margretes Bro and Æ'lei are the most recent structures.
They consist of two rows of stakes for mooring the floaters to the
bottom of the fjord and a floating barrage of oak beams held in
place by the stakes.[43] A dendrochronological study of the timbers
used to construct the 600-metre-long Æ'lei gives 403 as the year in
which the oak trees used as floating bars in the system were felled,
while the somewhat shorter (425-metre) Margretes Bro dates earlier, from the fourth century.[44] These dates can only be taken as a
rough indication of the date of construction, since these floating
bars may have been repaired as part of general maintenance after
the main construction had been finished (Figure 4).

In contrast to the apparent care that had been lavished on these
two barrages, the second- or third-century barrage at Gudsø Vig
seems to have been a temporary defence. It consisted of some
fifty trunks of oak trees that had simply been lashed together. The
structure seems to have had only a limited lifetime. The
Nakkebølle Fjord and Jungshoved Nor barrages on Fyn and
Sjælland still await detailed investigation but, like Margretes
Bro and Æ'lei they seem to have been the result of a concerted
and long-lasting effort by the local magnates: Nakkebølle Fjord
included some four or five hundred trunks and stakes for anchor-
ing the barrages at intervals of 1–3 metres – hardly a fortification
that was built as a temporary response to a military threat.[45]

ILLERUP ÅDAL

The period up to the third century saw a massive change in the
Roman army. It became professionalised and increasingly populated by mercenaries recruited from the tribes that the Romans
called 'Germanic'. However, such an increasing reliance on foreign mercenaries meant that the Empire became more and more

[43] Hedeager, *Danmarkshistorien*, Vol. II, p. 172.
[44] Jørgensen, Fortifications. In *Spoils of Victory*, see note 15 above, p. 198. F. Rieck,
Aspects of coastal defence in Denmark. In *Aspects of Maritime Scandinavia AD
200–1200*. Roskilde: Viking Ship Museum, 1991. pp. 83–96.
[45] Jørgensen, Fortifications. In *Spoils of Victory*, see note 15 above, p. 199.

Figure 4 Æ'lei
sea barrage. The
Æ'lei sea barrage
in Haderslev
Fjord (Jylland,
Denmark, c. AD
370–418). This
was one of
several sea
barrages built to
defend Denmark
in the fourth and
fifth centuries.
The barrage was
clearly intended
to be a
permanent
feature of the
access to the
bottom of the
fjord. The loose-
lying trunks
between the
stakes would
have made it
impossible to
enter the fjord
without a pilot to
guide the boat or
ship through.
The length of the
barrage is almost
600 metres, and
the depth of the
fortification is 25
metres, covering
an area of 1.5
hectares.

dependent on finding an emperor who could keep the troops happy. As a consequence, in the third century no fewer than twenty Roman emperors were deposed by commanders who made themselves emperors by acclamation of the army. This trend did not end until the reign of the Emperor Diocletian (284–305), who reformed the army in such a way that the majority of soldiers were recruited from the farthest reaches of the Empire in order to make it difficult for them to conspire against the emperor in Rome. Diocletian also expanded the army to almost twice its previous size and thus increased the possibilities for promotion for any soldier – even the mercenaries.[46] This new development allowed the Germanic and Scandinavian chieftains to learn military tactics directly from the Romans. This new military *nous*, with its attendant stratification of the line of command, is clearly visible in a series of weapon finds in Scandinavia, notably at Thorsbjerg, Nydam, Kragehul and Vimose (excavated in the nineteenth century) and in the more recent finds in Ejsbøl Mose and Illerup Ådal near Viborg in Denmark.

The Illerup Ådal site is one of twenty-five in Denmark and southern Sweden where weapons were sacrificed. The sacrificial sites are bundled together in a relatively small geographical area: half of them

---

[46] Hedeager, *Danmarkshistorien*, Vol. II, p. 249.

are concentrated in the eastern part of Jylland[47] or on the island of Fyn,[48] three sites are on Lolland and Sjælland,[49] two in southern mainland Sweden[50] and five on the relatively small islands of Gotland, Småland and Bornholm.[51] So far, comparable finds have not been made in the rest of Scandinavia, and the custom therefore seems to have been limited to southern Scandinavia. The custom was well known to classical authors such as Caesar, Tacitus and Strabo, but it seems to have died out on the continent by the first century AD. Some of the sacrificial sites were excavated in southern Scandinavia as early as the seventeenth century, but most were found in connection with peat-digging during the latter half of the nine-teenth century. Excavation techniques have improved substantially since then, and two sites in particular, Illerup Ådal near Viborg in Jylland and Ejsbøl near Vejle, have allowed archaeologists to refine and expand the interpretations of the finds from previous centu-ries.[52] (See Figure 5.)

The Germanic custom of destroying the vanquished foe's equipment is most eloquently described by the early fifth-century

[47] Trinnemose, Hedelisker, Illerup, Porskær, Dallerup, Vingsted, Tranebær, Ejsbøl, Nydam and Hjortspring. J. Ilkjær, Danish war booty sacrifices. In Spoils of Victory, see note 15 above, pp. 45–56; E. Jørgensen and P. V. Petersen, Nydam Bog: new finds and observations. Ibid., pp. 258–85; F. Rieck, The ships from Nydam Bog. Ibid., pp. 296–309; H. C. H. Andersen, New investigations in Ejsbøl bog. Ibid., pp. 246–57; F. Kaul, The Hjortspring find: the oldest of the large Nordic war booty sacrifices. Ibid., pp. 212–23.

[48] Krogsbølle, Kragehul, Vimose, Villestofte and Illemose. Ilkjær, Danish war booty sacrifices. Ibid., pp. 56–59; C. Engelhardt, Om Vimosefundet. In Aarbøger for nordisk oldkyndighed og historie. Copenhagen: Gyldendal, 1867. pp. 233–57; C. Engelhardt, Fynske Mosefund. Vol. II, Vimose-Fundet. Copenhagen; X. P. Jensen, The Vimose find. In Spoils of Victory, see note 15 above, pp. 224–39; Kaul, The Hjortspring find. Ibid., pp. 212–23.

[49] Sørup, Søborg sø and Ballerup Sømose. Ilkjær, Danish war booty sacrifices. Ibid., p. 59.

[50] Hassle-Bösarp and Finnestorp.

[51] Gudingsåkrarna, Dalby, Skedesmose, Knarremose and Balsmyr. Ilkjær, Danish war booty sacrifices. Ibid., pp. 59–60.

[52] J. Ilkjær and C. v. Carnap-Bornheim, Illerup Ådal. Vols. I–II, Die Lansen und Speere. Aarhus: Jutland Archaeological Society Publications, 25, 1990; J. Ilkjær, ibid., Vols. III–IV, Die Gürtel: Bestandteile und Zubehör; J. Ilkjær and C. v. Carnap-Bornheim, ibid., Vols. V–VIII, Die Prachtausrüstungen; J. Ilkjær, ibid., Vols. IX–X, Die Schilde. There is a well-illustrated website in Danish on http://www.illerup.dk, and a Danish summary analysis in J. Ilkjær, Illerup Ådal – et arkælogisk tryllespejl. Aarhus: Moesgård, 2000. (English translation: J. Ilkjær, Illerup Ådal: Archaeology as a Magic Mirror. Aarhus: Moesgård, 2003.) For Ejsbøl, see Hedeager, Danmarkshistorien, Vol. II, Danernes land, pp. 241–43; H. C. H. Andersen, New investigations in Ejsbøl bog. In Spoils of Victory, see note 15 above, pp. 246–57; C. v. Carnap-Bornstein, The ornamental belts from Ejsbøl bog and Neudorf-Bornstein. Ibid., pp. 240–45.

Figure 5 The weapons find at Illerup Ådal (Jylland, Denmark, AD 200–500) during excavation. The Illerup find is one of twenty-five sites that contain more than fifty weapon sacrifices following the defeat of an enemy. Most of these sites were excavated before the advent of modern archaeology. This find has made it possible to demonstrate that these weapon deposits were systematically destroyed and deposited in lakes as a result of regular, extensive warfare between the Scandinavian countries during the third to the sixth centuries AD. The weapons also show a clear command structure and a strong centralisation of military power in Scandinavia dating from the beginning of the first millennium.

priest–historian Orosius in his description of the Battle of Orange in 105 BC, which took place almost five hundred years before he wrote his account:

When the enemy had taken control of the two camps and an enormous booty they destroyed everything that had fallen into their control with renewed and unspent ferocity. Clothes were torn, ring mail was chopped to bits, harnesses were destroyed, gold and silver were thrown into the river. Horses were driven over precipices and men were suspended from trees with ropes round their necks so that in the end there was no more booty for the victors than the mercy they showed to the vanquished.

Caesar, Tacitus, Posidonius and Strabo all offer similar stories, although their descriptions are nowhere near as dramatic.[53]

The latest excavations have confirmed that the weapon finds were the result of a small number of large weapon depositions and not the accumulation of many small individual sacrifices. The twenty-five sites in Denmark and Sweden contain weapons from approximately fifty battles that took place in the area between the first and seventh centuries, mainly around the south-east coast of Jylland and the western coast of the island of Fyn. Illerup Ådal, which today is relatively dry, was once a lake where local warlords on at least three separate occasions sacrificed the military equipment of a vanquished foe. We cannot say exactly where the three battles took place, for the equipment was clearly collected beforehand and dumped in the lake as a major sacrifice.

The distribution of these weapon finds shows that, in Scandinavia, such a practice seems to have been limited to Denmark. The Illerup Ådal lake covered almost 100,000 square metres, and although it would be logical to expect the archaeological finds to be within throwing distance from the old banks of the lake, it has become clear that the finds were deposited into the lake from boats far from the banks. Every one of the fifteen thousand items had been deliberately destroyed before being deposited in the lake. An analysis of the finds gives some surprising information. First of all, the most popular weapon was not the sword: for every sword, three to four spears and lances have been found, some with barbs intended for throwing, and some without intended for stabbing in close combat, much like today's bayonet.

The oldest deposit in Illerup contained some 300 spear points of a type known as Venollum (from the name of a burial in Norway). Two of these spears are stamped with a die bearing the name *Wagnijo*, written in runes. This indicates that Wagnijo either manufactured or purchased these spears frequently enough to have a stamp die with his name on it. In other contexts

---

[53] Quoted in Hedeager, *Danmarkshistorien*, Vol. II, p. 223.

it is unknown for a Germanic object to be stamped like this, but it is common among Roman artifacts. We can therefore surmise that Wagnijo was familiar with industrial manufacturing and that he had either learnt the craft of a manufacturer or of a warrior from a Roman. We can also see that he could read – at least his own name. If Wagnijo is the name of the man who had the financial resources to equip this army of a thousand men, then we can put a name to one of the earliest magnates in Scandinavia. We find the same trend when we investigate the swords. Most of them are Roman blades, with Roman makers' marks. They had been bought half-finished abroad and given a hilt and other finishing touches in Scandinavia.[54]

Another aspect of the finds needs comment: although Wagnijo's men were dressed very much in the same manner, their equipment fell short of being a uniform. The shields, belts and scabbards found in Illerup indicate a stratification consisting of at least three levels. At the top level six shields from the earliest part of the site were decorated with bosses and handles made of silver, were edged with the same metal, and were often decorated with gold foil and painted bright red with cinnabar. Two even had runic inscriptions. The middle level is represented by 36 shields with bronze fittings, possibly gilt, while the lowest level consists of 320 shields with iron fittings.[55] Further evidence for the hierarchical structure of the army is found in the personal belongings of the soldiers. Each man had two belts; the first held up his trousers and was used to hold personal gear, such as money or a comb. Over their trousers many men wore a tunic and, over the tunic, another belt and a shoulder strap to hold their sword. These outer belts came in two varieties: adjustable and non-adjustable. The adjustable belts held the higher value swords with the most elaborate hilts, and survive in the smallest numbers. In other words, it is sensible to assume that the adjustable belts were reserved for commanding officers in the army, a natural enough thought given the size of the weapon deposit, which seems to have come from an army of about a thousand

[54] J. Ilkjær, *Tryllespejl*, pp. 43–47.
[55] J. Ilkjær, Centres of power in Scandinavia before the medieval kingdoms. In *Kingdoms and Regionality. Proceedings from the 49th Sahsensymposium 1998 in Uppsala.* Stockholm: Archaeological Research Laboratory, Stockholm University, 2001. p. 4, figs. 2.3, 2.4 (http://www.illerup.dk/documents/illerup_75.pdf).

men. The army that was vanquished near Illerup was thus a large, well-organised one whose weapons had come from a central armoury. But can we say more about it?

The most pressing question is, 'Where did it come from?' For an answer to that question we must turn to the private equipment of the soldiers which was carried in the outer belt. It was essential for a soldier to be able to light a fire, and for this he would carry some sort of implement. There are basically two versions of this tool: one is a flat piece of steel elongated into a handle, and the other is a narrow piece of steel set into a wooden handle. In both cases, one would strike the steel against a stone while holding it near combustible material such as tinder fungus or straw. The elongated piece of steel is characteristic of the continent at this time, while the other type is prevalent in Scandinavia. Some 129 tinderboxes have been found at Illerup; 5 were of the continental type, while 124 were Scandinavian. This is a strong indicator that the army came from another Scandinavian country. This is further substantiated by an analysis of the 124 combs found at Illerup. Combs at this time could be made of one, two or three pieces of antler from deer, elk or reindeer. The possibility that these were made from deer antlers must be rejected out of hand, as deer antlers do not grow to sufficient size. In other words, the combs found must have been made from either elk or reindeer antlers. Furthermore, a number of bone sword sheath-ends were found. These were too large to be made of deer antlers. As neither elk nor reindeer lived in southern Scandinavia in the third century, the vanquished army must have come from northern Scandinavia. It is even possible to be more specific, for among the combs is a pair made from two pieces of antler with a particular construction along the ridge. Combs of this construction have only been found in a grave in Tryti near Sognefjord north of Bergen in Norway.

The southern Scandinavian weapon sacrifices demonstrate how both southern and northern Scandinavia were highly organised and militarised. The changes in agriculture and village structure also point to a society that saw increased social stratification. This increased stratification is consistent with the increased building activity: better roads were constructed, and through their control of these roads, magnates could raise revenue to maintain their social status. The weapon sacrifices demonstrate that warlords, assisted by lesser leaders, were able to equip, train and command armies of up to a thousand men, and in the process their armies employed a clear line of command. As it is possible to identify where these armies came from, we can see that south-west Jylland endured several waves of attack: an early one came from what is now Poland, the others from areas in Norway and Sweden. The attackers must initially have sailed across the Baltic in large fleets consisting of up to fifty ships, and their very existence made it necessary for the kings and chieftains of Jylland to fortify their coastline and develop military techniques and strategies that could defend the land against such large-scale attacks.

The Illerup finds and the fortifications that have so far been found in southern Scandinavia also demonstrate that the area was subject to successive waves of attack that must be classified as full-scale warfare, and that a political movement towards centralisation and larger governmental units took place in Scandinavia from the first to the fifth centuries. In particular, there seems to have been a movement of political and military power from the west coast of Norway to the interior of the country: from the first to the third centuries the attacks came mainly from the north-west coast of Norway, but towards the end of the third century the origins of the attackers changed. Successive waves of attackers came from Norway, Sweden, Uppland (in present-day Sweden) and Finland from the fourth century on. The reason for these attacks is unknown, but it is clear that at the time south-west Jylland was rich in bog-iron and wood, which would have made it an important area for the production of weapons.

Early kingship

The early history of the consolidation and expansion of the Scandinavian kingdoms is documented in chronicles and annals that were mainly composed outside Scandinavia. The area was of interest to European chroniclers and annalists only when the 'Northmen' or 'Danes' impinged on their own countries. Their information is therefore very sporadic, and the connection between Scandinavian internal politics and the wider European scene is difficult to reconstruct reliably. Added to this is the fact that the continental sources do not distinguish consistently between the Scandinavian countries. For example, although all manuscripts of the Anglo-Saxon Chronicles mention the skirmish in Portland and the killing of the reeve Beaduheard, one manuscript tradition names the perpetrators 'Danes from Halogaland' (which is in Norway). Hence, what little we know about the 'kings of the Northmen' or 'the kings of the Danes' that are mentioned in the Annals of St Bertin and the Frankish Royal Annals we must presume refers to the kingdom of the Danes, and the following discussion is therefore mainly limited to the political situation in southern Scandinavia.

Although the Scandinavians begin to appear in the written sources with some regularity, the period from the late fifth to the late eighth centuries is less well documented in the archaeology. In southern Scandinavia we find a marked change in burial customs and settlements, while the Swedish and Norwegian finds indicate a continuation of previous social structures. Until this time burials across Scandinavia included ostentatious grave goods, so that the graves demonstrated the wealth of the dead person by the inclusion of large amounts of new, prestigious metalware or even slaves.[56] The change coincides with the possible return of the Heruli, described by Procopius as a wandering Germanic tribe whose remnants returned to Scandinavia as a consequence of their defeat at the hands of the Emperor Justinian around 512.[57] At the same time Gregory of Tours mentions a certain Chochilaicus, a Scandinavian chieftain, who was killed in a military skirmish in 515.[58]

The absence of ostentatious graves in southern Scandinavia during this period is also the result of a gradual process that had its beginning in the period of fortifications and clashes between the Scandinavian tribes outlined previously. Gradually the expensive grave goods were left out of interments, and by the sixth century we find predominantly cremations, with few if any

---

[56] K. Randsborg, *The Viking Age in Denmark: The Formation of a State*. New York: St. Martin's Press, 1980. p. 49.

[57] *Procopius with an English Translation*, trans. H. B. Dewing. Loeb Classical Library. Cambridge, Mass.: Harvard University Press; London: W. Heinemann, 1953–62.

[58] Gregory of Tours, *Libri Historiarum X*, ed. B. Krusch. Monumenta Germaniae historica: scriptores rerum Merovingicarum. Hanover: Hahn, 1965; Gregory of Tours, *The History of the Franks*, ed. and trans. L. Thorpe. Penguin Classics. London: Penguin, 1974.

grave goods. The relative lack of rich interments has been taken as an indication that the area was going through a demographic and economic crisis, but it is also possible to see this development as an indicator of early centralisation and kingship.[59] The lack of grave goods indicates a lack of a need for social differentiation in death, and this must be linked to a relatively peaceful existence for the people in general. The archaeological evidence also points in this direction. In all the Scandinavian countries agriculture became more regulated, and cattle paths, bounded by stone fences, were constructed to lead cattle away from cultivated fields. These cattle paths are ubiquitous throughout Scandinavia and can be found from Vestfold in Norway in the north, to the island of Gotland off the Swedish Baltic coast, to Vallensbæk outside present-day Copenhagen. Not only did these measures prevent the cattle from destroying the crops, but they also removed one of the major causes of friction between farmers.

There is also evidence of the centralisation of trade in the period 500–800. The most famous is the emporium at Birka on Helgö on Lake Mälar, south-west of present-day Stockholm. These emporia had a local manufacturing base: smithies, bronze casts and goldsmiths' workshops are invariably found in such places. But it is also clear that they were part of an extensive network of trade reaching far into the east and west: among the eighth-century finds on Helgö are a crozier from Ireland, a ladle from Egypt and a bronze statuette of the Buddha which had found its way to Sweden from India. Helgö also clearly served a more local market. Among the debris a number of moulds were found that correspond to items of jewellery found in other parts of the Baltic area.[60]

Attempts at conversion

The Scandinavian political scene in the eighth and ninth centuries is poorly documented in written European sources. We find entries mentioning kings of the 'Normans' or 'Danes' in the

[59] J. Steenstrup, *Normannerne*. Vol. I, *Indledning i Normannertiden*. Copenhagen: Rudolph Klein, 1876, pp. 182–90; Hedeager, *Danmarkshistorien*, Vol. II, pp. 291–323.

[60] D. M. Wilson, ed. *The Northern World: The History and Heritage of Northern Europe, AD 400–1100*. London: Thames and Hudson, 2003 [1980]. p. 132.

Royal Frankish Annals for the later years of the eighth century and the early years of the ninth, where the kings Sigefridus and Harioldus are mentioned for the years 782 and 812, and a further twenty-one mentions of similar kings are found in the century up to 891.[61] These entries can be supplemented by two contemporary German biographies of the first archbishops of Hamburg, St Anskar and Rimbert.[62] Carolingian and papal letters can also be used to outline the developing organisation of the archdiocese of Hamburg-Bremen.[63] Finally, especially for the later ninth-century history, the well-informed history of the diocese of Hamburg-Bremen written by the German cleric Adam of Bremen around 1075 is indispensible, in particular for the reign of Svein Estridsøn, whom Adam met and used as an informant for his history.[64]

The *Vita Anskarii* is remarkably low-key compared with other saints' lives of the period. Rimbert, who participated in Anskar's last mission to Sweden and collected information from other followers of Anskar, told the story of Anskar's life as a journey towards his martyrdom, which in Rimbert's version was not signified by a violent death but by Anskar's zealous dedication to his missionary work. In line with this low-key approach, Anskar converts by example and by educating his listeners, and Rimbert is meticulous about mentioning Anskar's superiors, such as Archbishop Ebo of Rheims, who was the first person to organise the mission to Scandinavia.

[61] *The Annals of St-Bertin*, ed. and annotated Janet L. Nelson, Ninth-Century Histories, 1. Manchester: Manchester University Press, 1991; R. Rau, *Ausgewählte Quellen zur deutschen Geschichte des Mittelalters*. Vols. V–VII, *Quellen zur Karolingischen Reichsgeschichte I–III*. Unveränderter reprografischer Nachdruck der Ausg. von 1955–60, ed. Reinhold Rau. Berlin: Deutscher Verlag der Wissenschaften, 1966 [1955–60]; I. Skovgaard-Petersen, Oldtid og vikingetid. In *Danmarks historie*. Vol. I, *Tiden indtil 1340*, exec. ed. A. E. Christensen, H. P. Clausen, Svend Ellehøj and Søren Mørch. Copenhagen: Gyldendal, 1980. p. 149.

[62] W. Trillmich and R. Buchner, *Quellen des 9. und 11. Jahrhunderts zur Geschichte der hamburgischen Kirche und des Reiches*. Vol. XI, Rimbert, *Leben Ansgars*; Adam von Bremen, Bischofsgeschichte der Hamburger Kirche; Wipo, *Taten Kaiser Konrads II*. Neu übertragen, trans. K. Nobbe and R. Buchner. Ausgewählte Quellen zur deutschen Geschichte des Mittelalters. Berlin: Rütten & Loening, 1961; Rimbert, *Anskar, the Apostle of the North 801–965*, trans. C. H. Robinson. Lives of Early and Mediaeval Missionaries. London: The Society for the Propagation of the Gospel in Foreign Parts, 1921.

[63] Most conveniently collected in Christensen and Nielsen, *Diplomatarium danicum*.

[64] Adamus Bremensis, *Monumenta Germaniae historica*. Vol. XVII, *Hamburgische Kirchengeschichte*. 3rd ed. B. Schmeidler. Scriptores rerum Germanicarum in usum scholarum separatim editi. Hanover: Hahn, 1977 [1917].

As has already been mentioned, such sources from the early Viking Age (700–900) do not allow us to distinguish clearly between the individual countries of modern-day Scandinavia. For example, the earlier of the two versions of Rimbert's *Vita Anskarii* tells us that Anskar's mission covered 'all the surrounding areas, and the peoples of the Swedes and Danes and also Slavs'. The later version adds the peoples of the Faroes, Greenland, Iceland, the Finns and 'all northern and eastern nations'.[65] The geographical location of Denmark ensured its predominance in the sources and made possible its many and varied contacts with the world outside Scandinavia, commercial as well as political. These influences brought new impulses and goods to the country and determined the directions of Danish outward expansion. For shipping, Denmark could either be seen as a gateway or a barrier between western Europe and the Baltic Sea. Seen from mainland Europe, Denmark provided connections between Britain and the coastal regions of the European continent, including Sweden and the Slavic countries south of the Baltic. And at the same time it was only a small journey by sea from Denmark to Norway. Water and ships tied the country and the whole of Scandinavia together, and these close links were the precondition for the unity of religion and culture of the three Nordic countries. Control over Scandinavian waters was the precondition for power over the kingdoms, and peace on the commercial highways by land and sea was the foundation for a flourishing trade.

The written sources fall into two periods and illustrate two different phases of the history of Scandinavia: the process of conversion and – after a hiatus – the period of ecclesiastical consolidation.

Denmark was closest among the Scandinavian countries to the Carolingian Empire and thus must have been a major concern for the Frankish kings. The Franks were concerned not only with securing their borders but also with spreading the Gospel. The mission to the north was a clear priority, at least from the

---

[65] A-text: In omnibus circumquaque gentibus Sueonum sive Danorum necnon Slavorum.
B-Text: In omnibus circumquaque gentibus Sueonum sive Danorum, Farriae, Gronlondon, Islondon, Scridevindum, Slavorum, necnon omnium septentrionalium et orientalium nationum. Adamus Bremensis, *Monumenta*.

year 689, when Pippin the Elder sent the Anglo-Saxon monk Willibrord to convert the 'Frisians', a phrase that may herald the beginning of a mission as far north as Denmark.[66] The Carolingians were closely associated with the Anglo-Saxon church, and in later centuries a rivalry grew up between the imperial German church centred around the archdiocese of Hamburg-Bremen, and the English and Scottish church, which was particularly sensitive about the liturgy of the Christian faith. In contrast to Christians in the Mediterranean, the Anglo-Saxons had acquired their knowledge of classical culture through the lens of learning, so to speak, rather than by living tradition. Their approach to Christianity was therefore more cerebral and based on the perfomance of the rituals of the Church.[67] At first this made the Carolingian mission focus on liturgy and maintaining particularly good ties with the pope in Rome rather than empha-sising the independence of the individual diocese. When the papacy and the Holy Roman Empire fell out in the eleventh century, the split was used for political purposes by the Scandinavians, as will be seen in Chapter 13. The theology and liturgy of the Carolingian church included elements of vernacular culture, and its teaching was based on a reading and interpreta-tion of selected parts of the classical heritage which was given a particularly Christian emphasis. In contrast, through the high general level of its learning and its emphasis on the education of converts and practising Christians, the Anglo-Saxon church became highly influential, and it supplied some of the most important European scholars, such as the Northumbrian Alcuin, to the imperial court at Aachen.

Throughout the period from the second to the eighth centu-ries, Denmark was the most highly centralised country in Scandinavia, closely followed by Norway. The archaeological evidence shows several far-reaching dynasties based in the coun-try, and it was the first Scandinavian country to develop royal centres of power that claimed in writing to rule a large part of the whole region.[68] It was also referred to as a clear geographical unit

---

[66] Skovgaard-Petersen, Oldtid. In *Danmarks historie*, see note 61 above, p. 48.

[67] F. M. Stenton, *The Oxford History of England*. Vol. II, *Anglo-Saxon England*. Oxford: Oxford University Press, 1947 [1943]. pp. 176–92.

[68] Randsborg, *Viking Age*; Hedeager, *Danmarkshistorien*. Vol. II, See the discussion of 'the birth certificate of Denmark', the Jelling monument, below, pp. 177–80.

by Ohthere in his sailing instructions included in King Alfred's translation of Orosius.[69] The country was thus of considerable age when it was first named in a native source, the Jelling monument, around 960 (see page 179). Some names of rulers can be gleaned from much earlier sources, and a very basic outline of some of the political history of the Scandinavian kingdom nearest to the continent can be constructed from the fragments. However, the dynasties and the motivations of the Danes must remain hazy.

The earliest kings in Scandinavia

We know the names of some early Scandinavian rulers, but how they were related to each other and how they interacted in Scandinavia we cannot say. As we have seen, weapons found at Illerup Ådal were stamped with the name of a certain Wagnijo in the third century. We do not know whether he was a king or a chieftain, or whether he was simply a wealthy soldier. As already stated, Gregory of Tours mentions a King Chochilaicus who was killed in France during the reign of Theoderic (511–26). And an anonymous seventh-century author from Ravenna informs us that the land of the Northmen was called Dania 'since old times'.[70] We have to go to Alcuin's Vita Willibrordi before we have the mention of a Rex Danorum called Ongendus. Alcuin informs us that Ongendus was in control of the lands north of the borders of the Frankish Empire in the early eighth century.[71] It is unknown how he was related to later kings, for the next mention of royal lineage in a continental source is of a King Sigefridus in 782.[72] From Paul the Deacon (who died around

[69] Two Voyagers at the Court of King Alfred: The Ventures of Ohthere and Wulfstan, Together with the Description of Northern Europe from the Old English Orosius, ed. N. Lund, trans. C. E. Fell. York: Sessions, 1984.

[70] A. E. Christensen, Vikingetidens Danmark paa oldhistorisk baggrund. Copenhagen: Københavns Universitets Fond til Tilvejebringelse af Læremidler i kommission hos Gyldendals forlag, 1969. p. 28.

[71] Alcuin, Willibrord, Apostel der Friesen: Seine Vita nach Alkuin und Thiofrid: Lateinisch-Deutsch, trans. and ed. H.-J. Reischmann. Sigmaringendorf: Glock und Lutz, 1989.

[72] Carolingian Chronicles: Royal Frankish Annals and Nithard's Histories, ed. and trans. B. W. Scholz and B. Rogers. Ann Arbor: University of Michigan Press, 1970. sub anno 782.

800) we learn that this Sigefridus was the son of Godefridus, a king of the Danes.[73]

Ongendus may thus have been responsible for the first part of a defensive wall built at the foot of Jylland during the eighth century. Only at this southern part of Jylland is there a solid, earth-bound connection between Scandinavia and the continent, and in the eighth century work began on a defensive wall which became the oldest part of the defences known as the Danevirke. As we have seen, the Danevirke was not the first construction of its kind, but this particular rampart became an important and highly visible symbol of the confidence and independence of the Danish kingdom. Dendrochronology shows that this earthen rampart was begun as early as 734[74] and was strengthened and extended many times during the Viking Age. By the High Middle Ages it had become a large complex of earthen ramparts spanning the length of the only part of the peninsula that presented a weakness to a potential enemy.[75] The Royal Frankish Annals inform us that it was King Godfred who built a rampart intended to run from the Baltic to the North Sea in 808, rather than Ongendus in 734, and that the aim was to make sure that the country presented only one gate to potential attackers.[76] This brief mention was written some two generations after the initial building works, and marks the point when the Carolingians became aware that the Danish nation would be a significant military and political adversary.

We cannot say when the areas that have been called Denmark since the ninth century were united. Unlike the annalists of Francia and England, medieval Scandinavian writers did not feel the need to provide a starting point for the unification of the Scandinavian kingdoms. This may have been owing to the fact that unification had happened such a long time before that it had ceased to be a matter to be commented upon. It is certainly clear that the archaeological record of the building of the Danevirke, the founding of the market town of Ribe around AD 700[77] and the

---

[73] Christensen, *Vikingetidens Denmark*, p. 27.

[74] H. H. Andersen, Et bolværk af træ. *Skalk*, 6, 1973, pp. 3–11.

[75] Its military significance to the country lasted up to 1864, when the rampart formed an important part of the Danish defences against the newly formed state of Germany.

[76] *Carolingian Chronicles, sub annis* 804–10.

[77] S. Jensen, *The Vikings of Ribe*. Ribe: Den Antikvariske Samling, 1991.

existence of an eighth-century artificial canal on the island of Samsø, which gave its owner control of much of the Store Bælt (the large stretch of water between present-day Jylland and the island of Fyn), must be taken as evidence of a strong centralising force even before the emergence of the nation states that were eventually called Denmark, Sweden and Norway. Certainly, the sparse written sources all indicate that the entire area was under the control of a comparatively small number of kings. However, the relatively unified country intimated by the written sources may not have been a constant in the European political scene throughout the Viking Age, for at regular intervals the area disintegrated into smaller kingdoms and re-aligned its forces or chieftaincies with their own rulers, only to be unified again under another ambitious king. It may be just such another unification by King Harald Bluetooth in the latter half of the tenth century that is mentioned on the Jelling stones, which report that 'Harald conquered all Norway and Denmark and made the Danes Christians'. The political and economic basis of early Scandinavian kingship has been widely debated. But it is clear that many Scandinavian kings were intent on moving along the process of unifying the twenty-nine kingdoms of the Scandinavian peninsula mentioned by Jordanes in the sixth century and becoming leaders of a larger geographical area. It is also clear from the Frankish annals (the *Annales Regni Francorum*) that a number of kings, such as Ongendus and Sigefridus, claimed to represent the 'Danes' or 'Normans' in negotiations with other foreign leaders and magnates.

These early kings doubtless also had the responsibility of keeping the peace across the country, especially in the trading towns and emporia of Haithabu (now Hedeby) and Ribe in southern Jylland, Birka in Sweden and Kaupang on the west coast of Norway, the foundations of all of which date from before the early ninth century. There is evidence of royal representation in Haithabu and Ribe from very early on in their histories. Haithabu was a royal foundation: the Frankish annals inform us that the Danish King Godfred destroyed the Obodrite town of Reric and moved its merchants to a place called Sliasthorp, which is doubtless the later Haithabu.[78] In 849 the German missionary Anskar

---

[78] Haithabu is located on Haddaby Nor at the mouth of the river Schlei in Germany, hence the alternative name *Schliasthorp*.

completed a church in the town, and in 873 the Danish King Sigfrid and the German King Ludwig agreed to allow merchants and their goods free passage across the Danish border. There is little doubt that Scandinavian kings would have fulfilled certain sacred functions as part of the pagan cults practised in the country, but initially their main income would have come from land, supplemented by tribute from conquered lands – in the case of Denmark often from Norway or from raids abroad, for example from Friesland and the land of the Obodrites south of the Baltic coast. The king's military prowess would then allow him to found or control spaces for the sale of goods. The early Scandinavian kingdoms thus found their focal points around the protection of trade and traders.

From around 804 we begin to hear more from the writen evidence. In that year Godfred was 'king of the Danes', and the Frankish sources tell of serious clashes between Franks and Danes at the Danish border in 804 and 805.[79] Godfred was killed by one of his own men in 810, and his successor, Hemming, concluded a peace treaty with the emperor, Charlemagne, the same year. When Hemming died in 812, civil war broke out,[80] and shifting alliances between Danes, Obodrites and Franks are attested in the sources, although none of these alliances seem to have finally brokered a lasting peace in the area. It was into this restless political landscape, in the year 826, that Anskar, a German missionary, arrived in Denmark in the retinue of a claimant to the Danish throne, Harald Klak, who had accepted Christianity and received baptism at Ingelheim (near Mainz) from the Emperor Louis the Pious in return for the emperor's support. Harald Klak was unsuccessful in his claim to the Danish kingdom and was expelled from the country, together with Anskar, in the following year. However, Anskar was invited back by Swedish emissaries to the emperor to perform a missionary journey to Birka in 830. When he returned from Sweden, he was appointed archbishop over a new archdiocese based in Hamburg, with special responsibility for the mission to Denmark and Sweden. Although Anskar was moderately successful in his efforts, the

[79] P. Sawyer, *Gyldendal og Politikens Danmarkshistorie.* Vol. III, *Da Danmark blev Danmark*, gen. ed. O. Olsen, trans. M. Hvidt. Copenhagen: Gyldendal & Politiken, 2002 [1986]; *Carolingian Chronicles*, sub annis 804–5.

[80] Ibid., *sub annis* 810–812.

hold of Christianity over Scandinavia was tenuous, and the new
religion had only taken superficial root in Denmark. Nowhere
was this more evident than in the fact that the town of Hamburg
was sacked by the pagan Danish King Haarik in 845.[81] After this,
Anskar transferred his episcopal see to the town of Bremen, and
henceforth the see became known as Hamburg-Bremen. Anskar
revisited Birka in 850 and continued his mission to Denmark.
Eventually, the sucessors to Harald, King Haarik and Haarik's
son, Haarik the Young, permitted Anskar to build churches in
Birka and Ribe (which, incidentally, indicates that the Danish
kingdom included parts of Sweden). Anskar died in 860 and left
his mission to his successors. Although he had been unsuccessful in his efforts to christianise Scandinavia, his mission meant
that the Nordic countries were counted among the subjects of the
archdiocese of Hamburg-Bremen until they succeeded in gaining
their own archdiocese in Lund in 1103/4.[82]

The personal power of a king during the Viking Age was to a
large extent determined by his personal esteem, his ability to
gather a hird of warriors around him who could add to his
prestige by plunder and military exploits, and by his ability to
co-operate with his nobles and thus keep them under control.
Opulent hospitality, panegyric poetry recited by skalds (court
poets) and the distribution of expensive gifts contributed to
royal power and increased its prestige. For example, in Lejre
near Roskilde on the island of Sjælland, a large royal compound
consisting of two halls almost 50 metres long, together with a
number of outlying houses, has been found that is remarkably
like the hall of the king of the Geats in *Beowulf* and the hall of the
Norwegian king in Niðaros.[83] The compound was in use for
almost three hundred years, from around 700 to the latter part
of the tenth century, and in contrast to most other buildings and
villages we know of from the period the layout of the compound
did not change, despite frequent repairs. Furthermore, we find
burial goods from this period consisting of richly decorated

[81] T. Reuter, ed. *The Annals of Fulda*. Ninth-Century Histories, 2. Manchester:
       Manchester University Press, 1992.
[82] Rimbert, *Anskar*.
[83] T. Christensen, Sagntidens Kongsgård. *Skalk*, 5, 1996, pp. 5–10; S. Heaney, trans.
       and ed. *Beowulf*. London: Faber and Faber, 1999; *Heimskringla: History of the Kings of
       Norway*, trans. L. M. Hollander. Austin: Published for the American-Scandinavian
       Foundation by the University of Texas Press, 1964.

riding gear, weapons and clothing that demonstrate the quality and opulence of goods, many of them imported from elsewhere in Europe, and to which the upper warrior-class were evidently accustomed.

It is difficult not to be struck by the scale and scope of the onslaught to which western Europe was exposed between the late eighth and mid-tenth centuries. Contemporaries were struck by the ferocity and relentlessness of the attacks, and sought to ascribe them to some flaw either in the alien culture or in their own. Dudo of St Quentin, who wrote around 1015 (when the Viking threat had long since subsided in his part of the world), had no doubt what caused the sudden appearance of ferocious warriors from the north: they were pagan polygamists who had left their country because there were too many of them:

> For these nations, greatly inflamed by lascivious unchastity, and ravishing very many women with singular baseness, by performing in this way, men beget from them countless filthy offspring through mingling in a union of unlawful sexual union. These offspring, who would have been superfluous had they continued to dwell in the inadequate land which they inhabited . . . after they had come to maturity . . . are driven out by lot . . . into the realms of foreign nations to obtain for themselves in battle realms wherein they might be able to live in never-ending peace, as did, for instance, the Getae, Goths who pillaged almost all of Europe up to where they now reside.[84]

Dudo's theory is clearly wrong: having more than one wife does not mean that birth rates go up, only that fewer men marry. So why did the Scandinavians suddenly take their wars outside Scandinavia in the eighth century? While not totally rejecting the idea that a population surplus might have been behind the Viking raids, Erslev and Steenstrup agree with Dudo that indeed there was a high population density in Scandinavia at the beginning of the Viking Age, but argue that more than one factor influenced the first Viking raids. Their suggestions, however, are vague and unsatisfactory.[85] Instead we must look at the evidence of settlement patterns and what we can surmise on the basis of the latest archaeological evidence.

[84] *Dudo of St. Quentin's Gesta Normannorum: An English Translation*, ed. and trans. F. Lipschitz, 1998. (Online) (http://www.the-orb.net/orb_done/dudo/02-vikings) Translation slightly emended by F. P.

[85] J. C. H. R. Steenstrup, Oldtiden og den ældre middelalder. In *Danmarks Riges Historie*, ed. K. S. A. Erslev, A. Heise, W. Mollerup, J. A. Fridericia, E. Holm, and A. D. Jørgensen. Copenhagen: Nordiske forlag, E. Bojesen, 1897–1904. pp. 223–24.

We have argued above that the Scandinavians played a crucial part in European politics, at least from the first century AD. The failure of the Roman army at the Battle of Teutoburg Forest caused a fundamental rethink of Roman foreign policy, and as a part of this process the Romans tried to contain the Germanic tribes north of the Rhine and Danube. They did so by forming diplomatic alliances with magnates to the far north of the Germanic tribes they tried to control. In this way the Romans became instrumental in accelerating an already existing development towards more stratified and unified kingdoms in the Scandinavian peninsula. These emergent dynasties participated as mercenary soldiers in the Roman wars against the Marcomanni in the late second century, and their Roman military training inspired new methods of military tactics and encouraged hierarchical structures among the Scandinavian chieftains. The combination of military renewal and a steady influx of wealth from serving in the Roman army meant that Scandinavian chieftains moved increasingly towards being petty kings with imperial designs on their neighbours. The weapon sacrifices in southern Scandinavia bear this development out. With their help it is possible to demonstrate that Scandinavia was constantly affected by war from the second to the sixth centuries. The Scandinavians not only sought out the finest weapons abroad but also imported half-finished, industrially produced weapons in large numbers. Contrary to the image of the roving Viking band, it is clear that the conduct of war was a highly centralised affair: the soldiers that perished in the incessant battles between Danes, Swedes and Norwegians in the third to sixth centuries did not bring their own weapons to the battlefield. They were equipped by their leader, and part of the measure of his success was his ability to maintain enough weapons to equip armies consisting of thousands of men.

Another aspect of these wars in Scandinavia was the sheer scale of operations: not only did magnates equip their armies, they also transported them over large distances. For this they needed ships. These ships were not the sleek Viking craft we think of now. Instead they were large rowing boats, each capable of transporting around thirty men. In other words, around fifty boats, representing a huge investment in time and money, would have been required to transport the army whose equipment was destroyed at

Illerup Ådal. These boats would have had a limited operating range, as their keels would not have allowed them to sail the open sea safely, and the pressure to succeed militarily probably lay behind a good deal of the developments in ship technology of the third to eighth centuries.

However, it is not only the weapon sacrifices that show that Scandinavia was developing into a highly sophisticated society. Fortifications sprang up across southern Scandinavia in the period as well. Sea barrages, both temporary and permanent, were built in the fjords and river mouths of southern Scandinavia, and ramparts were built across roads. In some places, mainly in the short strip across the neck of Jylland, these ramparts were designed to withstand massive attacks, but a series of lighter ramparts of limited use in military conflict are found constructed across some of the roads in the area, too. These allowed the already wealthy rulers to tax trade that was moving overland, and thus accumulate even more wealth. This wealth enabled them to guarantee the peace that was needed for markets and market towns to flourish, and so the sixth and seventh centuries saw the gradual establishment of trade posts and markets of international significance. Around the River Schlei in present-day Germany the town that later came to be known as Haithabu sprang up before 800, and on Helgö in Sweden an emporium was conducting lively trade from the late sixth century. Kaupang on the west coast of the Oslo Fjord was also active at the beginning of the Viking Age. The latest archaeological evidence from Ribe in Denmark indicates that this town was founded in the the early 700s. Ribe and Kaupang show clear evidence of a centralised power maintaining peace in the area, and chronicle evidence from Haithabu indicates that the town was founded in its final location as the result of a royal command around 800.

The paths of the regions of Scandinavia diverged in the sixth century. At that time Denmark saw a change in burial practices, while Sweden and Norway maintained the ostentatious magnate graves of the previous centuries. In Denmark, there was a movement towards less stratification, indicating that in this society the magnate class no longer needed to demonstrate its wealth through the display of magnificent sepulchres for the members of the ruling dynasty. The change may have had something to do with the return of the mysterious roving tribe of the Heruli, but it is enough for our purposes to point out that, whatever the cause, the change indicates falling prestige among the magnate class, while other archaeological evidence confirms there is no corresponding fall in the overall wealth of society. The logical conclusion must be that the magnate class in southern Scandinavia succeeded in creating a relatively peaceful and well-defended country. However, this success could have turned into disaster if the former fighting aristocracy had resumed the wars of the previous centuries. But, fortunately, being free of the disdain for trade that was such a part of Romano-Christian culture provided an outlet for magnates who were in danger of losing their *raison d'être*. Trading and raiding became an opportunity for creating further wealth for them, and with the development of the ocean-going Viking ship, with its sail, dropped keel and hydro-dynamic shape, the stage was set for the Scandinavians' dramatic entry into the annals of European history.

CHAPTER 3

First contact: England and the continent

Modern national historiography has given a vision of Scandinavian raiding and subsequent colonisation as a sharply compartmentalised series of geographically isolated events. Each area of the west did have different experiences of – and responses to – their encounter with the Danes and Norwegians, but to treat each in isolation is to ignore the common dimensions within this traumatic episode in European history. Despite, for example, the strongly Anglo-centric spin that drives most accounts of the Viking Age in Britain, the story is much more than the traditional account of Alfred, burnt cakes and a single-handed West Saxon resistance to a seemingly all-powerful enemy. The experience was not just an English one; nor, despite popular belief, was it largely confined to the waters around the British Isles. For all of western Europe, from Shetland to Algeciras, Pisa to Pamplona, the arrival of the Vikings heralded the bloody dawn of a new era of migration and state-building.

Early raids

The last decade of the eighth century saw an explosion of violence all around the shores of northern and western Britain: raids throughout the Hebrides in 794; Skye and St Columba monastery on Iona, Inishmurray and Innisboffin in 795; mainland Ireland and Argyll in 796; the Hebrides again and Ulster in 798; and Francia in 799.[1] While the forces involved may have been

[1] *The Annals of Ulster (to A.D. 1131)*, ed. and trans. S. Mac Airt and G. Mac Niocaill. Dublin: Dublin Institute for Advanced Studies, 1983. *sub annis* 794, 795, 798; *The Annals of Inisfallen (MS Rawlinson B.503)*, ed. and trans. S. Mac Airt. Dublin: Dublin Institute for Advanced Studies, 1951. *sub annis* 795, 796.

small – some of the raiding parties comprised the crews of as few as three ships – it is probable that there was already a considerable degree of planning and co-ordination behind these initial assaults. It has been suggested, for example, that the force that raided Lindisfarne in 793 was a splinter group from a larger fleet that rounded Cape Wrath in north-west Scotland in 794 and mounted the first raid on the Hebrides, recorded in the Annals of Ulster as 'the devastation of all the islands of Britain by gentiles'.[2] These raiders, probably Norwegian and operating from summer bases in Orkney, appear to have been probing for targets, gradually extending their range and starting to repeat their raids in directions where they had learned that soft targets were most numerous. However, although there is some evidence that reigning Scandinavian royalty was actively engaged in raiding in Hamburg and Friesland, it is likely that most early Viking raids were organised by individuals who acted without royal sanction (see Map 2).

Despite popular perceptions of raiders arriving unannounced in their sleek ships and slipping away before the smoke of their pillaging alerted the defenders of the wider locality, the first waves of Vikings did not have it all their own way. In 796 a small fleet entered the Tyne estuary and attacked the rich monastery at Jarrow. Encountering stiffer than expected resistance, in which their leaders were slain, the raiders fled, only for their ships to be driven ashore at Tynemouth and their crews slaughtered by the vengeful local populace. It is perhaps significant that this failure is the last securely attested Viking raid on England for nearly forty years, pressure instead building on Scotland and Ireland. In 802 Iona was sacked for a second time, and by 804 the monks there were preparing to move to the inland security of Kells in Ireland, but they had not made the transfer by 806 when a third Viking raid saw the slaughter of sixty-eight of their number. In 807, shortly after Iona was sacked for the fourth time, the abbot led the main part of his community to Kells, abandoning the island that for nearly 250 years had been the spiritual heart of Scottish Gaeldom (Figure 6).[3] The abbey, however, was not entirely abandoned, for a small body of monks under the leadership of the prior, Blathmacc Mac Flaind, a former warrior of

---

[2] *Annals of Ulster, sub anno 794.*
[3] *Annals of Ulster, sub annis 802, 804, 806, 807.*

Map 2 Viking Age British Isles.

aristocratic blood, remained in residence with the aim of seeking martyrdom. In 825 Iona was raided once more, and Blathmacc gained the end he craved. After killing most of his companions, the Vikings tortured Blathmacc for refusing to tell where the precious shrine of St Columba had been hidden:

[T]he violent cursed host came rushing through the open buildings, threatening cruel perils to the blessed men; and after slaying with mad savagery the rest of the associates, they approached the holy father to compel him to give up the precious metals wherein lie the holy bones of St Columba; but [the monks] had lifted the shrine from its pediments, and had placed it in the earth in a hollowed barrow, under a thick layer of turf; because they

Figure 6 Kells, Co. Meath, Ireland. Following the sacking of the island monastery of Iona on four successive occasions between 795 and 807 the monks moved to the comparative safety of Kells, taking with them the relics of Columba and the treasures of their community. The security of their new home was short-lived, the monastery falling prey to Viking raids, including major attacks in 920 and 951 by the Norse of Dublin.

knew then the wicked destruction [to come]. This booty the Danes desired; but the saint remained with unarmed hand, and with unshaken purpose of mind . . . therefore the pious sacrifice was torn limb from limb.[4]

It was evidently the death-blow for the monastery, which disappears from historical records for nearly 150 years (Figure 7). The picture we have, then, is of over a decade of sustained attack on the Western Isles and the Atlantic coast of Scotland, on islands off the Atlantic coast of Ireland and on sections of the

---

[4] A. O. Anderson, ed. *Early Sources of Scottish History, A.D. 500 to 1286*. Vol. I. Edinburgh and London: Oliver and Boyd, 1922. p. 264.

Figure 7
Martyrs' Bay, Iona. As one of the greatest and richest monasteries of Scotland, Iona was on the receiving end of a succession of Viking raids after 795. The third of these, in 806, saw the slaughter of sixty-eight of the monks on this sandy beach to the south of the abbey, where the raiders had beached their vessels.

north and west coasts of the Irish mainland. At first sight the implication that could be read into this pattern is that Viking war-bands had already begun to establish themselves in the northern islands of Scotland and the northern Hebrides, using these areas as bases from which to launch raiding expeditions down the western sea-lanes and ignoring the eastern coast of mainland Scotland, which at that time was controlled by the still powerful Pictish kingdom. In this view, it was soft targets that were being chosen, primarily the plunder-rich monasteries located conveniently on island and headland sites throughout the Gaelic west.

Francia

Down to the 830s the military strength of the Carolingian state could repel the seaborne raids. Scandinavian pressure in the west therefore appears to have fallen primarily on northern and western areas of the British Isles. However, as Frankish power declined and Charlemagne's heirs squabbled for mastery over their progenitor's empire, pressure began to shift southwards

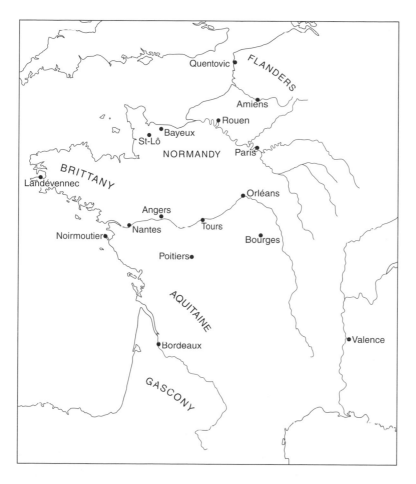

Map 3 Francia.

again to the English Channel and Atlantic coastlands of Francia. Almost inevitably, raids in that direction began to spill over into southern English districts that faced the continent, but the brunt of the attacks was borne by the Atlantic and Channel coasts of the Frankish Empire (see Map 3).[5] From 834 onwards chronicle accounts give the impression that the floodgates had been opened. Dorestad, near modern Nijmegen in the Netherlands, one of the great trading emporia of northern Francia, was plundered for the first time by a major force of Danes, an experience repeated in 835, 836 and 837.[6] Quentovic, a similar centre located near Etaples in northern France, fell

[5] E. Roesdahl, *The Vikings*. London: Penguin Books, 1998 [1987]. pp. 196–97; R. H. C. Davis, *A History of Medieval Europe from Constantine to Saint Louis*. London, New York; Longmans, Green, 1957. pp. 165–66.

[6] E. Roesdahl, *Vikings*, pp.196–98.

victim to a surprise raid in 842, and by the 840s Vikings had penetrated the Seine valley, sacking Paris for the first time in 845.[7] These were headline-grabbing events, used by mainly monastic chroniclers to lambast Carolingian rulers for their failure to provide protection and the Frankish people generally for their moral and spiritual degeneracy, for which these attacks were heaven-sent punishment. The image given is one of protracted crisis and a slide into anarchy and economic collapse as the great trading centres of the empire fell one by one before the onslaught. But it is a picture that draws little support from other evidence. Dorestad, for example, despite the slaughter and sack of the 830s seems quickly to have recovered its prosperity after each episode, and its disappearance in the 860s was a consequence of a shift in the course of the river channel along which its trade flowed rather than a result of Viking raids. Quentovic, too, suffered only temporarily in the aftermath of 842, and its steady decline in the tenth century was, like Dorestad, a result of environmental factors.[8]

A significant change in Viking tactics came about in 842 when a Viking war-band established a permanent base on the island of Noirmoutier near the mouth of the Loire.[9] From this strategic base they could penetrate deep into the heart of Francia up the navigable waterway and strike almost at will along the whole of the Atlantic coast from Brittany to northern Spain. More significantly, the taking of Noirmoutier marked the opening of a new phase in Viking activity, where the hit-and-run raids of the earlier ninth century gave way to longer-term predatory incursions and moves towards more permanent seizure of territory. By the late 840s the Loire-based Vikings had control of much of south-east Brittany and were turning the screw on Aquitaine, where they had penetrated the estuary of the Gironde and in 848 attacked Bordeaux.[10] Bordeaux's sack was symptomatic of a general

---

[7] Ibid., p.198.
[8] J. Haywood, *Encyclopaedia of the Viking Age*. London: Thames & Hudson, 2000. pp. 55, 151; J. L. Nelson, The Frankish Empire. In *The Oxford Illustrated History of the Vikings*, ed. P. H. Sawyer. Oxford: Oxford University Press, 1997. p. 24.
[9] *The Annals of St-Bertin*, ed. and annotated Janet L. Nelson. Ninth-Century Histories, I. Manchester: Manchester University Press, 1991. *sub anno* 843; Roesdahl, *Vikings*, p.198. For the movement of the fleeing monastic community of Noirmoutier, see H. W. C. Davis, *Medieval Europe*. Home University Library of Modern Knowledge. London, New York: Oxford University Press, 1960.
[10] Nelson, The Frankish Empire. In *The Oxford Illustrated History of the Vikings*, see note 8 above, p. 31.

problem within western Francia: few major centres had defences that could repel determined attack. Although most of the cities and smaller towns still possessed their late-Roman defences, the long era of internal stability in the west from the sixth to eighth centuries had seen their circuit walls fall into disrepair, and few were serviceable by the 800s. Frankish kings, moreover, were unwilling to allow cities to refortify as, with some justification, they feared that rebel magnates would turn them into fortresses to be used against the crown. It was only in the late ninth century that this policy was reversed, which led almost immediately to a dramatic decline in Viking successes.

Despite the highly coloured frothings of monastic writers, who presented the Vikings as heathen monsters of satanic character, some Frankish princes were prepared to deal with them as allies. The most prominent example of this is Pippin II of Aquitaine, a grandson of Emperor Louis the Pious. His failure to defend Bordeaux in 848 led to his deposition by his own people, and his cousin, Charles the Bald, forced him to enter a monastery.[11] Pippin, however, escaped from confinement in 857 and allied himself with the Loire Vikings in a bid to regain his patrimony, joining them in the bloody sack of Poitiers.[12] His actions outraged Frankish society, especially when it was reported that he had embraced both a Scandinavian lifestyle and adopted the Vikings' pagan religion. These accusations were used against him following his recapture in 864, and he was condemned and executed on charges of treason and apostasy.[13] Pippin's fate, however, did not prevent other rulers from seeking alliances with the Danes in the internecine struggle for power within western Francia or in order to keep Frankish power at arm's length. Count Robert of Angers hired Viking mercenaries to use in his wars with the Bretons, while Duke Saloman of Brittany in 866, for example, joined with them to reverse roles and defeat and kill Robert.[14] Clearly, despite the distaste with which they were viewed, the Vikings were to an extent being integrated into the political-military world of Francia.

[11] Nelson, The Frankish Empire, p. 31.
[12] Annals of St-Bertin, sub anno 858; Nelson, The Frankish Empire. In The Oxford Illustrated History of the Vikings, see note 8 above, p. 322.
[13] Annals of St-Bertin, sub annis 864, 869.
[14] Nelson, The Frankish Empire. In The Oxford Illustrated History of the Vikings, see note 8 above, pp. 32–33.

The activities of the Loire Vikings reached a new intensity from 862 when the Dane, Hastein, returned from a three-year raiding voyage around the western Mediterranean which saw the plundering of targets ranging from Mazimma in Morocco and Fiesole in Tuscany to Valence, nearly 200 kilometres inland on the Rhône. From Noirmoutier he waged a twenty-year reign of terror across a broad sweep of western and central Francia and Brittany. In 867 and 868 his raids penetrated as far east as Bourges and Orléans respectively, while in 872–73 he sacked Angers. It was only in 882 that, faced with the full might of the Frankish king, Louis III, Hastein agreed to withdraw and took his fleet north to the Channel coast.

There Hastein entered an increasingly crowded and steadily contracting theatre of operations, for the Frankish kings were also progressively closing off the region to Viking raids. As discussed above, the Channel coast had experienced an intensification of Viking activity in the 830s, and the Seine valley had been penetrated in the 840s. Paris was sacked for the first time in 845, then again in 857, 861 and 865. Charles the Bald's completion in 870 of a fortified bridge to control traffic on the Seine at Pont de l'Arche,[15] upstream from Rouen, provided fifteen years of respite for the upper reaches of the river. Similar bridges on the Oise and Marne attempted to close off the interior of northern Francia to raiding, but from 872 until 892 it was that region that bore the brunt of Viking attacks. For two decades, the country from the Rhineland, through Flanders and the Ardennes to the Seine valley, and the land around the Meuse, Scheldt and Somme were subjected to systematic devastation. In 881 the Danes began to penetrate the interior of northern Francia using tactics perfected in England in the 860s and 870s. Seizing horses from the local population, they were able to range far more widely through the countryside than had previously been possible for them.[16] In 882 a major fleet moved up the Scheldt to Condé, where a base was established and held for one year; from there, in 883, the army moved up the Somme to Amiens.[17] The following year the host divided, one group heading for England[18] while the main force moved east to sack Louvain before moving

[15] Haywood, Encyclopaedia, pp. 149–50.
[16] The Anglo-Saxon Chronicles, ed. and trans. M. J. Swanton. London: Phoenix, 2000. A, sub anno 881.
[17] Anglo-Saxon Chronicles, A, sub annis 883 [882], 884 [883].
[18] Ibid., sub anno 885 [884].

west again the following year to occupy a base on the Seine estuary.[19] The height of the crisis came in early winter 885, when the Danes moved up-river, stormed Pont de l'Arche and brought their fleet to besiege Paris once more. There, however, they were held at bay and forced into a protracted siege from November 885 until October 886, when Charles the Fat relieved the city. Rather than force a battle, however, Charles bought off the Vikings and gave them leave to proceed up the Seine and Marne to attack the Burgundians, supposedly as punishment for their disloyalty to him.[20] This action brought about the final turning of the Frankish nobility against the emperor, deposed in 887 by his nephew, Arnulf, who became king of the East Franks; meanwhile in western Francia Odo, the defender of Paris in 885–86, was elected king.[21] Both men began to take the offensive to the Danes, in marked contrast to their reviled predecessor. The Danes, meanwhile, over-wintered in the valley of the River Yonne.

There was no single Frankish victory that ended the Viking threat in the north. Odo did defeat the Danes at Montfaucon in 888, but the raiders were still able to threaten Paris again in 889, and it was rather a policy of constructing fortifications throughout the region between the Seine and the Rhine that sealed off the interior from Viking attack. With northern Francia becoming progressively less attractive as a theatre of operations, in 889 the Danes sailed west from the Seine estuary to St-Lô, from where they launched an assault on Brittany the following year.[22] The Bretons, however, repulsed the attack with a heavy defeat of the Danes, who then headed east again into Arnulf's territory. There, in 891, Arnulf inflicted a crushing defeat on them at the River Dyle near Louvain, where he overran the encampment of a force of Danes that had moved into Flanders from the Seine.[23] Faced with this unrelenting pressure and hard-hit by a severe famine in the winter of 891–92, the offer of tribute from Odo was sufficient to persuade most of the remaining Seine-based Danes to withdraw from Francia. Many, including Hastein, chose to try their luck in England.[24]

[19] Ibid., *sub anno* 886 [885].   [20] Ibid., *sub anno* 887 [886–7].   [21] Ibid.
[22] Ibid., *sub anno* 890 [889 and 890]; Nelson, The Frankish Empire. In *The Oxford Illustrated History of the Vikings*, see note 8 above, pp. 33–34.
[23] *Chronicle of Regino of Prüm*, printed in Davis, *Medieval Europe*, pp. 173–75.
[24] *Anglo-Saxon Chronicles*, A, E, *sub anno* 893 [892]. For a summary and analysis of the career of Hastein, see A. P. Smyth, *King Alfred the Great*. Oxford: Oxford University Press, 1995. pp. 117–19.

The withdrawal of the main Danish armies from Francia signalled the end of major Viking activity within Frankish territory,
but it did not mark the removal of the threat entirely. Two still-
substantial Scandinavian forces remained, one based in the Seine
estuary, the other at the mouth of the Loire. The leader of the
Seine Vikings, despite later Norman traditions, may have been
Norwegian rather than Danish. Icelandic saga sources identify
their leader as Göngu-Hrólfr, or Rolf the Ganger, son of
Rognvald, earl of Møre, who was exiled from Norway by King
Harald Hárfagri,[25] and the early eleventh-century Norman
chronicler Dudo of St Quentin dates his arrival on the Seine to
876, which is entirely compatible with that identification.[26] Rolf,
or Rollo as he is better known, pursued a predatory career down
into the early tenth century. In 911 he led his war-band in an
abortive attack on Chartres. The Frankish response to this move
was more astute than it has been painted by tradition, for at St-
Clair-sur-Epte the Frankish king, Charles the Simple, arranged a
treaty with Rollo which, in return for the Norseman's homage
and promise to defend the region against other Vikings, gave him
the title of count of Rouen, with control of that city and other
territories around the Seine estuary.[27] From this grant developed
the later duchy of Normandy, ruled by Rollo's lineal descendants.
Rollo became a nominal Christian in 912,[28] and was to receive
further grants of property from the crown down to 924, when he
was given Bayeux. He broke faith in 925 and launched a succession of attacks on neighbouring territories to the east, but was
defeated. While his son, William Longsword,[29] and subsequent
successors remained thorns in the side of later French kings,
their activities should be seen in the context of Frankish magnate
squabbles rather than as recognisably Viking behaviour. Indeed,
by the middle of the tenth century any distinctive Scandinavian
character had been lost by the Normans, who had largely adopted
the language and culture of the Franks.

Brittany had a different experience of the Vikings, having
endured phases of periodic occupation by the Loire-based army

---

[25] D. Crouch, *The Normans: The History of a Dynasty*. London: Hambledon and
London, 2002. pp. 1–8.

[26] Roesdahl, *Vikings*, p. 206.; Dudo of St. Quentin, *History of the Normans*, ed. and
trans. E. Christiansen. Woodbridge: Boydell Press, 1998.

[27] Crouch, *Normans*, p. 4.   [28] Ibid., p. 8.   [29] Ibid., pp. 8–14.

Figure 8 Landévennec Priory, Brittany. One of the chief spiritual and cultural centres of the Breton lands, St Winwaloe's monastery at Landévennec in its sheltered creek in western Brittany was destroyed by Viking raiders in 913. Its surviving monks fled with the saint's relics to safety in Francia, abandoning the monastery in a move symbolic of the near-collapse of the Christian society in regions subjected to sustained Viking attack.

but also on occasion allying with them against their common Frankish enemies. Breton strength, however, prevented any long-term incursions into their territory, and it was only as a result of a period of protracted weakness following the death of Duke Alan the Great in 907 that Viking interest in the duchy increased.[30] Pressure increased steadily and by 912 it was under constant attack, culminating in the effective collapse of the duchy in 919 and the flight of its leading families to England and Francia (Figure 8). The Vikings ruled Brittany from Nantes, but their takeover seems never to have developed beyond a military occupation. Certainly there is no indication of any significant rural colonisation, and Scandinavian rule appears to have remained as a kind of predatory lordship, sustained by tribute and raids rather than depending on agriculture and trade. Viking control,

[30] Nelson, The Frankish Empire. In *The Oxford Illustrated History of the Vikings*, see note 8 above, p. 33.; Haywood, *Encyclopaedia*, p. 37.

however, went unchallenged until 931, when the Bretons staged an unsuccessful revolt, but in 936 Alan Barbetorte, who had been living in exile in England, mounted an invasion that drove the Danes from Brittany within three years.[31] Low-level Viking raiding continued to plague Brittany into the early eleventh century, but the prospect of a second Scandinavian principality in northern France had effectively ended by 939.

Raids on England c. 840–c. 900

In the year 834, when the Frisian mart at Dorestad was first hit, a Viking war-band crossed the Channel and launched a plundering raid on the Wessex coast which saw a heavy defeat inflicted on Egbert, the West Saxon king. This raid appears to have been the first significant action in the region for four decades, and marked the beginning of what was to be an almost annual experience. As in Francia, it was the high-profile victims who were recorded, and a similar pattern of hit-and-run raids against the principal trading ports can be seen. In 840, for example, it was Southampton and Portland, while in 842 it was Rochester and London that were targeted. But it was not solely these plunder-rich communities that drew attack, for in 841 the whole coast from Sussex round to Lincolnshire experienced a succession of small but debilitating raids, Viking crews landing, plundering and then withdrawing to their ships before the local levies could be mustered against them. Although Anglo-Saxon sources almost uniformly label these western raiders 'Danes' or, more generically, 'heathens', it is possible that they were Norwegian and part of the steadily increasing northern Scandinavian presence in western maritime Britain. The raiders were not, however, entirely unwelcome, for the Britons of Cornwall saw them as useful allies to be employed against Wessex, and as early as 838 Vikings and Cornishmen had fought together against the West Saxons.[32] Although Egbert overcame this first Cornish threat, Wessex remained vulnerable in its remoter western

---

[31] Nelson, The Frankish Empire. In *The Oxford Illustrated History of the Vikings*, see note 8 above, pp. 33–34.
[32] *Anglo-Saxon Chronicles*, E, *sub anno* 835 [838]; for a general discussion of Viking activity in south-west England, see M. Todd and A. Fleming, *The South-West to AD 1000*. Regional History of England. London, New York: Longman, 1987. pp. 75–77.

districts, and it was in Dorset in 843 that his successor, Æðelwulf, suffered a heavy defeat.[33] Devon, Dorset and Somerset continued to suffer plundering raids throughout the 840s, but in 848 the local levies won a notable victory over a fleet of thirty-five ships that had based itself in the estuary of the River Parret.[34] Although the raids throughout this period had been regular, destructive and terrifying, they were also comparatively small-scale in comparison with those being experienced by northern Francia and Ireland. That, however, was soon to change.

The intensity of raids on southern England increased steadily throughout the 840s. Then in 850 came a significant change in tactics by the Danes: they over-wintered on English soil for the first recorded time (see Map 4).[35] Based on the Isle of Thanet, which at that date was still separated from the Kentish coast by a broad, marshy channel, they were secure from attack and free to launch raids around the outer Thames estuary. In the spring the largest Viking fleet yet seen appeared off the north Kent coast. The Kentishmen were overwhelmed and Canterbury sacked. Having plundered northern Kent, the Vikings pushed up the Thames and northwards into Mercian territory before turning south into Wessex. There, in a battle at the unidentified *Acleah*, King Æðelwulf routed the invaders 'and there made the greatest slaughter of a heathen host that we have ever heard tell of'.[36] The Kentishmen, too, enjoyed some measure of revenge, King Æðelstan defeating a Viking fleet in a naval battle off the coast at Sandwich. Despite the West Saxon successes of 850, however, the rich culture of southern England was too tempting a target for the raiders to ignore, and in 853 a Danish army again occupied Thanet, whilst in 855 a large force over-wintered in Sheppey.[37] By this date the raiding parties were growing larger still and their targets more audacious, until c. 861 a major force succeeded in sacking Winchester, the political and religious heart of Wessex.[38] Few, however, could have expected the full horror of the storm that was about to be unleashed upon the Anglo-Saxon kingdoms.

[33] *Anglo-Saxon Chronicles*, A, *sub anno* 840 [843].
[34] Ibid., *sub anno* 845 [848].   [35] Ibid., *sub anno* 851 [850].
[36] Ibid.   [37] Ibid., *sub annis* 853, 855.   [38] Ibid., *sub anno* 860.

Map 4 Viking
Age England.

THE GREAT ARMY AND THE CONQUEST OF ENGLAND

For southern and eastern Britain the mid-860s was a decisive
turning point, with a marked change in the character of the
Scandinavian raiding and a greater and clearer sense of purpose
on the part of the Vikings. The re-organisation of the Frankish
defences in the earlier 860s had begun to have an impact on the
Vikings' ability to harry northern Francia, and in 865, after a final
push up the Seine to sack Paris, their leadership recognised that it

was time to shift their focus elsewhere. As a result of this a great 'heathen host' of Danes sailed north and landed in Thanet. In return for a large cash payment they agreed to a peace treaty with the Kentishmen but, breaking their agreement, they left their encampment by night and started to plunder all of eastern Kent.[39] This attack coincided with the arrival of a much larger Danish force, commanded by Ivar the Boneless and Halfdan (whom tradition records as the sons of the semi-mythical Ragnar Loðbrók), which landed in East Anglia and established a winter base there. To later generations of Anglo-Saxons, this Danish host was known as the *micel here* or 'Great Army (or Host)', whose actions were to bring the patchwork of petty English kingdoms to the brink of oblivion.

Ivar and Halfdan brought a wholly new dimension to the Scandinavian onslaught on southern Britain. Their tactics over the next five years display a combination of keen awareness of the strategic military situation within England coupled with a firm grasp of the political position within each of the Anglo-Saxon kingdoms. Military shock tactics and acute intelligence-gathering brought the invaders to within an inch of eliminating organised resistance throughout England. The first indication of their aims came in the autumn of 865 when, having received the submission of the East Angles and the promise of tribute, they did not withdraw. Instead, they set up a fortified base and over-wintered in East Anglia.[40] Over the winter months they were evidently gathering information on the situation in Northumbria, and in the spring they struck with stunning savagery and speed.

Speed and mobility had been the keys to the Vikings' successful sea-borne raiding since the late eighth century. Their highly manoeuvrable ships enabled them to land, strike and withdraw with tremendous rapidity. Now they were transferring those same skills to land-based fighting. The source of their mobility was horses, which had been prominent amongst the tribute that they took from the East Anglians the previous autumn. On horseback, Ivar and Halfdan's Danes literally left the Anglo-Saxon infantry warriors standing.[41]

Leaving East Anglia, the Great Army moved rapidly north through Lindsey and round the head of the Humber. Their target was Northumbria, which was convulsed by a civil war between

[39] Ibid., *sub annis* 865, 866 [865].   [40] Ibid., *sub anno* 866 [865].
[41] Smyth, *Alfred*, p. 21.

King Ælle – whom legend records as having captured and executed Ragnar Loðbrók during an earlier Viking raid – and Osberht, a rival for his throne. In autumn 866 Ivar and Halfdan burst into York, the chief city of Northumbria, seat of one of the two Anglo-Saxon archbishoprics and the richest trading centre north of London (Figure 9).[42] Accessible by water up the River Ouse from the Humber and located in the midst of the rich agricultural land of the Vale of York, the city provided the Danes with plunder, security and a choice of escape routes should withdrawal prove necessary. Bitterly divided as they were, it must have seemed unlikely that the Northumbrians would be able to dislodge this unlooked-for new enemy and, as winter approached, the Danes settled down within their strongly fortified prize. Forced into co-operation by the common threat, Ælle and Osberht joined forces in March 867 and stormed York. Initial success turned to disaster for the Northumbrians as they were all but massacred in savage street-fighting through the burning city. When the fighting ended both Ælle and Osberht were dead, and the Danes' grip on York was stronger than ever.[43]

The taking of York marked a second new development in the Viking onslaught. While Scandinavian raiders had set up their own strongholds, such as the Irish *longphort* encampments (see Chapter 4), this was the first time that they had occupied and held a major native centre. After their defeat of the Northumbrian kings in March 867, moreover, it became clear that the Danes regarded York as an asset to be retained and one to which they would return. In the summer, as they prepared to move on, they installed a puppet king, Egbert, who was to rule until such time as Ivar and Halfdan returned to reclaim their prize.[44] Through the surrogacy of Egbert the Danes could consolidate their hold over the Northumbrian political heartland while they themselves turned elsewhere. With their rear secure, the Danes returned south of the Humber and penetrated deep into Mercia where, in the autumn, they seized a fortified Nottingham as their winter base.[45] A pattern was beginning to emerge.

---

[42] *Anglo-Saxon Chronicles*, A, *sub anno* 867 [866].
[43] Ibid., *sub anno* 867 [866].
[44] *Symeonis monachi opera omnia*, ed T. Arnold. Rerum britannicarum medii aevi scriptores, 75. New York: Kraus Reprint Ltd, 1965 [1885]. pp. 105–6.
[45] *Anglo-Saxon Chronicles*, A, *sub anno* 868 [867]; Smyth, *Alfred*, p. 23.

Figure 9 York, Anglian Tower. The old Roman fortifications of York were maintained and repaired by the Northumbrian kings down to the ninth century, as shown by the seventh to ninth-century 'Anglian Tower' in the city's western defences. Despite the walls, the Danes stormed their way into the city in 866.

Ivar and Halfdan remained at Nottingham over the winter of 867–68. Unable to dislodge them on his own, Burhred, king of Mercia, called for West Saxon aid to drive out the invaders. Æðelred of Wessex responded to the appeal by leading his levies to Nottingham, but even the joint strength of Wessex and Mercia was unable to take the fortification, and Burhred was eventually obliged to sue for peace.[46] The Danes withdrew to their secure base in York, which Egbert yielded up to them, and there they gathered their strength for a renewed onslaught on the southern English kingdoms.[47]

In autumn 869 Ivar and Halfdan again headed south with their host, bursting through eastern Mercia into East Anglia in what the Anglo-Saxon Chronicle presents as an orgy of looting and violence. In line with their established practice, they seized a defensible base at Thetford in which they over-wintered. Early in 870 the East Anglian king, Edmund, staged a counter-attack but was defeated, captured and, depending on the version of events preferred, either executed out of hand or offered as a sacrifice to Oðin.[48] His death effectively marked the end of the independent existence of East Anglia as an Anglo-Saxon kingdom and placed the Danes in control of a broad swathe of territory extending from York in the north almost to the Thames estuary in the south.

After his victory over Edmund there is no further mention of Ivar in any accounts, and it was Halfdan alone who carried the offensive southwards in the summer and autumn of 870. His target was Wessex, the only one of the Anglo-Saxon kingdoms yet to have escaped the attentions of the Great Army.[49] The Danes established a base at Reading, from which they fanned out across country. A series of bloody clashes between the West Saxons and the Danes at Ashdown, Basing and Marlborough – in the last of which King Æðelred I was mortally wounded – culminated in a Danish victory at Wilton over the new king of Wessex, Alfred.[50] Even allowing for the strongly West Saxon bias of our main surviving sources for this period, the fighting in 871 appears to have been particularly intense and savage. Despite the defeats suffered, Wessex was already establishing a status as the only one of the Anglo-Saxon kingdoms to have mounted any significant resistance to the invaders, a status that was to be much developed in later propaganda. The strength of the resistance, however, evidently took the Danes, who were more used to the rapid

[46] *Anglo-Saxon Chronicles*, A, *sub anno* 868 [867 and 868].
[47] Ibid., *sub anno* 869.
[48] Ibid., *sub anno* 870 [869 and 870]; ibid., E, *sub anno* 870 [869]; Smyth, *Alfred*, pp. 28–29.
[49] Ibid., pp. 30–36.
[50] *Anglo-Saxon Chronicles*, A, *sub anno* 871 [870]; Smyth, *Alfred*, p. 37.

Figure 10
St Paul's Churchyard, London, Scandinavian grave slab. The sculpture, which shows Sleipnir, Oðin's eight-legged horse, marked the burial place of a pagan Scandinavian within the Christian heart of London. It is a powerful image of the stranglehold maintained by the Danes on the chief commercial centre of southern Britain in the 870s.

collapse of native defences elsewhere, somewhat by surprise, and they readily accepted Alfred's offer of a truce. The shattered kingdoms of East Anglia and Mercia offered better prospects for plunder.

Success for Wessex in 871 spelled disaster for the rest of Anglo-Saxon England. After their treaty with Alfred, the Danes had withdrawn to London and remained there throughout 872, tightening their grip over the Thames estuary region and the river systems feeding into it from the north (Figure 10).[51] Then, in 873, after an absence of four years, Halfdan led his men back to York to exact tribute from Northumbria before heading south (into Lincolnshire) to establish winter quarters at Torksey in Lindsey.[52] Having effectively crushed Lindsey, the Danes re-entered Mercia proper and fortified Repton as their winter base (Figure 11). In the

[51] *Anglo-Saxon Chronicles*, A, *sub anno* 872 [871].
[52] Ibid., *sub anno* 873 [872].

Figure 11
St Wystan's Church, Repton, Derbyshire. The eighth-century crypt survives from the Mercian monastery occupied by the Great Army in the winter of 873–74. Excavation at the monastic site in the 1980s revealed a mass burial of what appeared to be Viking warriors killed in a winter epidemic.

spring the storm fell once more on Mercia, whose king fled before the onslaught, ending his days as a penitent in Rome.[53] Following the example used at York, Halfdan installed a puppet king in Mercia, Ceolwulf, described as 'a foolish king's thane', who swore that he would place the kingdom at their disposal and serve the needs of the Danish army as required.[54] By the end of 874 the Great Army had broken the power of Northumbria, East Anglia and Mercia, installed puppet kings over two of those

---

[53] Smyth, *Alfred*, p. 40.
[54] *Anglo-Saxon Chronicles*, A, *sub anno* 874 [873].

kingdoms, battered the West Saxons into submission, and stood poised to complete the conquest of England.

At this juncture the Great Army split. In 875 Halfdan took a portion of the army into northern Northumbria.[55] This district, Bernicia, which had been the dominant half of the old kingdom, had escaped the worst impact of the Viking invasion of 866–67. Despite the traditional portrayal of the fall of York in 866 as representing the end of Northumbria, the surviving northern portion of the kingdom – which stretched from Teesdale and central Lancashire in the south to the Firth of Forth in the north – still constituted a significant military power. It was, moreover, liberally endowed with wealthy churches and monasteries – prime targets for Viking attacks. Pressure was to be maintained on the region until Halfdan's death in 877.[56] In 875 he sacked Carlisle, Hexham and Lindisfarne, the community of the last-mentioned finally abandoning its monastery for a decade of semi-nomadic existence,[57] and rampaged through the country between the Solway and the Forth. His raid may have had a greater impact on Northumbrian political society west of the Pennines than the initial onslaught in 866–67, for the account of the wandering Lindisfarne monks and the relics of St Cuthbert gives little indication of organised government in the region. In autumn 875, having cowed the north, Halfdan led his men back to York, where the army finally dispersed, to settle both in the city and throughout the rich agricultural area between the Humber and the Tees (Figure 12).[58]

While Halfdan consolidated his hold over the north, the remainder of the Great Army under the command of Guthrum turned its attentions once more to the south. In 875 they based themselves at Cambridge; the following year Guthrum renewed the offensive against Wessex, where he seized Wareham in Dorset as a base from which to harry the western part of the kingdom.[59] As in 870–71 the West Saxons fought back deter-minedly and Alfred forced Guthrum into a truce but, in the midst of negotiations, the Danes broke away into Devon – pursued

---

[55] *Symeonis monachi opera*, 75, p. 110; *Anglo-Saxon Chronicles*, A, *sub anno* 875 [874].
[56] *Symeonis monachi opera*, 51, pp. 202–3.
[57] Ibid., pp. 53–54, 56–57; ibid., 75, p. 110.
[58] *Anglo-Saxon Chronicles*, A, *sub anno* 876 [875].
[59] Ibid., *sub annis* 875 [874], 876 [875].

Figure 12
Brompton, North Yorkshire, hog-back tombstone. The distinctive Scandinavian tombstones, whose curved backs represent the roof ridges of timber houses, mark the distribution of Danish settlers around York. Laden with pagan symbolism but Christian in context, they may mark a transitional stage in the integration of the colonists into Northumbrian society.

by Alfred – and took Exeter. Guthrum's move had been prompted by the presence of a large Danish fleet cruising along the Channel coast, with which he planned to link up, but the ships were scattered and many lost in a storm off Swanage in Dorset.[60] Deprived of either re-inforcements or a means of escape, Guthrum again submitted and withdrew into Mercia, where he obliged Ceolwulf to honour his oaths of 874. The Danes took possession of the area north and east of the River Welland, comprising the bulk of the kingdom, leaving Ceolwulf as king of a rump of territory.[61] It appeared that, like Halfdan's followers, the remnants of the Great Army were settling down, and a significant portion may indeed have done so, forming a Scandinavian colony dispersed around what became known in the tenth century as the Five Boroughs: Derby, Leicester, Lincoln, Nottingham and Stamford. Appearances, however, proved deceptive.

In the winter of 877–78 Guthrum broke his truce with Alfred and launched a surprise attack against Wessex from a base in Gloucester.[62] What appears to have been a co-ordinated attack on Devon and Somerset was launched by a separate Viking force that had been over-wintering in south Wales. Although the West Saxons defeated this force, Alfred was forced increasingly onto the defensive, and by Easter 878 Wessex stood on the brink of collapse. Gathering his forces at Athelney in the Somerset marshes, Alfred mounted an unexpected counter-attack and routed the Danes at Edington in Wiltshire.[63] Guthrum was now forced into

---

[60] Ibid., *sub anno* 877 [876].   [61] Ibid.; Smyth, *Alfred*, pp. 68–72.
[62] *Anglo-Saxon Chronicles*, A, *sub anno* 878; Smyth, *Alfred*, pp. 72–74.
[63] Ibid., pp. 74–75.

unconditional surrender and received Christian baptism as part of the price of peace. This time Guthrum honoured the treaty and withdrew from West Saxon territory into East Anglia, where his army finally dispersed and settled in a land-take similar to Halfdan's around York.[64] Wessex had survived, alone amongst the former Anglo-Saxon powers of southern mainland Britain, while a broad sweep of territory from the Thames to the Tees had been transformed effectively into a Danish colony.

ANGLO-SCANDINAVIAN YORK AND THE FIVE BOROUGHS

The Danes of York experienced a rapid integration into northern English society. Many had accepted Christianity before the end of the ninth century. Close co-operation rapidly emerged between the Northumbrian church and the Danish conquerors, whose rule the native church leaders regarded as a lesser evil than the civil war and royal plundering of church resources that had preceded the fall of York in 866. This relationship was cemented c. 882–84 when Guthfrith, a Christian Dane, succeeded to the kingship at York.[65] He took not only the church of York under his protection but extended his guardianship to the highly influential community of St Cuthbert, whose acceptance of his lordship gave him influence within the land beyond the Tees. The greater stability of Northumbria under its Danish rulers is underscored by the Lindisfarne community's decision to return after three decades of exile in the west and settle in 883 at Chester-le-Street,[66] in the heart of what had been hotly disputed territory between Angles and Danes in the 870s. Guthfrith's acceptance as a Christian king ruling over much of former Northumbria is emphasised by his burial in 895 in York Minster,[67] which the archbishop (Wulfhere) wished to establish as the symbolic and spiritual heart of northern England.

Guthfrith's immediate successors in York were either Christian or at least not hostile towards Christianity. This situation helped foster the fusion of Scandinavian and Anglian components within the kingdom, a development well advanced by

---

[64] *Anglo-Saxon Chronicles*, A, *sub annis* 878, 879 [878].
[65] *Symeonis monachi opera*, 51, pp. 68–71.   [66] Ibid., p. 69.
[67] F. M. Stenton, *The Oxford History of England*. Vol. II, *Anglo-Saxon England*. Oxford: Oxford University Press, 1947 [1943]. p. 262.

c. 900. Indeed, Christianised York had become such an accepted part of mainland political society that the exiled West Saxon prince Æðelwold, son of King Æðelred I, could ally with the Danes of York in a bid to win the throne of Wessex and not be regarded as a pariah by his own people.[68] This position stands in sharp contrast to that of the Norse of Dublin, whose aggressive paganism continued to set them apart within the political world of their host culture. By around 900, then, it appeared that an Anglo-Danish kingdom of Northumbria, little different from its pre-866 precursor, would emerge as a northern counter-balance to the growing power of Wessex in the south.

The political development of such an Anglo-Scandinavian kingdom was halted in its tracks in 909–10. York's support for Æðelwold had ended in defeat by Wessex in 905, but in 906 a treaty had been agreed between the two powers.[69] In 909, however, Edward the Elder, king of Wessex, who recognised the threat posed to his position by the northerners, sent his army into Northumbria and ravaged the kingdom for five weeks before eventually forcing its rulers to come to terms.[70] The following year the Danes of York broke the truce and, in alliance with the Danes of the Five Boroughs, launched an attack on English Mercia. The Danish army penetrated as far south as the Severn in a raid reminiscent of the Great Army's tactics, but, as it withdrew towards the north, it was intercepted by Edward the Elder and his army at Tettenhall in Staffordshire and annihilated. Amongst the dead were the brothers Halfdan, Eowils and Ivar, joint rulers of York.[71] With the elimination of the York leaders the Anglo-Danish kingdom all but collapsed, and Edward the Elder moved in swiftly to fill the vacuum and assert his lordship over the Danelaw (see p. 101 below).

THE ESTABLISHMENT OF THE DANELAW AND THE ANGLO-SAXON RECONQUEST

Alfred's victory in 878 provided Wessex with a long respite from significant raids and permitted the re-organisation of the kingdom's defences.[72] Alfred is also credited with wide-ranging

---

[68] *Anglo-Saxon Chronicles*, A, *sub anno* 901 [899].   [69] Ibid., E, *sub anno* 906.
[70] Ibid., A, *sub anno* 910 [909].   [71] Ibid., C. *sub anno* 910; D, *sub anno* 911.
[72] Smyth, *Alfred*, Chapter 4.

reforms of the military structures of Wessex, in particular his re-organisation of the *fyrd*, the system for providing military levies, which enabled him to keep a military force in the field virtually at all times. He also reformed the traditional royal right to labour services for the building of fortresses, roads and bridges in order to begin the development of *burhs*, fortified strongpoints that could be used as both offensive and defensive centres for local resistance to raiders. Amongst other measures adopted was the building of a fleet intended for the interception of raiders at sea. The ships proved their worth as early as 882, when they captured four ships off the Channel coast,[73] but they were insufficient in numbers to prevent a large Danish fleet from Francia landing in Kent in 884.[74] This fresh Danish force persuaded Guthrum to break his treaty with Alfred, but the threat from the Danish colonies in eastern England was contained without serious risk to Wessex. It was a traditional army that Alfred brought to Rochester in 885 to break the Danish siege, but he used his fleet to carry the offensive across the Thames estuary against a smaller Danish fleet based in Essex.[75] The West Saxon victory in Kent and Essex was rounded off with the occupation of London, which had been in Danish hands since 871, and the settlement of a new treaty with Guthrum which obliged him to grant equal rights under law to the English population of the Danish-held lands. The treaty survived Guthrum's death in 890 but failed in 892 when the Viking army from northern Francia arrived in England.[76]

The main Danish force attacked Kent, while Hastein and his men entered the Thames estuary with an eighty-strong fleet and established a base at Benfleet in Essex. Despite their pledges to Alfred, the Danes of East Anglia and York allied themselves with the new-comers, but constant harrying by the West Saxon army denied the invaders any opportunity of breaking out of their beachheads.[77] Danish sea-borne raids as far west as Devon were repulsed with heavy losses in 893 and, following a string of defeats in Essex and Kent, a large element of the army moved up Watling Street, the old Roman road running north-westwards from London, into north-west England, where they occupied the remains of the Roman

---

[73] *Anglo-Saxon Chronicles*, A, *sub anno* 882.   [74] Ibid., *sub anno* 885 [884].
[75] Ibid., E, *sub anno* 885.   [76] Ibid., A, *sub anno* 893 [892]; Smyth, *Alfred*, Chapter 5.
[77] *Anglo-Saxon Chronicles*, A, *sub anno* 894 [893].

legionary fortress at Chester.[78] This move took them far beyond West Saxon territory into Mercia, but since the death of King Ceolwulf in 879 what was left of that kingdom had fallen increasingly under Alfred's domination. In or around 883 a large part of Mercia west of Watling Street had fallen under the control of a nobleman called Æðelred, who took a strongly anti-Danish and pro-Wessex stance. Alfred capitalised on this position by marrying his daughter, Æðelflæd, to Æðelred, and the couple ruled Mercia jointly until Æðelred's death in 911.[79] Through this alliance the military pressure on the Danes was maintained.

Early in 894 the Danes, desperately short of supplies, abandoned Chester and headed west. They raided into Gwynedd in the north of Wales, but were again forced to withdraw eastwards in the face of stiff Welsh resistance and a lack of forage.[80] Harried all the way, they retreated through northern Mercia into East Anglia, where they drew fresh support from their kinsmen and made a temporary base on the island of Mersea (in Essex). This was followed by an attempt to establish a fortified base on the River Lea, north of London, but they were driven from there in 895 and forced westwards into Mercia, leaving most of their ships to be captured or destroyed by the West Saxon garrison of London.[81] The Danes finally succeeded in securing a winter base at Bridgnorth on the Severn but, faced with Alfred's army in spring 896, they dispersed, some heading for York, others to East Anglia, while the residue took to their ships and returned to Francia.[82] As colonists, this fresh wave of incomers served to consolidate the Danish hold over England north and east of the line of Watling Street – the area that was coming to be known as the Danelaw – with the most intensive colonisation occurring in East Anglia, the eastern Midlands, Lindsey and the Vale of York. Nevertheless, the failure of the 892–96 Danish army to repeat the successes of the Great Army of the 860s proved to be a turning-point in the conflict, and for much of the next century the initiative lay with the West Saxon kings.

---

[78] Ibid. This version of the chronicle gives a detailed account of the movements of the Viking force through Wessex and the nature and degrees of success of the local resistance to them.
[79] Ibid., C, *sub anno* 911.   [80] Ibid., A, *sub anno* 895 [894].
[81] Ibid., *sub anno* 896 [895].   [82] Ibid., *sub annis* 896 [895], 897 [896].

CHAPTER 4

Ireland and Scotland

The late 830s saw an intensification of Scandinavian activity in Scotland and Ireland, culminating in two events that had profound repercussions for the future path of British history. The first occurred in 838, when a small fleet of Viking ships entered the mouth of the River Liffey in eastern Ireland and established a fortified base or, as the native Irish called them, *longphort* on its southern bank at the place that in time would become Dublin. For Ireland, this small event marked the opening of four decades of intense Viking pressure, which saw further longphorts established at Cork, Limerick, Waterford and Wexford, Viking fleets operating on the great river and lough systems of the Irish interior, and raids that penetrated every corner of the island. The second event occurred in Scotland in 839. Few records survive to give any clear impression of the intensity of Scandinavian attacks on the Scottish mainland, but it is evident that activity increased significantly in the 830s. Settlement in the Hebrides provided bases from which raids were launched against the centres of Gaelic power in Dál Riada (Argyll), religious communities down the western seaboard, and against the heartland of the dominant political power, the Picts. In 839 a large Viking force, probably Norwegian rather than Danish, penetrated the Earn and Tay valleys in the heart of the Pictish kingdom and, somewhere in Strathearn, slaughtered Eóganán, king of the Picts, his brother, the vassal king of the Scots, and the cream of the Pictish aristocracy, 'almost without number'.[1] This elimination

[1] *The Annals of Ulster (to A.D. 1131)*, ed. and trans. S. Mac Airt and G. Mac Niocaill. Dublin: Dublin Institute for Advanced Studies, 1983. *sub anno* 839; for the significance of these events, see A. P. Smyth, *New History of Scotland*. Vol. I, *Warlords and Holy Men: Scotland, AD 80–1000*. London: Edward Arnold, 1984. pp. 180–81; B. E. Crawford, *Scandinavian Scotland. Scotland in the Early Middle Ages*. Leicester: Leicester University Press, 1987. pp. 48–49.

of the Pictish leadership destroyed the sophisticated kingdom that had been built up in what is now eastern Scotland by Eóganán's predecessors and started a chain of events that led within a decade to the Gaelic warlord Cináed mac Alpín's seizure of the Pictish kingship and establishment of the kingdom that would evolve into medieval Scotland.[2]

Scotland and Ireland to c. 900

Viking activity around Ireland had slackened after about 813, the lull possibly coinciding with the beginning of the colonisation of the Hebrides, but it also followed a string of defeats inflicted on various war-bands by native Irish kings in Ulaid, Munster and Connacht.[3] Raids intensified once more in the 820s, coastal monasteries once more being targeted, e.g. Cork was raided in 821 and 839.[4] Larger-scale operations commenced in the 830s,[5] coinciding with the intensification of Danish attacks on England and Francia. In 832 a fleet numbered at 120 – probably simply the chronicler's attempts to indicate 'a great many' – raided the coastlands of the kingdoms of northern and eastern Ireland. The larger fleets active from the early 830s may have marked a decisive shift in the nature of the onslaught. There is some evidence to suggest that provincial kings from Scandinavia were moving to secure control of the increasingly profitable western adventures. Members of the Vestfold dynasty, for example, may have been active in Ireland by the early 840s. Viking raiding strategy began to change in character in the mid-830s from attacks on primarily coastal or island localities to ones that penetrated deep into the interior up the many navigable water-ways. By soon after 840 they had also established a number of longphorts at various strategic locations around the country. The

---

[2] S. Foster, *Picts, Gaels and Scots: Early Historic Scotland.* London: B. T. Batsford Ltd/ Historic Scotland, 1996. pp. 108–17. Foster's book offers a brief overview of the state formation process.

[3] *Annals of Ulster*, *sub annis* 811, 812; AC [Annals of Clonmacnoise], *sub anno* 808 (recte 811), 809 (recte 812); FM [Four Masters], *sub anno* 807 (recte 812).

[4] *Coghadh Gaedhel re Gallaibh: The War of the Gaedhil with the Gaill: Or the Invasions of Ireland by the Danes and Other Norsemen: The Original Irish Text*, ed. and trans. J. H. Todd. Rerum britannicarum medii aevi scriptores, 48. Vaduz, Liechtenstein: Kraus Reprint, 1965 [1867]. p. 5.

[5] Ibid., p. 9.

Figure 13 River Liffey, Dublin. In 841 the Vikings established a base on the south bank of the Liffey beside the 'Black Pool', which grew into their chief centre in Ireland. Close to the sea and the main maritime trade routes, and located on the eastern edge of the routes into the heart of the island, Dublin's strategic position gave it tremendous political and economic power.

first and most successful was Dublin, built in 841, followed shortly after by bases at Limerick in the west, Cork in the south-west, and Waterford and Wexford in the south-east (Figure 13).[6] Only in the north of Ireland, where the northern Uí Néill mounted a highly successful defence against the Norse, were the raiders unsuccessful in establishing a permanent foothold. Longphorts were also created in the interior of Ireland. In

[6] J. Haywood, *Encyclopaedia of the Viking Age*. London: Thames & Hudson, 2000. pp. 50, 56–57, 121–22, 123, 204, 208.

844 a large fleet entered the Shannon river system and established a base on Lough Ree, from which raids struck out in all directions. Connacht to the west and Mide [Meath] to the east were particularly severely affected. One of the leaders of this fleet, known from Irish sources as Turgeis (representing Old Norse Thórgestr or Thórgils), later acquired a reputation amongst the Irish as the archetype of the demonic, heathen warrior, inspired by Satan and wholly inimical to the Christian religion. Later tradition has manufactured a picture of him as one of the main Viking leaders and, ultimately, king of all Vikings in Ireland. His career, however, was short and violent. In 845 he was captured by the southern Uí Néill king, Máel Sechnaill, and drowned in Lough Owel.[7] Turgeis' death signalled a shift in the tide of the conflict in favour of the Irish. The longphorts, although highly effective in enabling the raiders to maintain year-round operations, also made them vulnerable to counter-attack and, under Máel Sechnaill's leadership, the Irish kingdoms succeeded in inflicting a succession of heavy defeats on the Norsemen.[8] By 847 Irish successes and growing awareness of easier pickings to be had in Francia persuaded many of the Ireland-based Norse to depart. Not all, however, headed for the continent, and the coastal fringe of longphorts remained as bases from which predatory war-bands continued to mount devastating raids against their Irish hosts.

Throughout the first half of the ninth century Viking activity in Ireland had been almost exclusively Norwegian. In the early 850s, however, the situation in Ireland was further complicated by a new conflict between the Norwegians and the growing number of Danes who were turning their attentions there from Francia (see Map 5).[9] Gaelic Irish sources record regular clashes between the 'Black [Danish] Foreigners' and the 'White [Norwegian] Foreigners' with some glee, for while the Vikings were slaughtering each other they were not harming

---

[7] The most detailed account of Turgeis' activities occurs in the eleventh-century *Coghadh Gaedhel re Gallaibh*, where they may have been inflated for propagandistic effect to enhance the significance of the Irish victory over him. *Coghadh Gaedhel*, pp. 224–26, 248.

[8] *Annals of Ulster*, sub anno 847 [848].

[9] E.g. *Annals of Ulster*, sub anno 848 [849]. 'A naval expedition of seven score ships, of the people of the king of the Foreigners, came to take control over the Foreigners who were there before them; and then they disturbed all Ireland.'

Map 5 Viking Age Ireland.

good Christians. The newcomers' greatest success came in 851, when a Danish war-band succeeded in capturing Dublin, already the most important of the Norse longphorts: 'Black Gentiles came to Dublin, and they made great slaughter of the White Foreigners; and they plundered the fortress, both of men and of treasure.'[10] The Danes were to hold Dublin until their expulsion in 853 by a new Norwegian strongman, Olaf Guthfrithsson (also known as Ólafr Hvítr or Olaf the White),

[10] *Annals of Ulster*, *sub anno* 850 [851].

and his brother or kinsman, Ivar, who may have been sons of the king of Vestfold in Norway.[11]

Their arrival marked the opening of a new phase in Viking activities in Ireland, when the Norwegian toehold was to be turned into an almost strangling grip – and not just on Ireland, but on the whole of the western maritime zone of the British Isles. Olaf progressively shifted his main sphere of operations eastwards. Control of the Irish Sea was central to his designs, and it was possibly around this time that the Scandinavian settlement of the Isle of Man began. Olaf was also developing his interests in mainland Scotland, where before 858 he and Ivar had launched a series of plundering raids, sacking both Dunkeld and the nearby royal centre at Clunie.[12] It is possible that such pressure forced the Scots into a treaty sealed by a marriage alliance, and there is a strong annalistic tradition that Olaf married a daughter of Cináed mac Alpín, king of the Picts and Scots.[13] Marriage certainly played a key part in Olaf's reckonings and seems to have been used by him to seal important alliances that settled military conflicts and territorial disputes over spheres of interest and operation. In addition to the marriage to the Scottish king's daughter, he is also linked with Aud the Deep-minded, daughter of Ketil Flatnef, ruler of the Hebrides.[14] Olaf clearly used this marriage to neutralise or remove a potential rival for dominance within Ireland, but the marriage lasted only for as long as it served the purposes of both parties. In 857 Olaf and Ketil clashed in Munster,[15] and Olaf appears soon after that event to have repudiated Ketil's daughter. Aud was not his last wife, however, for he is linked subsequently with daughters of the dominant native Irish kings, Cerball mac Dúnlainge and Áed Findliath mac Néill.[16] Olaf was clearly a figure of consequence in the politics of both northern and western Britain and Ireland.

In the decade since Thórgils (Turgeis) had first established the Vikings as a political and military force within Ireland, the Danes

[11] *The Annals of Innisfallen, sub anno 853* in S. MacAirt, ed. and trans., *The Annals of Innisfallen*. Dublin: Dublin Institute for advanced Studies, 1951. 'Olaf, son of the king of the White Scandinavians, came to Ireland, and the Scandinavians of Ireland submitted to him, and tribute was given to him by the Gaels. Sigtrygg and Ivar, his two full brothers, came with him on that expedition.'

[12] *Chronicles of the Scots*, ed. W. M. Hennessy. *Chronicon Scotorum*. Rolls Series No. 46. London. p. 8.

[13] Smyth, *New History*, p. 156.   [14] Ibid.

[15] *Annals of Ulster, sub anno 856* [857].   [16] Smyth, *New History*, p. 156.

and Norwegians had become factors that could not be ignored in the reckonings of the native Irish rulers. One of the first Irish kings to recognise the potential of the Vikings in the endless struggles for hegemony between the native kingdoms was Cerball mac Dúnlainge, king of Osraige. In the course of his long reign (842–88) he succeeded in playing off rival Viking bands against each other and allied himself with some to give his kingdom the military capability to punch well above its weight. From 859 he was allied with Olaf and Ivar of Dublin, who provided him with armoured warriors for his wars against Máel Sechnaill mac Máele Ruanaid, the powerful king of the southern Uí Néill, and against the Gall-Gaedhil, whom he and Ivar crushed in Tipperary.[17] Although condemned by some monastic writers for his alliance with these pagans, Cerball had fought, and continued to fight, strenuously against Viking bands that threatened his kingdom. In 846–47 he had inflicted a heavy defeat on the Dublin Norse,[18] and in 860, 861 and 862 led forays against Norse bases. He also allied himself with the neighbouring king of Loígis to destroy a longphort that had been constructed on the River Barrow and was threatening his territory, and in 864 he slaughtered a force of Vikings that had plundered the monastery of Leighlin in Carlow. Later tradition claims that he even attempted to project his power into the Hebrides, identifying him with a Gaelic ruler called Kjarval by the Norse who was defeated in a naval battle off Barra c. 869.[19] Although it is unlikely that this Kjarval was Cerball of Osraige, Cerball certainly had ambitions to increase his influence in the Isles, from where Norse and Gall-Gaedhil bands launched raids into Ireland. The marriage of one of his daughters to Olaf was matched by that of another to Eyvind Eastman, a Hebridean chieftain, whose kin were highly influential in the Norse colony there.[20] The descendants of this marriage, all of whom

---

[17] Duald MacFirbis, *Annals of Ireland. Three fragments, copied from ancient sources by Dubhaltach MacFirbisigh; and edited, with a translation and notes, from a manuscript preserved in the Burgundian Library at Brussels*, ed. J. O'Donovan. Dublin: Irish Archaeological and Celtic Society, 1860. p. 140.

[18] *Annals of Ulster*, sub anno 846 [847].

[19] *Grettir's Saga*, ed. and trans. Denton Fox and Hermann Pálsson. Toronto: University of Toronto Press, 1974. Chapter 1.

[20] *Landnámabók*. In *Origines Islandicae: A Collection of the more Important Sagas and other Native Writings relating to the Settlement and Early History of Iceland*, ed. and trans. G. Vigfusson and F. Y. Powell. Oxford: Clarendon Press, 1905. Chapter 72.

emphasised their descent from Kjarvalr Írakonungr (Kjarval King of the Irish), were prominent in the Hebridean settlement of Iceland later in the ninth century.

Cerball was not the only Irish ruler to ally himself with the Norse. In 862 Olaf joined with the northern Uí Néill in an attack on their southern kinsmen, but increasingly effective Irish resistance gradually closed off the Dublin Norse's opportunities for plunder, and in the mid-860s they turned their attentions further afield. It is unlikely that the movements of the Great Army (see Chapter 3) and the campaigns of Olaf were co-ordinated even in the most general of ways, but in 866 or 867, whilst Ivar and Halfdan moved against York, Olaf launched an assault on the Scots. His invasion struck into the heart of the emergent kingdom of the mac Alpín kings centred on the old Pictish realm of Fortriu in Strathearn.[21] In common with the Great Army, this northern force also seized a base from which to operate and was eventually bought off with an offer of tribute and hostages. Olaf may have spent up to two years in Scotland, for he is not recorded in an Irish context until St Patrick's Day (17 March) 869, when, supposedly in retaliation for an Irish attack on Dublin, he launched a slave-taking and plundering raid against the greatest Irish ecclesiastical centre, Armagh. Late in the following year, however, he returned to mainland Britain in what was to prove his most spectacular raid of all. His target was Dumbarton, the citadel of the Strathclyde Britons, which he took after a four-month siege (Figure 14). In the seventeenth-century *Three Fragments* manuscript of Dubhaltach MacFirbisigh, some flavour of the scale of the operation can be gained:

In this year the kings of the Scandinavians besieged Strathclyde, in Britain. They were four months besieging it; and at last reducing the people who were inside by hunger and thirst (after the well that they had in their midst had dried up miraculously), they broke in upon them afterwards. And firstly, all the riches that were in it were taken; a great host [was taken] out of it in captivity.[22]

The significance of his success cannot be overstated, for it brought not only a large haul of plunder and captives to be transported for ransom or for the Dublin slave-market,[23] but it

---

[21] *Annals of Ulster*, sub anno 866 [867].

[22] MacFirbis, *Annals of Ireland*, p. 192. Duald's account builds on the more prosaic narrative offered by the *Annals of Ulster*, sub anno 869 [870].

[23] Ibid., sub anno 870 [871].

Figure 14
Dumbarton Rock, Dunbartonshire. The chief citadel of the Britons of Strathclyde, Dumbarton controlled the entry to the inner Firth of Clyde and access to the western end of the portage route across central Scotland. Its fall to the Norse after a four-month siege in 870–71 was a blow from which the British kingdom never recovered.

also established Scandinavian domination of the Clyde estuary and opened unrestricted access to central Scotland. Settlement of the coastlands around the Firth of Clyde may have followed swiftly on the heels of this victory (see Map 6).

Strathclyde took several decades to recover from the fall of Dumbarton, and its power contracted to a narrow core in Clydesdale proper. Before the disaster of 871 the authority of the Dumbarton-based kings extended over the river basin from which their kingdom derived its name. Their southern limit had probably lain on the watershed between the river-systems of the Clyde and Annan, but a southward shift in the political centre of gravity in the kingdom triggered by the sack of Dumbarton saw the emergence of Cadzow as a new centre of royal power. Although Dumbarton may not have been entirely abandoned – fragments of two tenth-century recumbent cross-slabs suggest some ecclesiastical activity on or near the rock – it disappears as a royal stronghold, probably because of its exposure to Scandinavian attack. This shift in the kingdom's internal dynamics may have encouraged its later tenth-century expansion into the river valleys that feed into the head of the Solway. In the late ninth century, however, Strathclyde was

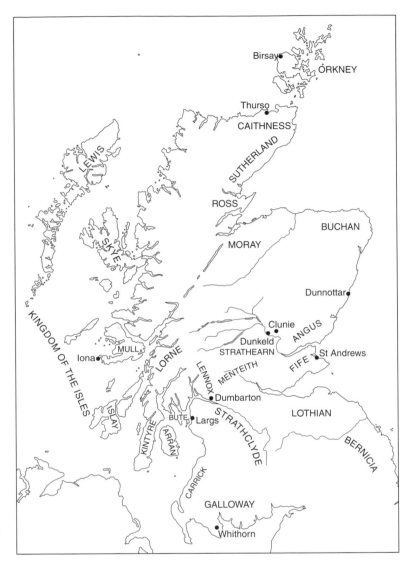

Map 6 Viking Age Scotland.

effectively removed from the reckoning in the political re-ordering of northern mainland Britain.

Olaf's attentions were not focussed solely on mainland Scotland, and through the late 850s he had been establishing Dublin-based domination of the Hebrides, thus setting in place a pattern that was to last into the eleventh century.[24] His aim was to curb the actions of the Isles-based Vikings, whose raids on

[24] Crawford, *Scandinavian Scotland*, pp. 49–51.

Ireland were posing as much of a threat to the stability of the Norse colony as to the native Irish kingdoms. Olaf's marriage to Aud the Deep-minded, daughter of Ketil Flatnef, may have been part of a move designed to strengthen Dublin influence over a man who had built up a powerful base for himself in the Isles and, through him, exert some control over the Hebrides-based war-bands. The alliance that went with the marriage proved short-lived, and in the late 850s Olaf was again in conflict with the Islesmen.[25] In 857 Olaf confronted and defeated a marauding force of Islesmen in Munster,[26] and it was around this time that he set aside Aud, who returned to her father's home in the Isles with her young son by Olaf, Thorstein the Red. Ketil's power disintegrated rapidly after this time in the face of the gradual spread of Olaf's influence into the Isles, and following Ketil's death Aud and her brothers were forced out of the Isles to settle instead in Caithness.[27]

Having established his domination of the western maritime zone of Britain and crippled the power of Strathclyde, Olaf disappears from British history. It is possible that he had simply died in the course of his Scottish raids, but late Irish sources claim that he returned to Norway to aid his father in a civil war there.[28] (Some scholars have attempted to identify him with the man buried in the Gokstad ship.) He was succeeded in Dublin by his brother, Ivar, who maintained the dominance achieved by Olaf, being described as 'king of the Northmen of all Ireland and Britain' at the time of his death in 873.[29] In Scotland the removal from the scene of Olaf saw the emergence of a powerful new leader in the person of his son, Thorstein the Red, who rapidly built up a powerbase in the western mainland and in the Isles. Most of what is known of Thorstein, and that is very little, is recorded in much later Icelandic

---

[25] Smyth, *New History*, pp. 154–58, 160–64; Crawford, *Scandinavian Scotland*, pp. 47–48.

[26] *Annals of Ulster*, sub anno 856 [857].

[27] *Landnámabók* offers a rather confused account of Aud's life, having her return to the Hebrides following the death of her husband in battle in Ireland. For Aud and Thorstein, see *The Saga of the People of Laxardal*, trans. K. Kunz. In *The Sagas of Icelanders*, ed. Ö. Thorsson. London: Penguin, 2001. pp. 278–79.

[28] D. MacFirbisigh, writing in the 1640s, claimed that 'Olaf went from Ireland to Scandinavia, to fight with the Scandinavians and to assist his father, Godfrey; for the Scandinavians were warring against [Godfrey]; and his father had sent for him.' MacFirbis, *Annals of Ireland*, p. 194.

[29] Ibid., p. 196; *Annals of Ulster*, sub anno 872 [873].

saga tradition. The sagas, however, claim that he briefly carved out a substantial kingdom for himself in Scotland and, in alliance with the Orkney Norse, established Scandinavian dominion over most of the country north and west of the Great Glen.[30] The sagas imply that the Scots submitted to him, but that they then treacherously tricked and slew him under trust. Whilst Thorstein's former ally, Sigurd of Orkney, was to go on to assert his lordship over northern Scotland, Thorstein's mother, Aud, and his remaining kinsmen were to quit their settlement in Scotland and join in the colonisation of Iceland.[31] The possibility of the emergence of a third Norse power centre in the north or west of the British Isles died with Thorstein.

By the close of the ninth century only Orkney survived from amongst the Norse colonies as a political and military heavyweight player. In Ireland Ivar's death was followed by a period of factional division amongst the Dublin Norse as various rivals contended for the kingship. For a while the alliance with Cerball mac Dúnlainge of Osraige staved off the threat to the Norse colony, but after his death in 888 Dublin lacked the patronage of a powerful external protector. This episode of weakness, which coincided with a period of decline in Viking activity in Ireland generally that came to be known as the Forty Years' Rest,[32] enabled the Irish kings to stage a recovery and carry the offensive to the invaders, who were further weakened by civil war in 893–94. The Irish resurgence reached a climax in 902 when Cerball mac Muirecáin, king of Leinster, stormed Dublin and drove the Norse into the sea.

Dublin's fall and the expulsion of the Norse sent reverberations around the Irish Sea. Although a great fleet led by Sigtrygg Cáech and his brother Ragnall returned from Brittany in 914 and based itself at Waterford, succeeding in 917 in re-occupying Dublin, the period 902–17 saw its power dispersed in new colonies around the northern Irish Sea basin. For example, Ingimund, a Dublin Norse warlord, made an abortive attempt to establish himself in north Wales before occupying the Wirral and attacking Chester. In Amounderness, where Norse and Norse-Gaelic place-names are clustered, there was a similar process. It was at the southern edge of this district that the Cuerdale hoard, deposited c. 903, was discovered. Its burial may be associated with political instability in York after Guthfrith's

---

[30] *Laxardal*. In *The Sagas of Icelanders*, see note 27 above, pp. 278–79.
[31] *Landnámabók*, Chapters 82–83.   [32] *Coghadh Gaedhel*, p. 27.

death in 895, but its rich Hiberno-Norse content is more consistent with an Irish origin. Because it lies at the western end of the trans-Pennine Ribble–Aire gap, control of Amounderness was vital to men aspiring to hold both York and Dublin. Its importance was underscored by its purchase in 934 from the Scandinavians by King Æðelstan and its grant to the church of York. Further effects of the aftershock of the fall of Dublin were felt all the way up the north-west coast of England. Norse and Norse-Gaelic settlement in Cumbria, whose Anglian rulers fled in the face of Scandinavian incursion, dates to the period c. 902–c. 914.

Norse, Gall-Gaedhil and the re-ordering of south-west Scotland c. 900–950

It has long been common to identify a ninth- or tenth-century Gaelic-speaking element as arriving in Galloway in conjunction with the influx of Norse settlers.[33] These settlers are usually labelled Gall-Gaedhil, portrayed inaccurately as Norse-Gaelic hybrids with a reputation for savagery and aggressive paganism. The tradition of their presence in Galloway stems from the assumption that the region was colonised in the later ninth century by large numbers of Norse, with Gall-Gaedhil following in their wake from Scandinavian settlements in Ireland or the Hebrides, or that some were native Gaelic-speakers who embraced Norse culture. Late Irish tradition viewed them as renegades and apostates, Gaels who had renounced their native culture and religion for those of the Norse. Our sole description of them is from a probably twelfth-century account preserved in the seventeenth-century *Three Fragments*:

They were a people who had renounced their baptism and they were usually called Northmen, for they had the customs of the Northmen, and had been fostered by them, and though the original Northmen were bad to churches these were worse, in whatever part of Ireland they were.[34]

In view of the absolute belief in a south-west Scottish locus for the Gall-Gaedhil, it is surprising to find that there is so little known about their origins and activities. Early Irish sources give them no clear geographical location, but the supposed sphere of

---

[33] The following discussion develops points first made in R. Oram, *The Lordship of Galloway*. Edinburgh: John Donald, 2000. pp. 6–9.

[34] MacFirbis, *Annals of Ireland*, pp. 138–39.

activity of their mid-ninth-century leader, Ketil Flatnef, points to
a Hebridean base.[35] Most modern authorities have suggested that
they were 'wandering bands of mixed Irish and Norse renegades',
or 'half-Irish half-Norse marauders', who preyed on Irish monasteries, and this view has met with few challenges.[36] Their
'homeland', however, is less certain. As Ireland was a major
target for their attentions, then unless they were associated
from an early date with the longphort settlements of the Norse
there, it is unlikely to have been their place of origin. A suggested
earlier Norse settlement of the Hebrides from c. 800 – for which
there is currently no concrete evidence – and the survival there of
a substantial Gaelic and Gaelicised population, however, have
been considered to offer the most obvious breeding-ground for
such hybridity.[37] The Western Isles, however, need not preserve a
monopoly over the Gall-Gaedhil, for similar conditions could be
found elsewhere in north-west maritime Britain and at later
periods for the generation of similar cross-breeds. North-west
England, indeed, has produced evidence for a substantial influx
of Hebridean or Irish Sea Norse in the early tenth century. Alfred
Smyth has highlighted the Gall-Gaedhil character of Cumbrian
society. It was 'half-pagan, half-Christian in religion; and ethnic-
ally . . . half-Norse, half-Celtic'.[38] The most striking monuments
of this hybrid culture are the Cumbrian high crosses, such as that
at Gosforth, with its oddly juxtaposed pagan and Christian motifs
(Figure 15).[39] Nick Higham developed Smyth's hypothesis and
highlighted the strong Gaelic component in the settlement of the
region.[40] Similar areas of mixed culture can also be identified on
the northern side of the Solway in Galloway.

[35] Crawford, *Scandinavian Scotland*, pp. 47–48.
[36] F. J. Byrne, *Irish Kings and High-Kings*. London: Batsford, 1973. p. 264;
D. O'Corráin, *Ireland Before the Normans*. The Gill History of Ireland. Dublin: Gill
and Macmillan, 1972. p. 70.
[37] Smyth, *New History*, p. 157; J. MacQueen, Picts in Galloway. *Transactions of the
Dumfriesshire and Galloway Natural History and Antiquarian Society*, Vol. 39, 1960–61.
p. 143.
[38] A. P. Smyth, *Scandinavian York and Dublin: The History and Archaeology of Two Related
Viking Kingdoms*. Vol. II. Dublin: Humanities Press, 1979. p. 265.
[39] R. N. Bailey, Aspects of Viking-Age sculpture in Cumbria. In *Scandinavians in
Cumbria*, ed. J. Baldwin and I. Whyte. Collins Archaeology. Edinburgh: Scottish
Society for Northern Studies, 1980. pp. 59–61.
[40] N. J. Higham, The Scandinavians in north Cumbria: raids and settlement in the
later ninth to mid-tenth centuries. In *The Scandinavians in Cumbria*, ed. J. R.
Baldwin and I. D. Whyte. Edinburgh: Scottish Society for Northern Studies, 1985.
pp. 37–51.

Figure 15
Gosforth Cross, Gosforth, Cumbria. The great tenth-century cross, with its blend of Scandinavian and Anglian styles and pagan and Christian motifs, is the chief monument to the hybrid culture of north-west England.

It is only in modern eyes that the equation of Galloway with the land of the Gall-Gaedhil has appeared suspect. The documentary evidence to support that identification is, admittedly, circumstantial and generally late in date, but it establishes that by the twelfth century it was a recognised fact that Galloway was the homeland of these 'Foreign-Gael'. In Irish sources, notably the Annals of Ulster, the heads of the Galwegian ruling house in

the twelfth and thirteenth centuries are accorded the title rí Gall-
Gaedhil.[41] Less certainty attaches to the same set of annals' use of
that style for an early eleventh-century individual, Suibne mac
Cinaedh, whose death is recorded in 1034, for there are no other
references to him through which to establish a firm provenance.[42] If any weight can be placed on the historically suspect
traditions of Ketil Flatnef and his associates in the Hebrides, it
is possible that Suibne may have been a Hebridean chieftain, but
there is no inherent improbability in his being a Galwegian
ruler. Independently of the Irish annal tradition, the early
thirteenth-century *Orkneyinga Saga* describes Galloway as
Gaddgeðlar, the Old Norse form of Gall-Gaedhil.[43] The unanswerable question is when did the name become narrowly
defined as referring to the south-west of the Scottish mainland?

On balance, the above evidence points to a continued influx of
colonists to Galloway after the initial settlement period in the late
ninth and early tenth centuries. The tenth-century colonisation
shows clear signs of having originated in regions where the
Scandinavian population had been exposed to considerable
Gaelic influences, as is evident in both their settlement vocabulary and in the saints' cults that they imported into their new
homelands. The chief zone of origin may have been the Hebrides,
posited as the early stamping-ground of the Gall-Gaedhil, but the
spread of Dublin and Waterford influence throughout the Irish
Sea in the tenth and eleventh centuries provides a clearer context
for the transplanting of Norse-Gaelic culture through Man into
Cumbria and Galloway.

The political relationships between these areas of Gall-Gaedhil
settlement stretching from the inner Clyde estuary to the inner
Solway zone and the kingdom of Strathclyde to its north and east
are obscure in the extreme. That the districts south and west of a
line from Renfrewshire to the Nith formed part of Strathclyde has
been argued for on the grounds that they fell within the twelfth-
century see of Glasgow and that they constituted part of the
principality controlled by the future King David I of Scotland
during the reign of his elder brother, Alexander I.[44] This latter

[41] *Annals of Ulster, sub annis* 1200, 1234.   [42] Ibid., *sub anno* 1034.
[43] *The Orkneyinga Saga*, ed. and trans. A. B. Taylor. Edinburgh: Oliver & Boyd, 1938.
p. 174 and note.
[44] Oram, *Lordship*, pp. xxiii, 25–26.

point is confirmed by charters of David and his grandson, Malcolm IV, which record David's grant to the churches of Glasgow and Kelso of elements of the yearly render of 'cain' (a tribute paid in foodstuffs) due to him from these districts. Significantly, however, the charters do not refer to the land from which these renders were drawn as part of Strathclyde or Cumbria, but as 'that part of Galloway' which David controlled.[45] At best, it would seem, the kings of Strathclyde exercised a loose and probably intermittent overlordship rather than direct lordship of the territory extending from Strathgryfe in what is now Renfrewshire southwards through Cunningham, Kyle, Carrick and Nithsdale – or at least they did so in the early 1100s. The suggestion that as late as the 1130s this territory was part of a wider Galloway again emphasises the western Norse-Gaelic links of this zone and its separation from the mainland Scottish world of Alba and Strathclyde. In common with Galloway proper, the naming of the discrete territorial units that comprised this region points again to a fragmentation rather than a coalescing of power, offering a parallel to the position evident within Galloway proper in the same period. Colonisation by external agencies, as occurred in Galloway, may likewise have been the determining factor in producing this fragmented political and cultural pattern in the districts fringing the eastern shore of the Firth of Clyde. Fellows-Jensen has pointed to the cluster of Scandinavian settlement names in Cunningham and Renfrewshire, a group which has been linked to Norse colonisation of the southern Hebrides and, possibly, to attempts to establish control over the Clyde estuary trading nexus.[46] Carrick, too, preserves traces of a Norse-Gaelic settlement in the tenth century, possibly linked to the kingdom of the Rhinns, but here Gaelic rather than Norse was the dominant cultural and linguistic type. Only in Nithsdale are we confronted with a ruling native dynasty, and here, too, it emerges only in the

---

[45] A. C. Lawrie, *Early Scottish Charters prior to A.D. 1153*. Glasgow: J. MacLehose and Sons, 1905. No. xxxv; G. W. S. Barrow, ed. *Regesta regum scottorum, 1153–1424*. Vol. I, *The Acts of Malcolm IV*. Edinburgh: Edinburgh University Press, 1960. No. 131; C. Innes, ed. *Registrum episcopatus Glasguensis munimenta ecclesie metropolitane Glasguensis a sede restaurata seculo ineunte XII ad reformatam religionem*. Edinburgh: Maitland Club Publications, 1843. No. 9.

[46] G. Fellows-Jensen, Scandinavians in southern Scotland? *Nomina: A Journal of Name Studies Relating to Great Britain and Ireland*, Vol. 13 (for 1989–90), 1991, pp. 41–60; Crawford, *Scandinavian Scotland*, p. 98.

early twelfth century in the person of Dunegal of Strathnith.[47] A scattering of potentially tenth-century British names in lower Nithsdale, centred on what appears to have been the main seat of lordly power at Dumfries, may indicate a western extension of Strathclyde influence from Annandale or the re-emergence of the old elites, but by the twelfth century this, like Carrick, was a thoroughly Gaelicised area.

What emerges from the above is the apparent ephemerality of the power of the kings of Strathclyde throughout much of the western Southern Upland zone outwith a corridor extending from Upper Clydesdale through Annandale to the Solway plain. This corridor was flanked to the west by territories that may, at times, have acknowledged the overlordship of Strathclyde, but that otherwise fell within the sphere of the western maritime powers and displayed a strongly Gaelic character liberally laced with pockets of Scandinavian. This hybridity no doubt gave rise to the labelling of this broader south-west as 'Galloway', the land of the Gall-Gaedhil, while the term *Galwalenses*, used by some twelfth-century authorities to describe the inhabitants of this zone, may reflect an attempt to rationalise a hybrid Gaelic-Brythonic or Scandinavian-Brythonic population which emerged in the wake of tenth-century migrations. Rather than comprising a unitary power bloc, Strathclyde-Cumbria was a congeries of minor lordships over which the men labelled kings of Strathclyde exercised a fluctuating control. Their comparative weakness acted as a magnet to external forces, notably to Alba and Wessex, for both of whom a politically fragmented and unstable Strathclyde constituted a major threat to their security. For the Scots, Strathclyde was the route by which the Norse entered Fortriu in the early 900s, while for the English it was the opening through which the grandsons of Ivar had seized control of York. It is as attempts to stabilise this dangerously disunited territory that the tenth- and eleventh-century manoeuvrings of Scottish and English kings should be read.

The submission of northern and western British rulers to Æðelstan of Wessex at Eamont Bridge in 927 (see p. 104) has long been interpreted as a 'border conference' on the southernmost limit of Strathclyde.[48] Nowhere in the contemporary record,

[47] Lawrie, *Early Scottish Charters*.

[48] *The Anglo-Saxon Chronicles*, ed. and trans. M. J. Swanton. London: Phoenix, 2000. *sub anno* 926 [927]; Smyth, *New History*, p. 201.

however, is it presented in such terms, and it should perhaps be seen simply as a meeting at a geographically strategic location where the old Roman road south from Carlisle met the roadways from York and Chester. Following swiftly on the heels of his seizure of York following the death of Sigtrygg and the expulsion of Guthfrith of Dublin from the city, the meeting shows Æðelstan seeking to consolidate his power north of the Humber and to re-define political relationships within the region through which challenges to his new position could be mounted. Significantly, the northern powers with whom he dealt were Causantin mac Aeda, king of Scots, and the Bernician ruler, Ealdred son of Eadwulf, the two men best placed to either wreck or secure the political settlement imposed by Æðelstan on the kingdom of York, with no mention being made of the king of Strathclyde.[49] Current historiography favours the conversion of Strathclyde, following the elevation to the throne there of an otherwise unknown brother of Causantin, Domnall mac Aeda, to little more than a satellite of Alba and, even with the native dynasty restored some time before 934, remaining subject to Scottish overlordship or at best firmly allied to its increasingly powerful northern neighbour. This scenario, however, has been shown to be built on a faulty reading of the relevant passage in the Poppleton Manuscript which refers to the death of Domnall mac Aeda, king of Ailech, and not to the elevation of a brother of Causantin mac Aeda to the kingship of the Britons.[50] Although this indicates that the native lineage continued to reign unbroken within Strathclyde, it does not rule out the probability that they

[49] Strathclyde's ruler at this time has been traditionally given as Domnall mac Aeda, an otherwise unknown brother of Causantin mac Aeda, king of Alba. He is presented as having been installed as king over Strathclyde in succession to the native king, Dyfnwal, c. 908–916. See A. MacQuarrie, The Kings of Strathclyde, c. 400–1018. In Medieval Scotland, Crown, Lordship and Community: Essays Presented to G.W.S Barrow, ed. G. W. S. Barrow, A. Grant and K. Stringer. Edinburgh: Edinburgh University Press, 1993. p. 14. This interpretation has been discredited (see below). The twelfth-century English chronicler, William of Malmesbury, gives the name of the king of the Cumbrians in 926–7 as 'Eogan' (for the British Ywain) and records how he joined with Causantin in giving refuge to Guthfrith following his expulsion from York (William of Malmesbury, Gesta regum Anglorum: The History of the English Kings, ed. and trans. R. A. B. Mynors. Oxford Medieval Texts, 1. Oxford, New York: Clarendon Press, 1998. p. 147). Ywain was evidently still king of the Cumbrians in 934 when he and Causantin were defeated by Æðelstan.

[50] B. T. Hudson, Elech and the Scots in Strathclyde. Scottish Gaelic Studies, Vol. 15, 1988, pp. 145–49.

were little more than vassals of Alba. This certainly appears to be the situation reflected in the events of 934 when, in response to Causantin's dealings with the new Dublin claimant of the throne of York, Olaf Guthfrithsson, Æðelstan staged a major raid by land and sea which defeated the Scots and the men of Strathclyde, penetrated Alba as far north as Dunnottar and saw the fleet ravage the coastlands of Caithness.[51] While Æðelstan secured a fresh submission and Causantin spent Christmas with him in southern England, the Scot was soon negotiating with Olaf. In 937, along with his Strathclyde vassals, he was the major mainland power to support Olaf in his bid for York that culminated in the crushing defeat of the Scots at Brunanburh.[52]

Æðelstan's victory at Brunanburh, spectacular though it was, evidently had little lasting impact on northern affairs, and following Æðelstan's death in 939 Olaf staged a fresh, and this time successful, bid for York.[53] Thus began a see-saw struggle for control of York and the country beyond the Humber between the kings of Wessex and a succession of Scandinavian aspirants for the northern kingship, culminating in 954 with the expulsion and death of Eirik Bloodaxe and the final annexation of York by Eadred of Wessex.[54] The struggle had seen a significant effort by the kings of Wessex to establish greater security on the northern extremities of their power, King Edmund's invasion of Strathclyde – whither Olaf Guthfrithsson had fled following his expulsion from York – and Edmund's subsequent 'grant' of the kingdom to the Scottish king, Máel Coluim mac Domnaill in 945.[55] A condition of the grant was that Máel Coluim should aid Edmund 'on sea and on land', which suggests that the king of Wessex aimed to end the now well-established connection between Strathclyde and Dublin, and close the Clyde and the Solway to Olaf and his successors. It was this Strathclyde–Dublin axis that had, for a quarter of a century, proved the undoing of English efforts to dominate the north. Presumably born out of fears that Wessex would seek to assert its role as the heir of Northumbria aggressively and regain control over those areas of

[51] Smyth, *New History*, pp. 202–03.
[52] *Anglo-Saxon Chronicles*, A, *sub anno* 937; Smyth, *Scandinavian York and Dublin*, Chapters 3 and 4.
[53] *Anglo-Saxon Chronicles*, D, *sub annis* 940 [939], 941 [940].
[54] Ibid., D and E, *sub anno* 954.
[55] Ibid., A, B, C, D, *sub anno* 945; Smyth, *New History*, pp. 222–23.

northern Cumbria and the Southern Uplands which Strathclyde had acquired from the Angles, and, possibly, re-assert the overlordship of this region which had been exercised by Northumbrian kings down to the 800s, the alliance had been designed to place a buffer between the Britons and the spreading might of the southern British superpower.[56] By ending this unholy alliance Edmund weakened the York–Dublin axis: when Eirik Bloodaxe seized York in 948 it was from the springboard of Orkney – not Dublin – that he launched his attack. Although a separate kingship of Strathclyde survived for over a further six decades, the violent intrusion of the Scandinavians into the political structures of the British Isles had claimed yet another casualty amongst the old order.

DISPLACEMENT AND RE-ORDERING, 903–920

The main Norse force expelled from Dublin, led by Ragnall, grandson of Ivar, roved over a wide area from central Scotland south to York, and may for a while even have been involved in the Scandinavian occupation of Brittany. Ragnall, however, first attacked Strathclyde before moving beyond the Forth–Clyde isthmus into the rich heartland of the Scottish kingdom. His men plundered the monastery and new shrine of Columba at Dunkeld in 903 but were defeated in Strathearn in 904, where Ragnall's brother or cousin was slain. Despite that reverse the Norse remained active within Strathclyde after that date. In 910, seizing the opportunity presented by the defeat and slaughter of the Danes at Tettenhall by Edward the Elder, Ragnall hurried south to take the throne of York. Accounts of what followed are confused and various scenarios can be built from them, but the most likely reconstruction is that the Norse hold on York was tenuous and lasted only a short while, possibly no later than c. 911. Ragnall, it would appear, returned to the west at about that time. Moving with great rapidity, he took ships from the Norse of Cumbria, won a sea-battle off Man against a Norse rival and imposed his rule on the Norse of Waterford. It is unknown whether he had managed to preserve some kind of hold over York, but control of the trans-Pennine routes in the late 910s may

---

[56] N. J. Higham, The Scandinavians in north Cumbria, pp. 41–43.

have enabled Ragnall and, after his death in 920, his brother
Sigtrygg, who had re-established the base at Dublin, to rule over a
kingdom that spanned the Irish Sea. Such a York–Dublin axis was
maintained intermittently down to the middle of the tenth century, foundering in 952 with Olaf Cuarán's second expulsion
from the kingship of York. While that event ended the direct
political link between the Norse colonies of Ireland and the
kingdom of York, the lines of communication were certainly
not severed. Indeed, it was while heading for the Norse colonies
in the west along the Stainmore route that Olaf's successor at
York, Eirik Bloodaxe, was attacked and killed in 954.

By the middle of the tenth century the Norse colonies in Cumbria
were well established. There was a semi-independent Scandinavian
lordship in north Westmorland in the second half of the 900s, and
intensive Norse settlement of the Solway coastlands. These colonies may originate in the post-902 dispersal, but the unsettled
military situation down to c. 920 was unfavourable for large-scale
settlement. From then until the invasion of Cumbria by Edmund of
Wessex in 945, however, was a comparatively stable period.

Ragnall's arrival in Waterford in 914 brought the Forty Years'
Rest in Ireland to a shuddering halt.[57] From this base he and his
brother Sigtrygg began to re-assert Norse power in the south of
Ireland, raiding widely through Munster.[58] Mounting pressure
on the Irish culminated in 917 with Sigtrygg's successful
re-occupation and re-fortification of Dublin after fifteen years of
abandonment, while Ragnall remained in control of Waterford.
Shortly afterwards Ragnall returned to mainland Britain, perhaps
drawn by the upheavals that stemmed from Edward the Elder and
his sister Æðelflæd's defeat of the Danes of Northampton and
Leicester in 916 and from Edward's successes against a major force
of raiders from Brittany in 917.[59] While Edward began systematically to pick off the remnants of the Danelaw, culminating in his
victory in 920 at Tempsford in Bedfordshire,[60] Ragnall moved
against York and succeeded in imposing his kingship on the
Danish colony there.[61] It was a momentous development, the

[57] Annals of Ulster, sub anno 913 [914].   [58] Coghadh Gaedhel, Chapter 26.
[59] Anglo-Saxon Chronicles, A, sub annis 917 [916], 918 [917].
[60] Ibid., sub anno 921 [920].
[61] Symeonis monachi opera omnia, ed. T. Arnold. Rerum britannicarum medii aevi
scriptores, 51. New York: Kraus Reprint Ltd, 1965 [1885]. pp. 72–73.

consequences of which were to reverberate throughout the British Isles for a further three and a half decades.

Ragnall's control of York was to face an almost immediate challenge both from within the city and from external enemies. One faction amongst the Danes of York approached Æðelflæd, the so-called Lady of the Mercians, with an offer of submission. Her rule was felt preferable to that of a Norseman (and pagan to boot). Æðelflæd's death,[62] however, ended negotiations, no approach being made to her brother, Edward the Elder, who moved swiftly to annexe Mercia to Wessex. Ragnall's presence in York, coupled with his effective domination of the Irish Sea, was a matter of grave concern for Edward, and the West Saxon occupation of Manchester was a clear attempt to sever the lines of communication between York and Dublin or Waterford. Faced with this growing threat from Wessex and troubled by hostility amongst the largely Christian Danish population of his capital, Ragnall struggled to maintain his grip on power. Early in 920, in a bid to secure his hold on the city, Ragnall made a treaty with Edward that promised to preserve the status quo in northern England. The deal, however, proved short-lived, for the Norseman was dead within the year and his successor at York had no intention of accepting any limits on his actions.

SCANDINAVIAN YORK AND DUBLIN 919–954

While Ragnall was building his kingdom in Britain, Sigtrygg had retaken Dublin from the Irish. In 919, at Islandbridge near Dublin, Sigtrygg, who was known to the Irish as Sihtric Cáech (the Squint-eyed), overwhelmed a large confederate Irish army led by Niall Glúndub, the northern Uí Néill high king, killing both him and five other kings.[63] His victory confirmed him as undisputed leader of the Norse in Ireland, and on Ragnall's death in 920 he swiftly and without challenge assumed the kingship of York also. Norse power now straddled the Irish Sea, Sigtrygg controlling two of the most important military and economic centres in the British Isles. Leaving his brother, Guthfrith, as king in Dublin, Sigtrygg headed for York, pausing only to plunder Cheshire en route.[64] By the mid-920s he had expanded Norse power south of the Humber to Lincoln, from where

[62] *Symeonis monachi opera*, 75, *sub anno* 919. [63] *Coghadh Gaedhel*, pp. 35–37.
[64] Smyth, *Scandinavian York and Dublin*, p. 1.

he could threaten the hold of Wessex over the southern Danelaw. In 926 at Tamworth, however, Sigtrygg entered into a treaty with the West Saxon king, Æðelstan, marrying his sister and accepting baptism as conditions of the agreement.[65] Within a year Sigtrygg was dead and Æðelstan moved swiftly against York, driving out the young Olaf Sigtryggsson. Rather than install a puppet king at York, Æðelstan annexed the city and its territory to his kingdom in a highly symbolic move that has often been taken as the point at which a unitary kingship of the English was established.[66] The next three decades demonstrated the hollowness of that notion, although the first challenge to West Saxon control proved short-lived, Æðelstan defeating and driving out Guthfrith, accompanied by his nephew, Olaf, who had arrived from Dublin in a bid to secure his brother's throne.[67] Guthfrith's continued paganism, in contrast to his brother's willingness to accept baptism as the price of his throne, may have been one of the many problems that prevented him from gaining unqualified acceptance at York, where the support of the archbishop was vital, and that made him unacceptable to Æðelstan. Without backing from the powerful Anglo-Danish elite of the city, York was effectively untenable for the Dublin-based interlopers. As is evident from elsewhere within the extended zone of Scandinavian activity around western Europe, paganism was not always a barrier to the forming of alliances with Christian powers. Other Christian rulers in Britain were not so particular about their allies, most notably the increasingly powerful Causantin II mac Áeda, king of Alba, whose support for Guthfrith was intended to provide him with a useful buffer against West Saxon ambitions. His support for the claimant to York, however, failed to translate into effective military resources. When the fugitives were pursued as far north as Eamont Bridge in modern Cumbria, Guthfrith and his allies Ywain, king of Strathclyde, and Causantin, king of Scots, came to terms with Æðelstan. As part of the settlement Guthfrith renounced his claims to York and was permitted to return to Dublin.[68]

[65] *Anglo-Saxon Chronicles*, D, *sub anno* 925; Smyth, *Scandinavian York and Dublin*, pp. 3–4.
[66] Ibid., pp. 9–10.
[67] *Annals of Ulster*, *sub anno* 927; *Anglo-Saxon Chronicles*, E, *sub anno* 927; Smyth, *Scandinavian York and Dublin*, pp. 10–11.
[68] *Anglo-Saxon Chronicles*, D, *sub anno* 926; Smyth, *Scandinavian York and Dublin*, pp. 11–13.

Guthfrith's fleeting reign and failure at York in 927 came midway through a longer but equally disappointing career in Dublin (921–34).[69] There his reign began on his brother's departure for England with a series of slave-taking and plundering raids around Ireland. His offensive met immediately with stern resistance from the native Irish under the leadership of Muirchertach mac Niall, king of the northern Uí Néill, whose father, Niall Glúndub, had been killed at Islandbridge in 919. It is clear that Guthfrith saw the Uí Néill as his chief opponents, for the target of the Dublin fleets, usually commanded by Guthfrith himself or his son, Halfdan Guthfrithsson, were concentrated in the north between Carlingford on the east coast and Inishowen (the centre of Uí Néill power).[70] Guthfrith's objective in 921 was the spiritual centre of Irish Christianity at Armagh, which lay under the protection of the Uí Néill king. His attack on St Martin's Eve (10 November) coincided with one of the major religious festivals at Armagh, where he could have expected to seize a rich haul of plunder and prisoners to be either ransomed or sold as slaves.[71] His expectations were rewarded in Armagh itself, but in the second stage of his raid, which saw three war-bands roving north and west through Ulaid into Uí Néill territory, the Norse fared less well; one raiding party was routed with heavy losses. This setback took the gloss off the success at Armagh. It was followed by a second blow to Dublin's position as the leading Norse centre in Ireland when in 922 Thormod Helgason and his war-band re-occupied the old longphort site at Limerick and established it as a permanent settlement from which raids up the Shannon valley were launched.[72] The newcomers also quickly established a strong role in the developing Atlantic trade routes between the Mediterranean and the Scandinavian regions, even beginning to rival Dublin as the key market for slaves. Thormod appears to have established a very effective intelligence-gathering network which informed him of the movement of leading figures amongst the native Irish clergy and nobility. Many were captured, and their ransoms served to swell the coffers of the Limerick Vikings. By

---

[69] For a discussion of Guthfrith's career at Dublin see Smyth, *Scandinavian York and Dublin*, Chapter 2.

[70] *Annals of Ulster, sub annis* 920, 921, 922.   [71] Ibid., *sub anno* 920.

[72] *Coghadh Gaedhel*, p. 39; Smyth, *Scandinavian York and Dublin*, pp. 20–21.

924 Thormod was challenging Dublin's domination of the Irish midlands, and Guthfrith made an attack on Limerick in an attempt to nip the threat in the bud. The result was another humiliating failure and the beginning of over a decade of bloody rivalry between the two Norse strongholds.[73]

The string of failures that followed most of Guthfrith's efforts – relieved only by the successful establishment of another son as king in Waterford and Halfdan's victory over the men of Ulaid in 924 – continued in 925 when he turned his attention once again to the north. He badly needed a success to bring in plunder and to re-inforce his battered authority. Instead, at Carlingford the Dublin army suffered one of its heaviest defeats, which resulted in the capture and execution of many of the Norse by Muirchertach and his men. Halfdan headed north with his fleet and war-band in September 925 to counter the growing threat from the Uí Néill, but further catastrophe followed in January 926 at Annagassan on the coast between Drogheda and Dundalk. There Muirchertach cornered Halfdan and his men, killing him and large numbers of his warriors.[74] The remnants of Halfdan's force fled north and were eventually rescued with difficulty by Guthfrith and the main Dublin fleet. It was against this background of recurrent military failure and declining political influence and personal prestige that Guthfrith headed for York on receiving news of Sigtrygg's death.[75] In an ironic twist, Thormod pounced on Dublin in 927 during Guthfrith's sojourn in Britain and succeeded in capturing the town, only to be driven out when Guthfrith made his despondent return. From 927 until 933 Guthfrith did succeed in re-asserting a degree of authority, backed by a string of small-scale but more successful raids around Ireland, starting with an attack on Kildare on 1 February 929 (St Brigit's Day), the chief festival at that monastery (Figure 16).[76] Limerick, too, was confronted and checked. In 928–9 the Limerick fleet had been operating on Loughs

[73] Annals of Ulster, sub anno 923.
[74] Ibid., sub annis 925, 926; Smyth, Scandinavian York and Dublin, pp. 19–20.
[75] Ibid., p. 22.
[76] J. O'Donovan, ed. and trans. Annálarioghachta Éireann: Annals of the Kingdom of Ireland by the Four Masters, from the Earliest Period to the Year 1616; Edited from MSS in the Library of the Royal Irish Academy and of Trinity College, Dublin, with a Translation, and Copious Notes. Dublin, 1851. sub anno 927.

Figure 16 Kildare, Co. Kildare, Ireland. St Brigit's monastery at Kildare was one of the great spiritual centres of Ireland and the focus of a rich pilgrim traffic. The pilgrims flocking to it on its patronal feast day (1 February) made it an irresistible target for Viking raiders, who in 929 carried off hundreds to the slave markets of Dublin.

Neagh and Corrib, within what had traditionally been Dublin's sphere, which had entailed transporting the ships overland from the Shannon waterways.[77] It was only in 931 that the Dublin men checked that spread.[78] But this slow recovery was shattered in 933 when a second major attack on Armagh met with the same lack of

[77] *Annals of Ulster, sub annis* 927, 928.
[78] O'Donovan, *Annálaríoghachta Éireann, sub anno* 929.

success as the first, with the added humiliation of
Muirchertach's successful recovery of all the plunder and prisoners that the Vikings had seized. It was a final blow for Guthfrith,
whom the Irish chroniclers gleefully recorded as having soon
after this raid contracted a painful wasting disease –'filthy and
ill-favoured'[79] – which resulted in his death in 934.

On Guthfrith's death, his son, Olaf, succeeded to the kingship
of Dublin, where he had already been providing leadership during
his father's long illness.[80] He gave no immediate indication of
any aspirations towards York, concentrating instead on re-estab-
lishing the dominant position of Dublin in Ireland. He began his
reign with an alliance with Áed, king of Ulaid, directed against
Muirchertach. This deal indicates a growing integration of the
Norse into Irish political life, where native dynasts saw them as
useful and acceptable allies in their own conflicts. Olaf and Áed
launched a joint attack on Muirchertach's ally, the king of
Airgialla, but suffered a heavy defeat.[81] At the same time Olaf
was obliged to maintain pressure on his father's old rivals in
Limerick, from where Olaf Scabby-head was leading highly effective raids across Ireland.[82] Olaf Guthfrithsson needed victories
and plunder to boost his authority, and he secured these through
raids against the royal centres of Brega at Lagore and Knowth in
935.[83] By the following year he was carrying the conflict into
Limerick's hinterland, sacking the monastery at Clonmacnoise
on the Shannon,[84] and in 937 he crushed the Limerick fleet in a
battle on Lough Ree and succeeded in imposing his cousin,
Harald Sigtryggsson, as king in Limerick itself. This victory
brought mastery over all the Norse settlements in Ireland into
Olaf's hands.[85] Only then, with his authority in Ireland secure,
was he able to turn his attention east.

Olaf had clearly been preparing the ground well in advance,
for later in 937, in alliance with his father-in-law and the king
of the Strathclyde Britons, he invaded northern England.[86]

[79] The Annals of Clonmacnoise, ed. D. Murphy. Dublin, 1896. 150.
[80] Smyth, Scandinavian York and Dublin, p. 31.
[81] Annals of Ulster, sub anno 932.   [82] Smyth, Scandinavian York and Dublin, p. 32.
[83] Annals of Ulster, sub anno 934.
[84] Ibid., sub anno 935; Smyth, Scandinavian York and Dublin, pp. 33–34.
[85] O'Donovan, Annálaríoghachta Éireann, sub anno 935.
[86] Annals of Ulster, sub anno 936 [937]; The Chronicle of Melrose, ed. A. O. Anderson,
    M. O. Anderson and W. C. Dickinson. London: P. Lund, Humphries & Co. Ltd,
    1936. sub anno 937; Smyth, New History, pp. 203–4.

Causantin's peace with Æðelstan had broken down by 934, probably as a consequence of the Scottish king's continued support for the Norse.[87] Æðelstan had responded by invading Alba, his army penetrating as far as Dunnottar on the east coast just south of Stonehaven, whilst his fleet struck even further north in a series of raids on the Norse colonies in Caithness.[88] It was possibly at this juncture that Causantin cemented his alliance with the Norse through the marriage of his daughter to Olaf.[89] Despite all of Æðelstan's efforts to the contrary, and also contrary to the propagandistic line offered by the Anglo-Saxon Chronicle, the West Saxon military effort failed to achieve any lasting, positive results. Instead, once Olaf had consolidated his kingship in Ireland he was able to turn his attention to York, secure in the knowledge that Causantin would give him his full military backing.

In autumn 937 Olaf and his army carried their ships across the Forth–Clyde portage and sailed for the Humber, while the warbands of Causantin and the Britons of Strathclyde marched south (Figure 17).[90] Overcoming a brief show of resistance by the pro-Wessex Danish element in York, they seized control of the city and the Scandinavian colonies in the Midlands. The confederate host appears to have penetrated far to the south of the Humber, possibly as far as Northamptonshire, where, at the unidentified Brunanburh, they finally encountered Æðelstan and the West Saxon army. Fortune, however, was not with Olaf on this occasion, and it was Æðelstan who won 'undying glory with the edges of swords'[91] in what West Saxon poetry portrayed subsequently as a crushing victory over the pagan king and his barbaric allies. Olaf, however, escaped with the remnants of his army, and the West Saxon king appears to have had little success in securing a tighter grip on the country beyond the Humber, despite his victory.[92]

There can be no doubt that Olaf's army had suffered significant losses in England in 937. Dublin was clearly considerably

---

[87] Ibid., pp. 202–3.

[88] *Anglo-Saxon Chronicles*, A, D, E, F, *sub annis* 933, 934; *The Annals of Clonmacnoise*, ed. D. Murphy. Dublin, 1896. *sub anno* 928 [934]; *Chronicle of Melrose*, *sub anno* 934.

[89] Smyth, *New History*, p. 192.   [90] *Symeonis monachi opera*, p. 125.

[91] *Anglo-Saxon Chronicles*, A, *sub anno* 937.

[92] For an analysis of the battle and the events surrounding it, see Smyth, *Scandinavian York and Dublin*, Chapters 3–4.

Figure 17 Logie Kirkyard, hog-back tombstones, Logie, Stirlingshire. The plain hog-back stones in Logie Kirkyard, close to the highest navigable reach of the River Forth at the eastern end of the portage route across central Scotland, probably reflect the importance of this area to the Norse in the tenth century as their leaders sought to assert their control over Dublin and York.

weakened and the native Irish kings saw this as an opportunity to eliminate the threat from this nest of vipers amongst them. Allying himself with his rival for the leadership of the Irish, Donnchad Donn, Muirchertach mac Niall and his army stormed and sacked the stronghold in 938.[93] The success, however, was

[93] *Annals of Ulster, sub anno 937.*

illusory, for the Irish failed to destroy the Norse fleet and warriors, and in 939 the Vikings gained their revenge with a stunning
attack on Muirchertach's own fortress of Ailech in Co. Donegal
which resulted in the capture of the Uí Néill king.[94] The plunder
from this victory (to which must be added the huge ransom
demanded for Muirchertach), the boost to his personal prestige
and the security it gave him in Ireland permitted Olaf to turn his
gaze once again to England, where the political situation had
changed profoundly.[95]

The fragility of the West Saxon hold on the Scandinavian
colonies in England was revealed with astonishing clarity in 939
when Æðelstan died and Olaf swooped from Dublin to take
York.[96] He was welcomed back to the city by Archbishop
Wulfstan, who saw the Norseman as the best-placed candidate
to hold West Saxon power at bay (Figure 18).[97] In a single episode
Olaf had not only reversed the result of Brunanburh but by 940,
when he had succeeded in establishing his lordship over the Five
Boroughs, had also pushed the Anglo-Saxon recovery back in
territorial terms to the position in which it had stood some two
decades earlier.[98] It was to take Edmund, Æðelstan's half-brother
and successor, years to re-establish West Saxon dominance in the
lands immediately south of the Humber. This re-advance of
independent Scandinavian power in the Midlands and north of
England proved short-lived, although the new king enjoyed a
string of successes between 939 and 941 which carried his
power not only deep into Mercia but also saw profitable campaigns against the Angles of Bernicia to the north.[99] His efforts in
Bernicia, which saw him sack the monastery at Tyninghame in
East Lothian, seem to have been more than just plundering raids:
they were aimed instead at securing the routes through the
Scottish midlands upon which communication between York
and Dublin relied.[100] In 941, however, Olaf Guthfrithsson died
after only two years as king of Dublin and York, to be succeeded

---

[94] O'Donovan, Annálaríoghachta Éireann, sub anno, 937; Annals of Ulster, sub anno 938.
[95] Smyth, Scandinavian York and Dublin, p. 90.
[96] Anglo-Saxon Chronicles, A, sub anno 941; D, sub annis 940, 941.
[97] For Wulfstan's role in the events of 940–41, see Smyth, Scandinavian York and
Dublin, pp. 91–94. For Wulfstan's participation in the campaigns in the
Midlands, see Symeonis monachi opera, pp. 93–94.
[98] Smyth, Scandinavian York and Dublin, p. 91.
[99] Anglo-Saxon Chronicles, D, sub anno 943.
[100] Symeonis monachi opera, p. 94; Chronicle of Melrose, sub anno 941.

Figure 18 York Minster. The symbol of the power of the medieval archbishops of York, whose early tenth-century predecessors exercised immense political influence in the north. A succession of archbishops, culminating in Wulfstan I (931–52), forged alliances with pagan Norse rulers in a bid to keep the encroaching power of Wessex at bay.

by his cousin, Olaf Sigtryggsson, who had participated in the Bernician campaign.[101] His father had ruled at York down until 927. He had been expelled from the city by Æðelstan when he annexed York on Sigtrygg's death, and had grown up in exile in Dublin, establishing a reputation there as a warrior in the continuing conflict with the native Irish. His character and career were moulded by the increasingly hybridised culture of Dublin, and he is better known by his Gaelic by-name of Olaf Cuarán ('sandal'). Whatever his successes in Ireland, Olaf was unable to repeat them in England, and by 942 he had lost control of the Five

[101] *Symeonis monachi opera*, p. 94.

Boroughs to a resurgent Wessex under King Edmund.[102] The following year Edmund pressed home the advantage north of the Humber, and Olaf sought peace terms that would permit him to retain control of York. Edmund accepted Olaf's submission, accompanied by his acceptance of Christianity, but in 944 he seized York and drove out both Olaf and his co-king Ragnall II Guthfrithsson.[103] The pre-939 status quo appeared to have been restored.

Following his expulsion from York Olaf withdrew to Strathclyde, where he sought allies against Edmund.[104] When Edmund continued his onslaught into the north and moved against Strathclyde, however, Olaf returned to Ireland, where in 945 he was accepted as king of Dublin.[105] It seemed that Edmund had succeeded in establishing a secure northern frontier with the Scots, had removed the Norse threat from southern mainland Britain and had imposed a degree of unity over the Anglo-Saxon territories, which were now emerging clearly as a kingdom of the English. His control over York, however, was quickly revealed as more apparent than real.

Despite Edmund's success in driving out Olaf Cuarán and imposing a degree of stability on the country between the Humber and the Clyde through treaties with the Scots, West Saxon rule in the former kingdom of Northumbria was not securely founded. Northumbria – both the Scandinavian-dominated southern half of the kingdom centred on York, and the northern portion based around Bamburgh – had a deeply entrenched tradition of independence and a long history of rivalry with kingdoms south of the Humber, a cleavage that also had a reality in terms of politics, culture and, quite strikingly, religion.[106] As in the later ninth century, one institution that gave a firm sense of separateness and regional identity was the Church, and more particularly the archdiocese of York. To both Christian Angles and the Danish and Norwegian elements in the population, most of whom had converted to Christianity by around 900, the archbishops of York offered local leadership that was strongly opposed to the spread of southern influences beyond the

---

[102] *Anglo-Saxon Chronicles*, D, *sub annis* 942, 943.
[103] Ibid., D, *sub anno* 944. For the peace treaty of 943, see Smyth, *Scandinavian York and Dublin*, pp. 94–95.
[104] Ibid., pp. 112–13. [105] Ibid., pp. 205–6; *Anglo-Saxon Chronicles*, D, *sub anno* 945.
[106] Smyth, *Scandinavian York and Dublin*, pp. 97–98.

Humber. This stance was driven as much by secular as religious considerations, the archbishops enjoying great political power in a region where royal authority was often ephemeral or, at best, intermittent, and where mainly pagan, foreign rulers needed a bridge between themselves and their local Christian subjects. With the spread north of the power of the West Saxon kings came the threat of the spreading influence of the southern archbishop, based at Canterbury, who was identified firmly with the Wessex dynasty. For Wulfstan I, archbishop of York, Edmund's success posed a threat on a multiplicity of fronts, but his personal authority was such that Wulfstan could do little other than chafe under West Saxon rule.

The opportunity to overturn the situation came in 946 with the death of Edmund and the accession of his younger brother, Eadred.[107] It may not, however, have been Wulfstan who seized the initiative. For the Scandinavian elite in York a more amenable, possibly compliant, king based in their city and sharing their world view, which was focussed on the Scandinavian north and its trade nexus, was infinitely preferable to a distant monarch whose cultural sympathies and outlook were turned towards Frankish Europe. Olaf Cuarán, it might have been thought, was the automatic choice for this role, but to the largely Danish population this half-Norse, half-Irish warlord was not an attractive proposition, not least because he would have come with a powerful military force at his back. That might have made him altogether too powerful, and therefore independent, for their liking. There was, however, one man present in the British Isles who seemed to fit the job requirements admirably.

In 936 Eirik Bloodaxe, king of Norway, had been forced to step down from the kingship by his half-brother, Hákon the Good, and sent into exile.[108] It seems that down to the mid-940s he had imposed himself on the earldom of Orkney, and the sons of Jarl Torf-Einar of Orkney were later to figure prominently in his service.[109] Eirik had some obvious attractions to the Danes of York. Although he was Norse and pagan, he lacked a

---

[107] Anglo-Saxon Chronicles, A, sub anno 946.
[108] Hakon the Good's Saga. In Heimskringla: History of the Kings of Norway, trans. L. M. Hollander. Austin: Published for the American-Scandinavian Foundation by the University of Texas Press, 1964. Chapters 3–5; Smyth, Scandinavian York and Dublin, Chapter 8.
[109] Crawford, Scandinavian Scotland, p. 61.

well-established powerbase in the British Isles and, presumably, the military resources of a ruler like Olaf Cuarán. Altogether he would have been more dependent upon and, potentially, manageable by the Scandinavian community within his kingdom. These same characteristics may have made him very attractive to Archbishop Wulfstan. In 948, therefore, Eirik was invited to assume the kingship of York. By then, however, the new West Saxon king, Eadred, had consolidated his hold on southern England and, despite the strong support of both Wulfstan and the Danish elite, Eirik was driven out of the city before the end of the year.[110]

Although it was Eadred who had secured the expulsion of Eirik Bloodaxe, the chief beneficiary was Olaf Cuarán. Following his expulsion from York, he had returned to Dublin, where he in turn expelled his cousin, Blacaire Guthfrithsson, who had been ruling there since 939.[111] He found the colony in a bad way. Olaf Guthfrithsson had stripped it of manpower to mount his bid for York, leaving Dublin dangerously exposed to the resurgent power of Muirchertach mac Niall. Muirchertach, indeed, had successfully capitalised on Norse weakness in the west of Britain to mount a highly effective naval campaign in 941 against Viking bases in the Hebrides.[112] In the same year Blacaire and his army suffered a crushing defeat in which 1,200 of the Norse were slain, further crippling the colony.[113] By 943, however, Blacaire had gathered sufficient men to consider a plundering raid against Armagh. As the Dublin-men headed north, Muirchertach and his army intercepted them at Clonkeen, expecting to eliminate the threat for good. In an unexpected reversal of fortunes, however, it was Muirchertach and his allies who were left dead on the field.[114] Blacaire, however, lacked the resources to follow up on this victory and suffered a string of defeats that saw Dublin itself sacked twice and its inhabitants forced to take refuge on Dalkey Island until their enemies withdrew.[115] His problems were compounded by the fact that the new dominant native Irish king, Congalach mac Máelmithig, king of Northern Brega, had his

[110] Anglo-Saxon Chronicles, D, sub anno 948.   [111] Annals of Ulster, sub anno 944.
[112] O'Donovan, Annálaríoghachta Éireann, sub anno 939 = 941; Smyth, Scandinavian York and Dublin, p. 116.
[113] Chronicles of the Scots, ed. W. M. Hennessy. Chronicon Scotorum. Roll Series No. 46. London. sub anno 940.
[114] Annals of Ulster, sub anno 942.
[115] Smyth, Scandinavian York and Dublin, pp. 118–19.

stronghold at Knowth, barely 50 kilometres from Dublin. It was probably this growing crisis in Dublin, the vital base from which Norse kings could project their power across the British Isles and from which they drew their military reserves, that forced Olaf Cuarán to return to Ireland in 945.[116]

Olaf worked hard to reverse the decline in Dublin's power. He moved immediately to establish a rapprochement with the native Irish, a remarkable move that reversed a century of deep-rooted enmity. Clearly, he recognised that Dublin could no longer survive alone in an Ireland of radically re-drawn political realities. The one power who could safeguard Dublin's existence was Congalach, and Olaf actively courted him and entered into an alliance with him. Alliance with Brega, however, forced a wider re-appraisal of Dublin's traditional activities, for the old plundering grounds of the north-east midlands were under the lordship of Congalach. Instead, Olaf and Congalach mounted joint raids against their common enemies in Leinster and Meath.[117] Olaf Cuarán, however, had not given up his interest in York, and late in 947 he recalled his exiled cousin, Blacaire, to resume the kingship in Dublin whilst he himself sailed east for a second attempt in England.[118] Moving swiftly from Dublin, Olaf arrived at York and assumed the kingship in 948.[119] Unlike Eirik, Olaf Cuarán had the resources and reserves to be able to rule independently of the political influences of either the archbishop or the Danish leadership of the city, a position that pitched him into confrontation with these twin pillars of northern separatism. In 952 Wulfstan was successful in uniting the opponents of Olaf Cuarán and engineered a coup that saw his permanent expulsion from the city.[120] Olaf's overthrow marked the end of nearly half a century dominated by the efforts of the Dublin dynasty to secure the kingship of York and severed the link that had attempted to forge an east–west axis within the British Isles.

Wulfstan's personal triumph was short-lived. His plan had clearly been to restore Eirik Bloodaxe to the throne of York, with real power resting in the hands of the archbishop rather than the king.[121] Eadred, however, succeeded in capturing

---

[116] Ibid., p. 119.   [117] *Annals of Ulster*, sub annis 943, 945, 946.
[118] Smyth, *Scandinavian York and Dublin*, pp. 119–20.
[119] *Anglo-Saxon Chronicles*, E, sub anno 949.   [120] Ibid., sub anno 952.
[121] Smyth, *Scandinavian York and Dublin*, Chapter 8.

Wulfstan before his ally could return to York, and the archbishop was forced to spend the remaining three years of his life south of the Humber, forbidden to return to his northern powerbase.[122] Despite the removal of the archbishop, however, Eadred was unable to prevent Eirik Bloodaxe from entering the city and resuming the kingship. Eirik's grip on power, however, was never effective without the strong backing of a man like Wulfstan and, although later saga tradition depicts him as a fearsome tyrant who 'kept his people wrapt up under the helmet of his terror'[123] and backed by his equally terrifying wife, Gunnhild, he lacked the means to give substance to his kingship. Outwith York, moreover, there was mounting hostility to the rule of this pagan Norwegian interloper, particularly amongst ambitious members of the northern Anglian nobility. In 954 Eirik and his supporters were driven from York a second time, this time in a coup engineered by Oswulf of Bamburgh, ruler of the northern remnant of old Northumbria.[124] As Eirik and his retinue headed west along the old Roman road across the Pennines, evidently seeking allies or refuge in the Norse-Gaelic territories of Galloway or the Isles, he was intercepted by Oswulf and his associates and slaughtered along with his allies, Arnkell and Erlend, the joint carls of Orkney.[125] His death 'in a certain lonely place called Stainmore'[126] was the final act in the bloody history of an independent Scandinavian kingdom based on York. With Eirik's demise, and Oswulf's acknowledgement of Eadred's overlordship, the West Saxon kings at last secured a firm hold on England north of the Humber and with it a quarter century of respite from Viking attack.

[122] *Anglo-Saxon Chronicles*, D, *sub anno* 952.

[123] *Egils saga, Íslenzk fornrit*, ii, 270, quoted in Smyth, *Scandinavian York and Dublin*, p. 183.

[124] *Anglo-Saxon Chronicles*, E, *sub anno* 952; Smyth, *Scandinavian York and Dublin*, pp. 172–73.

[125] *Symeonis monachi opera*, p. 197. *Hakon the Good's Saga*. In *Heimskringla*, see note 108 above, Chapter 4.

[126] Roger of Wendover, *Liber qui dicitur Flores historiarum ab anno domini MCLIV. annoque Henrici anglorum regis secundi primo*, ed. H. G. Hewlett. London: Printed for H. M. Stationery Office by Eyre and Spottiswode, 1886. p. 402.

CHAPTER 5

A water world

Nineteenth-century artists have given us the stirring image of the Scandinavian male of the Viking Age going to war in his horned helmet, sailing in his fearsome long ship, complete with dragon's head mounted on the prow and lusty Northmen straining at the oars. The painting we have in mind is that by Hans Gude, *Viking Ships under Sail in Sognefjord* (1889) in the Nasjonalgalleriet, Oslo. Equally absurd is a painting by R. Monléon, in the Museo Naval, Madrid, depicting King Olaf's fleet; here one of the vessels appears to be an unnatural hybrid somewhere between a Roman warship and Venetian galley.[1] And yet this image is not without some foundation. There were indeed long ships, some of them carried such ornamentation and oar power was used. But, more fundamentally, the popular view at least recognises that one of the defining characteristics of the Scandinavian peoples of the ninth to eleventh centuries was their sea-faring capability. This is not to minimise the significance of travel by land, and, more particularly, the role of land transport at the time.[2] However, the geography of Scandinavia (particularly that of Norway and Denmark), its situation on the edge of north-west Europe, its access to the markets in Britain, Francia and Frisian Dorestad on the lower reaches of the Rhine, and, indeed, to those in

[1] A dragon vessel, with a crew in assorted headgear (including horned helmets), and whose speed, judging from the manner in which the bow-wave is shown, appears to be that of a modern naval frigate, is to be found in the *Petit Journal* of 1911 and is reproduced in Y. Cohat, *The Vikings: Lords of the Seas*. New York: Harry N. Abrams, 1992. p. 26.

[2] On the relevance of land transport as well as the development of sea-faring from the first to the eleventh centuries, see U. Näsman, Sea trade during the Scandinavian Iron Age: its character, commodities, and routes. In *Aspects of Maritime Scandinavia AD 200–1200. Proceedings of the Nordic seminar on maritime aspects of archaeology, Roskilde, 13–15 March 1989*, ed. O. Crumlin-Pedersen. Roskilde: Vikingeskibshallen, 1991. pp. 23–40.

Scandinavia itself at Helgö, Hedeby (Haithabu), Kaupang, Ribe and Birka, all required a maritime focus. Without their vessels and, just as importantly, the seamanship and navigational expertise of their crews, the Scandinavians would not have had any empires in the sense employed in this book. There would have been no Normandy and thus no Normans to mount an invasion in 1066, and very possibly Gaelic, not the Scandinavian tongue, might now be heard in Iceland and the Faroe Islands.

Sources

As with any aspect of Scandinavian history during the Viking Age, there are problems associated with the sources dealing with ships and shipping. In the first instance there are the written sources, which may be grouped into three broad categories, namely: (1) the historical, legal and moral texts such as *Íslendingabók, Landnámabók, Grágás* and *Konungs Skuggsjá*; (2) the sagas such as *Grænlendinga Saga* and *Orkneyinga Saga*; and (3) skaldic poems such as *Hafgerðingadrápa*. Taken together, these not only furnish information about the voyages of discovery to Iceland, Greenland and North America but are also a rich source of detail on the different types of vessel used, ship names, ship-building, ship-wrecks, the sailing seasons, seamanship, navigation and weather conditions in the North Atlantic region. The problem with the literary component of these sources, however, is that many were only committed to writing after the classic Viking Age of the ninth, tenth and eleventh centuries had come to an end and when the dividing line between fact and fiction was not always observed.[3] Three points are nevertheless worth keeping in mind when evaluating the sagas in particular as a source for the maritime history of the Scandinavians. The first is that many were composed in Iceland and that Icelandic society in the twelfth

---

[3] A useful account of the reliability of the literary sources is found in L. Lönroth, The Vikings in history and legend. In *The Oxford Illustrated History of the Vikings*, ed. P. H. Sawyer. Oxford: Oxford University Press, 1997. pp. 225–49. Note also: G. Jones, *A History of the Vikings*. Oxford, New York: Oxford University Press, 1984 [1968]. pp. 36–37; J. Graham-Campbell, *The Viking World*. New Haven: Ticknor & Fields, 1989 [1980]. p. 68; E. Roesdahl, *The Vikings*. London: Penguin Books, 1998 [1987]. pp. 11–14. For a general critique of the sources, see P. H. Sawyer, *Kings and Vikings: Scandinavia and Europe, A.D. 700–1100*. London, New York: Methuen, 1982. pp. 10–38.

and thirteenth centuries was still very much a maritime culture. Modern ethnological research on, for example, Scottish fishing communities reveals that knowledge of the types of fish being caught, the location of the fishing grounds and the times of year when fish congregate on those grounds in large numbers is not confined to the fisher-men themselves but is exhibited by wives and those in ancillary trades such as processing, marketing and boat-building.[4] The Icelanders who composed the sagas, even if clerics, were still part of a wider community whose very existence depended on the sea; and they may, not unreasonably, be regarded as having had a pretty clear understanding of the maritime scenes included in the stories. And even if they did draw on contemporary knowledge, the difference between some of the vessels, seamanship and weather conditions described and those encountered in the 'heroic age' was almost negligible. The second point is that much of the information about the voyages and the seamanship deployed during them is scarcely in heroic vein. Ships cross the North Sea to England to trade and ply the waters of the North Atlantic and, in doing so, skippers sometimes lose their bearings and ships are lost at sea or wrecked. These are fairly matter-of-fact occurrences, narrated as such and unlikely to have been exaggerated by the saga writers of a later age. Thirdly, there is a relatively strong corroborative link between some of the information about ships in the sagas and what has been found in the archaeological record and demonstrated by the work of experimental archaeologists. This is not to argue that one should accept the sagas uncritically as a guide to ships and sea-faring but rather to suggest that they, and for that matter skaldic poetry, should not be dismissed out of hand.

As indicated above, archaeology offers another approach to understanding the types of vessel used. Many finds from our period and earlier have been made and, in particular, a number of remains from the Skuldelev and Roskilde sites in Sjælland (Zealand) in eastern Denmark have added immeasurably to our understanding of the ships and the manner of their construction (see Figure 19). Finds from Nydam in Denmark, Gokstad, Kvalsund and Oseberg in Norway and Sutton Hoo in East

---

[4] This is brought out particularly well in J. R. Coull, *The Sea Fisheries of Scotland: A Historical Geography*. Edinburgh: John Donald Publishers, 1996; and J. Nadel-Klein, *Fishing for Heritage: Modernity and Loss along the Scottish Coast*. Oxford: Berg, 2003.

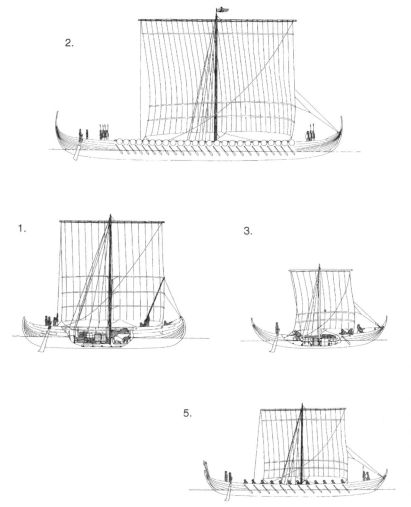

Figure 19 Four eleventh-century ships from Skuldelev, (Sjælland, Denmark): two warships (nos. 2 and 5) and two cargo ships (nos. 1 and 3). Reconstructions drawn at the same scale.

Anglia, for example, have permitted the evolution of ship design in north-west Europe to be studied and useful comparisons in ship morphology made. But archaeology has its limitations. Fittings such as rigging and sails are made from organic material, very little of which has survived. Masts and yards do not survive intact, leaving incomplete our knowledge of the sail area of the vessels recovered and, in consequence, the speeds at which they could be sailed.

Archaeological finds have, not unnaturally, encouraged the building of what are sometimes rather misleadingly referred to as 'replicas': in the absence of a fully fitted vessel one can hardly replicate exactly what that vessel looked like. Such reconstructions began with *Viking* (based on the Gokstad ship excavated in 1880) which sailed across the Atlantic in 1893: a prescient reminder that Scandinavian sea-farers reached North America almost five hundred years before Columbus made his much-celebrated crossing in 1492. A note of caution must, however, be sounded at this point. The fact that a reconstruction of the Gokstad ship successfully crossed the Atlantic should not be interpreted as indicating that this was the type of vessel that travelled the North Atlantic runs to Iceland and Greenland a thousand years ago. The fact that something can be done today does not prove that it was done in the past.[5]

Of all the reconstructions, perhaps the best known, and almost certainly the best researched, are those that were built or that were in the process of being built in Roskilde: in particular, the reconstructions of the two warships and the large cargo vessel found beneath the waters of Roskilde Fjord at Skuldelev.[6] As the science of interpreting ship remains continues to improve and the results are incorporated into the building of reconstructions of Viking Age vessels, these reconstructions help us to understand the methods employed in building the originals; the tools employed in their construction and their efficiency; and how well suited these vessels were to the purposes for which they were built. Most importantly, however, they give us a good idea of how the vessels were sailed and the sizes of the crews needed to man them. In short, reconstructions assist us to corroborate the accuracy of the iconographic evidence. One may also advance a strong case for the assistance that they provide in assessing the credibility of the literary sources dealing with sea-faring in the Scandinavian empires.

Iconography provides a third source of information about vessels and their equipment. Depictions of ships from the eighth to the eleventh centuries are to be observed in both formal and informal iconographic contexts. Formal images are, for example,

---

[5] O. Crumlin-Pedersen, Problems of reconstruction and the estimation of performance. In *The Earliest Ships: The Evolution of Boats into Ships*, ed. R. Gardiner and A. E. Christensen. Conway's History of the Ship. London: Conway Maritime Press, 1996. pp. 110–19.

[6] The remains of five vessels were found, and these are referred to as Skuldelev 1–6. The numbering appears slightly misleading: a single plank found after Skuldelev 3 was discovered led the investigators to think that they had found a new vessel, which they designated Skuldelev 4. After the fifth and sixth vessels were discovered it was realised that the plank was actually from Skuldelev 2, but it was decided not to renumber the other vessels.

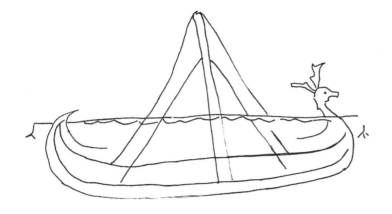

Figure 20 Ship graffito incised on stone near Trondheim, Norway. The image depicts a vessel with an animal head on the prow and a mast with furled sail and rigging.

to be found on carved monuments, such as the series of eighth-century stones from Gotland that portray vessels in some considerable detail, or, in the case of the Bayeux Tapestry, embroidered on textile and, once again, rich in detail.[7] Informal images, or graffiti, have also been discovered.[8] One of the ship graffiti scratched on a piece of soft rock found near Trondheim (and which may be eleventh century in date) depicts a vessel with an animal head mounted on the prow (Figure 20). Another, incised on a piece of wood known as the 'Bryggen stick', shows several ships, with dragons' heads and wind vanes (Figure 21). Ship graffiti have also been found on a number of wooden objects associated with the Oseberg and Gokstad burials, and on a piece of whalebone from northern Norway. As with the archaeological

Figure 21 Ship graffito incised on wood, known as the 'Bryggen stick', Bergen, Norway. The stick depicts a row of vessels lying abreast. Some of these have animal heads on their prows, others show vessels with wind vanes. It is possible that the vanes were mounted on the vessels' after-stems.

---

[7] On the Gotland stones, see D. Ellmers, Valhalla and the Gotland stones. In *The Ship as Symbol in Prehistoric and Medieval Scandinavia. Papers from an international research seminar at the Danish National Museum, Copenhagen, 5–7 May 1994*, ed. O. Crumlin-Pedersen and B. Munch Thye. Vol. I. Publications from the National Museum. Copenhagen: Nationalmuseet, 1995. pp. 165–70. On the Bayeux Tapestry, see M. Rud, *The Bayeux Tapestry and the Battle of Hastings, 1066*. Copenhagen: Christian Eilers, 1996 [1974]. pp. 60–67.

[8] On the value of graffiti as evidence, see L. Le Bon, Ancient ship graffiti: symbol and context. In *The Ship as Symbol*, see note 7 above , pp. 172–79; and A. E. Christensen, Ship graffiti. Ibid., pp. 181–85.

Figure 22
Picture stone
(3 metres high)
from Hammars
in Larbro,
Gotland, Sweden
(eighth to tenth
century). The
stone depicts a
double-ended
vessel with
identical stem
and stern. The
vessel also has a
single mast and a
fore-stay, and
carries a square
sail. The handle
of a tiller is
visible. The
pattern on the
sail gives rise to
considerable
speculation.

and literary sources, however, the iconographic evidence has its limitations. For example, the vessel carved on the Gotland stone (Figure 22) depicts a double-ended vessel with identical stem and stern. The vessel also has a single mast and a fore-stay; she carries a square sail, and the handle of a tiller is discernible aft. But how are the remaining details to be interpreted? Do the other lines depict rigging shrouds, giving the mast lateral support, or an after stay bracing the mast against the pressure exerted by a following wind on the sail? Then there is the sail itself. What do the lozenges on this suggest? Are these simply decoration? Do they represent strips of material, leather perhaps, designed to strengthen the sail? Are they simply artistic embellishment and no more? And what of the items omitted in the carving? Did this vessel have braces attached to the yard, enabling the angle of presentation of the sail to the wind to be altered? Were sheets also attached to the lower corners of the sail to prevent it lifting too high when filled with wind?

No single source of information on the vessels of the eighth to eleventh centuries can provide us with an exact picture of what these looked like and, just as importantly, how they handled at sea. One must glean what one can from all of the available evidence and, whenever possible, bench-test theory in the laboratory of the open sea.

Maritime northern Europe

The Anglo-Saxon Chronicles for 787 or 789 record rather tersely the arrival, possibly near Portland, of three ships – 'the first ships of the Danish men which sought out the land of the English race'.[9] This passage has frequently been interpreted as a raid,[10] because when King Beorhtric of Wessex's reeve questioned the Danes 'they killed him'. Another version of this event, however, states that Beaduheard, the reeve, 'spoke to them haughtily', and attributes his death to his overall manner of addressing the strangers.[11] Perhaps it really was a raid, although not all the versions of the *Chronicle*, unlike the accounts of the raids on Lindisfarne and Jarrow a few years later, actually say so or state that any atrocities were perpetrated. Æðelweard's account, however, also has the unfortunate Beaduheard making the assumption that the visitors were merchants. Perhaps this takes us closer to what may have happened. If the incident really did take place in the vicinity of Portland, this is fairly close to Hamwic (present-day Southampton), one of the two major Saxon ports of the eighth century. Portland itself lies to the south-west of Hamwic, and these three vessels may well have been those of traders who had been blown past their destination. There is, however, another possibility.

In the eighth century Dorestad on the lower reaches of the Rhine became the hub of an import/export trade with Hamwic in

---

[9] *The Anglo-Saxon Chronicles*, ed. and trans. M. J. Swanton. London: Phoenix, 2000. p. 54.

[10] F. M. Stenton, *The Oxford History of England*. Vol. II, *Anglo-Saxon England*. Oxford: Oxford University Press, 1947 [1943]. p. 239.; S. Keynes, The Vikings in England c. 790–716. In *The Oxford Illustrated History of the Vikings*, see note 3 above, p. 50; B. Cunliffe, *Facing the Ocean: The Atlantic and Its Peoples*. Oxford: Oxford University Press, 2001. p. 482.

[11] *The Chronicle of Aethelweard*, ed. A. Campbell. Medieval Texts. London: Nelson, 1962. p. 27; quoted in *Anglo-Saxon Chronicles*, p. 55, footnote 7.

Wessex, London, Ipswich in East Anglia, and with Quentovic and other ports in Francia.[12] From Dorestad goods were traded north to places such as Ribe and Hedeby (Haithabu) in Denmark, with a return trade from these markets and others, such as Birka in Sweden and Wolin on the Oder estuary, in northern produce such as amber, furs and walrus ivory. We cannot be sure what the Frankish vessels that engaged in this trade looked like. It seems, however, quite likely that they were not too dissimilar in appearance to the Celtic vessels that Julius Caesar commented on so favourably after seeing them in action in Gaul. Caesar emphasised their strong build (they were made of oak, he said), high sides and sea-keeping abilities under sail (they had no oars).[13] The remains of vessels found at Blackfriars in London and St Peter Port, Guernsey, in the Channel Islands confirm Caesar's account. The Blackfriars vessel, which may be dated to the late first or early second century, was around 18 metres in length and was built of oak; it had a mast and, as Caesar also noted, was flat-bottomed. The other vessel, dated to the third century, was 25 metres long and also had a mast and was flat-bottomed. Both boats could carry substantial amounts of cargo: the Blackfriars ship, for example, had about twenty-six tonnes of ragstones aboard when she sank. Vessels of this sort did not survive in England. After the Anglo-Saxon migrations they were replaced with vessels of which the early seventh-century Sutton Hoo ship is typical. This vessel exhibits points of similarity with the earlier, fourth-century one found at Nydam in Denmark in a context that makes it clear this was a votive offering by the winners of a battle in an on-going war between Denmark and Norway. Both vessels were powered by oars which were braced by thole pins: there were no oar ports. Both were also clinker-built, with overlapping planks fixed to each other by iron nails. Neither, however, had much by way of a keel, which of itself does not rule out the use of a sail, although there is

---

[12] On trade generally during this period, see U. Näsman, Sea trade during the Scandinavian Iron Age: its character, commodities, and routes. In *Aspects of Maritime Scandinavia*, see note 2 above, pp. 23–40. On the relationship between Scandinavia and other north European trade centres, see K. Randsborg, Seafaring and society in south Scandinavian and European perspective. In *Aspects of Maritime Scandinavia*, pp. 11–22.

[13] Julius Caesar, *The Gallic War* ed. and trans. H. Edwards. London: William Heinemann Ltd, 1986 [1917]. pp. 153–57. Julius Caesar, *The Conquest of Gaul*, Harmondsworth: Penguin Books, 1963. pp. 95–100.

no internal evidence of a mast or rigging.[14] Buried in all of this detail there is an attractive hypothesis advanced by Detlev Ellmers, who suggests that the Anglo-Saxons had their own ship-building tradition and continued to follow this once they were established in England. Consequently the Romano-Celtic vessels typified by the Blackfriars boat fell into disuse there. He speculates, however, that since the incoming Franks did not arrive in Gaul by sea and were not, initially, sea-farers, they would have been more likely to adopt the Romano-Celtic ship type.[15]

It is possible, however, to take this speculation a little further. At some point during the eighth century, perhaps even earlier, the carrying trade to Dorestad from Scandinavia ceased to be the exclusive prerogative of Frisian or Frankish merchants. Scandinavian vessels themselves came south to Dorestad and, very probably, to Francia and England. However, vessels of the Nydam type, which was approximately 27 metres long, with a beam of a little over 3 metres, and was equipped a steering paddle rather than a side rudder, were not well suited to trading in bulk commodities such as hides and furs. Indeed, even the very early eighth-century Norwegian Kvalsund vessel, with its low free-board, bluff, high stems and reliance on oar power, is not a likely choice for long-distance trading in the North Sea region.[16] Where goods are high value in nature, such as the Roman banqueting set found in Hoby on Lolland (discussed in Chapter 2), or the Indian statuette of the Buddha found at Helgö, cargo space is not an issue. In any event, the vessels employed to transport high-status

---

[14] On these and early vessels generally, see S. McGrail, *Ancient Boats in NW Europe: The Archaeology of Water Transport to AD 1500*. Longman Archaeology Series. London, New York: Longman 1997 [1987]. On the Sutton Hoo find, see R. L. S. Bruce-Mitford, *The Sutton Hoo Ship-Burial*. Vol. I. London: Published for the Trustees of the British Museum by British Museum Publications, 1975. On the Nydam vessel, see E. Jørgensen, and P. V. Petersen, Nydam Bog: new finds and observations. In *The Spoils of Victory: The North in the Shadow of the Roman Empire*, ed. L. Jørgensen, B. Storgaard and L. G. Thomsen. Copenhagen: Nationalmuseet, 2003. pp. 258–85. On a late ninth- or early tenth-century Saxon vessel, see V. Fenwick, and A. Morley, eds. *British Archaeological Reports*, Vol. LIII, *The Graveney Boat: A Tenth Century Find: Excavation and Recording; Interpretation of the Boat Remains and the Environment; Reconstruction and Other Research, Conservation and Display*. BAR British Series. Oxford, 1978.

[15] D. Ellmers, Celtic plank boats and ships, 500 BC–AD 1000. In *The Earliest Ships*, see note 5 above, p. 71.

[16] A. E. Christensen, Proto-Viking, Viking and Norse craft. In *The Earliest Ships*, see note 5 above, pp. 78–88.

emissaries and diplomatic gifts were more likely to have been military rather than commercial craft. On the other hand, bulk cargoes do require space and this, in turn, means smaller crews. Consequently vessels adapted to this trade required sails rather than oars for propulsion.[17] Once Scandinavian sea-farers became involved in the bulk carrying trade, the advantages conferred by sail over oar, not least in economies of scale, would have become evident by looking at the Frankish vessels which were now, in a sense, the competition. The transition to sail would, then, have appeared a logical one. The eighth century can therefore be viewed as a transitional one in Scandinavian ship design, and it has been portrayed as one in which the Kvalsund vessel and the early ninth-century Oseberg ship mark the beginning and the end of a period of experimentation.[18] The challenge facing the ship-builder at that time was how best to adapt the traditional Scandinavian hull to the use of the mast and sail. The vessel that ultimately emerged from this process was a highly successful blend of conservatism and modernity. All of which, in an elliptical way, brings us back to those three 'ships of the Danish men' lying off the Wessex coast.

Although it was not the only haven on the south coast of England,[19] Hamwic was still a major port of destination for vessels crossing the North Sea from Dorestad and northern Francia. It is unlikely that Scandinavian vessels were not involved in the carrying trade to and from England by the end of the eighth century; and Beaduheard's assumption that the Danes were merchants certainly makes sense if trading was already an established occurrence. In Scotland the presence of combs made from Norwegian reindeer antler horn certainly indicates economic links before the Scandinavian raiding phase began.[20] What seems to have sealed the reeve's fate was his arrogant manner, which sufficiently annoyed the Danes for them to kill him. Such a reaction does not ring true for merchants: killing royal officials is

---

[17] Näsman, Sea trade. In *Aspects of Maritime Scandinavia*, see note 2 above, p. 28. His suggestion that the sail was in use on Nordic vessels in the sixth century is improbable.

[18] Christensen, Proto-Viking, Viking and Norse craft. In *The Earliest Ships*, see note 5 above, pp. 78–88.

[19] B. Cunliffe, *Facing the Ocean*, p. 485.

[20] J. Graham-Campbell and C. E. Batey, *Vikings in Scotland: An Archaeological Survey*. Edinburgh: Edinburgh University Press, 1998. p. 23.

hardly sound mercantile practice. If, however, these men were not traders, and did not wish their presence to be known to the authorities, then might they not have been pirates?[21] Given the amount of commercial shipping plying the waters of the English Channel, the prospect of rich pickings both in goods and in coin from easy targets must have been a tempting one. The transition from oar to sail gave the Scandinavians perfect vessels for trading. The successful fusion of the southern sail and the sleek northern hull also gave them perfect vessels for piracy, raiding and military adventurism across the continent from the Baltic to the Mediterranean.

Together with the intriguing issue of the development of sea-going ships by the Scandinavians, there is the equally interesting matter of their knowledge of the topography of the North Sea. Cunliffe cites the comments of an eighth-century Frankish cleric who met some Scandinavians and noted how thoroughly conversant they were with 'the route and the harbours of the sea and the rivers that flowed into it'.[22] It is impossible to be sure whether that knowledge was the product of actual experience or had simply been gleaned from conversations with Frankish or Frisian traders in Scandinavian ports.[23] By the end of the eighth century, however, the Scandinavians certainly knew enough to direct the highly selective raids of its last decade, and those of the early ninth century, against prime economic targets – the monasteries and ports of England, Ireland, Scotland .and Francia. But interesting though their exploration of the North Sea is, the problems pale into insignificance when compared with the discovery of the islands of the North Atlantic archipelago.

It is popularly accepted that the very first residents of the Faroes and Iceland were the Irish monks or priests[24] referred to

---

[21] P. G. Foote and D. M. Wilson, *The Viking Achievement: The Society and Culture of Early Medieval Scandinavia*. Sidgwick & Jackson Great Civilizations Series. London, New York: Sidgwick and Jackson, St. Martin's Press, 1990. pp. 229–30. The authors mention piracy but appear to treat this as a synonym for raiding, which is not the case.

[22] Cunliffe, *Facing the Ocean*, p. 488.   [23] Ibid., p. 490.

[24] G. Jones, *The Norse Atlantic Saga, Being the Norse Voyages of Discovery and Settlement to Iceland, Greenland, and North America*, Oxford New York: Oxford University Press, 1986 [1964]. pp. 7–9; Jones, *A History of the Vikings*, pp. 275–76. More recent works that take this view are Cunliffe, *Facing the Ocean*, p. 503; and J. L. Byock, *Viking Age Iceland*. London: Penguin, 2001. p. 11.

by the Scandinavians as *papar*. Indeed, it has been argued that with regard to the early history of Iceland 'one of the few certainties' is that the island was 'discovered in the first instance not by Vikings but by Celtic monks'.[25] There exists a literary genre known as *immrama* which records the voyages of these men, mostly set in the sixth century,[26] seeking to find their own personal 'desert in the ocean' and salvation through pursuit of the eremitical life. In Adomnán's *Vita Sancti Columbae*,[27] for example, we are told that Cormac Ua Liatháin set sail in a curach on several occasions to find such a place. In the *Immran Curaig Maíle Dúin* mention is made of an island that is both mountainous and bird-infested; and of another where sheep were to be found in large numbers.[28] We should not, however, accept these works – particularly the *Navigatio Sancti Brendani Abbatis*, with its crystal pillars, tusked monsters and 'swarthy dwarves' (too easily equated with icebergs, walruses and, very offensively, native American peoples) – as genuine discovery narratives. Moreover, we should certainly hesitate before equating some of the islands described therein with the Faroes or Iceland: the rocky outcrops off the Atlantic coasts of Ireland and Scotland offer more plausible alternatives. Not even the accounts of *Thule* in Bede's *De temporum ratione* (725) or in the *Liber de mensura orbis terrae* by the Irish monk Dicuil (825), with its observation that during the light summer nights a man can see well enough to pick lice from his shirt, can be taken as unequivocal references to Iceland or the Faroes. Doubt may even be cast on whether these voyages, or at least the first successful ones, assuming that they took place at all, involved much more than entrusting oneself to the ocean in the hope that wind and tide would take one to a suitable rock.[29]

[25] A. P. Smyth, *New History of Scotland*. Vol. I, *Warlords and Holy Men: Scotland, AD 80–1000*. London: Edward Arnold, 1984. p. 16.

[26] W. F. Thrall, Clerical sea pilgrimages and the 'Imramma'. *The Manly Anniversary Studies*, 1923. pp. 278–83.

[27] Adomnán of Iona, *Life of St. Columba*, trans. R. Sharpe. Penguin Classics. London: Penguin, 1995. I.6; II.42.

[28] These voyages are set out more fully in G. J. Marcus, *The Conquest of the North Atlantic*. Woodbridge: Boydell, 1998 [1990]. pp. 16–32.

[29] For an excellent and trenchantly critical account of the stories about these voyages, see D. Dumville, The North Atlantic monastic thalassocracy: sailing to the desert in early medieval insular spirituality. In *The Papar in the North Atlantic Environment and History. The proceedings of a day conference held on 24 February 2001*, ed. B. E. Crawford. Vol. V: 1, The Papar Project. St. Andrews: University of St. Andrews, 2002. p. 121.

Indeed, the general thrust of recent studies suggests that not only is there no literary evidence for the presence of *papar* in Iceland and the Faroes, but that neither place-name nor archaeological evidence supports a pre-Scandinavian occupation of these islands either.[30] There is enough here to cast substantial doubt on the thesis that Iceland and the Faroes were already occupied before the arrival of the Scandinavians. This in turn renders debate on the sailing properties of curachs, the size of ocean-going curachs and whether or not the monks took passage on vessels crewed by professional seamen[31] rather irrelevant. More significantly, the claim that these clerics came from Ireland[32] may also be considered to be highly improbable. The Hiberno-centric discovery theory is not the only one, however, that requires to be considered in this context. There is also a view that the north-west Highlands and islands of Scotland were central to the exploration of the North Atlantic.

One version of this theory, which may be thought of as the Celtic-Norse discovery hypothesis, proceeds upon the following line of argument. Celtic clerics from the Hebridean islands reached Iceland and the Faroes first. We know this, the hypothesis continues, because of the numerous place-names in these islands which contain a *papar* element. Iona, it is claimed, played a pivotal role in establishing a route to these Atlantic islands, serving as a 'major base camp for wandering ascetics' who, on their return, provided information about their travels which could then be relayed to subsequent voyagers. Furthermore, again according to the hypothesis, Dicuil's *Thule* can be 'unhesitatingly' identified with Iceland. All of which, it is claimed, makes the case for the discovery of Iceland and the Faroes by Celtic (and Irish) monks 'sailing from the Scottish Isles in the seventh and eighth centuries ... unshakeable'.[33] Of course, this still leaves us with the matter of establishing a connection between the discoveries

[30] G. Sveinbjarnardóttir, The question of *papar* in Iceland. In *The Papar*, see note 29 above, pp. 97–106.
[31] Explored at great length in Marcus, *Conquest*, pp. 7–32.
[32] Jones, *A History of the Vikings*, pp. 269, 275; Marcus, The course for Greenland, pp. 16–32; Graham-Campbell, *The Viking World*, p. 66.
[33] Smyth, *New History*, pp. 166–69.

made by the *papar* and the rediscoveries of the Celtic-Norse. It is to this issue that we now turn.

The early Scandinavian raids on the Hebridean islands and Ireland targeted monasteries: an obvious source of wealth. But raiding did not preclude settlement and co-existence with the Celtic populations of both places. There was also intermarriage and concubinage, which brought the two races together and quickly created a hybrid Celtic-Norse ethnic group possibly identifiable in the Hebrides as the *Gall-Gaedhil* (the Foreign-Gaels – see Chapter 4).[34] In short, by the mid-ninth century the situation was ideal for the transmission of knowledge about the sea-faring adventures of the *papar*. All of which would have been eagerly fastened upon by Norse sea-farers and their Celtic-Norse cousins. It has not escaped notice that two of the (fictional) first voyagers to Iceland according to *Landnámabók*, Gardar Svavarsson and Flóki Vilgerdarson, had Hebridean connections. In the redaction of this work known as *Hauksbók*, Gardar's wife was Hebridean (whether she was a pure Celt or a Celtic-Norse hybrid is irrelevant) and he was bound from Norway to the Hebrides to claim her inheritance there from her father. In Flóki's case, according to both *Hauksbók* and *Sturlubók*, he had on board a Hebridean named Faxi. *Færeyinga Saga* names Grim Kamban as the first settler. 'Kamban' may derive from the Gaelic *camm*, meaning crooked, and this, in turn, may point to a mixed, Celtic-Norse ancestry. What is the conclusion to be drawn from all of this? The 'Scottish isles [were] the immediate starting point of the earliest Norse voyages of discovery and colonisation in the North Atlantic'.[35]

---

[34] Smyth, *New History*, p. 156. Smyth translates the term as 'Scandinavian Gaels'. Note also A. A. M. Duncan, *Scotland: The Making of the Kingdom. Vol. I, Edinburgh History of scotland*. Edinburgh: Oliver and Boyd, 1975. p. 89; J. Marsden, *Somerled and the Emergence of Gaelic Scotland*. East Linton: Tuckwell Press, 2000. pp. 1–22; R. Oram, *The Lordship of Galloway*. Edinburgh: John Donald, 2000. p. 1. For a general survey, see B. E. Crawford, *Scandinavian Scotland*. Scotland in the Early Middle Ages. Leicester: Leicester University Press, 1987. For place-name evidence, see G. Fellows-Jensen, Viking settlements in the Northern and Western Isles – the place-name evidence as seen from Denmark and the Danelaw. In *The Northern and Western Isles in the Viking World*, ed. A. Fenton and H. Pálsson. Edinburgh: John Donald, 1984. pp. 148–68. On archaeology, see J. Graham-Campbell, and C. E. Batey, *Vikings in Scotland: An Archaeological Survey*. Edinburgh: Edinburgh University Press, 1998. pp. 24, 70–92.

[35] Smyth, *New History*, p. 169.

It may well be the case that there was a substantial Celtic-Norse component in the original population of Iceland or the Faroes.[36] This does not, however, require one to believe that the discovery of these islands was an achievement of the Celtic-Norse. The hypothesis hangs, ultimately, on the argument that it was knowledge that the *papar* had reached Iceland and the Faroes which led to their discovery by the Celtic-Norse. As we have seen, however, all of the evidence discussed so far for this view suggests that there was no *papar* presence on the islands before their discovery by Scandinavians of some description. Moreover, the hypothesis, at least in some versions, ignores the point that, according to *Landnámabók*, the first discoverers of Iceland found it by accident and not by design, having been driven off-course from their intended destinations. Indeed, discovery by misadventure is a recurrent theme in the saga accounts of the first sightings of Greenland and North America also. Even so, and contrary to the arguments advanced against the Celtic-Norse hypothesis so far, there does exist a small possibility that the hypothesis is correct in its basic assumption.

Recent work[37] on caves in Seljaland in south-west Iceland indicates that these sites may have been occupied before 870 – the approximate date when the archaeological record suggests that Norse settlement began.[38] Particularly important in this respect are some crosses, incised on cave walls, which are in a style highly reminiscent of those found in Argyll in western Scotland.[39] These sites may be dated to the seventh and eighth centuries and may have been inhabited by clerics

[36] H. Pálsson, *Keltar á Íslandi*. Reykjavík: Háskólaútgáfan, 1996; Gísli Sigurðson, *Gaelic Influence in Iceland: Historical and Literary Contacts: A Survey of Research*. Studia Islandica 46. Reykjavík: Bókaútgáfa Menningarsjóð, 1988; H. Pálsson, Vinland revisited. *Northern Studies*, Vol. 35, 2000, pp. 11–38. Pálsson calls into question the 'Norse' discovery of North America, arguing that this distinction belongs to Icelanders from Breiðafjörður in Iceland, and pointing out that many of these Icelanders had come from the Hebrides and Ireland.

[37] K. Ahronson, Testing the evidence for Northern North Atlantic *Papar*: A cave site in southern Iceland. In *The Papar*, see note 29 above, pp. 107–20. K. Ahronson, One North Atlantic cave settlement: preliminary archaeological and environmental investigations at Seljaland, southern Iceland. *Northern Studies*, Vol. 37, 2003, pp. 53–70.

[38] This is reviewed by J. L. Byock, *Viking Age Iceland*. London: Penguin, 2001. pp. 89–91.

[39] E. Campbell, A cross-marked quern from Dunadd and other evidence for relations between Dunadd and Iona. In *Proceedings of the Society of Antiquaries of Scotland*. Vol. 117. Edinburgh: Society of Antiquaries, 1987. pp. 105–17.

or hermits. It has therefore been suggested, on the basis of these crosses and on a broader environmental survey of the sites, that the evidence is 'consistent with very early or Scotland-related settlement'.[40] This research is characterised by caution and a desire not to push the evidence too far, too fast. However, if on-going work does establish a pre-Norse settlement by religious, perhaps as early as 800, then it may be that the Celtic-Norse hypothesis for the 'discovery' of Iceland, certainly, and possibly even the Faroes, will finally rest on a more convincing basis than has been put forward for it so far.

Design

Many factors condition the design of a vessel, whether medieval or modern. One rather obvious factor is the construction material available to the ship-builder; another is the technology employed in the construction process; a third is consideration of the use to which the vessel will be put; and a fourth takes into account the sea conditions in which the vessel will operate. A vessel intended to raid should be built for speed. But length and beam (i.e. width) will vary depending on the number of raiders in the crew and on the destination of the raid. A fighting ship such as Skuldelev 2 (which was, incidentally, built in south-east Ireland in the Dublin/ Waterford area, probably in 1042),[41] with an overall length of approximately 30 metres and a beam of 4 metres, would be ideal for long-distance raids along the coastline of western Europe and into the Mediterranean (Figure 23). Her length allows her to carry a large number of warriors and high-value booty, while her draught, although deep enough to permit her to sail safely on the open sea, is not so deep as to

---

[40] Ahronson, Testing the evidence for Northern North Atlantic *Papar*: a cave site in southern Iceland. In *The Papar*, see note 29 above, p. 69.

[41] The dating of this and the other Skuldelev vessels is based on dendrochronological analysis described by O. Crumlin-Pedersen, Dendro-dating and analysis: dating and provenance of timber. In *Ships and Boats of the North*, ed. O. Crumlin-Pedersen and O. Olsen. Vol. IV: 1, *The Skuldelev Ships I, Topography, Archaeology, History, Conservation and Display*, by O. Crumlin-Pedersen, with contributions from E. Bondeson, P. Jensen, O. Olsen, A. Petersen and K. Stræetkvern. Roskilde: Viking Ship Museum, 2002, pp. 64–68.

prevent beaching in sheltered inlets or penetration up such rivers as the Seine, Elbe, Oder or Vistula. On the other hand, the second warship, Skuldelev 5, which is dated to the mid-eleventh century, is only a little over half the length and beam of Skuldelev 2, and vessels of this size may have been better suited to target victims closer to home or for use in a defensive capacity (Figure 24). A cargo carrier, however, must forgo sleek lines and a shallow draught in favour of the capacity to carry bulky cargoes. Vessels such as that exemplified by the (probably) early eleventh-century Skuldelev 1, with its deep draught, were ideal for the carrying trade across the North Sea and, in even larger versions, across the North Atlantic to the islands of the North Atlantic archipelago – the Faroes, Iceland and Greenland (Figures 25, 26). The much shorter Skuldelev 3 (built very probably between 1030 and 1040) with its shallow draught, might be more appropriate for carrying less bulky cargoes in the sheltered coastal waters of the Danish islands and the Baltic (Figure 19). But whatever the purpose to which a vessel was to be put, construction material and ship-building techniques were much the same throughout Scandinavia and the

Figure 23
Reconstruction of the warship known as Skuldelev 2 on the stocks in Roskilde, Sjælland. The illustration depicts clearly the inner strengthening of the hull.

Figure 24 *Helge Ask*, a reconstruction of Skuldelev 5, moored at Roskilde, Sjælland. This small vessel may have been a part of the national sea levy of the Danish kingdom and saw heavy use and many repairs. Vessels such as this would have been ideal for the more sheltered waters of the Baltic.

other parts of the Scandinavian world.[42] Double-ended with graceful, curving lines, these vessels are aesthetically pleasing in every respect. Yet, as with any wooden vessel, they had to be able to withstand the considerable force exerted by the sea. The hull had to be strong enough to bear the weight of crew, cargo, ballast and mast. It also had to be able to absorb the lateral pressure exerted by waves against the hull (yaw) and the upward motion (pitch) of rising and falling swells. Building a vessel that can float is not difficult. Building one that can carry 30 tonnes of cargo to Iceland or Greenland takes real skill. It is little wonder that the sagas narrate the value placed

[42] On ship-building generally in our period see Crumlin-Pedersen, and Olsen, *Ships and Boats of the North*, Vol. IV.1, see note 41 above, pp. 129–35. Much useful information is to be found in this publication, especially in Vol. IV: 1, and in Vol. III, *Ladby: A Ship Grave from the Viking Age*, by A. C. Sørensen in collaboration with V. Bischoff, K. Jensen and H. Henrichsen.

Figure 25 *Ottar*, moored in Roskilde, Sjælland, 26 April 2003. The knörr was a broad-beamed vessel with an impressive load capability. The reconstructed vessel carries just over 13 tonnes of stone ballast, although its historical payload would have been larger. This is in marked contrast to the ballast carried by the smaller, lighter and faster warship *Helge Ask. Ottar* was ideally suited for trading in the waters of the Viking Empires. Although capable of crossing the North Atlantic, even larger vessels than *Ottar* regularly travelled to the lands of the North Atlantic archipelago.

on the work of skilled shipwrights; and it is to their work that we first turn.

Ship-building[43]

An evocative passage in *Óláfs saga Tryggvasonar* describes the building of the king's ship, the *Long Serpent* (Old Norse *Ormrinn Langi*): 'Many people were gathered to do this task. Some cut down trees, others transported the timber, some smoothed the planks while others knocked in nails.' This suggest two things: that shipbuilding took place relatively close to the source of construction material; and that not all of the work was done at the construction site itself. It may, for example, be the case that cutting the planking in rough was done at the site where the trees were felled, which would make transportation from forest to the actual shipbuilding site easier to accomplish.[44] Gulathing Law confirms this

[43] For an excellent general account of what is covered in this section, though not confined to Scandinavia, or, indeed, to the Viking era, see J. Bill, Ship construction: tools and techniques. In *Cogs, Caravels, and Galleons: The Sailing Ship, 1000–1650*, ed. R. Gardiner and R. W. Unger. Conway's History of the Ship. London: Conway Maritime Press, 1994. pp. 151–59.

[44] A brief account of the quantities involved in building a reconstruction of Skuldelev 2 is given in S. Nielsen, The bottom is formed. *Maritime Archaeology Newsletter from Roskilde*, No. 17, 2001, pp. 41–42.

Figure 26 *Ottar* on Roskilde Fjord, Sjælland, 26 April 2003. This vessel – a *knörr* – is the reconstruction of Skuldelev 1. In contrast to the 650-kilogram ballast of *Helge Ask*, this vessel carries just over 13 tonnes of ballast. The large woollen sail has been treated to make it water-proof with a heavy coating of animal fat mixed with ochre. This mixture not only colours and weatherproofs the sail but also stiffens it.

general picture, indicating that the choice of site for building a vessel lay with the builders – subject to the proviso that 'no damage [should be] done to corn land or meadow'.[45] Gulathing Law also allocates different tasks to different artisans involved in the building process, identifying, in particular, shipwrights, the 'stem builder' and the 'plank cutter'.[46]

CONSTRUCTION MATERIAL

The construction material used for the planking (or strakes), internal strengthening, mast and keelson was wood.[47] Oak, which grew well in Denmark and southern Scandinavia,[48] and

[45] L. M. Larson, ed. and trans. *The Earliest Norwegian Laws, Being the Gulathing Law and Frostathing Law.* New York: Columbia University Press, 1935. p. 194. Gulathing Law survives in thirteenth-century manuscripts but dates to at least the eleventh century.

[46] Larson, *Norwegian Laws*, p. 195.

[47] On the woods used, see J. B. Godal, The use of wood in boatbuilding. In *Shipshape: Essays for Ole Crumlin-Pedersen*, ed. O. Olsen, J. Skamby Madsen and F. Rieck. Roskilde: Viking Ship Museum, 1995. pp. 271–82. This concentrates on Skuldelev 1 and also on the Bårset boat from Nord-Kvaløy, Troms, in Norway.

[48] A passage in *King Harald's Saga* reads: 'The oak keel ploughed the ocean all the way west from Russia . . . The oak ship carried the eager warrior prince from Sweden.' Snorri Sturluson, *King Harald's Saga: Harald Hardradi of Norway*, ed. and trans. M. Magnusson and H. Pálsson. Harmondsworth: Penguin, 1966. p. 66.

pine, which predominated in Norway, were favoured for these items. Indeed, the wood mainly used in the construction of the vessels found at Äskekärr, Gokstad, Klåstad and Oseberg was oak, which may indicate that these were constructed in southern Scandinavia. But although the keel of the cargo ship Skuldelev 1 is of oak, the original planking is pine; and this may indicate a northern provenance for the vessel.[49] Other woods, however, such as ash, alder and willow might be used to fashion smaller items and fittings. Some of the floor timbers on Skuldelev 1, for example, are of oak and lime.[50] The wood chiefly employed in the construction of the fighting Skuldelev 2 was oak: the after-stem (and very probably the fore-stem), the planking, the floor timbers, keel and keelson were all fashioned from this wood. However, some of the side timbers were of willow.[51] Oak predominates in the small cargo vessel known as Skuldelev 3 and in the smaller of the two warships known as Skuldelev 5: although beech and willow are incorporated in the former, alder, ash and pine have been used in the latter.[52]

WORKING WOOD

A thirteenth-century Norwegian treatise, Konungs Skuggsjá, itemises the tools used by ship-builders of the period.[53] These are: augers, broadaxes and gouges. The saw is not, however, mentioned. The Bayeux Tapestry also contains a scene (Figure 27) that depicts the construction of a vessel from the initial felling of timber to fitting her out. Here one sees axes being used to fell trees and branches and to cut out planking. A smaller axe, with a shorter handle and more elongated blade, is shown

[49] O. Crumlin-Pedersen, Ships, navigation and routes in the reports of Ohthere and Wulfstan. In *Two Voyagers at the Court of King Alfred: The Ventures of Ohthere and Wulfstan, Together with the Description of Northern Europe from the Old English Orosius*, ed. N. Lund, trans. C. E. Fell. York: Sessions, 1984. pp. 31–32.

[50] O. Crumlin-Pedersen, Description and analysis of the ships as found. In *Ships and Boats of the North*, Vol. IV: 1, see note 41 above, pp. 101–19.

[51] More extensive details are to be found ibid., pp. 148–87.

[52] Ibid., pp. 199–220.

[53] *The King's Mirror (Speculum Regale [or] Konungs Skuggsjá) Translated from the Old Norwegian*, ed. and trans. L. M. Larson. New York: The American-Scandinavian Foundation, 1917. The text was probably composed during the reign of Hákon IV (1217–63).

Figure 27 The Bayeux Tapestry, Normandy (eleventh century). The scene depicts the felling of timber and shaping of planks for the hull of a vessel to be used in Duke William's invasion fleet of 1066. The wood is cut and finished without the use of a saw.

being used to dress the planking.[54] Apart from these axes, also depicted are adzes, a bore and a router for cutting grooves in wood. No saw is to be seen. The best evidence for the absence of the saw, however, is the wood worked in the construction process. Certainly in the case of the Skuldelev vessels, some of the planks showed very distinct axe (and possibly adze) cuts. Also visible were the relatively smooth marks and occasional gouges typical of a plane, as well as those of drawknives (i.e. spokeshaves), scrapers and routers. Drilled holes are also in evidence.[55]

The Scandinavian shipwright worked very sympathetically with forest and woodland material. Recently cut timber was used, possibly immersed in water to render it sufficiently pliable to be

---

[54] A number of these have been found. One such axe, probably eleventh century in date, was uncovered in London. See G. Hutchinson, *Medieval Ships and Shipping. The Archaeology of Medieval Britain*. London: Leicester University Press, 1997 [1994]. p. 21.

[55] O. Olsen and O. Crumlin-Pedersen, *Five Viking Ships from Roskilde Fjord*. Copenhagen: National Museum of Denmark, 1990 [1978]. p. 130; O. Crumlin-Pedersen, Description and analysis of the ships as found. In *Ships and Boats of the North*, Vol. IV: 1, see note 41 above, pp. 101–19. Tools that might have been used by shipwrights, and that have been recovered from sites, include chisels, hammers, tongs and metal wedges: J. Graham-Campbell, *The Viking World*. New Haven: Ticknor & Fields 1989 [1980]. pp. 52–53.

bent to the shape of the hull. The natural shapes of trunks, branches and even roots were adapted to a vessel's construction. Tall, straight trees were ideal for fashioning into masts and planking or for cutting out a keel. The elegantly curved fore-stem and after-stem, whether on long ship or cargo vessel, could be sculpted as single units from curved trunks. Forked branches supplied the raw material for floor timbers, curved ones the internal frames. The join between trunk and root was ideal for fashioning into the knees – which were used to strengthen the fit between two pieces of timber set at an angle to each other.

Modern builders of wooden boats steam the planking before fitting it to the vessels' inner frames. The danger to be avoided here is that of the timber splitting or cracking as it is nailed to the ribs. But what necessitates steaming the wood is the fact that, today, planks are sawn lengthwise from a piece of timber. This cuts across the natural grain of the wood and weakens the plank considerably when it is bent to the natural curve of the hull unless properly steamed. Even under tension, a plank may subsequently crack or spring, with potentially disastrous consequences for the vessel. The Scandinavian shipwright of the Viking period, however, without benefit of saw or steam chest, solved the problem of planking the hull most ingeniously. The planks were split either radially or tangentially. The former method involved inserting chocks or wedges into the trunk and then splitting it along its length into roughly triangular-shaped strips, a method best suited to large-diameter trees such as oaks. The latter method entailed splitting the trunk in half and then, again along its length, abstract-ing a long strip from each half, a method better suited to pine and ash trees. Whichever method was used, the sections were then chopped by axe into a shape not unlike that of some cigars; and it was from these that the planking for the vessels was fashioned.[56] Radially formed planking, which is not cut against the natural grain of the wood, is in many ways superior to sawn planks: it is stronger (stronger even than tangentially cut planks); shrinkage is less (less even than tangentially cut planks); it is less prone to cracking; warping is less pronounced; and it produces a snugger fit

[56] The best account of this process remains Olsen and Crumlin-Pedersen, *Five Viking Ships*, pp. 132–33. See also O. Crumlin-Pedersen and O. Olsen, eds. Wood technology. In *Ships and Boats of the North*, Vol. IV: 1, see note 41 above, p. 57; Godal, The use of wood in boat-building. In *Shipshape*, see note 47 above, p. 280.

(and, therefore, more watertight hull) against the planks above and below it. But perhaps the greatest advantage of radially formed planking, particularly for warships, was the length and lightness of the planks that could be made and, within limits, their flexibility.

CONSTRUCTION PROCESS

Modern wooden boats are constructed frame first: the internal skeleton is assembled along the length of the keel and then the hull planking and decking are attached to this. The Scandinavians of the Viking Age did exactly the opposite. Their vessels were constructed on the shell principle, the hull planking being joined together before the internal strengthening was added.[57] What follows is an account of how vessels were probably constructed.

The keel was laid (probably on supporting wooden blocks). This was fashioned from a single trunk and chopped by axe into the broad 'T' shape characteristic of Scandinavian vessels. As these were double-ended, with pronouncedly curved after-stems and fore-stems, in the larger vessels the keel might be completed in three sections: a central section, and two gradually curving sections taking the keel up to meet the two stems.[58] These sections were then scarfed together, the ends of each being cut at complementary angles to the other, and bolted through the joints. Looking at the reconstructed vessels prompts a frequently asked question: how were the planks bent into shape to form such elongated and sharp curves? The answer is that they were not. The fore- and after-stems were fashioned as complete units from appropriately shaped tree trunks (Figure 28). These create the illusion of planks running the length of the vessel from stem to stern and joined to a stempost and a sternpost. The reality is that there is no stempost or sternpost in a Viking Age vessel as

[57] The shell method of boat-building took some considerable time to die out in northern Europe. The Bremen cog (c. 1380), typical of the vessel that was the workhorse of northern European waters in the fourteenth century, was built in this way: see Hutchinson, *Medieval Ships*, pp. 17–19. A Dutch painting of 1560 depicts shipwrights working on the lower planking of a small boat. The keel, stem and sternposts are shown, but floor timbers and frames are not. See I. Friel, *The Good Ship: Ships, Shipbuilding and Technology in England 1200–1520*. London: British Museum, 1995. p. 45.

[58] As was the case with the 30-metre Skuldelev 2. *Ships and Boats of the North*, Vol. IV: 1, see note 41 above, p. 148.

Figure 28 The fore-stem of the reconstruction of Skuldelev 2 on the stocks in Roskilde, Sjælland, 26 April 2003. The stems of this ship were fashioned from single pieces of timber which were later joined to the keel. The stepped profile of the fore-stem permitted the construction of vessels with graceful, sweeping lines. Ships were not purely functional: high-quality workmanship reflected the aesthetic aspirations of their owners and communicated status in a language that was immediately understandable to all.

such; there are only carved units scarfed at the bottom to the keel, and to whose stepped 'wings' the ends of the real planking were affixed. Such was the fore-stem of Skuldelev 3, the only one from the period to be found intact, and which bears a resemblance to the incomplete stems found on the Inner Hebridean island of Eigg and in Dublin and Waterford in Ireland.[59] The construction of these stems has also opened up a possible window into the mind of the shipwright and the approach to designing a vessel. If the stems were cut to shape first, then the vessel's lines would be predetermined by their form. From this it may be argued that

[59] Ibid., p. 231. On the Eigg find, see S. McGrail, *Ancient Boats in North-West Europe: The Archaeology of Water Transport to AD 1500*. London: Longman, 1997 [1987]. p. 124.

once the stems were created the shipwright then had a mental picture of what the hull of the finished vessel would look like. He would know how many planks the ship would have and the curvature of her hull between the stems. Such an approach, however, leaves very little margin for error. It may be, therefore, that the wings were not stepped initially when the stems were scarfed to the keel, thereby leaving the lines of the planking to determine the contours of the wings: a much more forgiving approach than the first.[60]

Once keel and stems were in place, planking was then begun. Since the vessel was built on the shell principle, and the internal strengthening of floor timbers, frames and crossbeams was not in place before planking began, the vessel was constructed from the bottom up. First to be fixed to the underside of the transverse part of the keel on both sides were the strakes, known as garboards. A second strake was then fixed to one of the garboards, the lower edge of which overlapped the outer, upper edge of the garboard, and the process repeated on the other garboard. The vessel was, therefore, built in the clinker (or lapstrake) style. The planks were held together by iron rivets,[61] inserted through pre-drilled holes, and clenched (i.e. the part of the rivet exposed on the inside of the plank was cut and hammered to form a head) over small iron roves or plates to prevent the fastenings from working free as the vessel rose and fell to the sea (Figure 29). On larger vessels the planks might not be long enough to run continuously from fore-stem to after-stem, which necessitated scarfing the requisite number of planks together, in which case the scarfs on the planks nearest the fore-stem were angled so as to ensure that water could not seep between the join as the vessel sailed or was rowed into the waves.

After several planks had been fitted in this way on either side of the keel and supported along their length by timber props, the first internal strengthening, the floor timbers, was added and the planks attached to these either by lashings or, more usually, by

[60] Ibid.
[61] On nails, see J. Bill, Iron nails in Iron Age and medieval shipbuilding. In *Crossroads in Ancient Shipbuilding. Proceedings of the Sixth International Symposium on Boat and Ship Archaeology, Roskilde, 1991*, ed. C. Westerdahl. Vol. XL. Oxbow Monograph. Oxford: Oxbow Books, 1994. pp. 55–63.

treenails (i.e. short wooden dowels), with wedges driven into a split on the inner end in order to ensure a watertight fit (Figure 30). It is possible that it was at this stage of construction that the keelson, incorporating the mast step, may have been fitted. Just below the point at which the waterline was intended to be, a somewhat thicker plank, known as a *meginhúfr* (literally 'a strong or thick plank'), was added, the purpose of which will be discussed later. As the upper planking was added, side frames and crossbeams, internal members giving lateral strength to the hull, were inserted. Despite overlapping planking, however, water will always find a way to penetrate the joints, and so the vessels had to be caulked. This was done (most probably before each plank was nailed to its neighbour) by packing twisted lengths of organic material such as wool or animal hair coated with tar along the length of the overlaps (the scarf joints were also caulked).[62] It is not certain, although it seems highly probable, that once the planking and internal strengthening was in place the rudder boss was then attached, usually to the starboard (i.e. right) side forward of the after-stem. This was carved from

Figure 29 Rivets on the reconstruction of Skuldelev 2, Roskilde, Sjælland, 26 April 2003. The rivets are driven through pre-drilled holes from the outside of the hull and fitted with metal roves on the inner hull before the point of the nail is removed. The remainder is hammered flat against the rove to provide a secure, waterproof fit. Note the scarfed (overlapping) joint on the upper planks.

[62] *Ships and Boats of the North*, Vol. IV: 1, see note 41 above, pp. 60–62.

Figure 30
Reconstruction
of Skuldelev 2,
Roskilde,
Sjælland, 26 April
2003. Viking Age
vessels were
constructed shell
first. It was only
after about half a
dozen of the
lower planks of
the hull had been
riveted together
that the internal
strengthening –
such as the floor
timbers above –
were added.
When this had
been done, more
planks were
added to the hull
and additional
strengthening
put in place.

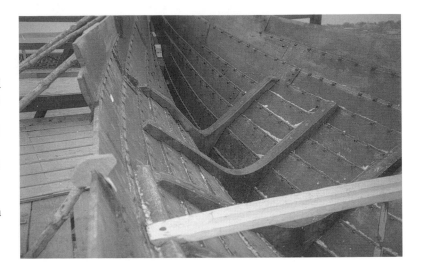

a single piece of wood, with a hole drilled through the middle, to which the rudder, side-mounted in Viking Age ships, would be attached.[63] The rudder itself, if attached at this stage (which, again, seems probable), would be strapped up clear of the ground prior to launching.

An interesting question at this stage is the extent to which the Scandinavian-built vessels from the Viking Age reflect a boat-building tradition in common with that in England, Ireland and Scotland. Skuldelev 2 was after all built in Dublin and the remains of ships' timbers found in Dublin, which were fashioned from Irish wood, also suggest that from the ninth to mid-twelfth centuries at the least Irish vessels from this area were built in the Scandinavian tradition.[64] Four boat burials have been found in Orkney, the latest being an oared vessel of approximately 7 metres found at Scar on the island of Sanday and dating to AD 875–950.[65] Mineral analysis suggests that this small vessel was probably built in Scandinavia.[66] Apart from the tenth-century stem found on the Hebridean island of Eigg, which need not mean that the vessel was built in the Western Isles, later iconographic evidence shows the unmistakable influence of

[63] On the side rudder, see O. Crumlin-Pedersen, Two Danish side rudders. *Mariners' Mirror*, Vol. 52, 1966, pp. 251–61.

[64] S. McGrail, *Medieval Dublin Excavations, 1962–1981*. Vol. III, *Medieval Boat and Ship Timbers from Dublin*. Dublin: Royal Irish Academy, 1993.

[65] O. Owen, A. Allen and M. Dalland, *Scar: A Viking Boat Burial on Sanday, Orkney*. East Linton: Historic Scotland in association with Tuckwell Press, 1999.

[66] A. Allen, The Boat. In *Scar*, see note 65 above, pp. 39–51.

Scandinavian vessels on the West Highland galley.[67] Even some eleventh-century Anglo-Saxon vessels, if the scenes depicting Harold Godwinson's vessel(s) in the Bayeux Tapestry can be trusted, may have been quite heavily influenced by Scandinavian ideas.[68]

PAINTING AND DECORATION

When [Earl Rognvald] reached Bergen . . . Lying at the quayside was the ship Jon Foot had built for the Earl, with thirty-five rowing benches. [She] was magnificently constructed, everywhere carved and inlaid with gold upon prow and stern, wind vanes and so on and there was no ship to compare with it in value . . . There came a day when they appeared to have a fair wind, so they left the harbour and hoisted sail . . . Next, they saw two large ships astern . . . One of them was a superbly built dragonhead, heavily inlaid with gold upon both stern and prow, brightly painted in the bows and all above the water-line.[69]

Orkneyinga Saga is far from alone in referring to the use of paint. In *King Harald's Saga* Svein Ulfsson's ships are also said to have been brightly painted.[70] And in the *Encomium Emmae*, vessels in the fleet of Svein Forkbeard in 1013 and, three years later, in that of Canute are said to have been magnificently decorated and tricked out in gold and silver.[71] These vessels may, of course, be considered somewhat special, the property of wealthy men or units in a royal fleet, and it has been pointed out that the common people would have owned or served in less showy vessels.[72] As a broad generalisation, and, indeed, as such vessels as Skuldelev 5 suggest, this is true. On the other hand, the hull of a *karfi*, used for a raid described in *Egils saga Skallagrímssonar*, is described as

---

[67] On these vessels, see D. Rixson, *The West Highland Galley*. Edinburgh: Birlinn, 1998.

[68] It has been observed that in each of the representations of Harold's vessel(s), the sheerstrake is cut down amidships, leaving it raised fore and aft: *Ships and Boats of the North*, Vol. IV: 1, see note 41 above, pp. 190–91. On early boats in England, note also P. Marsden, Early ships, boats and ports in Britain. In *Shipshape*, see note 47 above, pp. 171–72.

[69] *Orkneyinga Saga*, trans. and introd. by H. Pálsson and P. Edwards. Penguin Classics. Harmondsworth: Penguin Books, 1981. pp. 161–62.

[70] Snorri Sturluson, *King Harald's Saga: Harald Hardradi of Norway*, ed. and trans. M. Magnusson and H. Pálsson. Penguin Classics. Harmondsworth: Penguin, 1966. p. 182.

[71] *Encomium Emmae Reginae*, ed. A. Campbell. Camden Third Series, 72. London: Offices of the Royal Historical Society, 1949. I, 4; II, 4.

[72] Ibid., V, 95.

'richly painted' (or possibly 'stained') above her waterline.[73] In the Bayeux Tapestry the vessels' topsides and strakes, even those of the humble transport ships carrying horses, are picked out in different colours (Figure 31).

Archaeological science confirms the literary and iconographic record. Infra-red spectroscopic analysis carried out on the planking of the Skuldelev vessels has revealed the presence of pine tar, conifer resin and yellow ochre.[74] These may have been mixed, and their application to the hull would produce a covering at once both protective and decorative. The Ladby vessel, an early to mid-tenth-century military vessel, was also painted, probably yellow and blue, on the outside of her upper strakes and possibly even on their inboard faces. Pigments available in Scandinavia at this time were ochre, orpiment, lapis lazuli and copper. The first two, when mixed with linseed oil, produce a yellow colour; the latter produce a blue.[75]

Two of the sagas mentioned above refer to the carved decorations on the vessels, and in one mention is made of a dragon-head. The Bayeux Tapestry, the Bryggen stick and other graffiti also depict vessels with dragon or animal heads of some sort. Furthermore, a number of finds have revealed that the upper woodwork of vessels might be decorated. Perhaps the clearest example of this is the carving to be seen on both of the stems of the early ninth-century Oseberg ship from Norway. The upper strakes of the later ninth-century Norwegian Gokstad ship (Figure 32) have carved into them zigzag lines which may have been painted;[76] and the Ladby vessel from Denmark also appears to have had mouldings incised along the edges of some of her planking which were very similar, it is thought, to those on the Gokstad ship.[77] Evidence of mouldings has also been found on a number of other vessels from the Viking Age.[78] As for dragonheads, or for that matter other animal representations mythic or natural, we should feel inclined to trust the

[73] Egil's Saga, trans. B. Scudder. In The Sagas of Icelanders, ed. Ö. Thorsson. London: Penguin, 2001. p. 57.

[74] Ships and Boats of the North, Vol. IV: 1, see note 41 above, p. 61.

[75] Sørensen, ibid., Vol. III, see note 42 above, pp. 239–40.

[76] Ships and Boats of the North, Vol. IV: 1, see note 41 above, pp. 274–75.

[77] Sørensen, ibid., Vol. III, see note 42 above, p. 239.

[78] E.g. Hedeby (c. 980) and Klåstad (c. 1000). Earlier vessels found at Gunnarshaug (c. 700) and Kvalsund (c. 700) also had mouldings. See A. C. Sørensen, ibid., p. 239 (Figure 11.6).

literary evidence for these.[79] Associated with the Ladby find were several iron spirals reminiscent in style of those on a mould for a dragonhead ornament recovered in Birka in Sweden (Figure 33).[80] There is also good reason to think that in some cases, if not perhaps in all, the dragonhead may have been a separate unit that could be attached and detached at will. *Landnámabók* states that one of the earliest legal precepts in Iceland was that ships with figureheads should remove these when approaching shore:

At the beginning of that heathen law it says that men should not have ships with animal figure-heads at sea, but if they had them, they should unship them before they came in sight of land, and not sail near the land with

Figure 31 The Bayeux Tapestry, Normandy (eleventh century). This scene depicts several of the vessels of Duke William's invasion fleet crossing the English Channel. The hulls are brightly painted and the sails decorated in vivid colours.

[79] In *Einars þáttr Sokkasonar*, dealing largely with events in Greenland in the early twelfth century. A vessel is referred to as having a painted figurehead. See Jones, *The Norse Atlantic Saga*, pp. 191–203.

[80] Sørensen, *Ships and Boats of the North*, Vol. III, see note 42 above, p. 237. This does not mean that the dragonhead on the Ladby vessel must have been identical to that in the Birka mould. However, there is no reason to disbelieve that the decorations on vessels would not have been influenced by, or reflect in some way, the prevailing art styles throughout the Scandinavian world. On art generally, see O. Klindt-Jensen and D. M. Wilson, *Viking Art*. The Nordic Series, 6. Minneapolis: University of Minnesota Press, 1980.

Figure 32 The Gokstad ship, Norway, was built c. 880. It measures 23.3 metres in length. This ship may be typical of the vessels used in the long-distance raids across the North Sea and along the European Atlantic coastline. The sleek, graceful lines of this early example of Scandinavian design is a prime example of the way in which form follows function.

figure-heads with jaws gaping wide or grinning muzzles, which would terrify the land spirits.[81]

Perhaps the policy underpinning the legislation was not solely theological in nature. Scandinavians did raid each other, and an equally valid reason for requiring figureheads to be removed may have been to indicate to watchers on the shore that an approaching vessel was peaceful in intent. Of one thing we can be certain:

[81] The passage quoted is from the redaction known as *Hauksbók* (from its compiler Haukr Erlendsson), which was written c. 1306–8. The translation is that in R. I. Page, *Chronicles of the Vikings: Records, Memorials, and Myths*. Toronto: University of Toronto Press, 1995. p. 174.

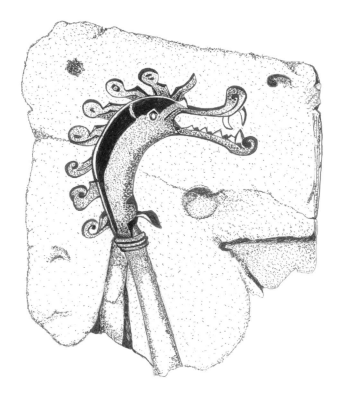

Figure 33 Dragon ornament mould from Birka, Sweden, unknown date. It is possible that a figurehead such as this was mounted on the ship used for the early to mid-tenth-century ship burial in Ladby, Fyn, Denmark.

with her hull tricked out in bright colours, stems elaborately carved in gilt, a painted dragonhead and brightly coloured sail, the vessel of a king or wealthy jarl would have been an awe-inspiring, as well as a most beautiful, sight. If a Scandinavian's first view of Constantinople inspired wonder in him, the approach of a Scandinavian fleet probably awoke much the same feelings in the ordinary Byzantine as he watched Harald Harðráði's fleet approach the city:[82]

Iron-shielded vessels
Flaunted colourful rigging.
The great prince saw ahead
The copper roofs of Byzantium;
His swan-breasted ships swept
Towards the tall-towered city.

SHIELD-RACKS

No stereotypical image of a long ship is complete without shields hung over the vessel's sheerstrake (i.e. the top strake of the hull).

[82] Snorri Sturluson, *King Harald's Saga*, p. 48.

Figure 34 The Bayeux Tapestry, Normandy (eleventh century). This scene depicts a military vessel in Duke William's invasion fleet. It is noticeable that the shields are not mounted outside the vessel, but rather carried inboard. The rudder is the distinctive shape of that associated with Viking vessels of the ninth and tenth centuries. The image gives a good impression of the complexity of the rigging.

That image is certainly not supported by the Bayeux Tapestry, where shields, when depicted, are only shown inboard (Figure 34). However, the elongated and tapered form of the Norman shield, unlike the round Viking shield, did not make it suitable for hanging in an outboard position. Both the Oseberg ship and Skuldelev 5 had shield-racks. In the latter, this was a relatively thin baton of wood attached to the sheerstrake at intervals, thereby leaving spaces between the points of attachment into which round shields could be dropped. But while coloured or decorated shields must have added to the spectacle enjoyed by the contemporary viewer, perhaps as the ships mustered for royal review, some thought must also be given to the practicality of mounting shields. On the positive side, these could have served as splashboards, giving the crew a little extra protection against spray or against enemy missiles during combat. Hanging shields outboard would also have reduced clutter on board as the crew moved about their tasks. On the other hand, judging by the positioning of the shield-rack on Skuldelev 5, the vessel could not be rowed when the shields were in the outboard position: a not inconsiderable drawback in an oared vessel.[83]

MOTIVE POWER: OAR AND SAIL

When Earl Rognvald left Bergen bound for the Holy Land we are told that the sail was hoisted after the vessel had left harbour, suggesting that it was rowed out of port and then made sail. Another scene from *King Harald's Saga* also depicts a fighting ship putting out to sea and still close to shore:[84]

As one King Harald's warriors
Lift long oars from the ocean;
The womenfolk stand watching,
Wondering at their sea skill.
We shall row ... without tiring,
Till the black tarred oars are broken,
Or the broad blades lie idle.

On the open sea, if the wind dropped, the crew of a fighting ship could always resort to the oars, and there are several episodes in *Egil's Saga* when the crews of warships off Norway's Atlantic coast are compelled to lower sail and ply their oars (Figure 35). However, rowing a vessel on the open sea, even with a large crew, is a tiring exercise;[85] and it is quite possible that advantage might have been taken of favourable currents to allow the ship to drift for long periods rather than to strain under the oars.[86] Apart from manoeuvring vessels in a sea-fight,[87] perhaps the best deployment of the oarsmen was in the context of raiding. A ship caught on a lee shore, with the wind and a flooding tide

[83] Crumlin-Pedersen, *Ships and Boats of the North*, Vol. IV: 1, see note 41 above, pp. 262–64; Sørensen, *Ships and Boats of the North*, Vol. III, see note 42 above, pp. 221–22.

[84] Snorri Sturluson, *King Harald's Saga*, p. 109. This was certainly the writer's experience as a guest crew member on *Helge Ask*, a reconstruction of Skuldelev 5, based in Roskilde. The vessel was rowed out into Roskilde Fjord before the sail was set, and the process reversed on entering harbour against wind and tide.

[85] In *Egil's Saga*, for example, a long ship is described as being 'hard to row'. See *Egil's Saga*, in *The Sagas of Icelanders*, see note 73 above, p. 99.

[86] 'Egil sailed out to sea at night ... and the next morning the wind dropped and it grew calm. They let the ship drift before the wind for a few nights.' Ibid., p. 103.

[87] As, for example, in the sea-fights described in *Orkneyinga Saga*.

Figure 35 *Helge Ask* being rowed out of harbour, Roskilde, Sjælland, 26 April 2003. In many vessels the crew operated in cramped conditions. There was limited room for movement and little space to store personal belongings and loot. In vessels of this size and construction the weight of the crew substitutes for ballast, and crew members would therefore need to be awake for a large part of the time when the ship was sailing the open seas.

against her, would make the raiders' speedy escape under sail difficult, if not impossible; the crew might have to turn and fight, with resultant loss of lives and booty. But adverse winds and tides are less serious if forty or sixty oarsmen can row their vessel quickly out of the range of arrows and spears. The positioning of the oarholes through which the oars projected may have varied according to individual preference. In the Oseberg ship these are located on the sheerstrake (i.e. the top strake along the hull); and this is also true of Skuldelev 5 and the Ladby military vessel.[88] In the Gokstad ship, however, the oarports were inserted through the third strake from the top of the vessel's hull.

Oars were also employed on cargo vessels. In their case, however, there is little doubt that deployment at sea would not have been very effectual. The broad-leaf (some might say, rather unkindly, 'tubby') shape of the larger carrier now referred to as a *knörr*, with its sunken cargo hold sandwiched between raised decks fore and aft, provides only limited space for oarholes along the sides of the latter. Moreover, the shape of this vessel renders it unsuitable for rowing over any other than very short distances. The smaller of the two cargo vessels known as Skuldelev 3 had only three oarholes through the port (i.e. left) side of the forward

[88] Crumlin-Pedersen, *Ships and Boats of the North*, Vol. IV: 1, see note 41 above, p. 262; Sørensen, ibid., Vol. III, see note 42 above, p. 232.

gunwale and two on the starboard. A single oarhole was found on either side of the vessel aft.[89] The lack of signs of wear and tear[90] around the oarports suggests only limited use was made of the oars: very probably only for manoeuvring around a quayside or onto and off an open beach. *Orkneyinga Saga*, describing a cargo vessel making passage across the Pentland Firth bound for the island of Rousay, tells how the vessel was sailed north along the west coast of Hoy and the mainland. It was only when she left the open sea and turned west, into the sheltered waters of Eynhallow Sound, that the crew took to the oars and 'rowed up to the shore'.[91]

The vessels under consideration here were also powered by sail. However, discussion of the sail alone, in the sense of an area of material filled by wind, simply does not begin to bring out the care and thought that went into developing the sailing capability of these Scandinavian vessels. Sailing a vessel efficiently depends not only on having a mast, a yard, a sail and rigging, but also on an internal structure capable of supporting the combined weight of mast and sail under stress of weather, and on her behaviour under the helm.

The keelson

It is essential that the foot of the mast of a sailing vessel should be securely fixed in position. A mast that 'jumps' in rough seas may weaken or knock a hole through the bottom planking of the hull, with disastrous consequences. The foot of the mast of a Viking Age vessel was, therefore, stepped (i.e. slotted) into a keelson, an object that is easier to depict than to describe (Figure 36). But the purpose of the keelson is clear: it distributed the combined weight of mast, sail and yard more evenly across a substantial portion of the lower hull and relieved the stress that would otherwise be exerted by these features.

The keelson, which might be carved from a single piece of timber or made up from more than one piece,[92] was not, contrary

[89] Olsen and Crumlin-Pedersen, *Five Viking Ships*, p. 114; Crumlin-Pedersen, *Ships and Boats of the North*, Vol. IV: 1, see note 41 above, pp. 224–45.

[90] Ibid., p. 245.   [91] *Orkneyinga Saga*, pp. 137–38.

[92] As, for example, with Skuldelev 2. See Crumlin-Pedersen, *Ships and Boats of the North*, Vol. IV: 1, see note 41 above, p. 166.

Figure 36 The keelson and mast partner on Skuldelev 2, Roskilde, Sjælland, 26 April 2003. The foot of the mast was a point of considerable stress exerted by a combination of mast height and sail area. This simple concept permitted the even distribution of these stresses over a large area of the keel. The keelson provided a secure base, locking and holding the mast in position, and it also protected the keel from wear arising from any movement at the foot of the mast.

to some,[93] attached to the keel itself. The underside was notched, and the notches were matched to several of the floor timbers, thereby preventing the keelson from slipping lengthways. Sideways movement was prevented by bracing the two central sides of the keelson with a series of knees attached both to the keelson and to several of the floor timbers. The forward side of the mast rested against a vertical projection fashioned as an integral part of the keelson. At deck-level a mast partner or mast fish (so named because of its fish-like shape) provided additional support for the mast itself. In an undecked vessel, a transverse mast beam served this function.[94]

In the cargo vessel Skuldelev 1, which was approximately 16 metres in length, the keelson is a little under one-third of her length. In Skuldelev 2, which was 30 metres long, the keelson

---

[93] Graham-Campbell, *The Viking World*, p. 45.
[94] As can be seen in Skuldelev 3. See Crumlin-Pedersen, *Ships and Boats of the North*, Vol. IV: 1, see note 41 above, p. 218 (Figure 27).

also occupied almost one-third of the vessel's overall length.[95] Such vessels could clearly carry a relatively high mast and large sail. In contrast, the keelson of the early ninth-century Oseberg ship, which was 21 metres long, was only about 2 metres. An even more telling comparison is that between the Oseberg vessel and the smaller military vessel, Skuldelev 5. The latter, whose length was a little over 18 metres, had a keelson of approximately 3.5 metres. The Oseberg ship is the first vessel to be found in Scandinavia that was definitely equipped with a mast.[96] One possible conclusion therefore is that the Oseberg vessel represents a stage in the development of Scandinavian vessels in which the transition from oar to sail was still incomplete. Another interpretation, however, and one that is preferable to the first,[97] is that the Oseberg ship was simply intended for a different purpose from that of the type of vessel used to raid the British Isles and Ireland. It was, after all, found in a queen's burial site and was probably more in the nature of a royal barge which was never intended for use on the open sea. In such a vessel the sail was ancillary to the main method of propulsion, which was oar power.

Rigging and sails

No Viking Age vessel has survived with rigging intact. For vessels carrying a large area of sail, however, careful rigging was necessary to provide support for the mast – holding it under tension as a vessel pitched and rolled on the open sea. Ropes of lime-bast and willow twigs have been found in association with the Skuldelev vessels. Twisted horsehair may also have been used for shorter ropes such as the sheets.[98] At one time, ship-ropes

---

[95] Ibid., pp. 119, 166.

[96] A. Binns, Ships and shipbuilding. In *Medieval Scandinavia: An Encyclopedia*, ed. P. Pulsiano and K. Wolf. Garland Encyclopedias of the Middle Ages, 1. New York: Garland, 1993. p. 579. Binns dates the Ladby ship to around AD 800, which if correct would support the implication in the text that Oseberg is not typical of masted ships at the beginning of the ninth century. Unfortunately, the Ladby find suggests a date somewhere in the period AD 885–1035: see Sørensen, *Ships and Boats of the North*, Vol. III, see note 42 above, p. 57.

[97] J. Bill, Ships and seamanship. In *The Oxford Illustrated History of the Vikings*, see note 3 above, p. 187. Bill is also sceptical, but possibly not for quite the same reasons as in the text above.

[98] Crumlin-Pedersen, *Ships and Boats of the North*, Vol. IV: 1, see note 41 above, p. 54.

fabricated from whale-hide and sealskin may have been used in the more northerly regions of Norway.[99]

Judging by their position on the upper hull of several finds, iron rings and ones made from withies indicate standing rigging, in the form of shrouds, on either side of the mast.[100] Holes and cleats imply the use of running (as well as standing) rigging, such as braces and sheets, to control the presentation of the sail to the wind.[101] Some of the iconographic evidence, such as the Bayeux Tapestry, depicts some vessels with mast stays running fore and aft and secured to the stems and some without. Graffiti on wooden planks from eleventh-century Dublin show vessels with yards lowered and standing rigging clearly visible.[102]

If we do not know as much as we should like about the rigging of these vessels, we know equally little about the sails. Without full masts and yards to supply a guide to the dimensions of the square sail carried, calculation (which may be a euphemism for educated guesswork) is all that can be attempted for each vessel found.[103] This is not, however, always factored in when making claims for the sailing capabilities of Viking Age vessels.

Remains or traces of *váðmál*, or wool ('wadmal'), have been found associated with the Oseberg and Gokstad ships, the Ladby ship and the twelfth-century Lynæs vessel, although one cannot be certain that this material was from their sails.[104] Other fabrics such as flax and hemp may also have been employed in

---

[99] These are mentioned in an account of a voyage by Ohthere from his home near Tromsø to the White Sea region in the later ninth century. See *Two Voyagers*, p. 20.

[100] For details on the Skuldelev vessels, see Crumlin-Pedersen, *Ships and Boats of the North*, Vol. IV: 1, see note 41 above, p. 62. For the Ladby ship, see Sørensen, ibid., Vol. III, see note 42 above, pp. 54, 224–27. The Frostathing Law refers to shrouds. See Larson, *Norwegian Laws*, p. 315.

[101] Crumlin-Pedersen, *Ships and Boats of the North*, Vol. IV: 1, see note 41 above, pp. 119, 220, 262. Larson, *Norwegian Laws*, p. 315, refers to braces and sheets.

[102] A. E. Christensen, Ship graffiti and models. In *Medieval Dublin Excavations, 1962–81*. Vol. II, *Miscellanea 1*, ed. P. F. Wallace. Series B. Dublin: Royal Irish Academy, 1988. pp. 13–26.

[103] For the calculations made in the case of the Ladby ship, see Sørensen, *Ships and Boats of the North*, Vol. III, see note 42 above, pp. 228–30.

[104] E. Andersen, Square sails of wool. In *Shipshape*, see note 47 above, pp. 258–59; Sørensen, *Ships and Boats of the North*, Vol. III, see note 42 above, p. 55. Note also L. B. Jørgensen, *North European Textiles until AD 1000*. Aarhus: Aarhus University Press, 1992. As an alternative to a sail, the material found might have come from a tent or awning rigged as protection against the weather. References to awnings are to be found, for example, in *Orkneyinga Saga*: see, *Orkneyinga Saga*, p. 190; Snorri Sturluson, *King Harald's Saga*, p. 69.

sail-making.[105] Clearly, such material had to be weatherproofed, and a variety of substances such as linseed, animal fat, tar or wax, either alone or in combination, may have been used.

Egil Skallagrimsson's uncle, Thorolf Kveldulfsson, is said to have owned a big 'ocean-going' ship, the hull of which was magnificently 'painted' and whose sail was 'black- and red-striped'.[106] Thorolf was, of course, a relatively powerful man, and the use of decorated sails (perhaps as depicted on several of the Gotland stones) on the vessels of the elite is highly plausible. The sails of humbler vessels, on the other hand, are more likely to have been monochrome.[107] However, it seems unlikely that sails were 'painted' in the modern sense of the word. They were probably woven in strips[108] which were dyed,[109] the dyes being produced from such plants as woad or from the juice of berries.

Because the upper edge of a square sail is attached to a yard, and the corners at the foot are attached to the sheets, and since either of the sides of the sail might be manoeuvred to present a leading edge to the wind, they have to be reinforced or they will simply fray and tear. Pieces of rope were collocated with the woollen material found at Oseberg and Gokstad, and it is possible, if the textile remains really were sails, that these ropes formed part of the bolt-rope which is fitted to a sail's edges as such reinforcement. It is thought that horsehair rope may have been used for the bolt-rope (and possibly the reef-points) on woollen sails, since this stretches well and would match the natural elasticity of wool.[110] As with the canvas sails of a later period there would have been an ever-present risk of damage, and *Konungs Skuggsjá* advises the sea-faring merchant of the thirteenth century to carry with him on his voyages a repair kit which included needles, thread and cord, all of which are items associated with the maintenance of the sail. More specifically, he is enjoined to have aboard two or three hundred ells of wadmal 'of a sort suitable for mending sails'.[111]

[105] Andersen, Square sails of wool. In *Shipshape*, see note 47 above, p. 267; Sørensen, *Ships and Boats of the North*, Vol. III, see note 42 above, pp. 54–55.
[106] *Egil's Saga*. In *The Sagas of Icelanders*, see note 73 above, p. 28.
[107] Not all of the sails on the vessels in the Bayeux Tapestry are striped.
[108] Andersen, Square sails of wool. In *Shipshape*, see note 47 above, p. 264.
[109] Sørensen, *Ships and Boats of the North*, Vol. III, see note 42 above, pp. 240–41.
[110] Elasticity is, however, a relative quality. A degree of stiffness is required in certain conditions. The matter is discussed later.
[111] *The King's Mirror*, p. 84.

The helm

The rudder on a ship of the Viking Age was, as already mentioned, a side rudder. As several of these have survived,[112] at least in part, we have a reasonably good knowledge of how the rudder was fixed to the hull and of its capabilities in use. It was mounted on a boss fixed (normally but not invariably) to the starboard quarter, attachment to the inside of the hull being achieved by passing a rope of twisted withies through holes bored in the rudder, the boss and a strake. This rope was knotted on the outside face of the rudder and secured to a timber member inboard (Figure 37). The tiller-arm, gripped by the helmsman,

Figure 37 Side rudder and mount on a Viking Age vessel.

[112] E.g. from Bergen, Gokstad and Oseberg in Norway, and Östra Aros in Sweden. Two rudders found at Vorså and Jungshoved in Denmark are described by O. Crumlin-Pedersen, Two Danish side rudders. *Mariner's Mirror*, Vol. 52, 1966, pp. 251–61. Two English side rudders, possibly eleventh century in date, and in a reasonably good state of preservation, were recovered near Southwold in Suffolk: see G. Hutchinson, The Southwold side rudders. *Antiquity*, Vol. 60, 1986, pp. 219–21; G. Hutchinson, Two English side-rudders. In *Shipshape*, see note 47 above, pp. 97–102; Hutchinson, *Medieval Ships*, pp. 50–53.

projected inboard at right angles to the upper part of the rudder stock, and the latter was held close to the gunwale by means of a leather rope or strap. This arrangement allows the helmsman to slant the rudder forward in shallow waters and to raise it altogether before the vessel is beached.

The ships in Duke William's invasion fleet are shown in the Bayeux Tapestry as having side rudders. Two features of these merit mention, namely that all have a small 'heel' on the after-edge of the blade, and each is deeper than the keel of the vessel to which it is attached. The first of these features may be connected to the fact that the blades of rudders such as the one found at Vorså in Jylland (Jutland), which also had a heel, are asymmetrical, the outer side being curved while the inner is straight. A rudder blade of this shape decreases resistance and the tendency of the vessel, even when sailing a straight course, to slide to star-board.[113] The heel may simply have been a further refinement, allowing the water to flow around and off the lower edge of the rudder with maximum efficiency. The second may be accounted for on the basis that the rudder must be deep enough to grip the sea even when the vessel heels over at an angle to the wind.

The side rudder was a great improvement on the steering oar used on the early fourth-century Nydam boat, and its use was common in northern Europe. However, by the mid-thirteenth century its replacement by the stern rudder was almost complete. Because we are accustomed to seeing vessels with stern rudders, and side rudders went out of general use eight centuries ago, there is a temptation today to view the former as being in some way technologically superior to the latter. This perception is quite incorrect. A rudder adapted for use on vessels that could sail over 1,300 nautical miles across the North Atlantic from Norway to Greenland is not inefficient, and it is most definitely not primi-tive. In a following sea, for example, it will not jam – an ever-present risk with the stern rudder that it replaced. The demise of the side rudder was a product of changes in ship design in northern Europe in the thirteenth century. The cog in its most developed form, with its higher freeboard and straight sternpost, was unsuited to the side rudder but perfect for the stern variety.[114]

---

[113] On the assumption that the rudder was mounted on this side. Discussed in greater detail in Crumlin-Pedersen, Two Danish side rudders, pp. 254–55.
[114] Hutchinson, Medieval Ships, p. 50.

Ship types

There is a scene in *Egil's Saga* in which a conversation takes place between father and son about the son's immediate plans. The young man says that he would like to go raiding and asks his father to let him have both a *langskip* (long ship) and a crew to go with her. As his son is something of a troublesome lad, his father refuses the request, saying that he will not provide him with a *herskip* (warship). However, as a less risky alternative, he states that he will give him a *kaupskip* (merchant ship) so that the young man can go to Dublin. As a further gesture, the father throws in a crew as well.[115] This passage identifies two main types of vessel – the fighting ship and the merchant ship. However, the same saga also applies a variety of other names to specific craft. These include the all-purpose ship (*skip*) and boat (*bátr*), and the more specific *skúta*; *snekkja*; *byrðingr*; *knörr*; *karfi*; and *fley*. To these one may add the *buza* and the *skeið*.

Because the vessels found in Scandinavia are of different types and built for different purposes, the wish to correlate names and types is understandable. It is not, however, an easy task to accomplish with accuracy. One problem is that the sagas in which we find references to these specific craft were not composed until the thirteenth century. The names, therefore, while they may reflect the terminology of the period of composition, need not necessarily represent that of the tenth or eleventh centuries. It has, for example, been pointed out that the authenticity of the passage that mentions *karfi* in *Egil's Saga* is suspect, and not composed in 900 as is often supposed.[116] The ninth-century Oseberg and Gokstad vessels have been said to be examples of *karfar*, whose function was essentially that of the troop-ship.[117] But the first 'reliable' use of *karfi*, we are told, does not occur until c. 1020 when it is used, not to describe the elegant vessels typified by Oseberg and Gokstad, but rather 'an unstable

---

[115] *Egil's Saga*. In *The Sagas of Icelanders*, see note 73 above, p. 53.

[116] P. G. Foote, Wrecks and rhymes. In *Aurvandilstá: Norse Studies*. Odense: Odense University Press, 1984. p. 225.

[117] O. Crumlin-Pedersen, Ships, navigation and routes in the reports of Ohthere and Wulfstan. In *Two Voyagers*, see note 49 above, p. 31. Crumlin-Pedersen does not repeat this assertion. He appears to regard the 11-metre Skuldelev 6 as a possible example of this type: see Crumlin-Pedersen, *Ships and Boats of the North*, Vol. IV: 1, see note 41 above, p. 325.

tub of a craft...met on some inland waterway'.[118] However, in the Irish poem *Cath Finntrágha*, describing the fictional Battle of Ventry, the *karfi* is encountered in its Irish form, *cairpthi*, as part of a Norwegian fleet preparing to descend on Ireland. This has been translated as 'troop carrier', but it might equally well be taken to signify a supply ship (perhaps such as those carrying horses in the Bayeux Tapestry).[119] So what was a *karfi*? Was it a small boat used only on lakes and rivers? Was it a large troopship (and if so, was it the same as a fighting ship)? Was it a supply ship (and if so, was it much the same as a *knörr*)? Or was it a cross between a royal barge and a 'fast warship of high merit'?[120]

One can repeat this exercise with the *byrðingr* and *skúta*. In two thirteenth-century legal texts from Gotland and Sjælland (Zealand), the *byrðingr* is contrasted with a larger cargo vessel (*kaupskip*) in the former, and described as a small boat in the latter.[121] A small eleventh- or twelfth-century whetstone from Gotland depicts a vessel with a sail and (possibly) oars with the runic inscription *byrðingr* incised on the right-hand side. As evidence for the size of the *byrðingr* this is far from conclusive, however. On the other hand, a *skúta*, as the name suggests, may have been a speedy vessel with sleek lines.[122] Is the available 'evidence' sufficient to conclude that Skuldelev 3 was either of these types?[123] At the risk of offending the textual scholars, but at least demonstrating the difficulties of ascription on the basis of the texts, there are passages in *Egil's Saga* in which this term is applied to vessels with crews of thirty and which were rowed. There are others where the *skúta* appears only to carry cargo. Given that the archaeological record has revealed fundamental design differences between cargo carriers and warships, the apparent interchangeability of this term to describe both types points once more to the dangers inherent in modern attempts to identify remains with records. In this

---

[118] Foote, Wrecks and rhymes. In *Aurvandilstá*, see note 116 above, p. 225.

[119] W. Sayers, The etymology and semantics of Old Norse knörr 'cargo ship'. The Irish and English evidence. *Scandinavian Studies*, Vol. 68, 1996, p. 284.

[120] R. Simek, Old Norse ship names and ship terms. *Northern Studies*, Vol. 13, 1979, p. 31.

[121] The two texts, *Guta Log* and *Eriks Sjællandske Lov*, are discussed by Crumlin-Pedersen in *Ships and Boats of the North*, Vol. IV: 1, see note 41 above, p. 313.

[122] In *Egil's Saga* one skúta is said to be 'exceptionally fast'. In *The Sagas of Icelanders*, see note 73 above, p. 99.

[123] Speed and sleek lines win for Crumlin-Pedersen, in *Ships and Boats of the North*, Vol. IV: 1, see note 41 above, p. 313.

particular context it also suggests the possibility that students of more modern craft encounter, namely that of regional variation in terminology. For example the term 'yawl', as applied to a small fishing vessel in Fife, on the east coast of mainland Scotland, referred to a quite radically different shape of vessel from that of the same name used in the Orkney Islands to the north of the Scottish mainland. Furthermore, their functions differed. The former was exclusively a fishing vessel; the latter, while usable for that purpose, also served to carry sheep and people. The same name, but for two quite different types of craft in terms of use and physical appearance.

The problem of ascription does not disappear when we come to two words used in the sagas, and in fairly common parlance today, to describe the archetypical warship and the merchant ship – the *langskip* and the *knörr*. The Anglo-Saxon Chronicles record that after Æðelstan's victory over Causantin of Scotland and his Dublin Norse allies at Brunanburh in 937, the latter fled back to Ireland in *nægled cnearrum*.[124] In this context these 'knörrs'[125] may be thought of as warships.[126] In *Egil's Saga*, however, the term is consistently applied to merchant ships and vessels that could carry entire households with their possessions to the new settlements in Iceland. The word appears, therefore, to have undergone a change in meaning by the early thirteenth century, the probable date at which this saga was composed. Where exactly does this leave us? What we can say with confidence is that in thirteenth-century Iceland a large cargo vessel of the ninth and tenth centuries was referred to as a *knörr*. However, this does not prove that it was known by this name in the Scandinavian world of that earlier period. Clearly there were merchant ships in use throughout the Scandinavian empires. The major markets at Dublin and York, and at Birka (Sweden), Hedeby (Denmark) and Kaupang (Norway) were supplied by sea; and the eleventh-century Skuldelev 1 and Hedeby ships as well as the possibly tenth-century Äskekärr vessel, were cargo carriers.[127] But we cannot be sure that the men who built and

---

[124] *Anglo-Saxon Chronicles*, p. 109.

[125] Swanton translates *nægled cnearrum* as 'riveted boats'.

[126] Bill, Ships and seamanship, see note 3 above, p. 190. Crumlin-Pedersen, in *Ships and Boats of the North*, Vol. IV: 1, see note 41 above, p. 325.

[127] Bill, Ships and seamanship. In *The Oxford Illustrated History of the Vikings*, see note 3 above p. 190.

sailed these referred to them as *knerrir* (plural of *knörr*): *byrðingr* and *buza* are equally possible alternatives.[128] Consequently, although the vessels that brought some of the colonists to Iceland during the settlement phase (c. 860–930) most probably were merchant vessels, to suggest that those merchant vessels were called *knerrir* may be incorrect.[129]

If the *knörr* saw service as a warship at one time, what sort of warship was it? Was it a *dreki* or a *snekkja*? Or was it a *skeið*? Can these vessels be thought of collectively as long ships? When was a *herskip* or fighting ship not a *langskip*? The terminology abounds and, once more, it has the potential to confuse rather than to elucidate.

In the literature the size of a warship is defined not by its length or beam but by the number of rooms into which it was divided or by the number of thwarts or oarsmen it had.[130] If, for example, Harald Sigurdsson's vessel, built to eclipse the size and splendour of Olaf Tryggvason's *Long Serpent*, had thirty-five rooms, then it had an equal number of thwarts, each seating a pair of oarsmen. This ship therefore had seventy rowers, as the saga later states.[131] If this seems to suggest an impossibly large size for these vessels, as was once believed to be the case, archaeology has corrected the misconception. Skuldelev 2, at 30 metres, probably had thirty rooms and could, therefore, be rowed by sixty men.[132] A vessel discovered recently in Roskilde itself is estimated to have had an approximate overall length of 36 metres.[133] Of course such vessels were, literally, long ships; and the Anglo-Saxon Chronicles for 896–97 mention the *langscipu* that Alfred had built and that 'were built neither after the Frisian design nor after the Danish'.[134] However, the word *langskip* is found only in

---

[128] *Skude* is identified as another possibility. Crumlin-Pedersen does, however, maintain that after 1000 the term *knörr* applies exclusively to vessels of the Skuldelev 1 type: see Crumlin-Pedersen in *Ships and Boats of the North*, Vol. IV: 1, see note 41 above, pp. 324–25.

[129] Byock, *Viking Age Iceland*, pp. 9–11.

[130] A room was the space between the thwarts upon which the oarsmen were seated. A. W. Brøgger and H. Shetelig, *The Viking Ships; Their Ancestry and Evolution*. Oslo: Dreyer, 1971. p. 187.

[131] Snorri Sturluson, *King Harald's Saga*, pp. 107–9.

[132] Crumlin-Pedersen, in *Ships and Boats of the North*, Vol. IV: 1, see note 41 above, p. 326.

[133] Ibid., pp. 107–9. J. R. Hale, The Viking longship. *Scientific American*, Vol. 2245, 1998, pp. 46–53.

[134] *Anglo-Saxon Chronicles*, p. 90. On Alfred's ships, see M. J. Swanton, King Alfred's ships: text and context. *Anglo-Saxon England*, Vol. 28, 1999, pp. 1–22.

the much later sagas and, apparently, is not encountered at all in medieval Danish and Swedish literature.[135] This does not mean that Scandinavians from the ninth to eleventh centuries did not refer to such vessels as long ships, but, for the present, we have no reliable evidence that they did. It has been suggested that such a vessel as Skuldelev 5 with thirteen thwarts and, therefore, twenty-six oars was the smallest craft that 'could be called a long ship'.[136] If even larger fighting vessels may not have been known as long ships, there is little point in arguing about how long (or short) a vessel had to be before it was referred to by that name. It is, however, possible that a large fighting ship of the tenth and eleventh centuries was referred to as a *skeið*. Contemporary usage of this word in skaldic verse supports the view that it refers to a large fighting ship;[137] and its Anglo-Saxon cognate, *scegð*, is used in an early eleventh-century context to refer to a sixty-four-oared vessel owned by Bishop Ælfwold.[138]

Our problems do not decrease when we turn to the vessel type referred to as a *snekkja*. Skuldelev 5 has been tentatively identified with the type of vessel referred to by this name.[139] The word appears in the sagas in a context that associates the vessel with a military purpose. *Egil's Saga*, for example, refers to a twenty-oared *snekkja* that had been used on 'Viking' raids. This does not mean of course that a *snekkja* was a vessel of twenty oars, but that this particular example of the type had that number of oars. Both the saga and archaeology flatly contradict the argument that vessels of fewer than thirteen thwarts should not be classified as fighting ships. Both also contradict the view that a *snekkja* was a vessel with forty oars and a complement of ninety.[140] But what the

[135] Crumlin-Pedersen, *Ships and Boats of the North*, Vol. IV: 1, see note 41 above, p. 314.

[136] Bill, Ships and seamanship. In *The Oxford Illustrated History of the Vikings*, see note 3 above, p. 191.

[137] Crumlin-Pedersen, *Ships and Boats of the North*, Vol. IV: 1, see note 41 above, p. 327. This view is based on R. Malmros, Leding og skjaldekvad. Det elvte århundredes nordiske krigsflåder, deres teknologi og organisation og deres placering i samfundet, belyst gennem den samtidige fyrstedigtning. *Aarbøger for nordisk oldkyndighed og historie*, 1985 p. 102.

[138] N. Hooper, Some observations on the navy in late Anglo-Saxon England. In *Studies in Medieval History Presented to R. Allen Brown*, ed. C. Harper-Bill, C. J. Holdsworth and J. L. Nelson. Wolfeboro: Boydell Press, 1989. p. 208. Crumlin-Pedersen, *Ships and Boats of the North*, Vol. IV: 1, see note 41 above, p. 327.

[139] Ibid., p. 317.

[140] Brøgger and Shetelig, *The Viking Ships*, p. 190. H. Falk, Altnordisches Seewesen. *Wörter und Sachen*, Vol. 5, 1912, p. 102.

archaeology cannot establish is whether Skuldelev 5 was termed a *snekkja* by its crew or anyone else at the time. Place-names containing a *snekkja* element are to be found in Scandinavia, Normandy, Orkney (Snaky Noust) and Shetland (Sneckerem). The first of these toponyms from the Northern Isles indicates a boat shelter, and the second a harbour for a *snekkja*.[141] Neither, however, provides clues as to what a *snekkja* actually looked like.

Although we cannot be confident about the names by which the vessels employed during the Viking Age were known at the time, it is striking that, to some extent, the names used represent a shared vocabulary in the areas touched by the Scandinavians. Whether it is in Irish poetry, Anglo-Saxon records or Icelandic sagas, some vessels were *knerrir*. The Scandinavians had the *snekkja*, the English their *snacc*, and the Normans the *isnechia*.[142] And if the Northman had his *skeið*, the Anglo-Saxon sailed in his *scegð*. Perhaps no Viking ever sailed on a raid or into battle in a 'long ship'; but his vessel might still have to face the *langscipu* of Alfred. The ships found at Skuldelev were not all Danish. The large merchant ship, for example, was built in Norway, as was the smallest vessel. Skuldelev 2, the long ship, is an Irish-Norse vessel, not a Scandinavian one. Regardless of place of origin, however, all ended their days at the bottom of a Danish fjord. There was a very cosmopolitan dimension to the shipping of north-west Europe during the Viking Age.

To know more about the types of vessel described in the sagas would indeed be gratifying; and it is irksome that, with so many vessels having been found, we cannot be sure how they would have been known to the peoples of the Scandinavian empires. But if we do not know with certainty how the vessels were described, we do at least know that some (perhaps all) were named by their owners. In the maritime culture of the Scandinavian world, where one's livelihood, or life, depended on a vessel, it was natural to wish to name vessels. Indeed, one sometimes glimpses the very close and deeply affectionate bond between man and ship typified by this runic inscription from Mervalla in Sweden: *Han oft siglt til*

[141] E. Ridel, Viking maritime heritage in Normandy from a British Isles perspective. *Northern Studies*, Vol. 35, 2000, pp. 80–84; O. Crumlin-Pedersen, ed. *Aspects of Maritime Scandinavia AD 200–1200*. Roskilde: Viking Ship Museum, 1991. pp. 233–40.

[142] *Anglo-Saxon Chronicles*, p. 179 (for the year 1052). Ridel, Viking maritime heritage, p.80.

Simgala / dýrum knerri um Domisnes – 'He sailed often to Semgallen / Around Domisnes in dearly prized knörr.'[143] This short, yet profoundly moving, sentiment speaks to the relationship between skipper and ship which is as true now as it clearly was then. The following is just a selection of the names given to individual vessels: *Álpt* (Swan); *Fálki* (Falcon); *Grágás* (Grey Goose); *Uxi* (Ox); *Visundr* (Bison); *Ormrinn Langi* (Great Serpent); *Svalbarði* (Cool Stem); *Fífa* (Arrow); *Skjöldr* (Shield). The names might, as this selection indicates, be those of animals or of inanimate objects. Place-names, such as *Hásaugabuza* (buza from Hausauge = Halsaa), might also be chosen for a ship from that place.[144]

Conclusion

This chapter has attempted to reconsider some of the views, both old and new, that have been expressed about this most definitive facet of Scandinavian material culture. The marine technology that raiding and trading in the Viking Age demanded did not emerge overnight, and its foundations lay in the fifth to seventh centuries, a period about which we still know relatively little. Moreover, some aspects of this technology, most notably the introduction of the sail, were the product of intercultural exchanges and not Scandinavian in concept. That said, the finished products, the *herskip* and *kaupskip*, provided models for imitation elsewhere and, indeed, these vessels still live on in the traditional wooden craft of the North Atlantic peoples. Moreover, if it is even remotely possible to describe Alfred's warships, the *langscipu*, as the first attempt to establish a Royal Navy,[145] it should not be forgotten that the catalyst for this was the success of the *herskip*. At almost every level of society ship and sea touched the lives of these people. The ship was their 'horse of the waves', 'sea-bull', 'sea-god's steed' and 'sea-king's swan'. These kennings appear so apt in describing the fine, purpose-built craft that offered their crews, passengers and cargoes the best chance of survival in turbulent waters. The sea, of course, was an avenue

---

[143] The inscription is quoted in Graham-Campbell, *The Viking World*, p. 164.
[144] Simek, Old Norse ship names, pp. 26–36; Brøgger and Shetelig, *The Viking Ships*.
[145] N. Rodger, *A Naval History of Britain*. Vol. I (660–1649), *The Safeguard of the Sea*. London: HarperCollins, 1997. pp. 9–13.

to adventure, plunder and conquest. Furthermore, it offered a road to trade and wealth as well as to freedom from centralising authority. But if it provided opportunities, it did not do so lightly. Perhaps it is fitting, therefore, to leave the last words to that old warrior, Egil Skallagrimsson:[146]

The sea-goddess
has ruffled me,
stripped me bare
of my loved ones,
the ocean severed
my family's bonds,
the tight knot
that ties me down.

---

[146] *Egil's Saga.* In *The Sagas of Icelanders*, see note 73 above, p. 153.

CHAPTER 6

Conquest and integration, c. 950–1260

During the ninth century the history of southern Scandinavia had been dominated by Viking raids. This meant raids along the coasts and rivers of mainland Europe and, later in the century, to the British Isles. Archaeological finds and a few written sources testify to renewed activity in the east as well. There is some evidence that reigning Danish royalty was actively engaged in raiding in Hamburg and Friesland, but it is likely that most of the ninth-century Viking raids were either private raids or that they were organised by members of the royal household and other chieftains who had been driven away from home as outlaws. So such Viking raids were private affairs, not state organised. During the ninth century such raids increased in frequency and size and became a veritable mass movement. Armies and raiding bands now not only raided during the summer but struck up permanent camps and, towards the end of the 870s, when large parts of England had been conquered, the army simply settled in that country. When the news of their good fortune spread, the Danish army was probably augmented by settlers from eastern Denmark, and many English and French place-names give evidence of this seizure and redistribution of land. The first wave of large-scale Viking raids petered out around 900, but the tales and experiences of those who had returned with gold and glory to their homelands during the 800s must have influenced their attitudes to royal power and politics strongly. These returning Vikings probably also helped pave the way for Christianity to become the main religion of Scandinavia.

There are many dates given for the end of the Viking Age: English historians end it around the time of the Norman Conquest in 1066, Danish historians see the end as coming in 1085, when King Canute IV had assembled an invasion fleet of 'a thousand ships' off the coast of Jylland (Jutland) but had to abort the invasion attempt because his father in-law, Count Robert of Flanders, did not supply the invasion army that Canute and the Danish expected. In Scotland Scandinavian earls continued to rule the islands and some of the mainland for hundreds of years. They were driven from the mainland in the mid-twelfth century but remained in the northern islands for another 300 years. The latest date for the end of the Viking Age is thus the one used by Scottish historians, who date it to the Battle of Largs (1263) and the subsequent Treaty of Perth (1266). The historians' accounts all have one thing in common: they have focussed on a single military event which has been taken as a convenient breaking-off point for the Scandinavian domination of a large part of Europe.

But the traditional account leaves an open question: why did the Scandinavians not bounce back? Why did the Norwegians not regroup to take England after 1066? Why was Canute IV's invasion attempt of 1085 not successful, and why was it not followed by other attempts? The answer lies in a more subtle approach to the end of the Viking Age: it did not go out with the bang most historians like to see, but rather with an apparent whimper. It is not possible to ascribe a single reason to the end of the Viking Age: instead a number of factors combined to change the Scandinavian outlook to one that was more in line with the rest of Europe. This process was drawn out over two centuries and was inextricably bound up with contemporary developments across Europe, in particular with the social and ecclesiastical reforms of the High Middle Ages. But by the end of this process the Viking threat to western Europe had been transformed into the Scandinavian kingdoms that formed a crucial part of that great common European project, the crusades. The Scandinavians opened up a new frontier and a new mission to convert the Slav peoples along the Baltic coast, an endeavour that the Scandinavians supported with their life-blood.

The expansion of the European economy

The challenges to the European world of the tenth to thirteenth centuries were fundamentally different from the challenges faced by the ninth-century Scandinavian armies in Europe. The European economy was booming, and so was the population: fertility in the countryside was rising and towns grew to sizes that had not been seen since the time of the Romans. The expanding population in the countryside fed a population boom in the cities, and the growing urbanisation of Europe, particularly around the Mediterranean Sea, engendered new ways of organising trade and shipping. Common to all these developments was that they were sparked by a new entrepreneurial spirit, amongst nobility and merchants alike, which paradoxically was founded on the fact that a concentration of capital in fewer hands meant that risks could be spread more evenly among several commercial ventures.[1] Towards the end of our period this can be seen in the proliferation of mills in the countryside. These signified both an increase in productivity and a concentration of capital and surplus in the hands of the mill-owners, i.e. those landlords who could afford to invest in the relatively new technology of the mills. On the other hand, the peasants also saw an increase in the complexity of their lives: the introduction of the heavy and expensive wheel plough and the re-organisation of the villages into three fields giving two crops a year made their lives more dependent on co-operation than had previously been the case.[2] The increased prosperity of the countryside and its importance to the magnates can be seen in the way that secular laws extended a specific protection – the *plough peace* – to peasant farmers. Overall, the upshot of the re-organisation of the countryside was that, like the landowners, the peasants faced a more prosperous life.

The broad European picture painted above contrasts with that painted by the German chronicler Adam of Bremen writing at the end of the eleventh century. Although he acknowledges the fertility of southern Scandinavia, he suggests that parts of Scandinavia – particularly Jylland (Jutland) – were barren, not because of the soil, but because of pirates:

The soil is barren there: apart from the river banks almost all of it appears like a desert, a salty marsh, and a wilderness of solitude. Even though every

[1] P. Anderson, *Passages from Antiquity to Feudalism*. London: Verso Editions, 1978.
[2] L. White, Jr. (1972) The expansion of technology 500–1500. In *The Fontana Economic History of Europe*. Vol. I, *The Middle Ages*, ed. C. M. Cipolla. London: Collins/Fontana Books, 1972. pp. 143–74.

locality of Germania is covered by frightening forests, only Jylland is more frightening than other parts of the country. There the land is shunned because of the lack of crops; the sea because of an infestation of pirates. Cultivated land is scarcely found in any location; it is scarcely fit for human habitation.[3]

It is, however, clear that land use increased in the eleventh century: pollen analyses from Scandinavia show that beech forests became more prevalent in southern Scandinavia, a fact that could indicate that the countries there saw a degree of depopulation. But the fact that pollen analyses for the fifth and sixth centuries – which saw the Saxons and Angles colonise England – show the same trend for most of southern Scandinavia makes it problematical to use them as indicators for the movements of peoples from Scandinavia. Instead it is likely that the pollen samples indicate that the *use* of the land changed. Unfortunately, the pollen of grasses (including cereals) has left too few indicators to demonstrate a corresponding increase in the productivity of cereal-producing land.

The concentration of trade

The change in land-use evident in the pollen samples reflects other changes as well. Throughout the Viking Age there was a move towards more restrictive trading practices which concentrated capital within a smaller group of people. This trend was already present in the first encounters between the English and the Danes in Portland in 789. The story has already been related (in Chapter 5), but it is worth repeating the surmise that the reeve Beaduheard was killed by Danish traders as he was trying to force them to go to Dorchester to declare the purpose of their visit, which was possibly to trade on the foreshore, as they had been accustomed to do in the past. Presumably, following tradition in

---

[3] Ager ibi sterilis; praeter loca flumini propinqua, omnia fere desertum videntur; terra salsuginis et vastae solitudinis. Porro cum omnis tractus Germaniae profundis horreat saltibus, sola est Iudlant ceteris horridior, quae in terra fugitur propter inopiam fructuum, in mari vero propter infestationem pyratarum. Vix invenitur culta in aliquibus locis, vix humanae habitationi oportuna.
Adamus Bremensis, *Monumenta Germaniae historica*. Vol. XVII, *Hamburgische Kirchengeschichte*, 3rd ed., B. Schmeidler. Scriptores rerum germanicarum in usum scholarum separatim editi. Hanover: Hahn, 1977 [1917].

other parts of Europe, they would have had to pay an entry fine to the local king for the privilege of trading under his protection.

In general a common trend towards a concentration of trade can be found across Europe: markets sprang up around monasteries, old Roman cities and – towards the end of the twelfth century – new, planned foundations, such as those at Lübeck, Freiburg im Breisgau and Bergen. In the development of cities as in so much else, Scandinavia imitated the rest of Europe. Early cities developed without prior planning, but some later ones were given a royal charter. Adam of Bremen mentions a number of old cities in Scandinavia: Schleswig (which by his time had taken on the role of nearby Haithabu (Hedeby)), Ribe, Aarhus, Viborg, Aalborg, Odense, Roskilde and Lund in Denmark, Trondheim and 'Vig'[4] in Norway, Skara and Sigtuna in Sweden.[5] These old cities were supplemented in the eleventh and twelfth centuries by new cities that were established under royal control. Other lists from the early thirteenth century mention a further seven cities in Scandinavia. Both Saxo Grammaticus and Snorri Sturluson mention cities that were founded by Danish and Norwegian kings in the eleventh century. Snorri even explains that the Norwegian kings took a personal interest in the physical layout of the towns.[6] We have no Scandinavian foundation charters for these cities, but one must expect that the eleventh-century foundations served the same functions as their twelfth-century chartered counterparts. These were primarily chartered to control trade in local markets and fairs, and to limit these markets and fairs to named days or specified periods. It became a royal prerogative to grant such privileges, and the city statutes legislated against forestalling the markets and protected the interests of the traders.[7]

European cities varied enormously in layout and in structure. However, most included a marketplace, a castle and several

[4] Possibly Tønsberg. G. A. Blom, Stad (Norge). In Kulturhistorisk leksikon for nordisk middelalder, ed. O. Olsen, P. Skautrup, N. Skyum-Nielsen and A. Steensberg. Copenhagen: Rosenkilde og Bagger, 1959–77.

[5] Adamus Bremensis, Monumenta, pp. II: 58, 61, III: 7, IV: 4, 5, 23, 25, 33; B. Fritz, Stad. In Kulturhistorisk leksikon, see note 4 above.

[6] Snorri Sturluson, Heimskringla, or The Lives of the Norse Kings, ed. E. Monsen, trans. A. H. Smith. New York: Dover, 1990. Chapter 70.

[7] G. A. Blom, Stadsprivilegier (Norge). In Kulturhistorisk leksikon, see note 4 above; E. Kroman, Stadsprivilegier (Danmark). Ibid.; L. Wikstrøm, Stadsprivilegier (Sverige). Ibid.

churches, and all had fortified walls that made it possible to control access to the market and fairs. Some cities had a network of streets that had grown organically out of the physical features of the ground they covered. Most cities were near waterways and had bridges that further controlled traffic within the town.[8] Houses were aligned with the streets or streams, but as time passed they were extensively re-aligned to allow more people and goods to live in the city. In practical terms this meant that the houses were originally parallel to the streets but were soon re-built to stand at right angles to them. This flexibility was made possible as much by necessity as by any conscious plan. Churches may increasingly have been built in stone or brick, but medieval dwelling houses were mostly built in wattle and daub, a material that had to be re-built at regular intervals. Although the city dwellings lacked permanence, they did allow the city dweller to constantly modify his house to reflect his status and, as time went on, the houses gained in height what they lacked in area at ground level. In Winchester houses were at least two storeys high by the twelfth century, and the human inhabitants had moved to the top floor while using the ground floor for storage or for shop fronts.

Although commercial centres developed in all parts of Europe, they developed more quickly in the regions near the main trade routes, which nearly always translated to near the main water-ways of Europe: the northern Mediterranean coast, along the Po Valley in Italy, the Rivers Rhône, Saône and the Meuse, the Rhineland, the English Channel and the shores of the Baltic. At the same time new roads crossing the countryside throughout Europe made most parts of the continent accessible to trade and commerce.[9] The revival of trade and the concurrent migration from the countryside to the urban centres was sustained by the increasingly influential class of merchants and, in particular, by the way in which they organised their trade and the privileges they secured for themselves. At the local level the traders might be monks who traded locally to sustain their monastery and make a

---

[8] R. Blomqvist, Stadsbebyggelse och stadsplan (Sverige och Skåne). Ibid.; H.-E. Lidén, Stadsbebyggelse och stadsplan (Norge). Ibid.; H. Søgård, Stadsbebyggelse och stadsplan (Danmark). Ibid.

[9] J. Bernard, Trade and finance in the Middle Ages, 900–1500. In *Fontana Economic History*, see note 2 above, Vol. I, pp. 274–338.

profit from their produce, or they might be long-distance traders, usually either Italian or Jewish, supplying spices, wines and fabrics to the magnates. Many long-distance traders came from as far away as Italy. As the Scandinavian North Sea empires slowly disintegrated, the merchants of the German cities – who were later to make up the hugely influential Hanseatic League – learnt to organise their trade in a way that allowed them to benefit from the new economies of scale made possible by new developments in shipping technology and finance.[10] Merchants invented new tools for pooling their resources. Although the Italian *commenda*, a partnership established for ventures at sea, and the *compagnia*, a means for pooling family wealth, may have had their counterparts in the Scandinavian *félag*, the Scandinavian traders never managed to reach the level of organisation found in Italy, nor did they ever understand the contracts for trade, exchanges and loans that formed the basis of the Italian dominance in the Mediterranean.[11]

The Scandinavians never learned to pool their resources in a manner that made large-scale productive enterprise possible, and the Baltic never saw anything like the cloth-making industries of the Low Countries or the deep mining that became a feature of the central German kingdoms. The guilds that did form as a consequence of the introduction of Christianity and the first Scandinavian saints never developed into the type of commercial guilds seen in other parts of Europe which supported their merchants when abroad. Instead, at most, they protected local interests by regulating hours, materials and prices and by providing an occasion for social gatherings.[12] Like their European counterparts they provided protection locally but never developed the power to become alternatives to magnatial – and later royal – power. Where their continental brethren struggled for and achieved urban independence, the Scandinavian towns did not develop a status of comparable freedom. However, the

---

[10] The best general introduction to the Hanse remains P. Dollinger, *The German Hanse*. London: Macmillan 1980. Cf. J. Bernard, Trade and finance in the Middle Ages, 900–1500. In *Fontana Economic History*, see note 2 above, Vol. I, pp. 274–338.

[11] F. Pedersen, The *fællig* and the family: the understanding of the family in Danish medieval law. *Continuity and Change*, Vol. 7 No.1, 1992, pp. 1–12.

[12] H. Søgård, Gilde (Danmark). In *Kulturhistorisk leksikon*, see note 4 above; S. Ljung, Gilde (Sverige). Ibid.; G. A. Blom, Gilde (Norge). Ibid.

development of free cities and their involvement in high politics in Italy and in Germany would eventually affect Scandinavia.

The birth of Scandinavia

This section will describe the history of southern Scandinavia in order to set the scene for the large-scale military ventures that enabled Scandinavian domination of the British Isles in the tenth and eleventh centuries, the period that saw the greatest successes of Viking expansion. There are only a few contradictory written testimonies about southern Scandinavia in the first half of the 900s. But we do know that an unnamed Scandinavian king was defeated by the German King Henry the Fowler in 934, and that this king accepted Christianity as a consequence. Although the political history is thus not very forthcoming on the early phases of the Christianisation of Scandinavia, it is clear that the process progressed with relative success. In 948 we learn that there were bishops in Haithabu (Hedeby), Ribe and Aarhus, and that these attended a synod called by the bishop of Hamburg-Bremen. This is the first mention of Aarhus, which seems to have been founded around this time and soon afterwards to have been fortified with a rampart. Both Haithabu and Ribe, although founded in the eighth and ninth centuries, were fortified around this time, a sure sign that notwithstanding the fact that the countries of the north had embraced the new religion, its message of peace had still to manifest itself in their old rivalries.

From the middle of the tenth century the political development of Scandinavia and the history of the Christian mission becomes easier to follow. A central source to these developments are the Jelling monuments (Figure 38). Both in conception and in execution these are unique. They are a carefully planned and executed monument to Queen Thyre, King Gorm the Old (d. 858/859) and their son Harald Bluetooth (d. c. 987). These three are the first known members of the royal dynasty that still rules Denmark today. The Jelling memorials were initially built as a pagan monument, probably by King Gorm, who erected the first of the two Jelling rune stones. The first stage consists of a ship-shaped stone ring (the largest in southern Scandinavia) and the rune stone to the memory of Thyre. It was enlarged by King

Figure 38 The royal monuments in Jelling, Jylland, c. 960–70. The Jelling monuments can be seen as a statement of the king's will to smoothe the transition from paganism to Christianity. The stones combine Christian and pagan iconography and are placed in the exact centre of a large, ship-shaped mound. The confident setting of the stones in the middle of a pagan burial place and the construction of a Christian church near the middle emphasise the king's intention of a smooth transition to the new religion.

Harald to include an impressive burial mound where Gorm was entombed in the pagan manner in 958 or 959. Some years later, around 965 when Harald had accepted Christianity, the Jelling mounds were adapted and changed into a Christian monument to Gorm and Thyre.[13] Incidentally, this is the time when we also hear about bishops of Haithabu, Ribe and Aarhus – all towns within the sphere of Harald's control.

Harald constructed a large wooden church in Jelling, and Gorm and Thyre's remains were transferred from their burial mound into the church. The ship-shaped stone circle was broken up and another memorial mound – even larger than the previous one – was constructed. In the exact middle of the ellipsis formed by the two mounds, Harald raised a large three-sided stone bearing the inscription 'Harald the king let these memorials be

[13] L. Hedeager and K. Kristiansen, eds. *Arkæologileksikon*. Copenhagen: Politiken, 1986. pp. 140–41.

Figure 39
Drawing of three
sides of the large
Jelling stone,
(Jelling, Jylland,
c. 960–70). The
two Jelling stones
have been called
'the birth
certificate of
Denmark'
because they
identify both the
country, the
ruling king and
his parents by
name. Note the
mixture of styles:
the Nordic runic
alphabet is
arranged
horizontally like
the Roman
alphabet, and the
two pictures
combine
Christian and
pre-Christian
stylistic elements
through their
depiction of
Christ and a
mythical beast.

made in memory of his father Gorm and his mother Thyre. The same Harald who won all Denmark and Norway and made the Danes Christian'(Figure 39).

The Jelling monuments are the embodiment of a new idea of the function of the strong king. And yet at the same time their seamless joining together of heathen and Christian elements signals a wish by King Harald to conduct a smooth transition from pagan to Christian worship. A confident mixture of traditions is seen in the rune stones themselves: the inscription is written in runes, not in the Roman alphabet, and the language used is Danish, not in Latin.[14] However, the text is arranged horizontally, like the lines of a book, and not in the haphazard ways that were normally used for runic inscriptions. The two large pictures found on the

[14] E. Roesdahl, Vikingetid og trosskifte (800–1050). In *Middelalderens Danmark*, ed. P. Ingesman, U. Kjær, P. K. Madsen and J. Vellev. Copenhagen: Gads Forlag, 1999. pp. 23–27.

stones – one of a large animal (perhaps a lion), the other of Christ – have been placed on the stones in a manner that is reminiscent of an illuminated book, like the ones found in contemporary monasteries and churches. The Jelling stone may be thought of as a 'book in stone' and heralds the Latin, book-based culture that was to follow the introduction of Christianity.[15]

But Harald Bluetooth did not just re-order and expand the monuments at Jelling. The Jelling monuments were of course a statement of his new-found religion, but they were also a bold statement of his confidence in the new religion as a tool of state-building. He may have accepted Christianity as a consequence of military pressure from the Holy Roman Empire, but his brand of Christianity was an inclusive one that allowed him to make conciliatory gestures in the programmatic statement of the stones. In this he stands in marked contrast to the Norwegian King Harald Hárfagri, who is generally described by later sagas as the cause of the Scandinavian expansion to the west because of his militant Christianity.

However, it is clear that Harald Bluetooth did not ignore the internal threats to his authority that his conversion may have sparked. A number of other large and unusual constructions saw the light of day during his reign, and these were more directed towards preserving his economic and military control of the country. In Ravninge meadows, not far from Jelling, a 5-metre-wide and 760-metre-long bridge was constructed across Vejle Aadal around 979. This is the oldest known bridge in southern Scandinavia, and by far the longest from the Viking Age. Within a few years four large and unique forts were built across the country as well: Trelleborg on Sjælland (Zealand), Nonnebakken on Fyn, Fyrkat in central Jylland and – largest of all – Aggersborg by Limfjord.[16] They were built according to the same overall plan: a perfectly circular rampart with gates opening up to the four corners of the earth, and a courtyard divided into

---

[15] Ibid., p. 23.
[16] L. B. Frandsen and S. Jensen, Kongen bød. Skalk, 4, 1988, pp. 3–8; P. Nørlund, Trelleborg. Copenhagen: Nationalmuseet, 1945; K. Randsborg, The Viking Age in Denmark: The Formation of a State. New York: St. Martin's Press, 1980; P. Sawyer, Gyldendal og Politikens Danmarkshistorie. Vol. III, Da Danmark blev Danmark, gen. ed. O. Olsen, trans. M. Hvidt. Copenhagen: Gyldendal & Politiken, 2002 [1986]; A. E. Christensen, Vikingetidens Denmark paa oldhistorisk baggrund. Copenhagen: Københavns Universitets Fond til Tilvejebringelse af Læremidler i kommission hos Gyldendals forlag, 1969.

four areas which held large houses set in a square pattern. They are the oldest royal buildings known in Denmark and, like the Ravninge bridge, they were built not only for military purposes but also to increase the prestige of the builder. The function of the forts is still the subject of hot debate in Scandinavia, but one may surmise that they were royal strongholds in an increasingly hostile environment (Figures 40, 41).

The pace of royal building construction during the reign of Harald Bluetooth is remarkable. It may even have included fortifying such cities as Ribe and Aarhus, and when Denmark faced renewed conflict with the Germans in 968 the Danevirke was extended (see Chapter 2).

Harald's army lost to the Germans in the shadow of the Danevirke in 974, and as a consequence Harald lost his grip on Norway and Germans settled in the border area between

Figure 40 The fortress of Trelleborg, Sjælland, Denmark (c. 980). This fortress was one of four constructed in the last decade of Harald Bluetooth's reign. Harald was responsible for an ambitious building programme across Denmark which included the half-mile-long Ravninge bridge in Jylland and the strengthening of the Danevirke.

Figure 41 The full-scale reconstruction of a 28.8-metre-long house from the Fyrkat fortress (Jylland, Denmark, c. 980) is the closest we can currently get to understanding the living conditions in Harald Bluetooth's four fortifications. The roof construction is conjectural. Not all the houses were used for living quarters: only about half had a fireplace.

Scandinavia and Germany. The German settlers were driven out of Denmark in 983 by an alliance consisting of Obodrite soldiers and troops loyal to Harald. Not long after this, Harald was killed fighting off a rebellion led by his son, Svein Forkbeard, and the large royal constructions were abandoned.

The second half of the 900s was in many ways a dividing line, of which the change in faith is the most important expression. Christianity was a fundamentally different religion from the one practised before, and in its wake the Scandinavian outlook changed. New relations are evident in attitudes to life, death, family, the individual and marriage, and in the cult of the gods. It took time for the changes to make themselves felt, but by the year 1000 Christianity was dominant in burial customs, and pagan symbols such as the hammer of Thor had been replaced by the Christian cross. The early years of Christianity must have seen churches and priests attached to the large royal households and the towns, but it was not until a century after the acceptance of Christianity that Scandinavia had a recognisable ecclesiastical structure with bishoprics, and it is likely that it took an equal amount of time before churches became common.

Many other aspects of life changed in the latter half of the 900s. Harald Bluetooth's monuments must be interpreted as an attempt to strengthen royal power, and his conversion to

Christianity can be seen in the same way. Although this was soon to change as a consequence of the Gregorian reform movement in the eleventh century, the organisation of the tenth-century Church was hierarchical and dependent on the support of the king for the power and livelihoods of the clergy. But perhaps more importantly the monuments also point to the fact that Harald claimed sovereignty of at least parts of Norway in the 960s and 970s. The Norwegians and the Danes were therefore locked in conflict, although the details of the internal politics of Scandinavia are impossible to unravel. Almost simultaneously, Svein Forkbeard and Olaf Tryggvason managed to establish personal control over Denmark and Norway respectively. Taking part in several expeditions, Olaf took the lead in extorting money from the English kingdom, and he was joined briefly by Svein Forkbeard. Together and separately, these two new Scandinavian kings became a fatal threat to the English king, Æðelred the Unready. Svein was an empire-builder: not only did he build up his fortune by allying himself with Olaf in early raids on England, but he was also prepared to break this alliance when an opportunity presented itself. Olaf and Svein fell out almost immediately over the Vik in Norway, which was old Danish territory and possibly the 'Norway' mentioned by Harald Bluetooth on the Jelling stone. Svein swiftly aligned himself with the Norwegian Earl Eirik Hákonson (who was another contender for the Norwegian throne) and the Swedish king, Olaf Skötkonung (who wanted control of Gautaland). Together they defeated and killed Olaf in the Battle of Svöld in the year 1000. The end result was to leave Svein with the ability to muster forces under Danish control to raid and ultimately conquer England.

CHAPTER 7

The Second Viking Age in England, c. 970–1066

The period from c. 950 to c. 975 saw the apogee of the West Saxon dynasty in England.[1] Eadred's success in securing lasting control of York and the submission of the Anglian rulers of Bamburgh removed from the scene the final competitors for their domination of southern mainland Britain and paved the way for a generation of stability in which to reconstruct and consolidate their kingdom. Within a year of his success in Northumbria, Eadred was dead and his kingdom had been divided between his two surviving nephews, Eadwig (who succeeded to the throne of Wessex) and Edgar (who received Mercia).[2] For a brief period it was possible that Anglo-Saxon England might split again into its primary components, but the early death of Eadwig in 959 handed the sixteen-year-old Edgar kingship over all England.[3]

The next sixteen years can be presented as something of a renaissance for the Anglo-Saxons, for Edgar, working closely in alliance with Archbishop Dunstan of Canterbury, initiated a programme of ecclesiastical reform and new monastic foundations that reversed the long decline that the Viking invasions and protracted warfare had brought.[4] This concentration on the spiritual needs of the people may appear odd in the eyes of a modern and largely secular society, but Edgar and his advisors carried the conviction that a sound Christian foundation was the essential basis upon which to rebuild a society that had been

---

[1] For overviews of the achievement of the late Anglo-Saxon state, see J. Campbell, *The Anglo-Saxon State*. London: Hambledon and London, 2000. Chapters 1 and 2.

[2] *The Anglo-Saxon Chronicles*, ed. and trans. M. J. Swanton. London: Phoenix, 2000. D, *sub anno* 955.

[3] *Anglo-Saxon Chronicles*, B and C, *sub anno* 959.

[4] P. Cavill, *Vikings: Fear and Faith in Anglo-Saxon England*. London: HarperCollins, 2001. Chapter 5.

traumatised and fragmented by a century of warfare and pagan threat. It was, of course, not just in Wessex that this programme of reconstruction took place, for the need was more pressing in the territories that had been conquered fully by the Danes and Norwegians, such as East Anglia and the eastern Midlands, where bishoprics had to be re-established, old monasteries restored and new religious communities founded. This process of spiritual reform went hand in hand with a cultural and economic regeneration, and by the 970s England was prospering and its culture flourishing.

The death of King Edgar in 975[5] proved in retrospect, therefore, to mark a watershed in the fortunes of the Anglo-Saxon kingdom. Factional discord between the supporters of Edgar's son by his first marriage, Edward, and those of his son by his second marriage, Æðelred, deepened after Edward's murder in 978 and cast a shadow over the beginning of what was to be the long, troubled reign of his half-brother, Æðelred II (978–1016), better known in popular tradition as Æðelred the Unready.[6] Recent re-assessments of his rule have been more upbeat than his traditional portrayal, stressing his achievement in holding his kingdom together in the face of mounting internal and external pressures for some three decades, but it cannot be denied that his reign witnessed the collapse of the West Saxon hegemony within Britain so painstakingly constructed by Alfred and his descendants.[7] Many of the crises of Æðelred's reign stemmed from the internal stresses of a kingdom that had been forced into an unnatural political union in the mid-tenth century – and from his mis-handled attempts to stamp his authority upon it – but the situation was greatly worsened by the coincidence of his succession with the re-opening of sustained Scandinavian attack on the British Isles in what is often referred to as the Second Viking Age. It was Æðelred's misfortune that he would face the formidable coming together of new ideas in Scandinavian religion and ideas of kingship that his predecessors had forged in their own contexts. The Scandinavian kingdoms of Norway and Denmark had gone through a parallel process of consolidation of royal power and organised religion. The second-generation Christian rulers

---

[5] *Anglo-Saxon Chronicles*, D, *sub anno 975*.   [6] Ibid., *sub annis 975, 978*.

[7] R. Lavelle, *Aethelred II King of the English, 978–1016*. Kings and Queens of Medieval England. Stroud: Tempus, 2002.

now had the authority that allowed them to equip and successfully pursue military adventures abroad and to attempt the first
conquest of England – not by Normans, but by Northmen.

Æðelred the Unready and the Scandinavian threat

In England the frequency and intensity of Scandinavian attacks
increased from 980. The Scandinavians – who initially were most
probably Norwegians, considering the fact that Denmark's
Harald Bluetooth appears to have been engaged in a civil war
with his son Svein until 986 – concentrated on the coast, targets
ranging as widely as Thanet, Southampton and Cheshire.[8] The
identification of the Scandinavian raiders as Norwegian is consistent with the fact that between 981 and 989 the Celtic principalities of Wales and Cornwall bore the brunt of the attacks, a
raid on Dorset in 983 being the only significant incursion
recorded in contemporary accounts into the West Saxon kingdom.[9] The prime focus, it would seem, was on the west and
south-west of the British Isles: West Saxon power was still an
ample deterrent to would-be attackers of England. In 991, however, the image of English invulnerability was shattered in a
defeat that revealed the fragility of the kingdom.

The attacker in 991 was Olaf Tryggvason, an exiled grandson of
King Harald Hárfagri of Norway who had been brought up
amongst the Rus and who had pursued a career as a war-leader
in the Baltic region. Turning west, he led a large fleet across the
North Sea on a plundering raid against the East Anglian and
Kentish coasts. Olaf seized Northey, an island in the estuary of
the River Blackwater near Maldon in Essex connected to the
mainland by a narrow and easily defended causeway. From
there he launched a succession of devastating raids around the
outer Thames estuary. The English counter-attack was led by the
ealdorman of Essex, Byrhtnoth, who gathered the *fyrd* of the eastern shires for an attack on Northey. Skirmishing across the

---

[8] *Anglo-Saxon Chronicles*, C, *sub anno* 980.
[9] *Anglo-Saxon Chronicles*, C, *sub anno* 982; M. Todd, and A. Fleming, *The South-West to
AD 1000. Regional History of England*. London, New York: Longman, 1987. p. 276.
For Wales, see W. Davies, *Wales in the Early Middle Ages*. Studies in the Early History
of Britain. Leicester: Leicester University Press, 1982. pp. 116–20.

causeway looked unlikely to yield a definitive result and, rather than risk the Vikings' simply taking to their boats and moving to a new base, Byrhtnoth opted to permit Olaf to bring his men over to the mainland, in the expectation that his superior force would wipe them out. Unfortunately for the English, however, Byrhtnoth was an early casualty in the fighting and, seeing their leader slain, the *fyrd*-men fled while the dead ealdorman's military retinue fought on until they were annihilated.[10] South-east England now lay open to the raiders, but at this point Æðelred opted to buy Olaf's withdrawal through payment of the cash bribe of 10,000 lbs of silver, the first payment of the tribute that came to be known as Danegeld. As a gamble in 991 it seemed to have worked, for the Viking fleet did not return the following year, but the tribute had bought a respite, not a permanent relief.

Olaf Tryggvason's success in extorting his buy-off in 991 drew the attention of other predators. In 994 an even larger fleet, commanded by Svein Forkbeard, king of Denmark, accompanied by Olaf, returned to England.[11] Again, when faced with the threat of invasion Æðelred and his advisors opted to buy off the attackers with payment of substantial tribute. On this occasion, however, Æðelred introduced conditions reminiscent of those used by his ancestor, Alfred, a century earlier, the chief of which was that Olaf should accept baptism.[12] Clearly, Æðelred was banking on the convert's acceptance of Christian moral codes and that he would refrain from future attacks on his co-religionists. Unexpectedly the gamble worked, for Olaf withdrew from England and headed for Norway to mount a bid for his grandfather's throne.[13] Although Olaf adhered to his new religion for the remaining six years of his life and started the process of imposing Christianity on the still largely pagan Norse, the deciding factor behind his withdrawal was probably his accumulation of sufficient wealth through his share of the Danegeld to finance his challenge rather than any

[10] *Anglo-Saxon Chronicles*, E, *sub anno* 991; I. Howard, *Swein Forkbeard's Invasions and the Danish Conquest of England, 991–1017*. Warfare in History. Woodbridge: Boydell Press, 2003. pp. 35–37; D. Whitelock, ed. *English Historical Documents*. Vol. I, *English Historical Documents, c. 500–1042*, gen. ed. D. C. Douglas. London: Eyre and Spottiswode, 1955. pp. 293–97.

[11] I. Howard, *Swein Forkbeard's Invasions*, Chapter 3.

[12] *Anglo-Saxon Chronicles*, E, *sub anno* 995.

[13] *Olaf Tryggvi's Son's Saga*. In *Heimskringla, History of the Kings of Norway*, ed. and trans. L. M. Hollander. Austin: University of Texas Press, 1964. Chapters 30–32, 47; *St Olaf's Saga*. Ibid., Chapter 96.

recognition of his Christian duties. His successes in Norway in 995 brought the added bonus of lifting Danish pressure on the English, for King Svein was forced to concentrate on attempting to shore up the pro-Danish element amongst the Norwegian nobility in a bid to maintain Danish domination of western Scandinavia.[14] From 995 Svein was chiefly concerned with containing Olaf, and it was only in 1000 in a sea-battle at 'Svöld', somewhere between Denmark and Norway, that the Danish king and his allies Eirik of Hlaðir and Olaf Skötkonung, king of Sweden, succeeded in defeating and killing him.[15]

Down to 1002 England enjoyed a respite from significant Viking attack whilst the struggle for the domination of Scandinavia unfolded. Æðelred, however, appears to have recognised that the elimination of Olaf in 1000 served notice of the likelihood of a termination of that respite, and he began to take steps to increase his diplomatic and military security. A major fleet offensive in the Irish Sea, designed to curb the activities of Isles- and Dublin-based Vikings, however, simply petered out for lack of decisive leadership.[16] One successful step in this process of building English security was the detachment of Normandy from its alliance or friendship with the Danes, for Norman ports could have afforded safe haven for Danish attacks on southern England. To secure Norman support for himself, the widowed Æðelred negotiated marriage to Duke Richard I of Normandy's daughter, Emma, who took the Anglo-Saxon name Ælfgifu.[17] Significantly, it was after negotiating this deal that on 13 November 1002 – St Brice's Day – Æðelred unleashed an attack against the substantial culturally Scandinavian population resident in his kingdom, supposedly to pre-empt a plot by them against his life and the security of the kingdom.[18] The main massacres probably occurred in the south and south-east of England, the chief victims being amongst the wealthy and prominent merchant classes. In the short term this action against

---

[14] Howard, *Swein Forkbeard's Invasions*, pp. 50–51.
[15] N. Lund, The Danish empire and the end of the Viking Age. In *The Oxford Illustrated History of the Vikings*, ed. P. H. Sawyer. Oxford: Oxford University Press, 1997. p. 169.
[16] *Anglo-Saxon Chronicles*, E, *sub anno* 1000.
[17] Howard, *Swein Forkbeard's Invasions*, pp. 60–61; D. Crouch, *The Normans: The History of a Dynasty*. London: Hambledon and London, 2002. pp. 32–35.
[18] *Anglo-Saxon Chronicles*, E, *sub anno* 1002.

a feared and suspect minority probably won Æðelred support amongst the Anglo-Saxons, but that support was gained at the cost of alienating the substantial Anglo-Scandinavian populations of the Midlands and north of the kingdom. In effect, the St Brice's Day massacre served to re-open the traditional fissures within the political structure of England.

Amongst the casualties in the slaughter was said to have been Gunnhild, a sister of Svein Forkbeard who was being held hostage in England as surety for her brother's adherence to the 994 settlement.[19] There is no corroborating evidence for this tradition,[20] and it would seem bizarre that Æðelred would order the killing of so significant a bargaining tool, but Svein's reaction to the massacre suggests that the story may be true. Whether or not he acted out of a desire to avenge his dead sister, or moved in response to an appeal from the Scandinavian population of north-east England, in 1003 Svein unleashed his assault on England.[21] If revenge was his objective, however, it quickly burned itself out, for in 1004 he allowed his anger to be assuaged by yet another massive Danegeld payment.[22]

Æðelred's aim in paying Danegeld was, from the beginning, to secure a respite from attack which could be used to rebuild defences and regroup his forces. This aim, however, seems never to have been realised, for each episode of raiding saw no significantly improved English military response. Such pay-offs, moreover, simply encouraged further attacks, which would be halted only by a significant military effort on the part of the English. That, however, never materialised, and so the Danes were encouraged to make further raids and demand larger and larger sums to withdraw. In 1006–7, when Svein launched a third wave of attacks on England,[23] the Danegeld offered for his withdrawal amounted to some 36,000 lbs of silver.[24] Following this, however, Æðelred attempted to set in place a military and naval re-organisation that could effectively counter any future attacks. In the course of 1008 he initiated a ship-building programme,

---

[19] Howard, *Swein Forkbeard's Invasions*, p. 62.
[20] William of Malmesbury, *Gesta Regum Anglorum: The History of the English Kings*, ed. and trans. R. A. B. Mynors. Oxford Medieval Texts, 1. Oxford, New York: Clarendon Press, 1998.
[21] *Anglo-Saxon Chronicles*, E, *sub anno* 1003.   [22] Ibid., *sub anno* 1004.
[23] Howard, *Swein Forkbeard's Invasions*, Chapter 5.
[24] *Anglo-Saxon Chronicles*, E, *sub annis* 1006, 1007.

again based on Alfred's earlier policies, with the intention of meeting and defeating the Danes at sea before they could land in England, and he attempted to overhaul the *fyrd* system, construct new fortifications and overhaul existing ones.[25] Unfortunately the continuing tensions within the royal family that had weakened English government since 975, and fresh strains between the king and his children by his first marriage, undermined his efforts.

It was in the aftermath of the failure of the 1008 efforts that a fresh Viking threat was unleashed on England in the form of the multi-national army led by Thorkell the Tall.[26] This was still a largely Danish venture but included Swedes and a large Norwegian contingent, amongst which was the twelve-year-old Olaf Haraldsson, another descendant of Harald Hárfagri. In 1009 Thorkell's force landed in eastern England and began to wage a highly effective and destructive campaign across the region, accumulating some 48,000 lbs of silver over four years in a series of locally negotiated Danegeld payments. A significant victory was scored in 1010 in Norfolk, where the ealdorman, Ulfcytel, and the East Anglian levies were defeated with heavy losses. The following year Thorkell and his allies achieved their most striking success when they raided Kent and captured Canterbury, where they seized many important prisoners. Chief amongst the captives was Archbishop Ælfheah, who had earlier converted Olaf Tryggvason to Christianity. His captors demanded a ransom of 3,000 lbs of silver for him, but Ælfheah refused to allow any payment to be made, and later tradition recounts how, as a consequence, he was pelted to death by some of the Vikings with meat bones in the midst of a drunken feast.[27] Thorkell appears to have been opposed to the killing of the archbishop and dissociated himself from the act and from his former allies, whom he soon abandoned. In 1012 he entered Æðelred's service, bringing with him forty-five warships and their crews, which were used to great effect in 1013 when he helped the Londoners repel an attack by Svein Forkbeard.[28]

[25] Howard, *Swein Forkbeard's Invasions*, pp. 76–82.   [26] Ibid., pp. 82–84.

[27] *Anglo-Saxon Chronicles*, E, *sub annis* 1009–13; Cavill, *Vikings*, pp. 297–98.

[28] *Anglo-Saxon Chronicles*, E, *sub annis* 1012, 1013; Howard, *Swein Forkbeard's Invasions*, pp. 97–98.

The Danish king's return to England in 1013 may have been triggered by two considerations and had a wholly different objective: conquest. Whilst English defences had never shown any real capacity to resist attacks from as early as the 980s, it was clear that Thorkell's onslaught in 1008 had brought the remaining defences to the brink of collapse. For Svein, whose domination of Scandinavia was at that point without any serious challengers, the opportunity to capitalise on English weakness was never likely to be better. Thorkell, too, was also a matter for concern, for his successes had brought him great personal wealth and earned him a reputation as a gifted war-leader that had secured him the loyalty of a substantial military following. Both features could be seen by Svein as potential threats that required to be eliminated or, at least, neutralised. The invasion force swept almost all before it; even Thorkell's successful defence of London could do no more than delay the inevitable outcome. By the end of December 1013 English resistance had collapsed and Æðelred, escorted by Thorkell, had fled to the safety of the Norman court with his family. The Danish conquest of England seemed complete.[29]

Svein did not enjoy his victory for long. In February 1014 he was at Gainsborough in Lincolnshire, in the heart of the Danelaw, when he took ill and died.[30] The Danish army was left in some disarray, and the English turned once more to Æðelred rather than to Svein's teenage son, Canute, who had accompanied his father on the campaign, or to Canute's elder brother, Harald, who succeeded to the Danish throne. Seizing the initiative, the remaining English leadership rallied their military forces, drove Canute out of England and invited their exiled king to return from Normandy.[31] Æðelred and the sons of his first marriage arrived in England in the early spring of 1014, whilst Emma and their young children remained in Rouen. Displaying almost immediately the ineptitude and bad judgement that had undermined his earlier rule, Æðelred quickly lost what support he had regained in England through his involvement in the politically inspired murder of leading Danelaw noblemen, whose property he then seized.[32] His position deteriorated rapidly thereafter and even Thorkell the Tall, whose loyalty to Æðelred in 1013 had secured the king's safe

[29] Ibid., Chapter 6.　　[30] Anglo-Saxon Chronicles, E, sub anno 1014.

[31] Howard, Swein Forkbeard's Invasions, Chapter 7.

[32] Anglo-Saxon Chronicles, E, sub anno 1015.

escape to Normandy, deserted to his enemies. In the autumn of
1015, backed by his brother, Harald II, and accompanied by
Thorkell and Eirik of Hlaðir, Canute returned to England.[33]

Æðelred's authority was already disintegrating before the arrival
of this new invasion force. Leadership of the English appears to
have fallen increasingly to his elder son by his first marriage,
Edmund, whose relationship with his father seems to have grown
progressively more strained after Æðelred's marriage to Emma and
the births of his half-brothers. It was Edmund, supported by the
powerful Northumbrian ruler Uhtred, who staged the most effective resistance to Canute.[34] As a result, when Æðelred died in April
1016 it was Edmund who was acclaimed king in the mainly Anglo-
Saxon areas of the kingdom.[35] In much of the Danelaw, however, it
was Canute who received that acknowledgement. Displaying the
energy and leadership skills that his father had so lacked, throughout the summer of 1016 Edmund waged a ferocious resistance that
earned him his later designation of 'Ironside', but at Ashingdon in
Essex on 18 October he was comprehensively routed by the
Danes.[36] The scale of the defeat was devastating, three English
ealdormen, a bishop and an abbot being amongst the slain of the
English political leadership, but its bitterest aspect was the role
played in Canute's victory by the desertion from Edmund's forces at
the height of the battle of Eadric Streona, ealdorman of Mercia, a
man whom Æðelred had raised to power. Badly wounded, Edmund
withdrew westward, pursued by the Danes, and was eventually
forced to sue for peace. At Alney in Gloucestershire the two kings
agreed to a partition of England, Canute taking everything north of
the Thames and Edmund being left with the rump of his father's
kingdom south of the river. Within a few weeks Edmund was dead,
probably as a result of wounds received at Ashingdon, although
there are also persistent traditions of assassination, and Canute
moved swiftly to take over the residual portion of the kingdom.[37]
Having won a conflict that had been both eased and prolonged by
political and cultural divisions within England, Canute had to
consolidate his position by restoring unity and strong government
to a kingdom wholly lacking those features.

---

[33] Ibid.   [34] Ibid., *sub anno* 1016.
[35] Ibid.   [36] Ibid.
[37] Florence of Worcester. In *English Historical Documents*, Vol. I, see note 10 above,
pp. 284–85.

The Anglo-Danish kingdom, 1016–1042

The young Canute set about consolidating his position within England and reconstructing royal authority after decades of decline under Æðelred II. He benefited from the relationship which he had developed as a teenager during the invasion of 1013 with Ælfgifu of Northampton, the daughter of Ælfhelm, ealdorman of Northampton, who had probably already borne him his first son, Svein Alfivason, by c. 1014.[38] Through Ælfgifu, Canute established links with an important segment of the Anglo-Saxon nobility, and the new king was to work hard to accommodate such men into his new regime (Figure 42). Canute understood the need for inclusive government of his new kingdom and, whilst his loyal followers expected and received rewards for their service, he was careful to avoid the creation of a colonial aristocracy ruling over the conquered English population. There were casualties as he weeded out some of the more dangerous figures from the old regime, most notably Eadric Streona, who was executed in 1017, and Uhtred of Northumbria, who had been one of Edmund Ironside's most active allies.[39] In place of Uhtred, Canute installed the Norwegian Eirik of Hlaðir as his northern strongman, to rule over the Anglo-Scandinavian population of York, whilst Thorkell the Tall was given control of East Anglia.[40] But Canute also had to deal with the remnants of the West Saxon dynasty, who could have posed a threat to his authority in England. Edmund Ironside's pregnant widow and young son were forced into exile, first of all in Sweden, where Canute instructed King Olaf Skötkonung to kill them, then subsequently at the court of Jaroslav the Wise in Novgorod.[41] Edmund's younger brother Eadwig, a youth in his teens, was simply executed on the king's orders.[42] Æðelred II's widow, Emma/Ælfgifu, however, offered Canute a means both of linking himself formally with the old

---

[38] Howard, *Swein Forkbeard's Invasions*, pp. 107, 108, 116, 137.

[39] S. Keynes, Cnut's earls. In *The Reign of Cnut King of England, Denmark and Norway*, ed. A. Rumble. Studies in the Early History of Britain: Makers of England. Leicester: Leicester University Press, 1993. p. 43; R. Fletcher, *Bloodfeud: Murder and Revenge in Anglo-Saxon England*. London: Penguin, 2002. pp. 86–110.

[40] S. Keynes, Cnut's earls. In *The Reign of Cnut*, see note 39 above, pp. 43, 54–58.

[41] G. Ronay, *The Lost King of England: The East European Adventures of Edward the Exile*. Wolfeboro: Boydell Press, 1989. pp. 24, 51–4.

[42] *Anglo-Saxon Chronicles*, D, sub anno 1017.

Figure 42
Winchester
Cathedral.
Canute
proclaimed his
succession to the
role of the West
Saxon kings
through powerful
symbolic acts.
Winchester, the
spiritual centre of
old Wessex,
benefited from
his patronage,
and when he died
in 1035 his body
was taken there
for burial.

regime and also of forging an alliance with Normandy, from where Æðelred had been able to secure support in the closing years of his reign. Emma was summoned to Canute's court and readily agreed to marry him.[43] This may have secured the survival of her two sons by Æðelred, Alfred and Edward, but they clearly did not figure that prominently in her plans, for both boys were left in Normandy and scrupulously ignored by their mother. If any child of hers was going to succeed Canute, Emma was determined that it would be fathered by him and have title to all of his dominions.

With these basic arrangements in place, by 1018 Canute's grip on England was sufficiently firm for him to be able to send home the bulk of his Danish army. A levy of 72,000 lbs of silver was raised to pay off the warriors, the king retaining the crews of only forty ships to provide a military force around him.[44] Canute then began to make conciliatory moves designed to reconcile the English to his rule, the most notable being an agreement to abide by the native lawcode as it had stood in the time of King

---

[43] Ibid.; Florence of Worcester. In *English Historical Documents*, Vol. I, see note 10 above, p. 286.
[44] Ibid.

Edgar. Whilst culturally his court would remain strongly Danish, and consequently would exert a powerful influence over Anglo-Saxon aristocratic culture, the basic character of Canute's kingship would be rooted firmly in Anglo-Saxon traditions. This character survived even his securing of the Danish throne following the death in 1018 of his brother, Harald II. From 1018 Canute ruled an empire that spanned the North Sea, and he was faced with the problems of developing a style of government that would allow for the smooth administration of the various portions of his far-flung domain.[45]

The empire assembled by Canute consisted of a series of overlapping overlordships rather than a unitary and centrally governed territory. Within each portion of his multi-national domain he was heavily dependent on continuity of native traditions in government and, consequently, on the native ruling elites. In England a key role was played by leading native churchmen, such as Archbishop Wulfstan of York,[46] and Canute's relationship with the English church saw little by way of 'Scandinavianisation'. Nevertheless, the need to secure his powerbase and also to reward his loyal supporters and kinsmen required him to create a new regime that would provide him with effective regional control.[47] In England between 1016 and 1018 the pressing need for stability had seen the establishment of four principal blocs of power: York under Eirik of Hlaðir; Mercia under the repeated turncoat, Eadric Streona; East Anglia under Thorkell the Tall; and Wessex under the king himself. Eadric's execution in 1017 and Canute's political settlement of 1018 allowed a re-ordering of those initial arrangements, producing a new pattern in which Anglo-Saxons featured more prominently. Indeed, men of recognisably Anglo-Saxon background were to dominate the governing community of England for the remainder of Canute's reign, and it is probable that many of the individuals bearing Scandinavian names were Anglo-Scandinavian natives of the Danelaw region of eastern England rather than Danish newcomers.[48] Control of politically – and militarily – sensitive areas, however, appears to have been vested in the

[45] P. Sawyer, Cnut's Scandinavian empire. In *The Reign of Cnut*, see note 39 above, pp. 10–26; N. Lund, Cnut's Danish kingdom. Ibid., pp. 27–42.

[46] M. K. Lawson, Archbishop Wulfstan and the homiletic element in the laws of Athelred II and Cnut. Ibid., pp. 141–64.

[47] S. Keynes, Cnut's earls. Ibid., pp. 43–88.   [48] Ibid., pp. 78–81.

hands of Scandinavians, although in parts of the country this may
have been dictated by the particular needs of new concentrations of
Danish colonists. One of Canute's most pressing concerns was for
the security of his kingdom during his necessary absences whilst
visiting other portions of his empire. The response to this was to
vest an over-riding responsibility for government in one of his
earls, who would govern in effect as a viceroy during his absence.
Down to 1023 this role was fulfilled first by Thorkell and then by
Eirik, but for the remainder of Canute's reign it was held principally by the great Anglo-Saxon *arriviste*, Godwin.[49] On the fringes
of his English kingdom Canute may also have employed his Anglo-
Saxon predecessors' traditional mechanism for control: the
manipulation of feud and rivalry between competing dynastic
segments or regional noblemen.[50] Above all, however, it was on
Canute's personal relationship with his lieutenants that the security of his empire depended. This can perhaps be seen best in the
arrangements that he made for the control of the western maritime
zone of the British Isles.

Canute's own experiences of the conquest of England had
impressed upon him the need to establish an effective overlordship of the other major powers within the British Isles, and this
view was strengthened further by his need to close off the possibility of support from these powers for potential challengers to
his own authority. The 1020s and early 1030s, although dominated by his efforts to impose his lordship within Norway, also
saw him extend his authority westwards into the turbulent waters
of the Irish Sea as part of that process. His aim may originally
have been directed towards containment of the ambitions of the
earls of Orkney, who, as nominal subjects of the Norwegian
kings, would have been brought under his overlordship after
1028. In 1014, after all, Earl Sigurd of Orkney had lost his life at
Clontarf outside Dublin in a bid to establish his authority within
Ireland, and his sons, Einar and Thorfinn, continued to seek a
similar position in the 1020s and 1030s. The unstable politics of
the western zone into which Orkney regularly intruded its
influence was fertile territory within which Canute's rivals
could build up their strength in advance of a challenge to his

[49] Ibid., pp. 82–88.
[50] For the position in Northumbria, for example, see Fletcher, *Bloodfeud*.

power.[51] There is no indication given in any saga source that Canute was able to establish an effective overlordship of Orkney, and he may instead have embarked upon a policy of containment of that would-be northern super-power. In what was possibly a pre-emptive move, he appears to have succeeded in placing one of his relatives, Hákon, son of Eirik, earl of Hlaðir, and representative of a Norse family with a long tradition of hostility towards the state-building Norwegian kings, in lordship over the Isles, perhaps as early as 1016–17. In about 1017 Canute also gave Hákon the earldom of Worcester, a strategic territory in land terms on the frontier between the Anglo-Saxon kingdom and the Welsh principalities, and in maritime terms by virtue of its access to the western sea-ways.[52] The sea-lanes through the Irish Sea and Hebrides led to Orkney and Norway and were of central strategic importance to Canute's imperial ambitions. Hákon Eiriksson was intended by Canute to control all the elements in this strategic chain, the final component being his installation as the king's deputy in Norway following the expulsion of Olaf Haraldsson in 1028.[53] The young earl, however, did not long enjoy his authority, for in late 1029 or early 1030, whilst on route to Norway for his marriage, he was drowned in a shipwreck in the Pentland Firth between Orkney and the Scottish mainland.[54]

The drowning of Hákon Eiriksson caused a crisis that Canute could not afford to ignore, for the attempted return of Olaf Haraldsson to Norway later in 1030, although ending with the Norwegian's defeat and death at the Battle of Sticklestad, had exposed the weaknesses in the Danish military regime. The earl's death may have stimulated Orcadian interest in reviving Sigurd's lordship in the Isles, but the earls of Orkney were not the only powers with an interest in this zone. It is surely no coincidence that in 1031 Canute led an army towards Scotland and, apparently

[51] B. E. Crawford, The dedication to St Clement and Rodil, Harris. In Church, Chronicle and Learning in Medieval and Early Renaissance Scotland. Essays Presented to Donald Watt on the Occasion of the Completion of the Publication of Bower's Scotichronicon, ed. B. E. Crawford. Edinburgh: Mercat Press, 1999. pp. 111–12.

[52] For the career of Echmarcach, king of Dublin and the Isles, see below, pp. 228–31.

[53] B. E. Crawford, The dedication to St Clement and Rodil, Harris. In Church, Chronicle and Learning, see note 51 above, pp. 119–20.

[54] Anglo-Saxon Chronicles, C, sub anno 1030; A. O. Anderson, ed. Early Sources of Scottish History, A.D. 500 to 1286. Vol. I. Edinburgh and London: Oliver and Boyd, 1922. pp. 569–70.

bloodlessly, gained the submission of the Scottish king, Máel Coluim mac Cinaeda, and two other kings.[55] One of the latter, 'Iehmarc', an Anglo-Saxon attempt at the Irish Echmarcach, was a member of the Waterford branch of the Uí Ímhair and ruler of a sea-kingdom that extended over much of the Irish Sea (see pp. 228–31). Through him Canute was to regain his security in the west, blocking the ambitions of the earls of Orkney for over a decade and even extending his reach further into the Norse-Gaelic world by virtue of Echmarcach's position within the Uí Ímhair dynasty.[56]

The success of Canute's arrangements for the government of his sprawling domain enabled him to exercise an unprecedented overlordship of Scandinavia and substantial parts of the British Isles. How effective or long-lasting his influence in Ireland or Scotland was is debatable, but his domination of Norway, England and the Isles ensured that the ambitions of the kings of Scots, the earls of Orkney and the Uí Briain kings in Ireland were held in check. In common with many of the 'empires' of this period, however, the union of its component parts was a very personal one and, regardless of how effective the arrangements for government had been during the lifetime of the ruler, it was unlikely that those arrangements would survive his death. Canute clearly intended his power to be passed on intact and, when he died at Shaftesbury in the heart of Wessex in 1035,[57] key figures in his circle of closest servants moved to ensure that the integrity of his legacy was preserved. Others, however, saw their opportunity to prosper under a changed regime.

There is no evidence to show that Canute had intended for his son by Emma, Hardacanute, to succeed to the thrones of both Denmark and England, although Emma was clearly determined that he should.[58] The fifteen-year-old Hardacanute, however, was in Denmark at the time of his father's death, and it was instead Canute and Ælfgifu of Northampton's son, Harold Harefoot, who mounted a bid for power, supported by the powerful Leofric, earl of Mercia, and the commanders of the English fleet.[59] Ranged against him were the queen-mother, Emma,

[55] Anglo-Saxon Chronicles, E, sub anno 1031 [?1027].
[56] For the career of Echmarcach, king of Dublin and the Isles, see below, p. 228.
[57] Anglo-Saxon Chronicles, D, sub anno 1035.
[58] F. Barlow, Edward the Confessor. Kings and Queens of Medieval England. Stroud: Tempus, 2000. p. 42.
[59] Anglo-Saxon Chronicles, E, sub anno 1035.

and Leofric's rival, Godwin, earl of Wessex, who forced a compromise that attempted to safeguard Hardacanute's interests.
Harold was at first recognised as regent in England for his half-
brother, but Hardacanute's pre-occupation with a succession of
challenges to Danish power in Scandinavia prevented him from
asserting his authority in England, and when Earl Godwin transferred his allegiance Harold was able to seize the throne and force
Emma into exile. The one significant challenge to Harold's power
came in 1036, when Æðelred II and Emma's son, Edward the
Confessor, left his exile in Normandy and returned to England.
The attempt proved to be a fiasco, and although Edward escaped
from that disaster, his younger brother, Alfred, who appears to
have made a similar bid on his own initiative, was captured and
blinded, dying shortly afterwards from his injuries.[60] Until his
unexpectedly early death in 1040, Harold Harefoot's grip on
England thereafter remained unshaken.[61]

Harold's death left his supporters leaderless, and Hardacanute
was quickly re-accepted as king in England. He and his mother
moved swiftly to establish control, displaying their contempt for
Harold by having his body exhumed and thrown into the Thames,
from which the dead king's supporters recovered and reburied
it.[62] It was an inauspicious start, and the new regime swiftly
further undermined its popularity by imposing a heavy tax on
the kingdom. This fresh levy was used to quadruple the size of the
royal fleet, probably for service against the rebellious
Norwegians.[63] Such moves, coupled with deep suspicion of the
young king's trustworthiness (he had ordered the murder of the
carl of Northumbria while he had been travelling to
Hardacanute's court under a royal safe conduct),[64] saw the
rapid development of a rival political grouping which looked
for leadership to Edward the Confessor. In 1041 Edward returned
from exile, was recognised as Hardacanute's heir and was associated with him in government.[65] The following year, whilst
attending a wedding feast at Lambeth, the twenty-three-year-old
Hardacanute suffered a seizure and died.[66] With him died the
Anglo-Danish kingdom.

---

[60] Ibid., D, *sub anno* 1036; Barlow, *Edward*, pp. 45–46.
[61] *Anglo-Saxon Chronicles*, C, *sub anno* 1040.   [62] Ibid.; Barlow, *Edward*, p. 48.
[63] *Anglo-Saxon Chronicles*, E, *sub anno* 1040 [1041].   [64] Fletcher, *Bloodfeud*, p. 137.
[65] Barlow, *Edward*, pp. 48–49.   [66] *Anglo-Saxon Chronicles*, E, *sub anno* 1041 [1042].

Cumbria, Scotland and England, 1000–1066

It was not just in the heartland of the Anglo-Saxon state that the power of the West Saxon kings faced potent threats in the opening decade of the eleventh century.[67] In northern England the political-military crisis of Æðelred II's government faced a second external threat in the form of the aggressively expansionist and opportunistic Scottish king, Máel Coluim mac Cinaeda. He began his reign with an 'inaugural raid' into Northumbria in 1006.[68] This ended with a crushing defeat at Durham. The victor, Uhtred, was appointed earl of Northumbria, to which King Æðelred added the earldom of York following his assassination of its earl in 1006.[69] The placing of both earldoms in the hands of one man reveals Æðelred's concern for English control north of the Humber. As Anglo-Saxon resistance crumbled before the Danish onslaught led by King Svein, Uhtred's support became vital to Æðelred. To ensure his continued loyalty, Uhtred was given the king's daughter, Ælfgifu, as his wife. This marriage may have proven Uhtred's undoing for, in 1016, as Canute consolidated his hold over England, he had Uhtred executed and replaced at York with his own follower, Eirik of Hlaðir.[70]

The destabilisation of the Pennine zone that this violent coup produced proved to be too powerful a lure for Máel Coluim mac Cinaeda to resist. Uhtred had been succeeded north of the Tees by his younger brother, Eadulf Cudel, who is portrayed in northern tradition as weak and lacking in capability. Eadulf, though, was in an unenviable position, for it is probable that he faced war on all fronts. While York was under the control of Canute's supporters, there is no evidence that the country beyond the Tees had submitted to the new king after Uhtred's murder while attempting to reach an accommodation with him. Eadulf, then, may have faced continuing warfare with Canute's powerful northern supporters. With York now occupied by a hostile Scandinavian earl, he lacked the military resources that had given his brother the ability to check any threats to the Northumbrian heartland. This was demonstrated to

---

[67] The following discussion develops points first presented in R. Oram, *The Lordship of Galloway*. Edinburgh: John Donald, 2000. pp. 29–34.

[68] *The Annals of Ulster (to A.D. 1131)*, ed. and trans. S. Mac Airt and G. Mac Niocaill. Dublin: Dublin Institute for Advanced Studies, 1983. *sub anno* 1005 [1006].

[69] *Anglo-Saxon Chronicles*, E, *sub anno* 1006.   [70] Ibid., D and E, *sub anno* 1016.

devastating effect in 1018, when Máel Coluim and his probable vassal, Ywain, son of Dyfnwal, king of Strathclyde, crushed a Northumbrian army at Carham on the Tweed, an event that was followed by the cession to the Scots of the country north of the river.[71] The defeat was followed by the death of Bishop Aldhun, a key figure in Northumbrian politics, and it appears that Eadulf, too, did not survive for much longer. His successor was Ealdred, the grandson of Bishop Aldhun and son of Earl Uhtred and Ecgfrytha, who evidently continued the resistance to Canute and his men in York.

Máel Coluim capitalised on this continuing upheaval. Welsh tradition records the violent death of Ywain, son of Dyfnwal, some time after 1015, and if the Durham tradition that records his presence at Carham is correct, then it is possible that he had been a casualty of the battle.[72] Ywain was possibly the last of his line, and it appears that his death saw the consolidation of Scottish power over Strathclyde and the beginning of the absorption of the western Southern Upland zone into the kingdom of the Scots. The process was to take over a century, not being completed until the reign of David I, but Canute's pre-occupation with consolidating his hold on the English heartlands and his lands in Scandinavia, and the political weakness of Northumbria after 1016–18, provided the Scots with the opportunity to entrench their power within a zone that kings of the English from the time of Edmund had considered vital to the security of their kingdom. It was not until the early 1030s that Canute was in a position to attempt to redress the shift in the balance of power in the north.[73] Recent arguments have proposed that his primary objective may have been containment of any threat to his authority

---

[71] Symeon of Durham, *De obsessione Dunelmie*. In Simeon of Durham, *Symeonis monachi opera omnia*. Vol. I, *Historia ecclesiae Dunhelmensis. Eadem historia deducta, incerto auctore, usque A.D. MCXLIV. Sequuntur varii tractatus, in quibus de Sancto Cuthberto et Dunelmo agitur. Epistola Symeonis de archiepiscopis Eboraci. Carmen Æolwulfi. Vita S. Bartholomae i. S. Vita Oswaldi regis et martyris.*, ed. T. Arnold. Rerum britannicarum medii aevi scriptores, 75. London: Longman, 1885. p. 218; Symeon of Durham, *Historia Dunelmensis Ecclesia*. In *Symeonis monachi opera*, Vol. I, p. 184; ibid., Vol. II, pp. 155–56.

[72] Symeon of Durham, *Historia Regum*. In *Symeonis monachi opera*, Vol. II, see note 71 above, pp. 155–56; *Annales Cambriae*, ed. J. Williams. London: Longman, Green, Longman, and Roberts, 1860. p. 22.

[73] See the discussion of Canute's motives and timing offered by B. T. Hudson, Knútr and Viking Dublin. *Scandinavian Studies*, Vol. 66 No. 3, 1994, pp. 319–35, and B. E. Crawford, The dedication to St Clement and Rodil, Harris. In *Church, Chronicle and Learning*, pp. 109–22.

in Norway from the rulers of Orkney, rather than rolling back Máel Coluim mac Cinaeda's power in Cumbria, but his campaign of 1031, which achieved the submissions of Máel Coluim, Echmarcach and, possibly, Macbeth (Macbethad mac Findlaích), represented a re-affirmation of English power north of the Humber and, more particularly, over the north-west.[74] From 1029 to 1030 Canute was certainly flexing his muscles in the Irish Sea zone, extending his influence to Dublin, directing campaigns against the Welsh and attempting to install Eirik of Hlaðir's son, Hákon, whom he had already made earl of Worcester, as king in the Hebrides. Hákon's drowning in late 1029 or early 1030 whilst sailing to his new territories via Orkney wrecked this plan and may have forced Canute into more direct action.[75]

Canute's 1031 campaign appears to have been highly successful. Not only did he secure his dominant position in the Irish Sea region and a treaty with the Scottish king, presumably in return for recognition of his possession of Cumbria, but he appears also to have forced Uhtred's son, Ealdred, into submission. That Canute now exercised some authority within Northumbria is supported by the record of his grant of property to Bishop Edmund of Durham.[76] This general settlement held until after the deaths of both Máel Coluim in 1034 and Canute in 1035 but was wrecked in 1038 by the murder of Ealdred. His successor was his half-brother, Eadulf, son of Uhtred and Sige, daughter of Styr, who reverted to the defiance of the Anglo-Danish regime in the south maintained by his family down to 1031. Like his earlier namesake, Eadulf faced challenges from all sides, the first significant threat coming from Donnchad mac Crinain, king of Scots. In 1039 Donnchad invaded Northumbria but, like his grandfather Máel Coluim before him, was heavily defeated at Durham.[77] Eadulf followed his success at Durham with a devastating raid into Strathclyde that may have won him temporary control of Cumberland,[78] but he was pragmatist enough to realise that Northumbria could not maintain

[74] Ibid., p. 112; Hudson, Knútr and Viking Dublin, pp. 319–35; Anglo-Saxon Chronicles, E, sub anno 1031.

[75] Theodricus monachus Nidrosiensi, De regibus vetustis Norvagicis., ed. B. C. Kirchmann and J. Kirchmann. Amsterdam: Apud Jansonio Waesbergios, 1684. sub annis 1028–30. See also the discussion of Canute's policies pp. 195–98.

[76] Symeonis monachi opera, Vol. I, see note 71 above, p. 213.   [77] Ibid., pp. 90–91.

[78] A. A. M. Duncan, Scotland: The Making of the Kingdom. Vol. I, Edinburgh History of Scotland. Edinburgh: Oliver and Boyd, 1975. p. 98.

its position indefinitely and, in 1041, attempted to come to terms with the new Anglo-Danish king, Hardacanute.[79] The king had plans for the country beyond the Humber, and Eadulf figured nowhere in these. On Hardacanute's instructions Eadulf was assassinated by the emerging strongman in the north, Siward, earl of York.

Siward, who had been established at York by Canute in 1033, added Northumbria beyond the Tees to his territories after 1041. From then until his death in 1055 Siward dominated the country north of the Humber, to some extent recreating a Northumbrian hegemony over the Southern Uplands and Cumbria. His position had been strengthened by the political upheavals in Scotland in 1040, which had seen the death of Donnchad at the hands of Macbethad and the flight southwards of the close kinsmen of the dead king. The key figures among the exiles were Donnchad's brother, Maldred, who had married Ealdgith, daughter of Earl Uhtred of Northumbria, and Máel Coluim mac Donnchada, eldest son of the late king. Siward, whose control of the region between the Tees and the Tweed had only recently been secured by marriage to Ælfleda, daughter of Earl Ealdred, now sought to project his authority beyond the limits of his earldom. In 1046 he invaded Scotland and succeeded in temporarily installing a rival – possibly Maldred – to Macbethad as king of Scots.[80] Although Macbethad drove out or killed this rival the same year, it appears that Siward held on successfully to some part of his kingdom, possibly in Cumberland, where Maldred's grandson, Dolfin, was to become a major figure at the end of the century.

Insufficient documentary evidence survives from which to build a chronology for the expansion and consolidation of Siward's power west of the Pennines, but some idea can be obtained of the mechanisms employed. A key figure in the political structure of Cumberland in the mid-eleventh century was a nobleman named Cospatric, who, probably after Siward's death in 1055, issued a writ in favour of one Thorfinn mac Thore concerning land in

[79] Symeonis monachi opera, Vol. II, see note 71 above, p. 198.
[80] Monumenta Germaniae historica inde ab anno Christi quingentesimo usque ad annum millesimum et quingentesimum, ed. G. H. Pertz, G. Waitz, W. Wattenbach, R. Pauli, F. Liebermann, Finnur Jónsson, M. Perlbach, L. V. Heinemann, O. Holder-Egger and A. Hofmeister. Vol. XVIX, Annales ævi suevici. Hanover: Hahn, 1826. p. 508; W. E. Kapelle, The Norman Conquest of the North: The Region and its Transformation, 1000–1135. Chapel Hill: University of North Carolina Press, 1979. pp. 42–43.

Allerdale.[81] The identity of this Cospatric is a matter of some controversy, the two main arguments naming him either as youngest son of Earl Uhtred or the son of Maldred, who was briefly to become earl of Northumbria between 1068 and 1072.[82] Alternatively he may have been the grandson of Bishop Aldhun's daughter, Ecgfrytha, through Sigrida, the daughter of her second marriage to Kilvert, son of Ligulf. Whatever the case, Cospatric was descended from one of the noble lineages of eastern Northumbria. The writ discloses that the lands with which it was concerned 'had been Cumbrian' but had been detached from Cumbrian control some time after 1041, possibly as a result of Eadulf's military operations after the defeat of Donnchad at Durham. The loss of what became Cumberland, however, may have resulted from a property transaction arising from the dynastic conflict in Scotland after 1040. The cession of this highly strategic zone to English control, which would have closed off the natural raiding routes into Siward's Northumbrian and York earldoms via the Tyne Gap and Stanemore, may have been the *quid pro quo* for his support for the cause of Maldred and Máel Coluim. It may be significant that Mael Coluim's father, Donnchad, had possibly held the kingship of the Cumbrians during the lifetime of his grandfather, Máel Coluim mac Cinaeda, although the main evidence for this comes from the late fourteenth-century tradition of John of Fordun.[83] Máel Coluim mac Donnchada, therefore, as his father's heir, may have delivered up to Siward, or formalised his seizure of, this territory as the price for the earl's support.

Further evidence for Siward's control of the Carlisle region is largely circumstantial. The scatter of Danish settlement-names north-westwards from the Vale of York into the Eden Valley and southern Annandale discussed above may represent an eleventh-century development rather than a late ninth- or tenth-century movement. Their spread certainly looks like an effort to control the routes from Strathclyde, Galloway and the wider Solway region into the political and economic heart of Siward's power in Yorkshire. A further indication of York-based influence over this

---

[81] F. E. Harmer, *Anglo-Saxon Writs*. Manchester: Manchester University Press, 1952. pp. 419–24, 531–6.

[82] Kapelle, *The Norman Conquest*, pp. 43–44; Duncan, *Scotland*, p. 98.

[83] W. F. Skene, ed., and F. J. H. Skene, trans. *The Historians of Scotland*. Vol. IV, *John of Fordun's Chronicle of the Scottish Nation*. Edinburgh: Edmonston and Douglas, 1872.

area of southern Cumbria in the mid-eleventh century is the rather garbled ecclesiastical record which states that Archbishop Cynsige of York (1051–60) consecrated two bishops 'of Glasgow' during his episcopate.[84] The consecration of these men, named as Magsuen and John, probably post-dates 1055, when Cynsige received his pallium from Rome, and it has been suggested that their appointment was in some way connected with Siward's invasion of Scotland in the previous year.[85] As in 1046, the invasion of 1054 secured control of the country south of the Forth as a base from which Siward's protégé, Mael Coluim mac Donnchada, was subsequently to launch his successful effort to depose Macbethad in 1056–57.[86] This was a somewhat Pyrrhic victory, for in the battle with Macbethad Siward lost his son by his first marriage, Osbeorn, his nephew, Siward, and a significant number of both his own huscarls (bodyguards) and of a detachment of King Edward's own bodyguard. Another evidently significant English casualty was Dolfin, Finntur's son, whom William Kapelle has identified as Dolfin Thorfinn's son, commander of a contingent from Cumbria.[87] Siward himself died in 1055, and, with his younger son by his second marriage to Ælfleda, Waltheof, probably still under fifteen years of age, the prospect of a continuation of his York-based dynasty collapsed.[88] Siward's successor at York was an outsider, Tosti, son of the powerful Godwin, earl of Wessex.[89] He lacked Siward's entrenched local position and close relationship with Máel Coluim, and it is likely that any York influence over the Scottish Southern Uplands quickly evaporated on the death of Siward. Under such circumstances it is improbable that Archbishop Cynsige could have realistically projected his metropolitan authority into northern Cumbria. This, however, begs the question of a see 'of Glasgow' as opposed to a see 'of Cumbria' at this time, and it is probable that Hugh the Chanter, writer of our source, was basing the political geography of his account on early

[84] J. Raine, ed. The Historians of the Church of York and its Archbishops. Rerum britannicarum medii aevi scriptores, 71. New York: Kraus Reprint, 1965 [1879–84]. p. 52.

[85] N. Shead, The origins of the medieval diocese of Glasgow. Scottish Historical Review, Vol. 48, 1969, pp. 220–21.

[86] Anglo-Saxon Chronicles, C, D, sub anno 1054; Annals of Ulster, sub anno 1054; Chronicle of Maianus Scotus. In B. MacCarthy, The Codex Palatino-Vaticanus. No. 830, Texts, Translations and Indices by B. MacCarthy. Todd lecture series, 3. Dublin: Royal Irish Academy, 1892. sub anno 1057.

[87] Kapelle, The Norman Conquest, p. 47.   [88] Anglo-Saxon Chronicles, D, sub anno 1055.

[89] Barlow, Edward, p. 193.

twelfth-century rather than eleventh-century structures. The twelfth-century partition of the old Cumbrian see into Scottish and English portions, with sees at Glasgow and Carlisle, may offer a partial solution to the problem of where Magsuen and John were based. Siward's control over the Carlisle area was probably more concrete than his influence over Máel Coluim's portion of Cumbria, and it is likely that it was in this area, where the bishops could serve as a further prop to the earl of York's power, that their see was fixed.

Analysis of Siward's activities outside his earldom has focussed almost exclusively on his king-making role in Scotland. The extension of his power into southern Cumbria, however, may have been related to other concerns, primarily the political developments that were taking place within the Irish Sea zone. As a York-based power, it is likely that Siward's authority had marched with the sphere of influence of the archbishop, who governed a trans-Pennine see that embraced south Westmorland and Lancashire. From the time of his establishment as earl of York around 1033 Siward may have been confronted with the repercussions of the shifting balance of power in the northern Irish Sea which his patron, Canute, had set in motion. Canute, for example, had brought Sigtrygg Silkiskegg into his clientage by 1030 and had used this Dublin alliance to good effect in his invasion of north Wales in 1030. This had seen the possible establishment of a Dublin colony on Anglesey, which may have been Sigtrygg's first destination after his final expulsion from Dublin in 1036.[90] This represented only part of a wider projection of Irish-based power eastwards across the Irish Sea. Perhaps the most significant threat to stability was posed by Echmarcach, with whom Canute had established some kind of treaty relationship in 1031. His control of Dublin and Waterford, Man and western Galloway provided him with a formidable powerbase, and it is possible that he may have been considered a potential challenger for control of York itself, where his Uí Ímhair ancestors had ruled as kings. The Solway region constituted a vulnerable point of entry through which Echmarcach could have driven, hence Siward's efforts to control the area. Some indication of his success here may lie in the strong links between eastern Galloway and the churches of Durham and York, links that are evident in the early

[90] Hudson, Knútr and Viking Dublin, pp. 327–35.

twelfth century. The establishment of lasting political control, however, was forestalled by the deaths of both Siward and his adult heir in 1054–55. Within five years of his death, the Northumbrian domain built by Siward had disintegrated.

The end of the Scandinavian dominance of England

It was only in retrospect that the sudden death of the twenty-three-year-old Hardacanute in 1042 came to be seen as marking the end of the Anglo-Scandinavian empire that his father had assembled after 1016. Whilst the English crown passed to Æðelred II's surviving son, Edward the Confessor, there were others who considered themselves to be the more legitimate successor. Chief amongst these were Canute's nephew, Svein Estridsøn, and Magnus Olafsson, king of Norway, with whom Hardacanute had apparently made a pact c. 1038 which stipulated that if either of them died without direct heirs their entire kingdom would pass to the survivor.[91] For Edward, it was the adult Magnus who posed the greater threat, and the danger was compounded by the machinations of his own mother, Queen Emma, who in 1043 was arrested on the king's orders and her property seized. It was later to be claimed that she was scheming on the Norwegian's behalf.[92] Fear of invasion from Norway remained high despite such measures: in 1044 and 1045 Edward himself took command of a fleet intended to counter an expected attack by Magnus.[93] The Norwegian threat came closest to materialising in 1045, when Magnus massed his forces to invade England, but his armada was diverted instead against Svein Estridsøn in Denmark. His successful expulsion of Svein from Denmark heightened the dangers to England, but the unexpected death of the Norwegian king in October 1047 lifted the immediate threat.[94]

That the anticipated Norwegian invasion in the 1040s never occurred should not detract from the perceived reality of the

---

[91] *Anglo-Saxon Chronicles*, D, *sub anno* 1069; D. C. Bates, *William the Conqueror. Kings and Queens of Medieval England*. Stroud: Tempus, 2000. p. 104.

[92] The Anglo-Saxon Chronicle suggests that there were other motives at work, principally a desire to secure control of her wealth, but she was also seen as having 'done less for him than he wished, both before his accession and afterwards' (*Anglo-Saxon Chronicles*, D, *sub anno* 1043); Bates, *William the Conqueror*, pp. 58–59, 76–78.

[93] Ibid., p. 79.   [94] *Anglo-Saxon Chronicles*, D, *sub anno* 1048.

threat at the time. Edward the Confessor certainly recognised the severity of the danger and took active measures to strengthen the defences of his kingdom. His preparations were deemed impressive, and in 1045, when he took his ships to Sandwich, we are told that 'so large a host was gathered there that no man had ever seen a greater naval force in this land'.[95] English military preparedness may have served as a deterrent to some extent, but its impact should not be overstated, for the coast from Kent to Essex was raided extensively in 1048 and Sandwich, where Edward had earlier marshalled his fleet, was sacked.[96] Irish-based Vikings also raided the inner reaches of the Bristol Channel in 1049.[97] Rather than the strength of the English defences, it was the fickleness of fortune that spared the kingdom from invasion in the early years of Edward's reign.

One clear shift in reactions to the threat to England in the period after 1042 was that Edward and his advisors recognised the dangers of treachery from within. This was no simple return to the paranoia of the twilight of Æðelred II's reign, for Emma's behaviour in 1043 had shown that potential security risks existed even at the heart of the royal family. Similar suspicions probably lay behind the expulsion from England in 1044 of Canute II's niece, Gunnhild, and her children; Gunnhild stood in the highest echelons of Anglo-Danish society, and her children had a claim to the various thrones once occupied by her uncle.[98] To some extent Edward's policy was vindicated in the 1060s and 1070s, for it was with the support of disaffected elements within the Anglo-Saxon and Anglo-Norman ruling elites that the last series of Scandinavian bids for the English throne was made.

Into the 1050s the main threat to England came not from Denmark, where Svein Estridsøn was gradually imposing firm rule amidst a protracted war with Magnus Olafsson's successor in Norway, Harald Harðráði, but from Norway. There is some suggestion that Svein may have been effectively Edward's vassal for part of this time, further re-inforcing English security, and that as he established his personal authority in Denmark he was able to rein back on the freedom of his nobles, effectively curbing their traditional raiding activities. In Norway a wholly different

---

[95] Ibid., C, *sub anno* 1045.   [96] Ibid., E, *sub anno* 1048.
[97] Ibid., D, *sub anno* 1050 [1049].
[98] Ibid., *sub anno* 1045; Bates, *William the Conqueror*, pp. 57, 79.

culture prevailed under Harald, who drove out men who would not submit to him and who failed to establish his unchallenged authority over all parts of his predecessor's kingdom. The result was an overspill of violence westwards, with Norwegian exiles active in Orkney and down the western seaboard into Ireland and Wales. Their activities threatened to destabilise the whole of the Irish Sea zone, a region which Æðelred II and Canute II had recognised as the soft underbelly of their kingdom and had accordingly sought to control. For Edward the great expedition into the west led by Harald's son, Magnus, in 1058 probably marked a re-articulation of Norwegian ambitions in the British Isles, possibly stimulated by the growing power of the Godwinsons in England. For Harald of Norway the sons of Earl Godwin of Wessex, and Harold Godwinson in particular, represented a threat to what he saw as his rightful place as Edward's heir. Although the Anglo-Saxon chronicler found the events of Magnus' expedition 'tedious to relate fully', the king saw the threat as sufficiently real to move his Easter court west to Gloucester, where he could be closer to events.[99] As it happened, Magnus Haraldsson's expedition never made a significant landfall in England, but the possibility of a Norwegian invasion continued to loom like a storm cloud on the horizon.

Already by the 1050s the probability of future Scandinavian intervention in England had been heightened by the growing suspicion that the ageing Edward the Confessor was not going to father an heir. Edward used his childlessness as a bargaining tool throughout the 1040s and 1050s, making promises of the succession variously to Harald Harðráði, Svein Estridsøn and, ultimately, William of Normandy, although he presumably reserved the right to bestow the succession elsewhere if he did not himself sire a child. Of course these promises also had the unwelcome consequence of heightening the expectations of the claimants, which would be brought to the fore in the crisis at the end of Edward's reign.

Events moved towards a climax when Tosti Godwinson, the exiled earl of Northumbria, turned to Norway to seek allies in a bid to regain his lost earldom. Tosti was an opportunist who first made an approach in autumn 1065 to his brother-in-law, the count of Flanders, and to the Danes. Then, following a failed

[99] Ibid., pp. 200–201; *Anglo-Saxon Chronicles*, D, *sub anno* 1058.

invasion of England in the early summer of 1066 and a brief spell in Scotland, he finally turned to Harald Harðráði for military aid. What finally prompted this move to Norway was the death in early January 1066 of the English king and the acclamation as his successor of Tosti's elder brother, Harold, for Tosti expected that Harald of Norway would stage his long-expected bid for the English throne. For Harald the arrival of this Anglo-Saxon exile must have appeared a heaven-sent gift, because Tosti opened a chink in the armour of English political unity against external threat that the late Edward had maintained since the early 1040s. Harald, however, had not simply been waiting for Tosti to act but had spent the summer months assembling the force that he planned to use to unseat Harold Godwinson from the English throne. Harald's invasion force crossed the North Sea late in the summer of 1066 and assembled in Orkney, where Earls Paul and Erlend submitted to him and added their strength to his army. From Orkney the fleet headed for Northumbria, arriving off the coast of Cleveland in early September.[100] After raiding down the Cleveland coast and burning Scarborough, Harald rounded Holderness into the Humber, and on 18 September he landed his army in England. Moving swiftly from a base at Riccall towards York, Harald was intercepted outside the city at Gate Fulford by the local *fyrd* commanded by the brothers Morcar, earl of Northumbria, and Edwin, earl of Mercia. In a bloody battle in the marshland by the River Ouse on 20 September, where 'the dead were piled up so thickly that the Norwegians could cross the swamp dryshod', Harald's army crushed that of Edwin and Morcar, and York prepared to surrender to the Norwegian king.[101]

Four days later Harald, who had expected to receive the submission of the city and hostages from the Northumbrians, was surprised by the arrival instead outside York of a new English army commanded by his rival, Harold Godwinson. Having left a large part of their own army, including Paul and Erlend, to guard the ships, Harald and Tosti had come to Stamford Bridge on the River Derwent east of York unprepared for battle, many of the warriors not even bearing their full equipment.[102] In the resulting carnage both men and the majority of the Norwegian army were

---

[100] *King Harald's Saga.* In *Heimskringla,* see note 13 above, Chapter 83.
[101] Ibid., Chapters 84–5.   [102] Ibid., Chapter 87.

slaughtered. The survivors, led by Harald's son Olaf, escaped to the ships and, having secured a truce from Harold, returned to Orkney, where they over-wintered. The following year Olaf and his brother, Magnus, asked for and obtained their father's body for reburial at home.[103]

Stamford Bridge was a crushing blow to Norse power. Neither of Harald's sons entertained any serious thoughts of reviving their father's claim to England despite the destruction of Anglo-Saxon military power at Hastings in October 1066 and the fragility of William of Normandy's hold on the kingdom down to 1069. Even had they considered such a move, their kingdom's military resources had been so depleted that it took almost a generation to recover from the slaughter of its warrior elite outside York. It was only in the 1090s that Olaf's son, Magnus III Barelegs, could seek to re-assert his grandfather's lordship over the Norse western colonies in the British Isles and contemplate mounting a challenge to Norman rule in England. In the generation after Stamford Bridge it was Harald Harðráði's old rival, Svein Estridsøn of Denmark, and his son, Canute IV Sveinsson, the later St Canute, who constituted the gravest threat to the Anglo-Norman realm.

In the first years of his reign in England William the Conqueror attempted to rule in the tradition of the late Saxon kings and to accommodate the surviving Anglo-Saxon leadership within his new regime.[104] William at first lacked the resources to impose a new military regime over the whole of the kingdom, and his powerbase in the north was especially weak. Beyond the Humber he was utterly dependent on the fickle loyalties of the native nobility, headed by Earl Cospatric of Northumbria. His policy was aimed at the integration of the new Norman elite with the old Anglo-Saxon aristocracy, and native lords enjoyed considerable favour at his court. This attempt to blend together the conquered and the conquerors failed utterly, brought to ruin in 1068–69 by the first of a series of rebellions by the native leadership which aimed at the expulsion of the Normans from England. In autumn 1068 much of the country beyond the Humber rose in

---

[103] Anderson, *Early Sources of Scottish History*, Vol. II, p. 18; *King Harald's Saga*. In *Heimskringla*, see note 13 above, Chapters 98–9.

[104] For a discussion of William's policy in the late 1060s, see Bates, *William the Conqueror*, pp. 99–103, 155–59.

support of Edgar Æðeling, the last male representative of the House of Wessex. William was forced to return to England from Normandy and conduct a winter campaign through Yorkshire. By April 1069 the northern rebellion had effectively collapsed and its leaders fled, but the threat to William's hold on England had not been lifted.[105] William had probably been long aware that disaffected elements within England had been in negotiations with foreign powers hostile to Normandy, and rumour had been rife that the Danish king, Svein Estridsøn, was considering an attempt to gain the throne which he claimed had been promised to him by Edward the Confessor several times and to which, as a kinsman of Canute the Great, he considered he had a legitimate right. In the summer of 1069 Svein Estridsøn at last made his move.

William clearly recognised the seriousness of the Danish threat to his position, for Svein was a formidable ruler who had successfully imposed his authority on Denmark and reconstructed its military potential. It is a sign of how gravely William viewed the situation in England in 1069 that he remained in the kingdom until late in 1070, the longest continuous period he was there of his entire reign. His concern was not misplaced. Early in the autumn a fleet reported as 240 ships in number arrived off the Kent coast and probed the defences of south-east England. Commanded by two of Svein's sons – Harald (Hen) and (the later St) Canute – and his younger brother, Osbern, it was a major fleet but it may simply have been intended by the king to secure a beachhead for his own later arrival. Moving up the east coast, it entered the Humber and made rendezvous with the English rebels led by Edgar Æðeling, Earl Cospatric and Waltheof, son of Earl Siward of York. Together they advanced on York and on 20 September captured the city, slaughtering William's garrison.[106] With the country beyond the Humber firmly under their control, the Danes crossed the estuary and established a fortified base on the island of Axholme, from which they extended their operations into northern Lincolnshire. Danish policy appears to have been to draw on the reserves of the northern English rebels while at the same time seeking to exploit any residual pro-Scandinavian sympathies amongst the population of Yorkshire. By focussing their strength beyond the Humber,

---

[105] Anglo-Saxon Chronicles, D, sub annis 1068, 1069.
[106] Ibid., sub anno 1069; Bates, William the Conqueror, p. 104.

however, William's enemies allowed him to effectively seal them off from his own centres of power in southern England. Moving from containment to neutralisation William advanced and forced the Danes to abandon Axholme and return to Yorkshire. Pushing beyond the Humber William then forced his enemies to abandon York, and by late December 1069 the Danish army, forced back to its ships on the Humber, was in dire straits, desperately short of supplies and unable to take to the sea to withdraw. Rather than risk everything in battle, Svein's sons negotiated a settlement whereby, for a hefty cash bribe and permission to forage for supplies over the winter months, they would leave England in the spring.[107] Confident of having dealt with the foreign threat, William proceeded to ravage northern England in the winter campaign known as the Harrying of the North, a brutal and systematic devastation which crippled the region economically and cut the ground from beneath the feet of the northern rebels.

Far from withdrawing from England in the spring, the Danes, now re-inforced by the arrival of Svein in person, shifted their focus to a new centre of rebellion against William. Moving south from the Humber Svein entered the Wash and landed part of his army. Pushing deep into Cambridgeshire they seized and fortified the Isle of Ely, where they were quickly re-inforced by the local Anglo-Saxon leadership. Chief amongst these was Hereward 'the Wake', a south Lincolnshire thegn (a middle-ranking nobleman), who although socially prominent was hardly representative of the top-most ranks of native society.[108] The failure of the rising to spread more widely, even amongst the Anglo-Scandinavian population of East Anglia, may have persuaded Svein that he had embarked on a venture that would be too costly in terms of manpower and resources to pursue. When William offered to negotiate Svein was ready to come to terms and, probably having swallowed another substantial cash bribe, the Danish king withdrew his men and left England.[109]

After the failure of Svein's invasion and the suppression of the revolts in England, William the Conqueror's grip on the English throne was tightened immeasurably. Svein had ruled for more than twenty-seven years and may have had other more pressing afffairs to deal with on the continent. During this period he was

---

[107] Ibid., pp. 218–20. [108] Ibid., pp. 221–22.
[109] Ibid., p. 222; *Anglo-Saxon Chronicles*, D, *sub anno* 1070.

engaged in securing the liberty of the Danish kingdom by political and religious means. A crucial part of his policy was the reorganisation of the Danish church, which depended on his appointment of English clerics to Danish dioceses in contravention of the rights of Hamburg-Bremen, who were strong supporters of the Imperial party. In fact, the archbishop of the diocese was one of the Imperial regents. It is probably in this context that Svein met Adam of Bremen, who appears to have visited southern Scandinavia sometime between 1068 and 1070. Svein may also have recognised that in 1070 William's position was well-nigh unshakeable, and, weighing his options, he calculated that he would not benefit from pursuing the claims that he had so regularly rehearsed in the past. His death in 1074, however, did not bring an end to the ambitions of his family, for in Denmark Canute Sveinsson now saw himself as heir to Canute II's Anglo-Scandinavian realm. As a young man he had participated in his father's 1069–70 invasion of eastern England, which had sought to capitalise on Anglo-Saxon revolts against their new Norman overlords. That attempt had ended in defeat when the rebels failed to make headway against the Norman military machine, but when in 1075 Canute Sveinsson was approached for aid by the leaders of a new rebellion against William the Conqueror, amongst whose number was Waltheof, earl of Northumbria, the son of Siward of York, and Ralph de Gael, earl of Norfolk, the prospect of the commitment of disaffected Anglo-Saxon and Norman nobles to his cause may have seemed to promise a better chance of success.[110] With the support of his elder brother, Harald III, Canute assembled a large invasion fleet, but by the time he arrived off the Norfolk coast the rebels in East Anglia had been defeated. Canute then headed north and entered the Humber estuary, presumably believing that he would find support in and around York. William's grip on the country north of the Humber, however, was tightening progressively, and even the independently minded Anglo-Scandinavian population of Yorkshire had been so effectively cowed by his ruthless military campaigns through their territories in the winter of 1069–70 that they failed to rally to Canute. The invasion force, however, had been gathered with the promise of the plunder of England and,

[110] Ibid., *sub anno* 1075. For the background to the revolt, see Bates, *William the Conqueror*, pp. 231–33.

with no other resources available to him to pay it, Canute unleashed his men on York, which was systematically ransacked.[111] It was hardly a move that would endear the Dane to his potential subjects and served rather to undermine further the remaining reserves of pro- Scandinavian sympathies in the north of England. Having achieved nothing of substance, Canute returned to Denmark.

Despite the setback of 1075 Canute continued to cherish ambitions for the English throne. Such was the antipathy towards William of Normandy from other regional rulers that Canute had little difficulty in finding allies. Chief amongst these was Count Robert of Flanders, a bitter rival of the Normans, and an alliance between Robert and Canute was sealed c. 1080 by the marriage of Canute to Robert's daughter, Adela.[112] That same year Harald III died, and Canute succeeded him as king of Denmark. With the resources of the kingdom behind him he could turn his focus once again towards England, but it was not until 1085 that he revived his claim to the English crown. In the intervening period, Canute had implemented wide-ranging fiscal reforms in an effort to boost royal revenue.[113] These measures were deeply unpopular at all levels in Danish society, and when he began to gather his invasion force in the Limfjord in 1085 the depths of that unpopularity began to make themselves apparent. Delayed by the threat of an invasion of Denmark by the Emperor, the fleet and army became the focus of opposition to Canute. In the summer of 1086 Canute fled in the face of the rebels, only to be cornered and murdered in St Alban's church at Odense.[114] With him died the last Danish ambitions towards the restoration of Canute II's Anglo-Danish empire, for the horizons of his successors lay in other directions. His death was not quite the 'final end of the Viking Age in England' that some have suggested,[115] for Norwegian royal fleets continued to cause

[111] *Anglo-Saxon Chronicles*, D, *sub anno* 1075. The chronicler records as divine judgement the deaths of those who had despoiled the Minster.
[112] Bates, *William the Conqueror*, p. 346.
[113] I. Skovgaard-Petersen, Oldtid og vikingetid. In *Danmarks historie*. Vol. I, *Tiden indtil 1340*, exec. ed. A. E. Christensen, H. P. Clausen, Svend Ellehøj and Søren Mørch. Copenhagen: Gyldendal, 1980. pp. 246–48.
[114] Bates, *William the Conqueror*, p. 356.
[115] A. E. Christensen, Tiden 1042–1241. In *Danmarks historie*, Vol. I, see note 113 above, pp. 246–47; J. Haywood, *Encyclopaedia of the Viking Age*. London: Thames & Hudson, 2000. p. 47.

alarums and excursions at the Norman court down to 1101 (see
pp. 238–40), and as late as 1152 King Eystein of Norway led a
plundering raid down the east coast of Britain, sacking Aberdeen,
Hartlepool and Whitby and raiding the coastlands of
Yorkshire.[116] Eystein's raid, however, was bent on plunder, not
conquest, and it is with this return to the spirit of the first Viking
onslaught that the English Viking Age finally closed. Elsewhere
in Britain, however, Scandinavian military power remained a
potent threat for over a century more.

[116] *Ingi's Saga*. In *Heimskringla*, see note 13 above, Chapter 20.

CHAPTER 8

The Irish Sea

Olaf Cuarán ruled as king of both Dublin and York.[1] His intermittent reign at Dublin spanned four decades from 941 to 980 and witnessed the consolidation of the Norse colonies around the Irish Sea.[2] It also, however, saw revived Gaelic Irish activity within this zone of Scandinavian settlement for the first time in about a century and closed as new Norse and Danish powers encroached on the region. Olaf's departure for York in 940 to aid his cousin, Olaf Guthfrithsson, coincided with renewed Hebridean raids on Ireland: 941 saw a raid on Downpatrick by Islesmen.[3] It may have been such raids that stirred Muirchertach mac Niall, king of Ailech, to stage a naval expedition into the Hebrides that year.[4] The events of 941 marked the beginning of a new trend: the intrusion of Hebridean- and Orkney-based powers into the Irish Sea basin. It is even possible that Eirik Bloodaxe used control of Orkney to master the Hebridean colonies in the early 950s.[5] He could not use this position, however, to win control of the Scandinavian colonies in Ireland.

---

[1] The following discussion is developed from R. Oram, *The Lordship of Galloway*. Edinburgh: John Donald, 2000. pp. 9–12.

[2] See A. P. Smyth, *Scandinavian York and Dublin: The History and Archaeology of Two Related Viking Kingdoms*. Vol. II. Dublin: Humanities Press/Templekieran Press, 1979. Chapter 6.

[3] *The Annals of Ulster (to A.D. 1131)*, ed. and trans. S. Mac Airt and G. Mac Niocaill. Dublin: Dublin Institute for Advanced Studies, 1983. *sub anno* 941.

[4] J. O'Donovan, ed. and trans. *Annálaríoghachta Éireann; Annals of the Kingdom of Ireland by the Four Masters, from the Earliest Period to the Year 1616; Edited from MSS. in the Library of the Royal Irish Academy and of Trinity College, Dublin, with a Translation, and Copious Notes*. Dublin, 1851. *sub anno* 939 = 940.

[5] B. E. Crawford, *Scandinavian Scotland. Scotland in the Early Middle Ages*. Leicester: Leicester University Press, 1987. p. 61.

Ireland, Man and the Isles c. 950–c. 1000

After the Eirikssons' departure from Orkney, there is little clear evidence for the political structure of the Western, as opposed to the Northern, Isles until the 980s. There are indications, however, that the late 960s and early 970s had seen the emergence of a powerful kingship in the Hebrides that may have been flexing its muscles further to the south. This may have been one of the factors behind the assembly of a fleet at Chester in 973 by the English king, Edgar.[6] According to the Anglo-Saxon Chronicle account of this event, six (un-named) kings came there, submitted to him and swore 'to be his fellow workers by sea and land'. In later Worcester tradition one of the kings, named 'Maccus', was lord of 'very many islands', a description that is strongly suggestive of a Hebridean base. Who this 'Maccus' was is unknown, but his name may be a garbled form of a Norse name. In this context, the M[agnus?] Haraldsson who raided the monastery of Inishcathy (Scattery Island in the Shannon) in 974, accompanied by 'the Lawmen of the Islands', evidently as part of a wider conflict with the Ostmen of Limerick whose king had taken refuge there, presents himself as a candidate.[7]

Haraldsson appears to have extended his influence south from the Hebrides into the northern Irish Sea basin in the 960s. In 969 and 970 he is named as Macht or Mact – and his younger brother and successor in the kingship, Godred Haraldsson, invaded Anglesey, perhaps establishing lordship over the small but economically important Scandinavian colony established there.[8] The Haraldssons' power was presumably based on control of the increasingly important trade routes that ran north through the Irish Sea and Hebrides from Dublin and Biscay. To secure these routes they had probably established lordship over the Scandinavian colonies of western Galloway, there being no record of conflict on the Ulster coast that might otherwise have

---

[6] *The Anglo-Saxon Chronicles*, ed. and trans. M. J. Swanton. London: Phoenix, 2000. E, *sub anno* 97; Florence of Worcester. In D. Whitelock, ed. *English Historical Documents*. Vol. I, *English Historical Documents, c. 500–1042*, gen. ed. D. C. Douglas. London: Eyre and Spottiswoode, 1955. *sub anno* 973.

[7] O'Donovan, *Annálaríoghachta Éireann*, *sub anno* 972 = 974. 'Ostmen' was the term used for the 'Norse' inhabitants of Dublin, Limerick, Cork, Waterford, Wexford and Drogheda.

[8] A. O. Anderson, ed. *Early Sources of Scottish History, A.D. 500 to 1286*, Vol. I. Edinburgh and London: Oliver and Boyd, 1922. pp. 478–9 and note.

indicated an effort to dominate the western flank of the North Channel bottleneck. There is, likewise, no evidence for conflict with Olaf Cuarán's Dublin, for whom the security of trade along the western British sea-lanes may have been more important. Indeed, the fact that Olaf chose, following his crushing defeat at Tara in 980 by Máel Sechnaill mac Domnaill, to retire to Iona,[9] the re-emergent spiritual heart of the Hebrides, is an indication of his affiliation with the Isles.

The renaissance of Iona's influence along the western sea-ways is one indication of the spread of Hebridean Norse power in the later tenth century. Although heavily influenced by local Scandinavian culture, as the fine tenth- and early eleventh-century sculptures from the monastic site indicate,[10] this was still an Irish-style community, cultivating Gaelic saints and participating in the wider religious life of Gaelic Scotland and Ireland through its place within the Columban *familia*. The establishment of churches dedicated to Columban saints, particularly to individuals active after the mid-seventh-century decline in the fortunes and prestige of Iona, gives some indication of the revival under Scandinavian patronage. In Galloway, where the strong Northumbrian ties of the local church were hardly conducive to the establishment of the cult of later Columban saints before the tenth century, dedications to Ionan saints may signal a political re-orientation, at least on the part of the Scandinavian colonists (Figure 43).

Dedications to Columban saints, such as Colman at Buittle, Urr and Colmonell in Carrick, Aed mac Bricc at Kirkmabreck, Bride at Blaiket, Cormac at Kirkcormack and Cummène at Kirkcolm, display a striking correlation in distribution to the main zones of Scandinavian settlement noted above, particularly to the zone around Kirkcudbright. The Cummène dedication alone lies remote from the concentrations of Norse settlement-names, being located on the eastern side of the Rhinns.

---

[9] *Annals of Ulster, sub anno 979 [980]; The Annals of Tigernach, Being Annals of Ireland, 807 B.C. to A.D. 1178*, ed. W. Stokes. *Revue Celtique*, pp. 16, 17, 18, 342. Paris: Librairie Emile Bouillon (Off-prints), 1895–97.

[10] Crawford, *Scandinavian Scotland*, p. 178 and fig. 67; for detailed discussions of the monuments on Iona, see Royal Commission on the Ancient and Historical Monuments of Scotland, *Argyll: An Inventory of the Ancient Monuments. Vol. IV, Iona*. Edinburgh: Royal Commission on the Ancient and Historical Monuments of Scotland, 1982.

Figure 43
Hammerhead cross, Whithorn, Wigtownshire. By the later tenth century the Scandinavian colonies in Galloway had probably adapted the Christianity of their host culture. Church dedications to Irish and southern Hebridean saints in Carrick and Galloway point towards a close association between the Norse in south-west Scotland and the Isles. Crosses of this form are characteristic of the period and have been found at several centres of Norse settlement in the region.

Significantly, however, the western side of the medieval parish of Kirkcolm, which straddles the peninsula, bears the name of The Airies (Summer Pastures), which may indicate settlement by Hebridean *Gall-Ghaedhil*, and the whole of the peninsula was integrated in the eleventh century into the Isles-based domain of King Echmarcach.

Six years after the death of Olaf Cuarán at Iona, the monastery was plundered and the abbot and fifteen senior monks slain.[11] The Annals of Ulster linked the attack with an account of a raid by 'Danes' on the shores of Dál Riada, an event that heralded a new phase in the struggle for domination of the Hebridean and Irish Sea zone. In 987 Godred Haraldsson was attacked in Man by 'Danes' and drove them off with heavy casualties while, in what appears to have been a separate action, the 'Danes' who had attacked Iona the previous Christmas were slaughtered.[12] Continuing disturbances in the Isles culminated in 989 with Godred's death at the hands of the men of Argyll.[13] Barbara Crawford has pointed out the link between the 987 attack on Man and the account in *Njal's Saga* of Kari Solmundarson's fight with King Godred/Gofraid and taking of plunder from the island, and has argued that the term 'Dane' has been used simply to

---

[11] *The Annals of Inisfallen (MS. Rawlinson B.503)*, ed. and trans. S. Mac Airt. Dublin: Dublin Institute for Advanced Studies, 1951. *sub anno* 986; *Annals of Ulster, sub anno* 986.
[12] *Ibid., sub anno* 987.   [13] *Annals of Tigernach*.

denote 'pirates'.[14] The aggressors in these actions appear to have been Orcadians under the leadership of Sigurd the Stout, earl of Orkney, who according to saga tradition had established his domination of the Hebrides in the 980s, ruling through a vassal-earl, 'Gilli'.[15] Sigurd, until his forced conversion to Christianity in 995 by Olaf Tryggvason, king of Norway, was aggressively pagan, hence his readiness to target – and shed blood at – the monastery that had become the spiritual focus of the Christianised Hebridean Norse (Figure 44).

Orkney influence, according to saga tradition, extended to Man. Here Godred had been succeeded by his son, Ragnall, who was to reign until 1005.[16] Orcadian domination of the western sea-ways may initially have been less attractive to the Dublin Norse under their new king, Sigtrygg Silkiskegg, younger son of Olaf Cuarán. By the early 990s the Ostmen cities were showing signs of favouring the new high-status interlopers from Norway and Denmark, Olaf Tryggvason and Svein Forkbeard, both of whom made raids on Man c. 995.[17] The late tradition of *Orkneyinga Saga* narrates how Olaf had married a sister of Olaf Cuarán of Dublin, an account dismissed by Anderson as romantic and unhistorical but perhaps preserving a memory of an early bid by the king of Dublin to gain control of Man and extend by proxy his influence over the Irish Sea trade routes.[18] Olaf also, however, may have been preparing the ground for himself, for it was in the western colonies that he raised the army and fleet with which he sailed for Norway to reclaim his father's throne, stopping off in Orkney to receive Sigurd's submission.[19] Olaf's success in securing support within the Isles and the Scandinavian colonies around the Irish Sea was evidently a cause for concern in

---

[14] Crawford, *Scandinavian Scotland*, p. 66; *Njal's Saga*, ed. and trans. M. Magnusson and H. Pálsson. Penguin Classics. London: Penguin Books, 1960. pp. 183–84. 196.

[15] *Njal's Saga*, pp. 182, 341.   [16] *Annals of Ulster*, sub anno 1005.

[17] B. T. Hudson, Knútr and Viking Dublin. *Scandinavian Studies*, Vol. 66 No. 3, 1994, pp. 320–21; *Heimskringla: History of the Kings of Norway*, trans. L. M. Hollander. Austin: Published for the American-Scandinavian Foundation by the University of Texas Press, 1964. Chapter 30.

[18] *Orkneyinga Saga: The History of the Earls of Orkney*, trans. Hermann Pálsson and P. Edwards. London: Hogarth Press, 1978. Chapter 12; Anderson, *Early Sources of Scottish History*, Vol. I, p. 506, note 2.

[19] *Olaf Tryggvi's Son's Saga*, Chapter 47; *Flateyiarbók*, i, 229; and *St Olaf's Saga*, Chapter 96. In *Heimskringla*, see note 17 above.

Figure 44
St Audoen's Church, Dublin. Although Dublin's rulers remained aggressively pagan until the later tenth century, Christianity had taken root amongst their people in the early 900s. St Audoen's, dedicated to St Ouen, the seventh-century bishop of Rouen and patron of Dublin's Norman conquerors, was built after 1190 on the site of an older church dedicated to St Columba, an association that underscored the strong connections between Dublin and the Hebrides in the tenth and eleventh centuries.

England, which had been on the receiving end of the Norwegian's attentions since 991. Olaf Tryggvason withdrew to Norway, where he was killed in 1000. In the same year Æðelred II staged a major offensive against Cumbria, presumably to neutralise the Scandinavian colonies around the Solway, while his fleet, which had originally been intended to act in concert with his army, operating out of Chester, raided Man.[20] In the event the western colonies were to play no significant part in Svein Forkbeard's

[20] *Anglo-Saxon Chronicles*, E, *sub anno* 1000.

plans for the conquest of England; they were to become caught up instead in a protracted struggle for control of the commercial wealth of the Irish Sea routes and the military wealth it generated.

Even as the Scandinavian era in southern mainland Britain was drawing to its bloody climax at Stamford Bridge, the fate of the Norse western colonies was being bound ever closer to political developments in Ireland and Scotland. By the middle of the eleventh century there was very little about these colonies that was still distinctively culturally Scandinavian, for the processes of intermarriage and exchange that had been under way since the early tenth century between natives and colonists had brought about their integration into the Gaelic world of Scotland and Ireland. Irish chroniclers might still preserve a notion of difference between the inhabitants of Dublin and the other former longphort settlements and the indigenous population of the island, and the folk of Dublin could seek to maintain their distinctiveness by maintaining old links or forging new bonds – political and ecclesiastical – outside Ireland, but notions of separateness extended little deeper than the labelling of their citizens as the 'Ostmen' or 'Gaill' to distinguish them from the Gaedhil amongst whom they dwelt. As the events of the first half of the eleventh century had demonstrated in Ireland, the Norse settlements had been drawn into a relationship that was at first symbiotic with, then purely dependent on, the Irish kingdoms in whose midst they had been planted. Control of the economic and military potential of the former Viking bases gave the kings of Munster and Leinster distinct advantages in the seemingly endless internecine conflicts between the native rivals for dominance of their island. There is some irony that one factor that may have contributed to the eclipse of the Uí Néills' centuries-old political hegemony in Ireland may have been their success in ensuring that no Scandinavian community succeeded in putting down permanent roots within their northern heartlands, whilst their southern rivals had been forced to endure the fixing of predatory bases around their coasts. Gradual acceptance of the presence of these parasitic communities turned slowly to dominance, and by the eleventh century Munster and Leinster had come to vie for control of the greatest prize, Dublin. But Irish eyes were fixed on a goal beyond possession of Dublin alone, for through control of that city Irish kings could project their power into the western sea-ways that for over two centuries had been the preserve of Scandinavian rulers. It was an ambition that would bring them into collision with other expansionist powers.

Irish renaissance

By the 980s and 990s native Irish potentates were projecting their authority into the once Norse-controlled Irish Sea region.[21] At the dawn of the eleventh century Irish provincial kings were exercising an increasing domination of the rich trading towns that had grown out of the longphort settlements of the ninth century. Despite the Irish annals' artificial separation of their world into distinct spheres of *Gaedhil* and *Gall*, it was evident that there had been, and would continue to be, a remarkable degree of integration of the Norse into Irish native society and culture. Such integration was an unmistakable feature of the reign of Sigtrygg Silkiskegg, king of Dublin from c. 989 to 1036, who was the son of Olaf Cuarán and the Leinster princess Gormflaith ingen Murchada. After Olaf died in 981 Gormflaith married in turn Máel Sechlainn II and Brian Bóruma, which gave her son links with the Uí Néill high kings and their Munster rivals. Such ties, however, did not bring Sigtrygg political security, and in 995 he was driven temporarily from Dublin by his kinsman Ímar of the Uí Ímair of Waterford; then, in 1000, he was forced to submit to Brian Bóruma. Dublin remained under Munster overlordship until 1013, when Sigtrygg rebelled in alliance with his maternal uncle, Máelmorda mac Murchada, king of Leinster.

Munster and Leinster interest in Dublin was driven by the simple aim of controlling the wealth and the military and naval resources of the greatest trade centre in Ireland. Control of Dublin was seen as the key to swinging the balance of power decisively in one direction in the seemingly endless struggle to secure the symbolic status of high king of Ireland. Sigtrygg, however, was determined not to be simply swallowed by either his Leinster ally or his Munster rival, and actively courted alliances with other Scandinavian colonies around the Irish Sea and in the Hebrides, and also sought the aid of the powerful Orkney

[21] The following discussion develops points first made in Oram, *Lordship*, pp. 12–18.

earl Sigurd the Stout. It is grossly inaccurate, however, to portray this quest for allies as one Scandinavian power seeking aid from another, for, like Sigtrygg, Sigurd was a man with Gaelic-Irish, Leinster ancestry, his mother being Eithne, daughter of Cerball, son of Lorcán, son of Donnchad, the heir to Leinster. Despite later Irish tradition, best represented in the twelfth-century account known as *Cogadh Gaedhel re Gallaibh* (The War of the Irish with the Foreigners), which presents the conflict in strictly ethnic terms, partly with the aim of inflating the role of the Uí Briain dynasty as saviours of Ireland from the Norse yoke, the struggle in the early eleventh century was between native Irish rivals for the political domination of Ireland and the Gaelic world generally. Although still perceived as a distinct element within Ireland, the Scandinavian colonies had become fully integrated with the political, economic and cultural life of their host society.

Sigtrygg found his allies. Sigurd and the others were drawn to aid the Dublin king by more than just the promise of plunder that the *Cogadh* implies. The growing influence in the late tenth and early eleventh centuries of Brian Bóruma, king of Munster, cannot but have been felt in Galloway and in the kingdom of Man and the Isles. Brian's triumphal visit to Armagh in 1005 had confirmed his exercise of the high-kingship which he had wrested in 1002 from the former Uí Néill high king, Máel Sechnaill mac Domnaill.[22] We can see how he viewed his own power at that time from the description of him in the *Book of Armagh* as *Imperator Scotorum*, 'emperor of the Gaels'.[23] Too much can be read into the title, but it is possible that Brian was voicing a claim to the headship of all *Gaedhil*, in Scotland as well as Ireland. Brian could already project his power far beyond his homeland in Munster by sea as well as land, for he controlled Limerick and Waterford and, intermittently from 981 and more or less permanently from 999 to 1013, Dublin. The Norse galleys greatly enhanced Brian's military capacity, as he demonstrated in 1005 when he led a host round the coasts of the north of Ireland.[24]

The threat from Munster lay behind the support offered to Sigtrygg Silkiskegg in 1014 from the rulers of the Isles and

---

[22] S. Duffy, *Ireland in the Middle Ages*. British History in Perspective. New York: St. Martin's Press, 1997. pp. 33–34; *Annals of Ulster, sub anno* 1004 [1005].
[23] Duffy, *Ireland in the Middle Ages*, p. 34.   [24] *Annals of Ulster, sub anno* 1005.

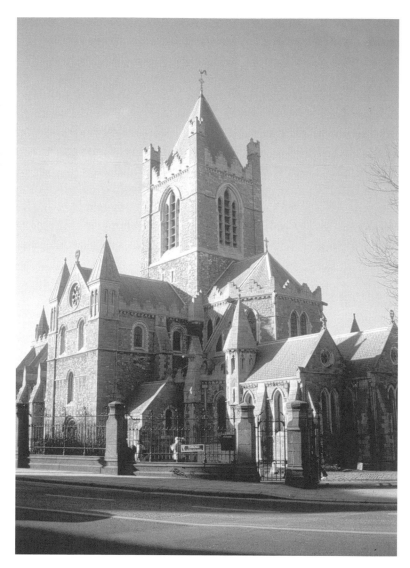

Figure 45
Christchurch Cathedral, Dublin. Although they had become integrated into Irish political and cultural life by the later tenth century, the rulers of Dublin sought to preserve an idea of their separate identity. One aspect of this was the establishment of a separate bishopric of Dublin in the eleventh century, free of any ties to the native Irish church and looking instead to Anglo-Scandinavian England and the Church of Canterbury for its lead.

Galloway (Figure 45).[25] Presented in the *Cogadh* as the climax of a 200-year-long war between Gaedhil and Gaill for mastery of Ireland, the struggle that culminated in the bloody battle of Clontarf on 23 April 1014 was driven more by economic than political ambitions. Certainly, Sigurd's alliance with Sigtrygg was probably conditioned more by a desire to re-establish control of the commercial traffic along the western sea-ways that Orkney

[25] *The Annals of Loch Cé: A Chronicle of Irish Affairs from A.D. 1014 to A.D. 1590*, ed. and trans. W. M. Hennessy. Rerum britannicarum medii ævi scriptores, 54. London: Stationery Office, 1871. *sub anno* 1014.

had held in the 990s than to impose his lordship over the Irish. In the end, both Sigurd and Brian perished in the battle and, whilst Munster's power was seriously weakened by the loss of its dynamic ruler, Orkney's dominance of the western sea-lanes was thrown into dramatic decline (see below). Ironically, while Sigtrygg enjoyed a brief period of revived freedom of action, he also proved in the long term to be a casualty of the battle.

The death of Brian Bóruma at Clontarf created a power vacuum in the Irish Sea zone which others were quick to exploit. One such figure was Canute, king of Denmark and England, whose leadership of the Scandinavian world gave unique influence over the western colonies and whose control of their commercial arteries gave an economic edge to political domination. His death in 1035 was followed by a series of upheavals in the Irish Sea region, not all of which were co-incidental on the demise of the dominant figure in British politics. The removal of his strong hand unleashed a domino effect of consequential events. One immediate consequence of the contraction of Anglo-Danish influence was a re-assertion of Dublin's independence, signalled in 1035 by Sigtrygg Silkiskegg's revival of conflict with the Ostmen kings of Waterford, a dynasty which may itself have been a branch of the Uí Ímhair of Dublin, descended from Olaf Cuarán. Rivalry between these Ostmen cities had climaxed in 982, when Sigtrygg's elder brother and predecessor as king of Dublin, Glúniarainn, in alliance with his half-brother and brother-in-law the Ua Néill high king, Máel Sechnaill mac Domnaill, had defeated Ímar of Waterford and his ally or overlord, Domnall Cloen, king of Leinster, killing Ímar's son, Gilla-Pátraic.[26] In 993 the hostility had been renewed by Sigtrygg and Ímar's son, Ragnall, and apparently ended with Sigtrygg's temporary expulsion from Dublin and the killing of Ragnall by the Leinstermen.[27] Forty-two years later Sigtrygg killed Ragnall mac Ragnaill, king of Waterford, in Dublin and triggered the final crisis of his long and turbulent reign.[28] The following year Sigtrygg's reign ended in deposition, exile and death.

[26] *Annals of Ulster, sub anno 982.*
[27] *Annals of Inisfallen, sub anno 993; Annals of Ulster, sub anno 993.*
[28] *Ibid., sub anno 1035.*

Sigtrygg's fall precipitated a crisis in Dublin that provided a member of the Waterford dynasty with an opening that he was quick to exploit, no doubt aided and encouraged by his brother-in-law, Donnchad mac Briain, king of Munster, who was keen to re-establish the control of the city that his father had enjoyed. What followed was a see-saw struggle for power in Dublin by representatives of the rival Dublin and Waterford dynasties, itself an extension of the rivalry between their respective patrons, the kings of Leinster and Munster. In 1036 Echmarcach mac Ragnaill, a brother or son of the man killed by Sigtrygg, seized the kingship of Dublin and held the city until his expulsion in 1038 in favour of Ímar mac Arailt, who may have been Sigtrygg's nephew.[29] Ímar, in turn, held the kingship until 1046, when Echmarcach regained control the city, a hold that he was to maintain until his expulsion in 1052 by Diarmait mac Maíl na mBó, king of Leinster.[30]

Echmarcach's ejection from Dublin ended the Waterford dynasty's involvement in the affairs of the city, but not its significant role in Irish Sea politics. It was evidently from a position of established power in the region that he had mounted his bid for the Dublin kingship in 1036. The question is, where was that power based and how had it been achieved? The Anglo-Saxon Chronicle offers one clue. In 1031 Canute had mounted a major expedition into northern England and Scotland and, evidently without battle, had brought the Scottish king, Máel Coluim mac Cinaeda and two other kings into submission.[31] One of these kings was named 'Iehmarc', clearly an Anglo-Saxon attempt at rendition of the Irish Echmarcach. His association with Máel Coluim in this context suggests a southern Scottish or northern Irish Sea location for his kingdom. Two possibilities present themselves: Man and Galloway.

Sean Duffy has outlined the probable domination of Man by Dublin in the early eleventh century.[32] Sigtrygg Silkiskegg may have based himself there following his flight from Dublin before

---

[29] Annals of Tigernach, sub anno 1038. The Annals of Ulster note the death in 998 of 'Aralt mac Amlaim' along with other Dublin and Waterford Norse leaders at the hands of Brian Bóruma (Annals of Ulster, sub anno 998).

[30] Annals of Tigernach, sub anno 1046; S. Duffy, Irishmen and Islesmen in the kingdoms of Dublin and Man, 1052–1171. Eriu, Vol. 43, 1992, p. 98.

[31] Anglo-Saxon Chronicles, E, sub anno 1031.

[32] Duffy, Irishmen and Islesmen, p. 98.

the advancing power of Brian Bóruma and maintained a close association with the island and its affairs into the 1020s. While there is no direct evidence for Sigtrygg's possession of the joint kingship of Dublin and Man, twelfth-century Welsh tradition presented his son, Amlaib (or Olaf), either the individual killed in battle with the Munstermen in 1013 or the one killed in 1034 in England en route to Rome, as ruler of a domain that stretched into Galloway.[33] Unsupported though this statement is by any corroborative evidence, it preserves a tradition of Dublin domination of the northern Irish Sea zone during at least part of Sigtrygg's reign. That domination may have been challenged in the past by the Waterford dynasty, and Echmarcach was certainly based in Man following his second expulsion from Dublin in 1052. His control of the island, if he is to be identified with the mac Ragnaill defeated by Murchad mac Diarmata, son of the all-powerful Leinster king, lasted until 1061.[34] This hold on Man appears well established, and it can be safely assumed that he was ruling both Dublin and the island during his second reign in the city. When, though, had control of Man been achieved? In view of the Dublin naval action that followed his overthrow in 1038, with their fleet campaigning in the North Channel/Rathlin Island area, it is possible that Echmarcach was already established in that region before 1036 and had used Man as a launchpad for his first attempt on Dublin. This may be the powerbase that had attracted the attention of Canute in 1031.

Canute's interest may also have been drawn by the spread of Echmarcach's power into south-west Scotland. At the time of his death in 1065 Echmarcach was described as *rex innarenn*, i.e. king of the Rhinns.[35] It has been argued plausibly that the Rhinns of Galloway constituted the rump of Echmarcach's kingdom, in which he had based himself following his expulsion from Man in 1061.[36] There is little record of Irish activity in this region in the eleventh century, but there are indications that the Ostmen of Dublin may have sought to control this highly strategic peninsula

---

[33] *Annals of Ulster*, sub anno 1013; Duffy, Irishmen and Islesmen, p. 99.

[34] *Annals of Tigernach*, sub anno 1061.

[35] *Monumenta Germaniae historica inde ab anno Christi quingentesimo usque ad annum millesimum et quingentesimum*, ed. G. H. Pertz, G. Waitz, W. Wattenbach, R. Pauli, F. Liebermann, Finnur Jónsson, M. Perlbach, L. V. Heinemann, O. Holder-Egger and A. Hofmeister. Vol. V, *Annales ævi suevici*. Hanover: Hahn, 1826. p. 559.

[36] Duffy, Irishmen and Islesmen, pp. 99–100.

that commanded the eastern side of the straits that separated the Irish Sea from the Sea of the Hebrides. Sigtrygg Silkiskegg's son, Olaf, may have added the Rhinns to his Manx-based dominion before 1013, for the somewhat fanciful account in the Annals of Loch Cé record that in 1014, at Clontarf, the Dublin host was joined by contingents from Man and the Rhinns. Echmarcach evidently sought to control a similar powerbase, presumably taking advantage of established links between the Scandinavian colonies in western Galloway and those in Man and Dublin. The chronology for the formation of Echmarcach's maritime domain is unknown, but there are no substantial grounds upon which to argue, as Seán Duffy does, that his control of the Rhinns post-dated his expulsion from Man by Murchad mac Diarmata in 1061.[37] The spread of the Waterford dynasty from Man into the Rhinns may well have been the development that attracted Canute's attention to the north-west peripheries of his realm thirty years earlier.

The spread of Waterford influence in the second quarter of the eleventh century should be seen as part of the developing struggle for power between Donnchad mac Briain, king of Munster, who was seeking to re-establish his family's control of the high-kingship, and Diarmait mac Maíl na mBó, king of Leinster. The Ostmen of Limerick and Waterford were, by this time, simply satellites of the Dál Cais kings of Munster, who could call upon their reserves of heavily armoured warriors and galleys. The slaying of Ragnall mac Ragnaill of Waterford in Dublin in 1035 is probably to be seen in the context of Munster–Leinster rivalry, coloured by the long-standing feud between the Ostmen dynasties. Ragnall's presence in the city is not explained, but it might be seen against a backdrop of warfare in the Irish Sea that had not gone all Dublin's way. Certainly, Sigtrygg appears to have lost control of Man before 1036, for it did not provide him with a refuge after his expulsion from Dublin. While there is no evidence to support the suggestion, it is a distinct possibility that Ragnall mac Ragnaill and Echmarcach mac Ragnaill had established Waterford's maritime supremacy in the 1020s. Here the maritime war waged between the Ostmen of Dublin and Ulaid hints at the circumstances through which this was achieved.

---

[37] Ibid., p. 100.

The major naval defeat inflicted on the Dublin fleet by Niall mac
Eochaid, king of Ulaid, in 1022, followed by a hosting of the
Ulstermen into Fine Gall in 1026,[38] must have severely weakened
Sigtrygg's power, while his defeat and capture by the king of
Brega in 1029 brought his authority to a new low. If not actively
assisting Niall in 1022 – Ulaid is not otherwise noted as a
significant maritime power – then the meic Ragnaill may have
capitalised on the eclipse of Dublin's naval power to seize control
of Man. From that base Ragnall or Echmarcach extended their
influence over the lesser Scandinavian colonies along the northern coastlands of the Irish Sea.

MAN IN THE MIDDLE

Just as Man-based kings recognised that control of Dublin was
vital for their own security and could open Ireland to their
ambitions, so the Irish kings understood that Man represented
the key to domination of the western sea-lanes. In the middle of
the eleventh century it was Leinster that had succeeded in taking
control of Man. The man who drove Echmarcach from Man in
1061, Murchad mac Diarmata mac Maíl na mBó, had already in
1052 been installed as king of Dublin by his father. Murchad was
an energetic ruler, and through his control of the city sought to
project Leinster power into the maritime world of the Ostmen.
His taking of tribute from the island and the expulsion of
Echmarcach, who may still have cherished ambitions to regain
control of the resources of Dublin, signalled the opening of a
new phase in which Gaelic Irish potentates sought to take
control of the seas from the Scandinavians who had dominated
the sea-ways for so long. Murchad's own success in that direction can be seen in the title 'king of Leinster and the Foreigners'
given to him in his obituary in 1070.[39] On Murchad's early death
Diarmait mac Maíl na mBó assumed personal control of Dublin,
and possibly also the overlordship of Man, for the kingship of
Man was by 1066 in the hands of Godred or Gofraid mac
Sitreaca, probably the son of Sigtrygg Silkiskegg. The kings of
Leinster, it seems, controlled the island through a splinter of the

---

[38] *Annals of Ulster, sub annis* 1020, 1026.   [39] *Annals of Ulster, sub anno* 1070.

Uí Ímair, the remnants of whom had been reduced to the status of client kings.[40]

The eleven years of Leinster dominance in Man did not end the Waterford dynasty's aspirations to rule there. Echmarcach's sons and kinsmen held to their alliance with the Uí Briain and perhaps clung to power in the Rhinns of Galloway, for after Diarmait's death in 1072 they re-appeared as contenders for the rulership of both Dublin and Man. The dynastic links between Waterford and Munster were clearly established: Donnchad mac Briain had married a sister or niece of Echmarcach, while his second grandson, Tadg mac Toirrdelbach Ua Briain, married one of Echmarcach's daughters.[41] This kinship may explain the speed with which Munster moved to regain control of Dublin and Man on Diarmait's death. Toirrdelbach Ua Briain seized Dublin in 1072 and, although recognised as king by its people,[42] chose instead to insert one of his meic Ragnaill cousins, Gofraid mac Amlaim meic Ragnaill. Furthermore, in 1073 one 'Sitriuc mac Amlaim and two grandsons of Brian [Bóruma]' were killed in a raid on the Isle of Man.[43] This attack on King Finghal mac Gofraid was presumably a follow-up to the takeover of Dublin, led by a brother of Toirrdelbach's vassal-king and two grandsons of Ragnall.

After the abortive Ua Briain attack on Man there were no further mainland Irish attempts to seize the island kingdom for two decades. Finghal mac Gofraid's grip on power, however, may have been politically weakened after 1073. By c. 1075 Finghal had been overthrown by Gofraid Crobán, a kinsman and opportunist mercenary who had begun to assert his influence in Man as early as 1066,[44] soon after the collapse of Orkney's Hebridean overlordship following the death of Thorfinn. Gofraid, founder of the dynasty that ruled Man until 1265, was a great-grandson of Olaf Cuarán[45] but had his powerbase in the Isles rather than Dublin. Indeed, the Manx kings enjoyed lordship over the rest

---

[40] Ibid., sub anno 1072 describes Diarmait as 'king of Leinster and the Foreigners'. Annals of Tigernach add the Isles to his territory, which Duffy interprets as meaning at least the Isle of Man: Duffy, Irishmen and Islesmen, p. 101; Chronica regum Manniae et Insularum: The Chronicle of Man and the Isles: A Facsimile of the Manuscript Codex Julius A. VII in the British Museum, ed. P. A. Munch. Douglas: Published at the Museum, 1924, sub anno 1047 [1066]. In the text, Sitriuc has been struck out and replaced with Fingal, the name of Gofraid's son and successor in the kingship.

[41] Duffy, Irishmen and Islesmen p. 105.   [42] Annals of Inisfallen, sub anno 1072.

[43] Annals of Ulster, sub anno 1073.   [44] Chronica regum, sub anno 1047 [1066].

[45] Duffy, Irishmen and Islesmen, p. 106.

of the Isles, at least until Somhairlidh of Argyll challenged that position in the mid-twelfth century, and until the failure of Gofraid's line their power stretched along the sea-ways from Man to Lewis. In Gofraid's reign this power was more than a nominal overlordship, for he maintained an active presence in the Isles and it was there that Gruffudd ap Cynan, king of Gwynedd, met him c. 1094 when seeking allies for his war with the Normans Hugh of Avranches, earl of Chester, and his brother, Robert de Bellême, earl of Shrewsbury.[46] It was also in the Isles, on Islay, that Gofraid died in 1095.[47]

Gofraid represents a return to late tenth-century trends: his power was intruded into the region from the Hebrides. He clearly had a deep reservoir of support in the Western Isles, founded presumably upon the ties forged by his ancestor, Olaf Cuarán. His reign may be seen as an Isles-based attempt to regain control of the southern end of the important trade routes from the south through the Irish Sea, Dublin and Man, which led ultimately to Orkney and Norway itself. Gofraid clearly intended to control all the elements in this nexus, as is evident from his seizure of the kingship of Dublin in 1091.[48] Although there is no documented evidence for such a move, it is probable that he would have sought control of the Rhinns, thereby safeguarding his domination of the sea-lanes through the North Channel. Certainly, the church dedications in western Galloway and southern Carrick to saints of the Ionan church may relate to strong Isles' influence in this period, but this cannot be attributed specifically to Gofraid.[49] However, his earlier activity in this region is hinted at in records of an attack launched on Man in 1087 by the son of the king of Ulaid and two meic Ragnaill dynasts, possibly sons of Gofraid, former king of Dublin, or of Echmarcach himself,[50] mirroring the response from Ulaid in the early eleventh century to Dublin's efforts to dominate the North Channel.

Control of Dublin, Man and the Isles established Gofraid as a power-broker in the politics of western maritime Britain. In its

[46] A Mediaeval Prince of Wales: The Life of Gruffudd Ap Cynan, ed. and trans. D. S. Evans. Felinfach: Llanerch, 1990. pp. 40, 72.
[47] Chronica regum; Annals of Ulster, sub anno 1095.
[48] Chronica regum, p. 6. Annals of Tigernach, sub anno 1091.
[49] D. Brooke, Wild Men and Holy Places: St. Ninian, Whithorn and the Medieval Realm of Galloway. Edinburgh: Canongate Press, 1994. pp. 74–76.
[50] Annals of Ulster, sub anno 1087.

eulogy of the king, the Chronicle of Man claimed that 'the Scots' were so daunted by his power 'that no ship- or boat-builder dared to insert into it more than three bolts'.[51] However this entry is interpreted, the implication is that he exercised a naval supremacy over his neighbours in northern Britain. This naval power is implicit in the sixty vessels Gofraid lent to Gruffudd ap Cynan in 1094, an action which in itself was an indication of his readiness to project his authority into western mainland Britain. His position, however, did not go unchallenged, and the 1087 attack by the Ulaid (i.e. the Westernmen) and Ragnall's descendants could indicate that there remained elements within his far-flung dominions whose loyalties lay elsewhere. It has been argued that the attack on Man lies in the context of a developing struggle after 1086 within the Uí Briain kindred for the leadership of that family between the sons of Toirrdelbach Ua Briain, and that it was aimed at preventing Muirchertach mac Toirrdelbaigh Ua Briain from establishing his control over the island by placing a supporter of his rivals for the kingship of Munster, his nephews, Tadg's descendants, in power there.[52] Whether Muirchertach was, however, in any position before 1089, despite his victory at Howth Head over the Ostmen of Dublin in 1087, to attempt to project his authority into Man while Gofraid Crobán was at the height of his power is doubtful: from 1087 to 1089 Muirchertach's priority was to secure possession of Munster itself. Ulaid's (Ulster's) place in the conflict is equally uncertain. While the king of Ulaid (Ulster) had marital connections with a rival branch of the Uí Briain descended from Donnchad mac Briain, for them Tadg's descendants were as much the enemy as Muirchertach. Co-operation between Ulaid and Tadg's descendants, therefore, seems highly unlikely.

In 1091 Gofraid Crobán seized the kingship of Dublin. His possession of the city lasted barely three years and ended with his expulsion in 1094 by Muirchertach Ua Briain. The occupation of Dublin represented the climax of Gofraid's steady accumulation of power in the Irish Sea and Isles but was, in its timing, nothing more than a splendid piece of opportunism which capitalised on the conflict in Ireland that was keeping both Munster and Leinster weakened. His control of the city was evidently

[51] *Chronica regum*, pp. 5–6.
[52] Duffy, Irishmen and Islesmen, pp. 104–5 and note 60.

prolonged through alliance with Domnall son of Ardhgar mac Lochlainn, king of Ailech, Muirchertach's chief rival for hegemony in Ireland. In 1094 mac Lochlainn and Gofraid defeated Muirchertach's first attempt to recapture the prized city, but the Munster king returned once his opponents had disbanded their armies. Driven out of Dublin, Gofraid fell back on his Hebridean powerbase, dying there of plague the following year.[53]

It has been suggested that Muirchertach succeeded in driving Gofraid not only from Dublin but from Man as well,[54] heralding an era of unprecedented Munster power in the Isles. This is an ambitious claim, for it is evident that Gofraid was succeeded as king in Man by his eldest son, Lagmann.[55] The Chronicle of Man, noted for its suspect arithmetic and chronology, credits Lagmann with a seven-year reign that ended 1096 or 1098 with his death on crusade.[56] Even allowing for the vagaries of the chronicler's calculations, it appears that he had assumed the kingship of Man before his father's death. Indeed, it can be inferred that Lagmann's reign commenced with his father's departure for Dublin in 1091, a clear indication of the perception of the status of the kingship of that city amongst the Gaill. Even before the events of 1094, however, Lagmann's rule faced a challenge from within his family, his younger brother, Harald (or Aratt), staging a prolonged rebellion that ended with the latter's capture, blinding and castration. According to the Manx chronicle it was remorse for the mutilation of his brother that led to Lagmann's resignation of the kingdom and departure for the Holy Land. There are indications, however, that more worldly pressures persuaded him to abandon his kingdom.

By 1096 Lagmann was facing mounting hostility to his rule from within the Isles, represented by a noble faction that had formed around his young brother, Olaf (or Amlaim). Perhaps unable to topple Lagmann through their own efforts, this group turned to Ireland for aid and made an approach to Muirchertach Ua Briain. The deciding factor in this must have been Muirchertach's recent capture of Dublin and control of its naval power. According to the Chronicle of Man, the chief men of the

---

[53] O'Donovan, Annálaríoghachta Éireann, sub anno 1095.
[54] Duffy, Irishmen and Islesmen, p. 108.   [55] Chronica regum, p. 6.
[56] For discussion of the chronology of the reigns of Gofraid and his sons, see Anderson, Early Sources of Scottish History, Vol. II, p. 98, note 1.

Isles asked Muirchertach to provide them with a member of his own kin to rule over the Isles until Olaf reached adulthood,[57] although this is more likely to have been the price for his support imposed by Muirchertach. The man he chose was Domnall mac Taidg Uí Briain, earlier one of his rivals for the kingship of Munster but, more importantly, a grandson of Echmarcach and, since the death of Ragnall's descendants in Man in 1087, possibly the senior male representative of that line. Domnall's intrusion into Man, however, was not as easy as the chronicle implies, for the killing there in 1096 of his brother, Olaf,[58] indicates that rule by Tadg's descendants was opposed by some, presumably the supporters of Lagmann.

Domnall mac Taidg is credited with a three-year reign over Man and the Isles, c. 1096–98, but it is apparent that the kingdom built up by Gofraid Crobán had begun to disintegrate under his rule. Indeed, it is questionable how extensive his authority was in the northern island territories of the kingdom at any time. Manx tradition records that shortly before the expedition of Magnus Barelegs, king of Norway, into the west in 1098, the king had sent a deputy, Ingimund, with instructions to seize the kingdom. Based in Lewis, which in the twelfth and thirteenth centuries was to constitute the principal northern portion of the kingdom of Man and the Isles, he attempted to usurp the kingship but was killed in the process by the chieftains of the Isles. In Man itself the factional tensions that had led to the imposition of Domnall erupted into civil war in 1098, a conflict in which Domnall himself evidently played no part, which probably indicates that he had already lost control of the island.[59] How that conflict would have resolved itself is one of Manx history's great 'what ifs?', for the internal struggle for power was swiftly overtaken by external events: the arrival of King Magnus Barelegs in the Isles.

ENGLAND, NORWAY AND THE IRISH SEA 1092 TO C. 1100

According to the Chronicle of Man, probably towards the end of 1097 King Magnus of Norway, grandson of Harald Harðráði, chose to re-assert Norwegian influence in the Hebrides and

---

[57] *Chronica regum*, sub anno 1075 [1096–1098].
[58] O'Donovan, *Annálaríoghachta Éireann*, sub anno 1096.
[59] *Chronica regum*, sub anno 1098.

sent his representative, Ingimund, to take the kingship. Ingimund did not last long.[60] After taking control of Lewis, the Islesmen rose in rebellion and killed him.[61] The following year Magnus' brought his fleet to the Isles and, according to the chronicle, based himself in Man.[62] His aim was to establish Norwegian lordship over the Isles and, perhaps, over mainland areas that had close links with the main centres of Scandinavian colonisation. The chronicle records him progressing southwards from Lewis, to Skye, Tiree, Mull and Iona, then on again to Islay and Kintyre before arriving in Man, plundering and receiving submissions as he went.[63] During this voyage, he captured King Lagmann, and his release may have been conditional on his departure from the Isles and joining the First Crusade. Magnus' ambitions did not end there, however, for he launched raids into Anglesey and Gwynedd, where he confronted the spreading power of the Normans. According to *Heimskringla*, in Anglesey he fought against a 'Welsh' army commanded by two earls, named as Hugh the Noble and Hugh the Fat, who can be identified as Hugh de Montgomery, earl of Shrewsbury, and Hugh d'Avranches, earl of Chester.[64] These earls were the chief figures in William Rufus' expansion of Norman rule in Wales. In the resulting battle Hugh de Montgomery, who 'was covered with armour, so that nothing in him was exposed, save the eyes only', was slain by Magnus himself, who shot him through the eye with an arrow. Hugh's death in conflict with 'pirates from overseas' is corroborated by the Anglo-Saxon Chronicle.[65]

Heimskringla claims that Magnus added Anglesey to his domain following his victory there, but it is probable that he was simply stepping into Gofraid Crobán's shoes as protector of Gruffudd ap Cynan, who had been defeated by the earls and driven into exile in Dublin.[66] From Anglesey Magnus headed north. He had already received the submission of the Gall-Gaedhil and received a tribute of cut timber from them.[67] Now, though, Magnus

---

[60] The discussion is a development of ideas first presented in Oram, *Lordship*, pp. 39–44.
[61] *Chronica regum, sub anno* 1077 [1097].   [62] Ibid., *sub anno* 1098.
[63] *Magnus Barefoot's Saga*. In *Heimskringla*, see note 17 above, Chapters 8, 9.
[64] Ibid., Chapter 10.   [65] *Anglo-Saxon Chronicles, sub anno* 1097 [1098].
[66] Duffy, *Irishmen and Islesmen*, p. 110 and note 82; F. Barlow, *William Rufus*. London: Methuen, 1983. pp. 389–90.
[67] *Chronica regum, sub anno* 1098; *Magnus Barefoot's Saga*. In *Heimskringla*, see note 19 above, Chapter 9.

consolidated his position in the west through a treaty with the Scottish king, Edgar, which confirmed Norwegian possession of all the Hebrides.[68] Although no supporting evidence for such a treaty survives in Scottish sources, twelfth- and thirteenth-century Scottish recognition of Norwegian suzerainty in the Isles indicates a pre-existing arrangement. In one event-filled year, then, Magnus had ended Irish interests in the Isles, halted Norman aggression in Gwynedd and given notice to the English and Scottish kings that a new power had arrived in the west.

How much of a threat did Magnus Barelegs represent to Norman power in 1098? His brief appearance in mainland British affairs and the collapse of his schemes for control in Ireland on his death in 1103 have seen his significance played down in most modern analyses of his career. Yet in the late eleventh century he appears to have been regarded as a very real threat to Norman security. As the grandson of Harald Harðráði, who had died in 1066 in his attempt to seize the English throne, and with the bid of King Svein Estridsøn to regain his uncle Canute's English dominion in 1069–70, and Canute IV's planned invasion of c. 1080 as examples, Magnus must have appeared to William Rufus as a rival.[69] William of Malmesbury certainly believed that Magnus intended to make a bid for the English throne, and claimed that Harold, son of Harold Godwinson, the last Anglo-Saxon king, accompanied Magnus on his campaign.[70] Contemporary observers were not to know that the successes of Canute were never to be repeated. Magnus Barelegs' domination of the Irish Sea gave him a powerful position on the western flank of England, where Norman power was less well developed than on the east. The submission of the Gall-Gaedhil in Galloway, his treaty with the Scottish king and his re-establishment of Isles-based influence in Gwynedd were very real threats that had to be confronted and contained. The rapid development of Ranulf Meschin's power in the north-west, stretching from Carlisle south into Lancashire, must surely have been a response to this additional challenge. Despite the concerns of the English in

[68] Ibid., Chapter 10.
[69] D. C. Douglas, *William the Conqueror: The Norman Impact on England*. English Monarchs Series. London: Eyre & Spottiswode, 1966. pp. 164–66, 213–22.
[70] William of Malmesbury, *Gesta Regum Anglorum: The History of the English Kings*, ed. and trans. R. A. B. Mynors. Oxford Medieval Texts, 1. Oxford, New York: Clarendon Press, 1998. p. 376.

1098–99, these arrangements were never tested against a Norwegian invasion.

As a threat, the expected challenge from Norway failed to materialise. Magnus over-wintered in the Isles to consolidate the gains made in 1098. The following summer he returned to Norway and did not sail west again until 1102. The timing of his second campaign may have been intended to capitalise on the weakness of Henry I, but Magnus' primary objective on this occasion appears always to have been Ireland, particularly Dublin.[71] His arrival in Man with a large fleet, noted by the Annals of Ulster, was followed by a possibly successful attempt to seize Dublin, accompanied by demands for the submission of the then dominant political force in Ireland, Muirchertach Ua Briain, the same man as had been attempting to extend his influence through Dublin into Man and the Isles.[72] Negotiations led to a truce, formalised through the marriage of Magnus' nine-year-old son, Sigurd, to Muirchertach Ua Briain's five-year-old daughter, Bláthmín.[73] While the saga account places this marriage in 1098–99, it has been demonstrated that it fits better into the context of 1102, when Magnus and Muirchertach became allies.[74] An alliance between these two men may appear unlikely in view of their competing ambitions in Dublin and the Isles, but the establishment of Sigurd, Muirchertach's new son-in-law, as king over the territories that his father had won would have immeasurably strengthened Munster power in the region, which would in turn have removed the main potential challenger to Norwegian overlordship. It also united Magnus and Muirchertach against the one man in a position to challenge their power in both Ireland and the Isles: Domnall son of Ardghar mac Lochlainn, king of Ailech. Muirchertach and Domnall had been at war since 1094, and as recently as 1100 Domnall had raided the country around Dublin, which was then under Ua Briain control. Furthermore, his family exercised considerable influence within the Hebrides: the meic Lochlainn were a very real threat to Magnus' new-won lands. As Magnus intended to return to Norway, there is

---

[71] Duffy, Irishmen and Islesmen p. 111.

[72] *Annals of Ulster*, *sub anno* 1102; *Chronica regum*, *sub anno* 1098 [1102]; Duffy, Irishmen and Islesmen p. 111.

[73] *Magnus Barefoot's Saga*. In *Heimskringla*, see note 17 above, Chapter 11.

[74] R. Powers, Magnus Bareleg's expedition to the west. *Scottish Historical Review*, Vol. 65, 1986, pp. 107–32; Duffy, Irishmen and Islesmen p. 112.

no question as to where the main benefit of the arrangement would fall.

In spring 1103 conditions seemed set for Munster dominance of Ireland and the extension of that power into the Isles and western mainland Scotland. While sailing north, however, Magnus raided the Ulster coast, although the Ulstermen were allied with Muirchertach. In a skirmish there Magnus was killed.[75] His death ended both his grand design and Muirchertach's dreams. Sigurd did not share his father's vision for the western colonies but was eager to return to Norway to secure his share of the kingdom alongside his brothers. Repudiating Bláthmín, he sailed north, never to return to his nominal kingdom in the Isles. Behind him he left a vacuum that neither Ua Briain nor mac Lochlainn were in a position to fill. Although Muirchertach regained control of Dublin and, through it, some degree of domination of the western seas, there was no return to the pre-1098 position. Instead, in the decade after his death, as Magnus Barelegs' sea-kingdom disintegrated, warlords rose on the flotsam to contend for power, building and losing petty empires.

[75] *Magnus Barefoot's Saga*. In *Heimskringla*, see note 17 above, Chapters 23–26; *Chronica regum*, *sub anno* 1098 [1103].

CHAPTER 9

Scotland and the Vikings

The political structures of the western sea-ways had begun to be redrawn in the second quarter of the twelfth century as two new mainland Scottish-based powers extended their spheres of influence. From the east, King David I had consolidated his grip on what had been the heartland of the old kingdom of Strathclyde and in the 1130s and 1140s had started to extend his control into the district to its west, running from Renfrew south through Cunninghame and Kyle into Carrick, a zone once dominated by the Gall-Gaedhil. His steady encroachment on the Scandinavian west marched in parallel with his expansion into the Scandinavian northern mainland of Scotland (see below, pp. 283–89) and revealed a determination to eliminate all rivals to his political domination of the northern half of Britain. Notice was being served to the kings of Norway that even their nominal mastery of the Western Isles was no longer to be tolerated. The second key player was Somhairlidh mac Gilla Brighte (Somerled), the ruler of Argyll, whose relationship with the kings of Scots was ill-defined and of only nominal dependence at best. In parallel with David's consolidation of control to the east and south of the Clyde, Somhairlidh was extending his power out of a heartland in northern mainland Argyll to create a personal lordship that stretched from Kintyre northwards to the head of the great sea-inlet of Loch Linnhe.[1] By c. 1150, therefore, the kingdom of Man and the Isles had as neighbours two ambitious and aggressive mainland-based powers who evidently cared little for the claims to overlordship of this zone held by the Norwegian crown.

[1] R. A. McDonald, *The Kingdom of the Isles: Scotland's Western Seaboard in the Central Middle Ages, c. 1000–c. 1336*. Scottish Historical Review Monographs Series. East Lothian: Tuckwell Press, 1997. pp. 39–67.

New patterns: Somhairlidh mac Gilla Brighte and the Scots

Conflict became inevitable as the three power blocs collided in the outer zone of the Firth of Clyde, the expanse of sea between Kintyre and the western coast of the mainland that contained the islands of Arran, Bute, the Cumbraes and their smaller satellites. The trigger for collision within the region was the deaths within months of each other in 1153 of both David I and Olaf Godredsson (*alias* Olaf the Black). Although Olaf's son, Godred, was soon able to muster Norwegian aid to secure his father's throne, the old king's assassination by his Dublin-based nephews and the resulting political instability in the kingdom of the Isles blew apart the status quo that had prevailed for nearly half a century. Parts of Olaf's kingdom may have quickly broken away from Manx control as local lords sought to build personal empires. One such area where Manx lordship evidently disintegrated was in the Firth of Clyde.

A hint of new alignments can be seen in brief references to a struggle far-removed from the stormy waters of the Clyde. In 1154 a long-running conflict for the domination of Ireland between Toirrdelbach Ua Conchobair, king of Connacht, and Muirchertach Mac Lochlainn, king of Cenél nEógain, erupted into renewed violence.[2] Ua Conchobair's fleet had plundered Mac Lochlainn's territories in what is now Co. Londonderry and in response Mac Lochlainn recruited a mercenary fleet from 'Galloway, Arran, Kintyre, Man and the shores of Scotland also'.[3] The distinct reference to Arran as well as to Man suggests that the Clyde islands were perhaps seen as forming a separate powerbloc, although it is possible that the annalist was simply attempting to make the list of powers who gave Mac Lochlainn their support as impressive as possible. The simplest reading of the account, however, is that the cohesion of the sea-kingdom was breaking down and external forces now sought to capitalise on those divisions.

For the Scots, the relationship with Man down to 1153 had been one of mutual benefits. A strong, stable Manx kingdom able to keep the ambitions of predators as diverse as the kings of Norway,

---

[2] R. Oram, *The Lordship of Galloway*. Edinburgh: John Donald, 2000. p. 73.
[3] A. O. Anderson, ed. *Early Sources of Scottish History, A.D. 500 to 1286*. Vol. II. Edinburgh and London: Oliver and Boyd, 1922. p. 227.

England and Gaelic Ireland, as well as the earls of Orkney, at bay provided the Scots with security on their otherwise vulnerable western flank whilst they consolidated their domination of the mainland. After Olaf's death, however, the political instability of his kingdom was seen to pose a threat to Scottish interests, as several of these other powers moved to fill the political vacuum. The Scots themselves, however, were in a position to capitalise on the situation, for David's political settlement of the region had provided a launchpad for more aggressive intervention in the area. The key development in this had been the grant c. 1147 to one of David's friends from his days at the court of King Henry I of England, Walter I fitz Alan, founder of the Stewart family fortunes in Scotland, of a lordship based on Renfrew.[4] A build-up of Stewart power in this district continued under Malcolm IV (1153–65) and into the reign of William I (1165–1214).[5] In the 1150s and 1160s Walter received further grants that created a substantial lordship along the southern shores of the Clyde around Renfrew and a second lordship in northern Kyle; and before his death in 1177 he had begun to extend his power into Cowal on the northern side of the Firth, the Cumbraes and, possibly, Bute. With the encouragement of the crown, Scottish power was being extended to the fringes of Argyll.

Such rapid extension of Stewart influence provoked a direct confrontation with Somhairlidh mac Gilla Brighte (Figure 46). Somhairlidh is a somewhat shadowy figure who, in the 1140s and 1150s, through a combination of military aggression and diplomatic marriages created a substantial sea-based kingdom that controlled most of Argyll and the southern Inner Hebrides centred on Mull and Islay.[6] In 1153 he revealed his hostility towards the descendants of David I in Scotland by backing a rival claim to the throne, signalling the start of what was to be a decade of alternating antagonism, conflict and unstable peace between Somhairlidh and the Scottish crown into which powers as remote as Orkney and Galloway were to be drawn.[7] Somhairlidh, however, was the ultimate opportunist, and in

[4] G. W. S. Barrow, ed. *Regesta regum scottorum, 1153–1424*. Vol. I, *The Acts of Malcolm IV*. Edinburgh: Edinburgh University Press, 1960. No. 87.
[5] Barrow, *Regum scottorum*, Vol. I, nos. 184, 310.
[6] See McDonald, *The Kingdom of the Isles*, pp. 39–67 for a discussion of Somhairlidh and his wider context.
[7] Oram, *Lordship*, p. 74.

Figure 46
Rothesay Castle, Bute. In the late twelfth and early thirteenth centuries the kings of Scots began to re-assert their lordship in the western mainland and Isles. Scottish nobles were encouraged to expand their territories into the region of nominal Norwegian overlordship in the Isles. The most aggressive of these nobles were the Stewarts, whose castle at Rothesay lay at the heart of a domain carved from island territories. In the invasion of 1230–31, Rothesay was a prime target for the Norwegians, falling to them after they hewed through its sandstone walls with their axes.

1157 he abandoned his allies in Scotland to pursue a plan to wrest the kingship of Man from Godred Olafsson, who was his brother-in-law, for his own son, Dubgall mac Somairlid, Godred's nephew.[8] According to the Chronicle of Man, Dubgall was recognised as king in the islands, and, after a naval battle off Man with Godred's supporters, Somhairlidh succeeded in forcing the Manx king to partition his kingdom and cede most of the island territories to his nephew.[9] It is most likely that the Clyde islands formed part of this settlement. By 1157–58, therefore, Somhairlidh had gained control, through his son, of a highly strategic group of islands in a territory that the Scottish crown considered vital for its own security. Given Somhairlidh's fractious relationship with the Scots, further conflict was highly likely.

Somhairlidh's settlement with Godred lasted only until 1158, when the Argyllman launched a surprise attack on Man, defeated Godred and drove him out.[10] Godred fled first to England and then to Scotland in search of aid against Somhairlidh, but failed

[8] Anderson, *Early Sources of Scottish History*, Vol. II, pp. 231–33. For a discussion of the background to this conflict, see Oram, *Lordship*, pp. 75–76.

[9] *Chronica regum Manniae et Insularum: The Chronicle of Man and the Isles: A Facsimile of the Manuscript Codex Julius A. VII in the British Museum*, ed. P. A. Munch. Douglas: Published at the Museum, 1924. *sub anno* 1144 (recte 1154–56). See also A. A. M. Duncan and A. L. Brown, Argyll and the Isles in the earlier Middle Ages. *Proceedings of the Society of Antiquaries of Scotland*, Vol. 90, 1956–57, pp. 192–220.

[10] *Chronica regum, sub anno* 1158.

to secure help in either kingdom.[11] By late 1160 or early 1161 Godred was in Norway, where he distinguished himself fighting on behalf of King Ingi I.[12] Somhairlidh, therefore, was left to consolidate his hold over the kingdom of Man and the Isles for a period of years. He did so secure in the knowledge that the Scots were not going to interfere with his plans, for by Christmas 1159 Somhairlidh had reached an understanding with King Malcolm IV.[13] It was perhaps negotiations leading to this agreement that prevented the Scots from backing Godred earlier in that year. For the Scots, perhaps, the stability that Somhairlidh had imposed on the region was preferable to the threat to them posed by the internal problems of Godred's kingdom.

Somhairlidh's understanding with Malcolm IV was short-lived. In 1164 Somhairlidh gathered a fleet and army from Ireland, Man, Argyll and the Hebrides and led it across the Clyde.[14] Why exactly he launched what was clearly a well-prepared attack on the Scots remains unknown, but its direction offers us some clues. According to the Chronicle of Melrose, the invasion force made its landfall at Renfrew.[15] Clearly, Somhairlidh's target was the centre of the Stewarts' lordship, and it is likely that he was striking at a family whose own ambitions in the region were in direct conflict with his own.[16] The chronology of the spread of Stewart power at this time can only be sketchily reconstructed, but it was probably Walter fitz Alan's extension of his influence into Cowal, perhaps with Malcolm IV's encouragement, that provoked Somhairlidh. The good fortune that had followed the ruler of Argyll to this point now deserted him, and in what appears to have been a rather confused skirmish by the Clyde both he and one of his sons were killed. With the removal of his strong hand, the kingdom that he had built in the west disintegrated, but the fragmentation of

---

[11] J. Hunter, ed. *The Pipe Rolls of 2–3–4 Henry II*. London: HMSO, 1930. pp. 155, 168. Barrow, *Regum scottorum*, Vol. I, no. 131; Oram, *Lordship of Galloway*, pp. 76–77.

[12] *Hakon Broad-shoulder*. In *Heimskringla: History of the Kings of Norway*, trans. L. M. Hollander. Austin: Published for the American-Scandinavian Foundation by the University of Texas Press, 1964. Chapter 17.

[13] Barrow, *Regum scottorum*, Vol. I, no, 175.

[14] *The Annals of Ulster (to A.D. 1131)*, ed. and trans. S. Mac Airt and G. Mac Niocaill. Dublin: Dublin Institute for Advanced Studies, 1983. *sub anno* 1164.

[15] *The Chronicle of Melrose*, ed. A. O. Anderson, M. O. Anderson and W. C. Dickinson. London: P. Lund, Humphries & Co., Ltd, 1936. *sub anno* 1164.

[16] Duncan and Brown, *Argyll and the Isles*, pp. 192–220.

power that resulted was to prove more troublesome for the Scots than the unitary authority wielded by Somhairlidh, for a succession of would-be successors to his mantle brought protracted instability to the whole of the western seaboard of Scotland.

THE HEIRS OF SOMHAIRLIDH AND STEWART EXPANSION

Somhairlidh's death heralded decades of instability and a kaleidoscope of political re-ordering. Within months of the events at Renfrew, Godred Olafsson had returned from Norway to reclaim his kingdom, and succeeded in re-imposing his power over most of the northern Hebrides and Skye as well as Man.[17] While the Manx kings may have aspired to regain some limited overlordship of the other Hebridean islands into the thirteenth century, their authority never recovered from the blow it had received at Somhairlidh's hands. Although much of what their father had gained in the late 1150s passed quickly from their possession, Somhairlidh's family, however, did succeed in retaining control of some of his conquests, in particular in Kintyre and the southern Hebrides, including Mull, Jura and Islay. Arran and Bute, too, may have remained in their grasp, but the evidence for that is late and unreliable. Leadership of Somhairlidh's kin fell to his eldest surviving son, Dubgall, who succeeded to his father's patrimony in Lorn and who also controlled the adjacent islands. Ragnall, Somhairlidh's second son, claimed the title of lord of Kintyre and king of the Isles, which appears to have involved control of Islay, Jura and, possibly, Arran. His efforts to consolidate his hold over this southern portion of Somhairlidh's domain, however, led to decades of conflict with other, more shadowy members of his family and prolonged the instability that had begun in 1164.

The void left by Somhairlidh was something that Walter fitz Alan and, after his death in 1177, his son, Alan fitz Walter, were eager to fill. This was a dangerous ambition, for while the Stewarts may have enjoyed royal encouragement in the past, the political climate had changed considerably after the 1170s, and the expansion of Stewart influence was itself considered a threat to Scotland's security. The Stewarts, however, were being actively courted by other powers in the region and were forging alliances

---

[17] McDonald, *The Kingdom of the Isles*, pp. 70–71.

with other kindreds who had ambitions to expand their influence in the northern Irish Sea and Firth of Clyde zones, such as the lords of Carrick. Their most significant ally, however, was Ragnall mac Somhairlidh, who controlled Islay, Kintyre, Arran and Bute, and who appears to have turned to Alan fitz Walter for aid in his struggle to impose his overkingship on his own kin.[18] In 1192 Ragnall was defeated in battle by his brother Aongus.[19] Shortly afterwards Ragnall made a grant to Paisley Abbey of the annual render of one penny from every house on his lands that had a hearth,[20] possibly a move by Ragnall to secure an alliance with the powerful head of the Stewart family, the patrons of Paisley. The emergence of a Stewart lordship in Bute around this time suggests that either they had exploited the conflict between Ragnall and Aongus to seize control of the island or that it had been given to the Stewarts by Ragnall as the price for their support in a struggle that he was clearly losing in 1192. Before 1200, then, it seems that the Stewarts had extended their western frontier to the waters between Bute and Kintyre, intruding a mainland Scottish presence into a region that had been ceded to Norwegian overlordship a century earlier.

Royal concern at Stewart activities can be read clearly in King William's decision to allow Roland, lord of Galloway, to inherit his brother-in-law's lordship of Cunninghame in 1196, and the plantation of a royal castle at the mouth of the River Ayr in 1197.[21] The king was certainly aiming to curtail Stewart expansion, and when in November 1200 Alan fitz Walter used William's absence in England to complete the marriage without royal permission of his daughter, Avelina, to Earl Donnchad of Carrick, his displeasure was made immediately obvious.[22] As part of the measures insisted upon by King William to limit Stewart power, Alan was required to grant the church and chapel of Bute to the monks of Paisley Abbey, a move perhaps designed to neutralise the problem of Stewart control of a territory that was not only technically

[18] See N. Murray, Swerving from the path of justice: Alexander II's relations with Argyll and the Isles, 1214–49. In Scotland in the Reign of Alexander II, ed. R. Oram. Leiden: Brill, 2005.

[19] Chronica regum, sub anno 1192.

[20] Registrum Monasterii de Passelet, ed. C. Innes. Edinburgh: Maitland Club, 1877.

[21] Oram, Lordship, p. 106.

[22] Chronica Magistri Rogeri de Houedene, ed. W. Stubbs. Vol. IV. Rerum britannicarum medii aevi scriptores, 51. London: Longmans, Green, Reader, and Dyer, 1868. p. 145; Murray, Swerving from the path of justice.

outwith the Scottish kingdom, but that lay under the jurisdiction of a foreign archbishop.[23] Alan fitz Walter was still in disgrace when he died in 1204, and with his son, Walter II fitz Alan, a minor, Stewart expansion in the Clyde estuary was brought to a grinding halt.[24]

MEIC RAGNAILL, MEIC RUAIDHRÍ AND ALEXANDER II

The activities of Ragnall mac Somhairlidh's children were a cause of growing concern to the Scottish crown from the 1180s onwards, but events in 1209 underscored the threat that this powerful military kindred posed to the stability of the maritime west. In that year there had been growing disturbances in the region caused by Ruaidhrí mac Ragnaill and his brothers' efforts to extend their influence into Skye.[25] Warfare in the Isles was always the harbinger of disorder in the adjacent mainland, for a sept known as meic Uilleim ('Uilliam's descendants'), claimants to the Scottish crown, had become adept at using the regional destabilisation caused by such events as launchpads for successive bids to win the throne. A further complication was the arrival in 1210 of a predatory Norwegian force in the Isles.[26] When in the same year King John of England invaded Ulster and drove out its earl, Hugh de Lacy, and sent his fleet to raid Man,[27] the destabilising of the region was complete.

In the 1220s it was the young Scottish king, Alexander II, who was the principal aggressor in the west. In early 1221 Alexander conducted a campaign in the Highlands from a base at Inverness against one Domnall mac Néill, a man whose name might indicate a connection with the Ulster Uí Néill. This campaign was the opening round of a protracted struggle of which few recorded details have survived. Although the contemporary Melrose Chronicle contains no reference to further campaigning, the late fourteenth-century chronicler John of Fordun notes a naval campaign against Argyll in the weeks immediately following the

---

[23] *Registrum Monasterii de Passelet*. The diocese of the Isles was part of the Norwegian archdiocese of Nidaros and was not considered to be part of the 'ecclesia Scoticana'.

[24] Oram, *Lordship*, p. 133.

[25] *Annals of Ulster*, sub anno 1209.

[26] Anderson, *Early Sources of Scottish History*, Vol. II, pp. 378–79, 380–81.

[27] Oram, *Lordship*, pp. 115–16.

king's marriage at York in June 1221.[28] Fordun implies that this operation ended in failure, with Alexander's fleet scattered by storms, and that the king mounted a second naval campaign in the west in 1222. These campaigns almost certainly targeted the meic Ragnaill, who had perhaps provided the meic Uilleim with military aid.[29] Although there is some circumstantial evidence to support these claims of major naval operations in the Clyde estuary in 1221–22,[30] what we know of Alexander's itinerary for both years makes it difficult to provide a time frame for his personal involvement in an extended fleet-based campaign in either year.

We can only conjecture what the consequences of Alexander's campaign in the region in 1221–22 were. It appears that his principal target had been Ruaidhrí mac Ragnaill, who had certainly controlled Kintyre at least in the early 1200s. He seems to have been ejected from Kintyre by Alexander, who instead granted the lordship to Domnall mac Ragnaill, Ruaidhrí's brother.[31] The king followed this up with the construction of a castle at Tarbert, controlling the important portage way across the neck of the Kintyre peninsula.[32] In July 1222 Alexander also erected Dumbarton into a royal burgh and granted it trading privileges that extended to the head of Loch Long,[33] and may also have given formal recognition to the Stewarts of their position in Cowal. In basic terms the result of the campaign appears to have been a consolidation of Scottish authority over the territories flanking the northern and western sides of the Firth of

[28] W. F. Skene, ed. and F. J. H. Skene, trans. *The Historians of Scotland*. Vol. IV, *John of Fordun's Chronicle of the Scottish Nation*. Edinburgh: Edmonston and Douglas, 1872. *sub anno* 1221; A. A. M. Duncan, *Scotland: The Making of the Kingdom*. Vol. I, *Edinburgh History of Scotland*. Edinburgh: Oliver and Boyd, 1975. p. 528.

[29] Oram, *Lordship*, p. 122.

[30] *The Annals of Loch Cé: A Chronicle of Irish Affairs from A.D. 1014 to A.D. 1590*, ed. and trans. W. M. Hennessy. Rerum britannicarum medii ævi scriptores, 54. London: Stationery Office, 1871. p.264. *Registrum S. Marie de Neubotle: Abbacie cisterciensis Beate Virginis de Neubotle chartarium vetus, 1140–1528*, ed. C. Innes. Bannatyne Club Publications. Edinburgh: Bannatyne Club, 1849. no. 27, which shows Thomas of Galloway, earl of Atholl, and some of his vassals in Cunninghame, possibly in connection with the campaign.

[31] McDonald, *The Kingdom of the Isles*, p. 84.

[32] A. A. M. Duncan and J. Dunbar, Tarbert Castle: a contribution to the history of Argyll. *Scottish Historical Review*, Vol. 50 No. 1, 1971, pp. 1–17.

[33] See E. Dennison, Burghs and burgesses: a time of consolidation? In *Scotland in the Reign of Alexander II*, ed. R. Oram. Leiden: Brill, 2005.

Clyde, coupled with a consolidation of Stewart power in Bute and Cowal.

So far the Scots had been able to extend their influence without provoking a response from their principal rival for domination of the Isles, the Norwegians, for Norway at this time was undergoing a prolonged period of internal political instability. When Alexander II returned his attentions to the west in the late 1220s, however, Norwegian domestic weakness had been replaced by the firm rule of Hákon IV. Alexander presumably recognised the changed circumstances, but he clearly cherished ambitions to expand his authority into the nominally Norwegian Isles, from where the meic Uilleim had earlier drawn mercenary aid. The Scottish king also wanted to prevent the further spread of Uí Néill influence from west Ulster into the Hebrides. To help keep the Uí Néill in check he encouraged Alan, lord of Galloway's efforts to win the kingship of Man and the Isles for his bastard son, Thomas, whose marriage to the daughter of Rognvald, king of Man, he had secured as the price of aid for Rognvald Godredsson against the demands of his half-brother, Olaf, for a share in the kingdom. King Alexander manipulated Alan's ambitions to bring the crisis to a head, but he got more of a reaction than he had bargained for. Instead of the quick victory that Alexander expected, Alan's chief opponent, Olaf Godredsson, escaped to Norway, where his report of Alan's onslaught won King Hákon's active support, and he returned to the Isles at the head of a Norwegian fleet.

In spring 1230 Olaf and his nephew Godred Dond sailed from Norway with a fleet commanded by another Hebridean warlord, Gilla Esbuig mac Dubgaill (known to the Norwegians as Uspak Hákon), who had been given the kingship of the Isles by King Hákon of Norway (Figure 47). Gilla Esbuig's twelve ships were joined by a further twenty from Orkney, and the initial stages of the campaign in the west passed relatively successfully, with the capture of some of Gilla Esbuig's rival half-brothers who had joined Alan of Galloway's attack on Olaf the previous year. Word of the expedition was brought to Alexander II, who immediately headed for Ayr, which was to become his headquarters during the unfolding crisis and where he was met by several of his principal commanders, including Alan of Galloway. While Alexander gathered his forces, however, the Norwegian fleet was bearing down

rapidly on the Firth of Clyde, where the Stewarts became their next target.

According to the saga accounts of the campaign, Gilla Esbuig's fleet had by this stage swollen to about 80 ships, probably carrying in excess of 3,000 men. Leaving the waters around Lorn, where Dubgall's descendants had their powerbase, the ships rounded the Mull of Kintyre and entered the Firth of Clyde, probably in early June. There is no reference to any other action during this stage of the campaign than the invasion of Bute and the siege and capture of Rothesay Castle. The steady expansion of Stewart power into the outer Firth of Clyde was clearly a matter of grave concern to the leading descendants of Somhairlidh, and they easily persuaded their Norwegian allies that the Stewarts' encroachment on territory recognised as being under King Hákon's overlordship merited specific action. According to the most detailed saga account, probably composed soon after the events it described:

they sailed south round the Mull of Kintyre, and so in to Bute. The Scots were there in the castle; and a certain steward was over the Scots. [The Norwegians] attacked the castle, but the Scots defended it, and they poured out boiling pitch. The Norwegians hewed the wall with their axes, because it

Figure 47
Dunvegan Castle, Skye. Many Hebridean chieftains in the Middle Ages traced their ancestry to Norse colonists and maintained a traditional – if nominal – allegiance to the kings of Norway. Amongst such families were the Macleods of Skye, who claimed descent from a Norse warrior called Ljot, the supposed builder of the early stronghold at Dunvegan.

was soft. The torch-bearer who was called Skagi shot the steward to death. Many of the Norwegians fell before they won the castle. There they took much treasure, and one Scottish knight, who ransomed himself for three hundred marks of refined silver.[34]

Their next move, however, was to withdraw in the face of the news that Alan of Galloway was moving north against them with a fleet rumoured to be 200 strong. They fell back into Hebridean waters, where Gilla Esbuig, who had apparently been wounded during the three-day siege of Rothesay, died and was taken to Iona for burial.[35] Following his death, command of the fleet fell to King Olaf, who now directed it towards his own purpose of regaining his kingdom in Man. In the autumn he succeeded in capturing the island with little opposition, and his Norwegian allies over-wintered in Man before heading for home in the spring.[36] On their north-bound voyage the Norwegians raided Kintyre but were driven off with heavy losses.

The events of 1230–31 coincided with the last bid by the meic Uilleim to secure the Scottish throne. It appears that Ruaidhrí mac Ragnaill may have used this rising as a means of renewing his pressure on the Scottish king, and the lord of Garmoran should probably be identified with the ally of the last meic Uilleim pretender in that venture.[37] It is unclear whether he died along with meic Uilleim in 1230–31, but there is no other evidence for his actions after that date. By the 1240s the descendants of Ruadhrí, while remaining a powerful military and naval force in the west Highlands and Islands, with a lordship centred on Garmoran and the Uists, ceased to play any part in the political life of the Clyde estuary region. Ragnall's descendants, however, were not the only casualties of the crisis of 1230–31, for, despite Alexander's clear encouragement of men such as Alan of Galloway to pursue conquests in the Scandinavian west, the king had clearly been caught off-guard by the scale of the Norwegian reaction. It was fortunate for the Scots that the Norwegians secured their objectives in restoring Olaf to his throne, and equally fortunate that the

---

[34] Eirspennill's Hakon Hakon's Son's Saga. In Anderson, Early Sources of Scottish History, Vol. II, pp. 473–78. One version of the text states that the siege lasted for three days.

[35] Ibid., pp. 476–77. The Chronicle of Man account states that Gilla Esbuig was hit with a stone during the siege and died immediately: Anderson, Early Sources of Scottish History, Vol. II, p. 472.

[36] Ibid., p. 477.   [37] Oram, Lordship, pp. 130–32.

ambitious Gilla Esbuig mac Dubgaill had died, for what could
have escalated into a more general war fizzled out in 1231.
Alexander, too, had attained his objectives, for in the course of
the war he had succeeded in finally eliminating a family that had
proved to be a persistent threat to his line's possession of the
Scottish throne and curbed the activities of one of Somhairlidh's
most turbulent descendants. His objectives achieved, Alexander
withdrew his support from Alan of Galloway and his policy of
aggressive expansion in the west, turning instead to the Stewarts,
the principal victims of the war, to provide him with counsel.
Alan's war-mongering was replaced with a more measured strategy that saw the half-Norse lords of the western mainland and
islands drawn increasingly into a Scottish orbit through a mixture
of carrot-and-stick methods. Grants of formal title to their lands
as vassals of the king of Scots and marriage into leading Scottish
aristocratic families was balanced by the intrusion of royal castles
into the zone and the establishment of new lordships for loyal
crown servants throughout the western Highlands. Within fifteen
years the west-coast sea-kingdoms, once remote from the centres
of Scottish royal authority, had to face a new reality that saw the
king of Scots as their immediate neighbour. The old independence of the Norse-Gaelic sea-lords was disappearing in just the
same way that Orkney was experiencing at the hands of the
Norwegians.

The 1240s saw Alexander's authority within Scotland reach its
zenith. On the mainland only the Mac Dubgaill lordship of Lorn
still had an ambiguous relationship with the crown, and beyond
it beckoned the Hebrides. For Alexander the Isles constituted
both unfinished business and a continuing challenge, for so
long as they remained under even nominal Norwegian overlordship they posed a potential threat to the security of his kingdom.
Although the people of the Isles were overwhelmingly Gaelic in
their culture by this date, the design of their ships, some loan
words from Norse into the Gaelic dialects of the region and some
Gaelicised personal and place-names were the chief reminders of
their Scandinavian past. They had pursued their own political
agendas independent of the interests of the kings of Norway;
their theoretical status as vassals of the crown of Norway offered
them some defence against Scottish ambitions in their direction.
In times of threat, such as during Alan of Galloway's campaigns

against them, it suited the Islesmen to remember their otherwise ignored overlord. Alexander must have chafed at this restraint on his actions, for the west remained a zone of vulnerability to his kingdom's security for so long as it remained outwith his full control. The perennial instability of the region had long provided a breeding-ground for challengers to his segment of the royal dynasty, and although the meic Uilleim had been eliminated, the region remained a potential source of succour to disaffected elements within mainland Scotland. In 1244 Alexander offered to buy the Isles from Norway, an offer rejected out of hand by the Norwegian king, Hákon IV, who was steadily re-asserting his own authority after the ending of the long civil wars that had so debilitated his kingdom. Hákon similarly dismissed subsequent offers.[38] Suspicions that the meic Dubgaill, who were vassals of the kings of Scots and Norway, were also involved in negotiations with Henry III of England prompted Alexander to end the ambiguity once and for all. In the summer of 1249 a royal fleet set out from the Clyde ports and cruised the waters of the Inner Hebrides. In early July it anchored off the island of Kerrera in Oban Bay, poised to strike against the heart of meic Dubgaill power at nearby Dunstaffange Castle.[39] On 8 July, at the height of his power, Alexander II died suddenly in his tent on Kerrera, struck down, it was claimed, after receiving warnings in his dreams from St Olaf of Norway and St Magnus of Orkney, before finally being felled by the power of St Columba, protector of the Isles.[40]

The king's death brought the campaign to an abrupt conclusion, with most of its objectives unrealised. While arrangements were set in place for the transportation of Alexander's body to Melrose for burial,[41] the political elite scrambled to establish their positions in control of the child Alexander III's administration. Indeed, the old king's corpse was all but abandoned as his former lieutenants raced to Scone for the inauguration of the boy king. From the first it was clear that the political stability that Alexander had imposed would be subjected to great stress as the

[38] Anderson, *Early Sources of Scottish History*, Vol. II, pp. 539–40.
[39] *Chronicle of Melrose*, sub anno 1249; W. Bower, *Scotichronicon in Latin and English*, ed. D. E. R. Watt. Vol. V. Aberdeen: Aberdeen University Press, 1987. p. 191.
[40] Anderson, *Early Sources of Scottish History*, Vol. II, pp. 556–57.
[41] *Chronicle of Melrose*, sub anno 1249.

political community of the kingdom began to manoeuvre for power. With his heir a child of eight, it remained to be seen whether the realm that Alexander II had welded together through blood and violence would remain intact through the inevitably long minority that would follow. From the perspective of the Islesmen, Alexander II's death brought to a halt the Scottish advance into the west, but it must have been clear that the collapse of the 1249 campaign had been a postponement of the inevitable rather than the permanent end of the threat from Scotland. The mainland from Kintyre to Caithness, it was clear, was firmly under Scottish royal authority, but the question of the status of the Isles remained unresolved. Even although Stewart control of the Clyde islands had been consolidated before 1249, technically the area remained under Norwegian sovereignty, and although there is no indication that the Stewarts had ever offered their homage to the king of Norway for their island possessions, it was this kind of ambiguity that Alexander II had striven to eliminate. Unfortunately for the Norse-Gaelic lords of the west, the families who dominated the politics of the minority of Alexander III included the Comyns and the Stewarts, two very powerful families with ambitions in western Highland and Hebridean Scotland. Largely through their efforts Scottish influence over the islands was considerably strengthened in 1255 when Eoghan of Lorn was received into Alexander III's peace and restored to his mainland territories.[42] The meic Dubgaill chief quickly became a pillar of the Scottish political community, marrying into the Comyn family, attending councils and parliaments, and serving as a loyal agent of the crown.[43]

SCOTTISH SOVEREIGNTY ACHIEVED 1261–1296

The Scottish offensive in the Isles was resumed in 1261 on the coming of age of Alexander III. The opening moves in the campaign were again played out in the Firth of Clyde, where the Menteith branch of the Stewart family, headed by Walter Stewart, earl of Menteith, received royal encouragement to move against the powerful meic Suibne kindred, who controlled northern Kintyre and Knapdale from Castle Sween on Knapdale's

---

[42] Duncan and Brown, Argyll and the Isles, p. 212.
[43] McDonald, The Kingdom of the Isles, pp. 116–18.

west coast.[44] The meic Suibne were a powerful military kindred whose resources made them an unwelcome and unpredictable neighbour for the Stewarts. Under the fiction of a grant of property by the meic Suibne to Earl Walter, this destabilising agent was removed from the power structure of Argyll.[45] Crown and Stewart interests probably coincided in respect of the fate of this unpredictable Norse-Gaelic mercenary family. Whether large-scale military action was involved is unknown, but the meic Suibne were progressively stripped of their remaining lands. Later clan tradition records how the meic Suibne subsequently pursued successful careers as mercenaries in Ireland and the Isles. Menteith had succeeded spectacularly in creating a new, Stewart-controlled lordship in southern Argyll, signalling his success by confirming earlier meic Suibne gifts of the churches in his newly acquired territories to the monks of Paisley.[46] The deprivation of the meic Suibne should, then, be seen as a final component in a sustained Scottish strategy in the Firth of Clyde which had seen either the expulsion or destruction of families whose loyalties were suspect, the forging of new political relationships with others, especially the emerging meic Dubgaill and meic Domnaill kindreds amongst the heirs of Somhairlidh, and the intrusion of committed allies of the Scottish crown into key lands and castles throughout the region.

That control of the southern Hebrides, Argyll and the Clyde islands was now felt to be secure can be seen in the direction of the renewed onslaught. While Alexander II had directed his efforts against the south-west Highlands, Alexander III's pressure was on the north-west and the adjacent islands, especially Skye.[47] It was this attack, amongst other issues, that prompted King Hákon IV of Norway to mount his expedition to the Isles, which culminated in early October 1263 in the inconclusive skirmish on the beach at Largs.[48] The campaign drew support from Dubgall mac Ruarídh, the ruler of the outer Isles, and his

---

[44] E. Cowan, Norwegian sunset – Scottish dawn: Hakon IV and Alexander III. In *Scotland in the Reign of Alexander III*, ed. N. Reid. Edinburgh, 1990. p. 122.

[45] McDonald, *The Kingdom of the Isles*, p. 143.

[46] *Registrum Monasterii de Passelet*.

[47] Anderson, *Early Sources of Scottish History*, Vol. II, p. 605.

[48] For discussion of the campaign, see Cowan, Norwegian Sunset, pp. 103–31; D. Alexander, T. Neighbour and R. Oram, Glorious victory? The Battle of Largs, 2 October 1263. *History Scotland*, Vol. 2, No. 2, 2002, pp. 17–22.

brother Alan, both of whom had claims through their father to lands in Kintyre and, probably, the Clyde islands also. Aongus Mor and Murchaid mhic Domnaill, sons of Domnall mac Raonaill, lord of Islay, submitted to Hákon under threat of having their lands ravaged, which gave the Norwegians a powerful grip over the Argyll side of the Firth of Clyde.[49]

By mid-August Hákon's fleet lay in the Sound of Kerrera, where it menaced the lands of Eoghan mac Dubgaill, but the lord of Lorn refused to come into the Norwegian king's peace against his other lord, Alexander III, as he 'held larger dominions of him than of the king of Norway'.[50] From there he sent fifty ships south to plunder in Kintyre and five ships round the Mull to raid Bute. A short while afterwards Hákon also headed south with the remainder of his ships and took up station off Gigha, where he received a deputation from 'a certain abbot of a monastery of Grey-friars',[51] presumably the abbot of Saddell in Kintyre, who asked for the king's protection for himself, his community and their property. Hákon clearly considered himself to be gaining the upper hand through such submissions, each of which appeared progressively to roll back the advances made by the Scots over the last century. While at Gigha Hákon received word that Bute, as in 1230, had fallen to the Norwegians and that the castle at Rothesay had again surrendered. Hákon granted the island to a certain Ruaidrí, who claimed the island as part of his birthright.[52] The identity of this man has never been confirmed beyond doubt, but he is probably a son or grandson of the Gilleasbuig who seized Bute in 1230, or a descendant of Ruaidrí mac Raonaill, who had been ejected from Kintyre by Alexander II in the 1220s.[53] Quite clearly, those Hebridean kindreds who had lost out in the course of Alexander II's ruthless annexation of the western mainland were seeking restoration of their inheritance under the aegis of the Norwegian crown.

With Bute securely in Norwegian hands the invaders carried the war into Scotland. The Norwegian garrison of Rothesay and Ruaidrí's men launched raids against the mainland, presumably

[49] Anderson, *Early Sources of Scottish History*, Vol. II, p. 617.
[50] Ibid., p. 617.   [51] Ibid.   [52] Ibid., pp. 620–21.
[53] McDonald, *The Kingdom of the Isles*, pp. 120–21. Cowan, Norwegian sunset, pp. 103–31.

Figure 48 Loch Lomond. As late as 1263 Scandinavian warriors were still practising the skills of their Viking forebears. During Hákon IV of Norway's campaign a detachment of Norwegians sailed up Loch Long, dragged their ships over the portage route from Arrochar to Tarbert on Loch Lomond, and raided the rich farmland of the Lennox around the shores of the loch.

attacking Stewart properties in Cowal and Ayrshire.[54] Hákon himself now rounded Kintyre and brought his fleet to Arran, where it anchored in the sheltered waters between the island and Holy Island. Throughout September 1263 Hákon was involved in protracted negotiations with Alexander III, who like his father in 1230–31 had based himself at Ayr.[55] The negotiations centred on the issue of sovereignty and possession of Arran, Bute and the Cumbraes. When it became clear that the Scots were spinning out the talks in anticipation of the deterioration of weather with the arrival of autumn, Hákon decided to turn up the pressure on the Stewarts and sent a detachment of his fleet up Loch Long, across the portage point at Arrochar and into Loch Lomond, where it proceeded to raid throughout Lennox and Menteith, while he and the main force moved to a new anchorage between the Cumbraes and the mainland (Figure 48).[56] Unfortunately for Hákon on the night of 30 September–1 October his fleet was battered by gales. A merchantman moored amidst the ships dragged its anchor overnight and was driven aground in

[54] Anderson, *Early Sources of Scottish History*, Vol. II, p. 621.
[55] pp. 622–23.   [56] Cowan, Norwegian sunset, p. 121.

the shallows off Great Cumbrae. It was floated off by the tides and, drifting with the current, ran aground on the morning of 1 October on the mainland shore, together with four other vessels from the fleet.[57]

THE 'BATTLE' OF LARGS[58]

A small force of local Scots began a series of running skirmishes with the crews of the beached ships, inflicting a number of casualties, but withdrew when Hákon sent a strong party of warriors ashore. This force remained with the beached ships overnight, but under cover of darkness the Scots plundered what they could from the merchantman. On the morning of 2 October Hákon himself came ashore to supervise the salvage of what remained of the merchantman's cargo and oversee the efforts to refloat the ships. While the king was on land a large Scottish force was seen approaching, most probably from the south from a muster-place at Ayr. The most detailed account of the battle that followed is offered from the Norwegian perspective in *Hákonar Saga*, the epic praise-poem for the king composed either by an eye-witness or by a man with close dealings with several individuals who had been central to the main action. It reports that a Norwegian force some 200 strong, under the command of Ogmund Crow-dance, were assembled on 'a certain mound' some way inland from the beach, while the remainder, around 700–800 strong, were with the king 'below, upon the beach'. Ogmund's force was then attacked by the vanguard of the Scottish army, at which point the Norwegians advised Hákon to withdraw to the ships.[59]

As the main Scottish force, comprising some mounted knights and mainly poorly equipped infantry, all under the leadership of Alexander the Steward, head of the Stewart family,[60] approached, Ogmund withdrew from the mound to avoid being encircled and cut off from those on the beach. The presence of King Alexander in September at Ayr, the location of

[57] Anderson, *Early Sources of Scottish History*, Vol. II, pp. 626–28.
[58] For the most recent detailed analysis of the battle, see Alexander, Neighbour and Oram, Glorious victory? pp. 17–22.
[59] Anderson, *Early Sources of Scottish History*, Vol. II, pp. 628–29.
[60] G. Barrow, The army of Alexander III's Scotland. In *Scotland in the Reign of Alexander III*, ed. N. Reid. Edinburgh: John Donald, 1990. pp. 138–40.

the Steward's major power-centre at Dundonald in Kyle, and his position as sheriff of Ayr all point towards this Scottish force advancing northwards from Ardrossan and Irvine towards Largs rather than pushing southwards down the coast from Inverkip or having come westwards from the Garnock Valley across the moorland of northern Cunninghame. An advance northwards would have threatened to drive a wedge between Ogmund and his compatriots on the beach. What appears to have been a planned Norwegian withdrawal degenerated into a chaotic scramble as the detached force descended from the 'mound' to a 'dell' between it and the beach. Seeing Ogmund's force apparently fleeing, those on the beach made a rush for the boats, many being drowned in the undisciplined rout.[61] Parts of the Norwegian force, however, made a stand at the vessels that had been driven ashore by the storms at various points along the beach, using the vessels as makeshift fortifications, and succeeded in driving back the Scots, killing a knight named 'Perus', who has been identified tentatively as Piers de Curry, an Ayrshire vassal of the Stewarts.[62] The Scots now withdrew to the mound previously occupied by Ogmund's men. The next few hours were spent in desultory exchanges of arrow-shooting, stone-throwing and the occasional skirmish, until late in the afternoon the Norwegians launched a full-scale assault on the mound and forced the Scots into a headlong retreat. The Norwegians were than able to stage a controlled withdrawal to the fleet, returning to shore unopposed on the morning of 3 October to recover their dead and to burn the beached vessels.[63]

Inconclusive though the fight at Largs had been, Hákon knew that time was against him (Figure 49). Short of supplies, he withdrew first to Holy Island off Arran, then south round Kintyre to Gigha and Islay. He clearly intended to return in the spring to continue the campaign and, as he withdrew towards winter quarters, he confirmed his earlier disposal of lands. Ruaidrí was granted Bute and Murchaid mac Domnaill, lord of Kintyre, was also given the lordship of Arran.[64] With Norwegian assistance, this reversal of Scottish fortunes,

[61] Anderson, *Early Sources of Scottish History*, Vol. II, pp. 630–32.
[62] Ibid., p. 632. Barrow, *The army of Alexander III's Scotland*, p. 139.
[63] Anderson, *Early Sources of Scottish History*, Vol. II, pp. 633–34.
[64] Ibid., pp. 634–35.

Figure 49 Largs, Ayrshire. The Irish round tower was erected in the late nineteenth century as a monument to the Battle of Largs. Celebrated as both a Norwegian and a Scottish victory, the indecisive clash on the foreshore at Largs in October 1263 represented the final flourish of imperial Norway's ambitions to assert its grip over the Norse western colonies.

which the saga-writer claimed 'had won back again all the dominions that King Magnus Bareleg had acquired and won, from Scotland and in the south',[65] may have been made more substantial, but in mid-December 1263 King Hákon died in his winter quarters in the bishop's palace at Kirkwall in Orkney, the deeds of his ancestors being read to him as he lay on his deathbed,[66] and the last great Norwegian campaign into the west fizzled out (Figure 50).

Deprived of Hákon's driving will and military resources the Hebrideans knew that they stood no chance against the superior resources of Alexander III. Although Hákon recovered physical possession of the islands during the autumn of 1263, the withdrawal of the Norwegian fleet after Largs handed the initiative back to the Scots. It is clear that in the following campaigning season control of the Clyde islands and Kintyre had swiftly been restored, evidently by a force commanded by the Earl of Mar.[67] Recognising the new political realities, that same year King Magnus of Man travelled to Scotland and, at Dumfries, made his formal submission to Alexander III's

---

[65] Ibid., p. 635.   [66] Ibid., pp. 639–42.

[67] Skene and Skene, *John of Fordun's Chronicle, sub anno* 1264; R. Oram, Continuity, adaptation and integration: the earls and earldom of Mar, c. 1150–c. 1300. In *The Exercise of Power in Medieval Scotland c. 1200–1500*, ed. S. Boardman and A. Ross. Dublin: Four Courts Press, 2003. pp. 63–64.

Figure 50
Bishop's Palace
and St Magnus
Cathedral,
Kirkwall, Orkney.
Withdrawing
northwards after
the indecisive
clash at Largs,
Hákon IV of
Norway planned
to over-winter in
Orkney before
resuming his
campaign in
1264. He took up
quarters in the
Bishop's Palace
at Kirkwall, dying
there after a short
illness on 15
December. His
body was buried
temporarily in the
nearby cathedral
before being
taken to Norway
in the spring.

overlordship.[68] When the king died the following year[69] the Scots annexed Man with the intention of establishing it as an apanage for the heir to the throne. The annexation did not sit easily with the fiercely independent Manx, and as late as 1275

[68] Skene and Skene, *John of Fordun's Chronicle*, sub anno 1264; Anderson, *Early Sources of Scottish History*, Vol. II, p. 649; *Annals of Furness*. In *Chronicles of the Reigns of Stephen, Henry II, and Richard I*. Vol. II, *The Fifth Book of the 'Historia Rerum Anglicarum' of William of Newburgh. A Continuation of William of Newburgh's History to A.D. 1298. The 'Draco Normannicus' of Etienne de Rouen*, ed. Richard Howlett. London: Longman, 1884. p. 549.

[69] *Chronica regum*, sub anno 1265.

they were prepared to rebel in support of the claims to the kingship of Man of Godred, a bastard son of Magnus.[70] But Scottish power in the west had grown immeasurably since 1263, and the rebellion was swiftly and brutally crushed. There was to be no future for an independent kingdom in the Isles. Scottish sovereignty over the Western Isles was finally secured by the 1266 Treaty of Perth, which ceded lordship over the kingdom of Man and the Isles, and all its territories, from the Norwegian to the Scottish crown. The *de facto* control of the previous decades was converted into *de jure* possession.[71]

The significance of the fight at Largs does not appear to have been recognised at the time. The contemporary Scottish account in the Chronicle of Melrose devotes only a few lines to the battle,[72] not even naming its location, while the whole Norwegian expedition passed with little comment in Irish and Manx sources,[73] and in England, which was pre-occupied with the civil war between the supporters of Simon de Montfort and King Henry III, it escaped detailed record. In the late fourteenth century the conflict was inflated into a struggle of epic proportions as the climax in a life-or-death struggle between Hákon and his Norwegian warriors, who were intent on the conquest of Scotland, and Alexander, who was fulfilling his role as defender of the kingdom.[74] This presentation was largely a propaganda and image-forming exercise, designed to strengthen the thesis being formulated by John of Fordun of the benefits of a strong, centralising monarchy, in which Alexander III was being cast as the ideal of kingship to be aspired to by later Scottish monarchs. This thesis was developed through the fifteenth century,[75] but by the seventeenth the battle had once again been relegated to comparative insignificance. Indeed, it was only in the nineteenth

[70] Oram, *Lordship*, p. 156.
[71] McDonald, *The Kingdom of the Isles*, pp. 119–24; Cowan, Norwegian sunset, pp. 123–26.
[72] *Chronicle of Melrose, sub anno* 1263.
[73] The Chronicle of Man (*Chronica regum, sub annis* 1263–64) noted simply that 'Hakon, the king of Norway, came to the districts of Scotland; but achieving nothing he went back to Orkney, and he died there at Kirkwall.'
[74] Skene and Skene, *John of Fordun's Chronicle, sub anno* 1263.
[75] W. Bower, *Scotichronicon in Latin and English*, ed. D. E. R. Watt. Vol. V. Aberdeen: Aberdeen University Press, 1987. pp. 337–41. Bower extends his discussion with references back to Norse raids on Scotland in the time of the Picts in the following pages (pp. 341–47).

century, with the awakening of antiquarian and academic interest in this period, culminating in the publication in translation of *Hákonar Saga*, that the Battle of Largs was 'rediscovered'. From that point it was accorded the status of a conflict of international significance, an interpretation that is now questioned by most academics. Regardless of the scale of the battle and its significance as a set-piece engagement, it is acknowledged in retrospect that it – or more particularly the campaign of which it was just part – was a decisive turning-point in the history of Scotland, the kingdom of the Isles and, indeed, of Norway. It was the final proactive element in the Scandinavians' involvement in the Hebrides, and revealed to Hákon and the Norwegian nobles with him the limited influence still held in the region by the crown of Norway and the evanescent nature of the Islesmen's acknowledgement of his overlordship: within three years Norwegian sovereignty over the Isles had been ceded to the Scots in the Treaty of Perth. The main consequences of the battle were the effective completion of the medieval kingdom of the Scots and confirmation of the domination by Scotland, not Norway, of the north-west maritime zone between Britain and Ireland. After four hundred years the epic struggle for control of the British Isles between Scandinavian and native powers had been brought to a final, decisive conclusion.

CHAPTER 10

Orkney and Shetland

It is generally assumed that the northern isles of Scotland, especially Orkney, provided the launchpad for the sustained episode of Viking raids around northern Britain and Ireland that began in the 790s.[1] The origins of Scandinavian settlement in the islands are shrouded in myth, but it is probable that Orkney and Shetland had suffered the attentions of their eastern neighbours throughout the later eighth century, and tradition recounts that they had become the base for piratical bands who had left Norway in an effort to escape the increasing authority of the kings there.

The earliest times

Scandinavian activity in the Northern Isles down to the later ninth century may have been little more than the seasonal occupation of headlands and easily defended islets by pirate bands. There is no concrete evidence for widespread or systematic colonisation until the late 800s. A shift towards permanent settlement is linked by historical tradition to the influence of Olaf the White and the efforts of the kings of Vestfold in Norway to curb the activities of island-based pirates.[2] Early thirteenth-century saga tradition identifies Harald Hárfagri (born c. 850) as the main agent behind this change. The sagas depict Harald as the man who first imposed unified monarchical rule on Norway, in the process forcing into exile numerous regional rulers and their war-bands. Some of these, tradition records, used Orkney and Shetland as bases from which to attack Norway. As a consequence Harald was said to have taken a

---

[1] B. E. Crawford, *Scandinavian Scotland. Scotland in the Early Middle Ages.* Leicester: Leicester University Press, 1987. pp. 40–41.
[2] Crawford, *Scandinavian Scotland*, pp. 51–53.

fleet to the islands, eliminated the threat and established his lordship over Orkney.[3] Modern scholarship has dismissed the campaign as largely a fiction built on later elaboration of traditions of
Harald's growing power *within* Norway, but recognises that there
is a substantial core of fact lying behind the myth.

Establishment of a recognisable earldom of Orkney is attributed by saga tradition to Earl Rognvald of Møre.[4] The saga
account claims that Rognvald was given Orkney by Harald as
compensation for the death there of Rognvald's son in the course
of the king's campaign against the pirate bands, but a more
plausible interpretation is that Harald sanctioned a Møre-based
expedition to impose Norwegian rule over the exiled Vikings.[5]
The most favoured line, however, is that the venture was an
independent initiative organised by Rognvald and his sons.
Certainly, Harald grew to consider Rognvald's expanding power
as a threat to his own and, as the king sought to impose his
authority over Møre, precipitated a crisis in Norway. Harald's
actions resulted in a protracted feud which first saw Rognvald's
son, Rolf the Ganger, exiled (later to settle in Normandy), then
Rognvald himself perishing in the burning of his hall by Halfdan
Haraldsson.[6] In turn Halfdan was allegedly captured and blood-
eagled in Orkney by Rognvald's youngest bastard son, Einar
(better known as Torf-Einar), who, despite Harald's best efforts,
was able to keep the Norwegians at bay and hold on to Orkney.[7] It
was not Einar, however, but his uncle, Sigurd, who had turned
the Northern Isles of Scotland from an outlier of Norwegian
power into the centre of a new political force in northern Britain.[8]

Sigurðr hinn ríki (Sigurd the Mighty), as he was remembered
in saga tradition, was the effective creator of the Norse earldom
(or jarldom) of Orkney. According to saga tradition he had been
given Orkney by his elder brother, Rognvald, who wished to focus

[3] *Harold Fairhair's Saga. In Heimskringla: History of the Kings of Norway*, ed.
L. M. Hollander. Austin: Published for the American-Scandinavian Foundation by
the University of Texas Press, 1964. Chapter 22; *Historia Norvegiæ*, ed. G. Storm.
Monumenta historica Norvegiæ: latinske kildeskrifter til Norges historie i middelalderen.
Kristiania: A.W. Brøger, 1880. *pp. 89–90*.
[4] Crawford, *Scandinavian Scotland*, pp. 53–57.
[5] *Harold Fairhair's Saga. In Heimskringla*, see note 3 above, Chapter 22.
[6] Ibid., Chapter 30.
[7] Ibid., Chapters 31–32. For 'blood-eagling', see E. Roesdahl, *The Vikings*. London:
Penguin Books, 1998 [1987]. p. 192.
[8] Crawford, *Scandinavian Scotland*, pp. 57–58.

his attentions instead on his position within Norway. An ambitious and capable man, Sigurd began to convert what may have been a small-scale Norse presence in northern mainland Scotland into a more effective regional lordship within Caithness. From this start, in alliance with Thorstein the Red, son of Olaf Hvítr of Dublin, Sigurd began the wider conquest of northern mainland Scotland. The sagas present in outline the progressive expansion of Møre power into Caithness and Sutherland.[9] Details of this spread are lost, but it was certainly military in nature and clearly violent, although it is also evident that alliances were forged with native lineages such as that of Donnchad, lord of the district around what is now Duncansby in northern Caithness, whose daughter Thorstein married. Gaelic annals recording the 'wasting of Pictland' in the reign of the Scottish king Domnall mac Custantín (889–900) are probably referring to the activities of Sigurd and Thorstein.[10] By the 890s Sigurd's domain extended as far south as the River Oykell, which formed the border between Ross and Sutherland. Thorstein and Sigurd's aim may have been to establish control of the strategic routeway, portage and trade artery of the Great Glen, which bisects the Scottish Highlands and offered a link between Thorstein's kinsmen's territories in the Western Isles and Sigurd's lands in the far north-east of the mainland and Orkney. In Ross, however, his ambitions collided with those of a native magnate, Máel Brigte 'Tooth', and although Sigurd defeated and killed the Gaelic warlord in a skirmish that resulted from a failed peace negotiation, he himself died of wounds sustained in the fighting.[11]

Sigurd's death resulted in a brief crisis in Orkney under his less capable successors, his short-lived son, Guttorm,[12] and his nephew, Hallad, which led to a contraction of Norse power in the northern mainland. Around 895, having failed miserably to mount a realistic defence of his lands and people against other

---

[9] *Harold Fairhair's Saga*. In *Heimskringla*, see note 3 above, Chapter 22; *Orkneyinga Saga*, trans. and introd. by H. Pálsson and P. Edwards. Penguin Classics. Harmondsworth: Penguin Books, 1981. Chapter 5; *Landnámabók*. In *Origines Islandicae: A Collection of the more Important Sagas and other Native Writings relating to the Settlement and Early History of Iceland*, ed. and trans. G. Vigfusson and F. Y. Powell. Oxford: Clarendon Press, 1905. Chapter 82; Crawford, *Scandinavian Scotland*, p. 57.

[10] W. F. Skene, *Chronicles of the Picts, Chronicles of the Scots, and Other Early Memorials of Scottish History*. Edinburgh: HM General Register House, 9, 1867.

[11] *Orkneyinga Saga*, Chapter 5.   [12] Ibid.

Viking marauders, Earl Hallad is said in saga tradition to have resigned the earldom, which Rognvald then bestowed on Hallad's half-brother, Torf-Einar, his youngest bastard son.[13] Before the new earl's arrival, however, the sagas claim that Danish Vikings had begun to colonise the islands, echoing the conflicts between the two groups in York and in Ireland. Torf-Einar, it is reported, based himself first in Shetland, where he gathered his military resources before launching his invasion of Orkney. In the resulting conflict the Danes were eliminated and Torf-Einar established his position as lord over the islands.[14] The new earl, claim the sagas, faced a serious threat from King Harald Hárfagri, who sent his son Halfdan Longleg to take possession of the islands. The fighting, however, resulted in a major sea-battle amongst the islands which ended with the capture and ritual killing of the king's son. Harald was unable to dislodge his enemy and was eventually obliged to come to terms with Torf-Einar, who was confirmed in possession of the earldom.[15] Torf-Einar's successful defence of Orkney gave him the authority to impose his rule over the Norse settlers in the Northern Isles, and his energetic organisation of the military potential of the earldom gave him the resources to assert Orcadian dominance of Caithness, Sutherland and the waters of the Moray Firth. Over the course of the tenth century Orkney was to emerge as the powerbroker in northern British politics.

Orkney and Shetland, c. 900 to c. 1065

Under Torf-Einar and his successors the political significance of Orkney was firmly established. It was militarily powerful and possessed a formidable fleet with which to project that strength. Furthermore, the earls had forged strong dynastic and diplomatic ties with other Norse colonies, especially Normandy – where their kinsmen ruled as dukes – and the Western Isles, Man and Dublin. But Orkney's power was not simply military: it was also economically significant as a hub of routes for the Atlantic trade, a nexus for a network that stretched from Dublin and York to Norway, Iceland and Greenland. This wealth and power, however,

[13] Ibid., Chapters 5–6.   [14] Ibid., Chapter 7.
[15] *Harold Fairhair's Saga*. In *Heimskringla*, see note 3 above, Chapters 31–32.

attracted interlopers, the most important of whom was Eirik Bloodaxe, another son of Harald Hárfagri, who had been driven out of Norway. Eirik used Orkney as a springboard for his bid for the kingship of York in the mid-tenth century (see above, pp. 114–15), and Torf-Einar's sons, Arnkell and Erlend, were key figures in his military retinue, dying with him in the slaughter on Stainmore in 954.[16] Orkney's role in Eirik's designs brought the earls into conflict with both the kings of Scots and the Norse of Dublin, whose leader, Olaf Cuarán, was Eirik's rival for the throne of York and Orkney's rival for mastery of the Hebrides. It is possible that Eirik's widow and sons remained in control of Orkney, in association with Earl Thorfinn Skull-splitter, down to 962,[17] and continued as allies in the struggle with the Scots for control of the northern mainland. Indeed, it was probably raiders from Orkney who in 962 killed the Scottish king, Idulb, at Cullen on the Moray coast.[18]

The domination of Orkney by such interlopers as Eirik was facilitated by the strong traditions of rivalry within a ruling dynasty where any male descendant of an earl, through male or female lines, could claim land and a share in the earldom with the title of earl (Old Norse jarl). Conflict within the dynasty was a major hazard, and rivals sought external alliances, frequently sealed by marriages, to bolster their positions. Earl Skuli, for example, is said to have sought recognition from a king of Scots of his lordship over Caithness,[19] thereby providing himself with a powerful ally, but the relationship with the Scots remained generally hostile into the eleventh century. Marriage alliances, however, helped to spread Orkney's influence as well as secure its rulers' positions. The regular marriages of members of the ruling family into native Gaelic dynasties spread the net of kinship and mutual interest into the western mainland and the Isles. By the late tenth century the earls of Orkney were the most powerful warlords outwith Norway. The spread of their influence was further aided by the progressive absorption of the Dublin Norse into the political and cultural world of Ireland and a concomitant decline in their authority in the Isles. In the 980s and 990s it was

---

[16] *Hakon the Good's Saga*. In *Heimskringla*, see note 3 above, Chapter 4.
[17] Ibid., Chapter 5.   [18] Skene, *Chronicles*, p. 151.
[19] *Orkneyinga Saga: The History of the Earls of Orkney*, trans. Hermann Pálsson and P. Edwards. London: Hogarth Press, 1978. Chapter 10.

Orkney that filled the power vacuum in the west, and domination of the Hebrides enabled the earls to project their influence into both Scotland and Ireland.

Under Sigurd II (the Stout), earl from c. 985 to 1014, Orkney's power reached its apogee. He resumed a policy of aggressive expansion on the Scottish mainland, where Caithness was finally secured by the defeat of the last significant Gaelic ruler, Moddan of Duncansby. Orkney territory now stretched from Shetland to the Dales of south-east Sutherland. This warfare in the east was matched by renewed raiding in the Hebrides, where Sigurd came into conflict with the Irish kings of Leinster and Munster, whose struggle for domination of Ireland had spilled over into the Isles, and with their Norse tributary kings in Man and the Isles. Orkney fleets penetrated far to the south. In 986 Sigurd raided Iona,[20] and in 989 he defeated the Norse-Gaelic king of Man and plundered the island.[21] Saga tradition reports that he exacted tribute from Man and the Isles and established a vassal earl to rule over them. Inevitably his power attracted the unwelcome attention of other aspiring powers. In 995 Olaf Tryggvason, who had been active in the Irish Sea region during the renewed Scandinavian offensive against England, headed north on his way to staging what was to be an ultimately successful bid for the Norwegian throne. Probably recognising the importance of the earldom as a base from which to mount his challenge and from which a check could be kept on Danish activity in northern Britain, Olaf aimed to assert his lordship over Orkney, and he succeeded in forcing Sigurd's submission and conversion to Christianity:

When the earl came to speak with the king, they had spoken but little before the king said that the earl must have himself baptised, and all the people of his land, or as alternative he should die on the spot, immediately; and the king said that he would go with fire and burning through the islands, and devastate the land unless the people were baptised. And since the earl was thus pressed he chose to take baptism; so he was baptised, and all the people who were there with the king.[22]

Olaf Tryggvason's defeat and death at Svöld in 1000 heralded a period of weakness in Norway that freed Sigurd from Norwegian

[20] The Annals of Ulster (to A.D. 1131), ed. and trans. S. Mac Airt and G. Mac Niocaill. Dublin: Dublin Institute for Advanced Studies, 1983. sub anno 986.
[21] R. Oram, The Lordship of Galloway. Edinburgh: John Donald, 2000. p. 11.
[22] Olaf Tryggvi's Son's Saga. In Heimskringla, see note 3 above, Chapter 47.

overlordship. It was after this point that he reached the pinnacle of his power, perhaps signalled by marriage to a daughter or sister of the Scottish king, Máel Coluim mac Cinaeda, by which he may have legitimated his conquests in northern Scotland. As the dominant Scandinavian power in the west, he was a natural ally for Sigtrygg Silkiskegg, king of Dublin, and his Irish ally, the king of Leinster, in their struggle with Brian Bóruma, king of Munster and high-king of Ireland. Sigurd moreover, through his mother, Eithne, was a kinsman of the Leinster king. For Sigurd the opportunity to expand his influence in the Norse colonies in Ireland, a natural progression for Orkney's already powerful position within the Atlantic trade nexus, could not be ignored. His ambitions, however, ended in disaster on Easter Day 1014 at Clontarf, when he and the cream of his army perished in battle against Brian. Sigurd's death marked the end of an age, and Orkney passed into a period of decline that was halted only with the emergence of Thorfinn the Mighty in the late 1020s. While he certainly measured up to the achievements of his great Viking ancestors, he was a Christian ruler, and in his ambitions he was bedded firmly into the political world of the rapidly expanding Scottish kingdom.

In line with established custom there was no single successor to Sigurd's domain, the earldom instead being divided between the three eldest of his sons, Sumarlidi, Brusi and Einar 'Wrymouth'. The youngest of Sigurd's sons, Thorfinn, who was probably only about five at the time of his father's death, was taken to Caithness and brought up there. Later Scandinavian tradition suggests that the Scottish king, Máel Coluim mac Cinaeda, gave his young kinsman Caithness and Sutherland and the title of earl,[23] but this seems to be a projection backwards from the later twelfth century of the extended reach of Scottish royal power into the Norse-dominated north. Of the elder brothers Einar, remembered in saga tradition as 'obstinate, cold and unfriendly; ambitious, and covetous, and a great warrior',[24] was by far the most ambitious to re-assert his father's lordship in the western sea-ways, and in 1018 he launched a major expedition down through the Hebrides to Ulaid. There, at Úlfreksfjörðr (modern Larne), he was heavily defeated by a native Irish army and its Norse allies.[25] The failed

[23] St. Olaf's Saga. In Heimskringla, see note 3 above, Chapter 96.
[24] Ibid., Chapter 97.   [25] Ibid., Chapter 86.

ambition evident in this campaign characterised Einar's rule, and
although he pursued a more successful Viking career plundering
around northern and western Britain, he became ever more
dependent on the resources of his own earldom to maintain his
status. Even allowing for the strongly anti-Einar bias of the later
sources, it is clear that his unappealing personality, lack of military success and financial exactions contributed to his mounting
unpopularity. Following his brother Sumarlidi's early death, Einar
took over his third of the earldom, denying the right of the youngest brother, Thorfinn, to a share and stating that Caithness and
Sutherland were a more than adequate inheritance. Einar's other
brother, Brusi, however, handed over a share of his third to
Thorfinn.[26] This partition produced a strained peace between
the brothers, but Thorfinn's supporters, the chief amongst
whom was Thorkell Amunderson, known as Thorkell the
Fosterer, a man who had earlier clashed with Einar over his
excessive tax demands, cherished greater ambitions for his
young earl.[27] In 1020 Thorkell brokered a deal with King Olaf
Haraldsson of Norway, who perhaps saw in Thorfinn someone
through whom he could regain the overlordship of Orkney that
Olaf Tryggvason had enjoyed briefly in the late 990s. The king
may have been complicit in Einar's murder at Thorkell's hands in
autumn 1021; certainly he approved of the deed and supported
Thorfinn's claim to a full one-third share of the earldom against
his brother, Brusi. There was, however, a *quid pro quo* for his
brokering of a settlement between the brothers: both, albeit
grudgingly, acknowledged Olaf's rights over the earldom.[28]

The Norwegian hold over Orkney lasted until 1028, when Olaf
was driven out of his kingdom by Canute of Denmark and his
allies. Orkney had already been suffering from Danish raids
through the 1020s, and the teenage Thorfinn used the crisis
that this had triggered as a means to extract a further third of
the islands from Brusi, completely disregarding the 1021 settlement.[29] Around 1030 Brusi died and Thorfinn seized the remainder of the earldom, effectively disinheriting his nephew, Brusi's
son Rognvald. With the support of King Magnus Olafsson of
Norway, Rognvald laid claim to his share of Orkney and took
from Thorfinn the third that Brusi had held at the time of his

---

[26] Ibid., Chapter 97.   [27] Ibid., Chapters 98–99.
[28] Ibid., Chapters 100–102.   [29] Ibid., Chapter 103.

death. Rognvald, however, wished to have the 1021 settlement honoured and, although he and his uncle appear to have co-existed for several years and even co-operated on raiding expeditions, a new political crisis was triggered in the earldom which led to civil war and Rognvald's death in 1046 at the hands of Thorkell the Fosterer.[30] King Magnus, at this point, was facing a challenge to his rule from his uncle, Harald Harðráði, and was at war with the Danes, leaving him impotent to avenge the death of his protégé. As a result Thorfinn was able to entrench his authority, and he ruled over the re-united earldom almost unchallenged until his death c. 1065. Nevertheless, what is evident, despite the best gloss that the sagas could put on Thorfinn's career, is that the earldom had become increasingly vulnerable to the aggressive intrusion of Norwegian royal authority. Although Thorfinn had, ultimately, been able to remove Rognvald Brusason without suffering retribution from his rival's Norwegian sponsors, his inability to resist Rognvald's crown-sanctioned claims underscore the real limits on his authority.[31]

Despite the shadow of Norwegian overlordship it cannot be denied that under Thorfinn Orkney reached the apogee of its power, exceeding even the degree of influence exerted by Sigurd down to 1014. According to the sagas Thorfinn 'had the greatest dominion' of all the earls, encompassing Orkney, Shetland and the Hebrides, and 'a great dominion in Scotland and Ireland'.[32] Evidence for conflict as far south as Man in this period (see pp. 227–31) suggests a return to the aggressive exertion of Orkney power that had characterised his father's rule and a revival of the military successes of that time after the failures of Earl Einar. In mainland Scotland he extended his influence south at the expense of the native Gaelic rulers, who have been identified with Macbethad and his father, Findlaech, and possibly also in competition with his own kinsmen. *Orkneyinga Saga*, beneath the distortions caused by its projection of thirteenth-century political circumstances back into the eleventh century, records a major contest for control of the northern mainland between Thorfinn and a man referred to as 'Karl Hundason', usually though possibly

[30] Anderson, *Early Sources of Scottish History*, Vol. II, pp. 584–86.
[31] Crawford, *Scandinavian Scotland*, pp. 78–79.
[32] St. Olaf's Saga. In *Heimskringla*, see note 3 above, Chapter 103; Crawford, *Scandinavian Scotland*, pp. 71–73, 75–76.

incorrectly equated with Macbethad, whom Thorfinn defeated in two key battles at Deerness on the east coast of Orkney mainland and at the unidentified 'Torfnes' somewhere in the inner Moray Firth zone.[33] Regardless of whether 'Karl' was Macbethad or not, it is clear that there was deep enmity between Thorfinn and Macbethad, and the Orkney court may have for a time provided refuge for the Scottish king's rivals for his throne. Certainly, Máel Coluim mac Donnchada, son of King Donnchad I mac Crinain, appears to have found safe haven at the courts of Thorfinn in Orkney and Siward at York, exposing him to strong Scandinavian influences that shaped his policies once he became king in 1058. Máel Coluim, indeed, was to marry Thorfinn's widow, Ingibjorg, in the later 1060s, through her cementing an alliance with her sons, the co-earls Paul and Erlend.[34] Even allowing for the exaggeration and anachronisms of the sagas, it is evident that Thorfinn had succeeded in establishing himself as one of the chief power-brokers of northern Britain by the later 1040s, holding the balance of power in the conflicts between rival dynasts in Ireland, the Isles and mainland Scotland.

The 'Viking' character of Thorfinn's rule that *Orkneyinga Saga* presents, with the earl leading plundering raids deep into the south of Britain,[35] gives a misleading picture of the cultural development of the earldom in the eleventh century. Orkney, in Thorfinn's day, was no mere predatory culture supporting itself through the systematic looting of the wealth of its neighbours. Raiding still played an important part in Scandinavian society generally for a century or more yet, but the evolution of more sophisticated government, coupled with the intellectual shifts and diplomatic ties brought by the conversion to Christianity, saw a gradual change in the nature and intensity of raiding and a steady diminution of its significance to the elite in Scandinavian society. Thorfinn's reign marked the point of a decisive shift in the cultural balance of Orkney, reflected in the crystallisation of the structures of administration within his earldom and in his efforts to establish a matching structure of

---

[33] *Orkneyinga Saga*, Chapter 20. Torfnes is most commonly identified with Tarbatness, the headland at the north-eastern extremity of the peninsula that separates the Dornoch and Cromarty Firths, but there is nothing in the saga that allows so definite an identification. Crawford, *Scandinavian Scotland*, pp. 71–72.

[34] Anderson, *Early Sources of Scottish History*, Vol. II, p. 4.

[35] E.g. *Orkneyinga Saga*, Chapter 23.

ecclesiastical government. Under Thorfinn, while the earl's authority still rested on personal attributes and success as a war-leader, that authority became increasingly formalised through the creation of a machinery of government.[36] Thorfinn appears to have had ambitions to impose greater unity over his far-flung dominions, welding together his Norse territories in Orkney and Shetland, mixed Norse-Gaelic Caithness and Sutherland, and the largely Gaelicised colonies in the Western Isles into a stable and enduring entity. A key component of this effort was the establishment of an episcopal see embracing all of his territories and the close association of the Orkney-based bishop with the political power of the earl.[37] This close association between the spheres of authority of the secular and spiritual powers was a common feature of European state-building ventures of the period, where it can also be seen in the context of the spreading influence of the Gregorian reform. Within the British Isles, Thorfinn's diocese stands alongside the attempts of the Scottish crown from the middle of the eleventh until the late twelfth century to secure the establishment of a separate Scottish ecclesiastical province; the creation of a bishopric at Dublin with a territory encompassing the range of the king's authority; towards the close of the eleventh century the creation of a diocese in the Isles; and, in the early twelfth century, the creation of a diocese in Galloway, with the express purpose of excluding foreign ecclesiastical or political influences from these areas.[38] The failure of Thorfinn's scheme in the late eleventh and twelfth centuries should not detract from the vision that lay behind it.

Thorfinn's policies reveal him to have been very receptive to the spreading influence of western European (Frankish) culture. Whilst in the past he has been presented as the last of the great Viking earls of Orkney, closer consideration of his achievements shows him to have been a figure who quite successfully straddled a cultural divide. On the one hand, his background was rooted firmly in the traditions of the Scandinavian past, but on the other he strove to present himself as a figure of European stature. In

---

[36] For a discussion of the administrative structures of the eleventh-century earldom, see Crawford, *Scandinavian Scotland*, pp. 79–91.

[37] *Orkneyinga Saga*, Chapter 31, stresses the physical juxtaposition of the earl's residence at Birsay and the minster of Christ Church, the seat of the bishop.

[38] See Oram, *Lordship*, pp. 164–74. For a discussion of similar developments in a Scandinavian context, see Chapter 13.

part this may have been a product of his cross-cultural back-ground, further re-inforced by an effort to find a counter-balance to the influence of the Norwegian crown in his earldom, but it is also symptomatic of the process of acculturation, or Europeanisation, of Scandinavian society that followed on from its conversion and progressive integration into wider European society.[39] One striking indication of the extent to which the elite class of mid-eleventh-century Orkney had embraced its role within wider European society was Thorfinn's journey to Denmark, his meeting with the Holy Roman Emperor Henry III in Saxony, and his pilgrimage to Rome and audience with Pope Leo IX,[40] all probably undertaken in 1050. In embarking upon this venture he was placing himself on a par with Canute the Great and with Macbethad, who also undertook a pilgrimage to Rome in 1050, where he 'scattered money like seed to the poor'.[41] Although not of royal status, Thorfinn was clearly seeking to register his significance on the European stage, and meetings with King Svein in Denmark and Emperor Henry III in Germany may have been used as opportunities to demonstrate his wealth and might to two of the most influential powers on the continent. Alliances with both or either of those powers would have given Thorfinn great leverage against Norwegian influence within his earldom.

For all Thorfinn's attempts to weld his far-flung dominions into a cohesive entity, his ríki was still very much a personal empire. Foreign alliances and domestic administration could not hold that empire together in the absence of such a command-ing personality as Thorfinn's. Saga tradition clearly considered his reign to have represented a high-water mark and that after him Orkney entered an era of protracted and often painful decline. What his death revealed was how shallowly his control of the outlying portions of his domain was rooted and the extent to which he had held it together by simple force of personality.

[39] For a discussion of the process of 'Europeanisation', see R. Bartlett, *The Making of Europe: Conquest, Colonization, and Cultural Change, 950–1350.* London: Penguin, 1994. pp. 5–23, 269–91.

[40] *Orkneyinga Saga*, Chapter 31.

[41] Marianus Scottus, *Chronicon*, ed. G.Waitz. In *Monumenta Germaniae historica scrip-tores: rerum Germanicarum in usum scholarum separation editi.* Vol. V. Hanover: Hahn, 1844. pp. 495–564, 558.

Without him the network of Orcadian overlordship began rapidly to unravel:

> The earl was much lamented in his inherited lands; but in those lands that he had laid under himself with warfare, many men thought it great servitude to live under his dominion. Then many of the dominions that the earl had laid under himself were lost; and men sought for themselves the protection of the chiefs that were there native-born to the dominions. Loss followed quickly upon the decease of earl Thorfinn.[42]

As with all empires it was not until the process of decline had become manifest that it was recognised that the death of Thorfinn the Mighty had marked the passing of Orkney's golden age. To be sure, the earldom remained a potent force in the politics of the British Isles into the twelfth century and staged a striking revival in its fortunes in the second half of the 1100s under its remarkable and long-lived earl, Harald Maddadsson, but its history post-Thorfinn is one of progressive marginalisation and increasing domination by external powers. To Orkney's south the kings of Scots were steadily tightening their grip upon the northern mainland, extending their effective reach further and further into the Scandinavian zones of Sutherland and Caithness, and forcing grudging recognition of their overlordship on Thorfinn's successors for their mainland dominions at least. The kings of Norway, too, who had long exercised an oscillating domination of Orkney and Shetland proper, often playing off the competing segments of the ruling family against each other by sending a favoured candidate to rule in his name or by coming in person to take the submission of the ruling earl, had begun to assert their lordship more effectively over the Norse western colonies. The internal politics of the earldom made it easier for these external powers to interfere in its affairs, for competition between the various claimants to the earldom title saw them seek the patronage of their powerful neighbours.

For most of the remainder of the eleventh century peace prevailed within the earldom under the joint rule of Thorfinn's sons, Paul and Erlend. Their reign had started fairly inauspiciously with their involvement in King Harald Harðráði's disastrous bid in 1066 to win the throne of England (see p. 210), but both earls escaped the carnage at Stamford Bridge and returned safely to

---

[42] Anderson, *Early Sources of Scottish History*, Vol. II, p. 2.

Orkney. Their involvement in Harald's venture, which has been represented as a sign of an 'amicable relationship' between Orkney and Norway and the king's recognition of the value of such militarily potent allies,[43] is indicative of the extent to which Norwegian royal power had extended its effective reach in the eleventh century as Harald and his predecessors had manipulated the politics of the earldom to their own advantage.[44] That enhanced royal reach survived the slaughter of 1066 and was to play a key role in the re-emerging internecine conflict in the ruling dynasty at the close of the century.

Unlike the relationship between Thorfinn and his elder brothers and nephews, that between Paul and Erlend appears to have been stable and amicable. Until their sons reached adolescence and began to jostle for influence, the brothers jointly ruled an undivided earldom. Saga tradition, clearly with an eye on the violence that later scarred the earldom, presents their rule as a time of peace and stability, but it is equally clear that it saw the progressive erosion of the territorial authority that Thorfinn had exercised in mainland Scotland, and through the Hebrides and Man. It is unlikely that this contraction of Orkney influence went uncontested, but it is evident that in the later 1070s and 1080s Thorfinn's role in the west had been assumed by Gofraid Crobán, who by the 1090s ruled a kingdom that extended from Dublin to Lewis (see pp. 232–35). This progressive erosion of the domain created by Thorfinn may have been one of the factors that contributed to the animosity between Paul and Erlend's sons, Hákon and Magnus, as they faced the prospect of co-existence within a shrunken earldom. The friction between the cousins opened fissures within the family which, according to saga tradition, revolved around the question of the precedence of one branch over the other.[45] Eventually – the precise timing of events is unclear – Paul and Erlend partitioned the earldom between them 'just as in the time of Thorfinn and Brusi'.[46] The division, however, did not end the rivalry and by c. 1090 there appear to have been concerns that Hákon's actions would provoke a civil war. This was averted only by his departure for Norway following

---

[43] W. P. L. Thomson, *History of Orkney*. Edinburgh: Mercat Press, 1987. p. 54.

[44] For a discussion of the growth of Norwegian royal power in Orkney, see Crawford, *Scandinavian Scotland*, pp. 78–79.

[45] *Orkneyinga Saga*, Chapter 78.   [46] Ibid., Chapter 79.

the intervention of the influential land-holding class.[47] Hákon's visit to Norway, however, was not simply a voluntary exile or extended holiday trip, for he at once set about cultivating his influential Norwegian relatives and courting the favour of the new king, Magnus III Barelegs. Clearly, Hákon planned to secure Norwegian assistance and authority for his establishment as sole earl in Orkney. He was to be disappointed bitterly. In 1098 Magnus Barelegs embarked upon the first of his great expeditions to the west. Rather than installing Hákon Paulsson as sole earl in Orkney, however, the king had settled on a radically different solution to the problem: he had decided to suppress the earldom. On arriving in Orkney he seized both Paul and Erlend and sent them back to Norway, where both died that winter.[48] He placed instead his own eight-year-old son, Sigurd, in nominal control of the islands with a council of advisors to govern in his name.[49] Taking Magnus Erlendsson, his younger brother Erling and Hákon Paulsson with him, Magnus Barelegs headed for the Hebrides, intent on imposing his authority over the kingdom of the Isles and the valuable trade routes that threaded through them, and extending his power from there into both Ireland and mainland Britain. The saga version of the events of this campaign generally place a religious gloss on Magnus Erlendsson's behaviour (he refused, for example, to participate in the Norwegian attack on Anglesey and the battle at the Menai Straits with the Norman earls of Chester and Shrewsbury), but it is more likely that his hostility towards King Magnus stemmed from the recent events in Orkney and royal partiality for Hákon, and there are also indications that the young Orcadian had already established political relationships with the native Welsh rulers that ran contrary to current Norwegian policy.[50] Deeply out of favour with King Magnus, Magnus Erlendsson turned to the one power that he saw as offering a counter-balance to both Norwegian influence in Orkney generally and also the king's favouring of Hákon Paulsson specifically – the king of Scots.

---

[47] Thomson, *History of Orkney*, pp. 54–55.
[48] *Orkneyinga Saga*, Chapters 39 and 42.   [49] Ibid., Chapter 39.
[50] Ibid., Chapters 38 to 44; W. P. L. Thomson, *History of Orkney*. Edinburgh: Mercat Press, 1987. pp. 55–57.

Magnus Barelegs' sudden intervention in the already complex political world of the British Isles had repercussions far beyond Orkney. English historians have tended to downplay the significance of his campaign, largely because it resulted in little of lasting consequence,[51] and its impact on Scotland has been viewed with some ambivalence for similar reasons.[52] There has been a tendency to dismiss the effects of a re-assertion of active Norwegian royal interest in Orkney and the Isles and a suggestion that the treaty of 1098 between Magnus Barelegs and the Scottish king, Edgar, cost the Scots little, as they had no significant interest in either area. Such a view, however, ignores the whole thrust of Scottish diplomacy in the eleventh century, which aimed at containment and control of Orkney and the establishment of pro-Scottish rulers in an earldom that had traditional interests in both the northern mainland of Scotland and down its entire western seaboard. The arrival of Magnus Barelegs and his effective absorption of these territories into his own domain overturned Scottish policy and introduced a new and aggressive dynamic into the already complex political mix. Magnus Erlendsson's arrival at the Scottish court, therefore, must have seemed like a heaven-sent political gift.

With King Edgar's backing, Magnus Erlendsson was established as earl in Caithness. Gaining the support of the king of Scots in this way had been a device used by earlier Orkney earls to secure their place in the succession, as in the case of Thorfinn in the 1020s and 1030s, but Magnus' arrangement with Edgar represented a refinement of that device, in that it established a tradition where rival segments sought legitimation and support for their pretensions from either the kings of Scots or the kings of Norway. It showed, without question, that the future of the earldom was bound up inextricably in the political affairs of two rival expansionist powers and how far the independence enjoyed by the tenth- and eleventh-century earls had been compromised. Down to the death of Magnus Barelegs in 1102 two

---

[51] E. g. F. Barlow, *William Rufus*. London: Methuen, 1983. pp. 389–90.; R. Bartlett, *England under the Norman and Angevin Kings, 1075–1225*. The New Oxford History of England. Oxford: Clarendon Press, Oxford University Press, 2000. p. 72.

[52] A. A. M. Duncan, *Scotland: The Making of the Kingdom*. Vol. I, Edinburgh History of Scotland. Edinburgh: Oliver and Boyd, 1975. p. 127; G. W. S. Barrow, *Kingship and Unity: Scotland, 1000–1306*. Edinburgh: Edinburgh University Press, 1989. p. 106, where less than a paragraph is devoted to the events of 1098–1102.

hostile forces eyed each other warily across the Pentland Firth. In Orkney sat Sigurd Magnusson and his council, forming the Norwegian interest, whilst in Caithness Magnus Erlendsson was entrenched as the pro-Scottish representative of the Orkney dynasty. The death of the king brought an immediate change in this arrangement, for young Sigurd returned immediately to Norway to claim his place as co-ruler alongside his elder brothers.[53] It appears that he may have attempted to govern Orkney from Norway without establishing a representative to act in his name, but this arrangement proved to be unworkable. In 1104 Hákon Paulsson arrived in Norway from Orkney and secured the grant to him of the earldom by Sigurd and his brothers.[54] *Orkneyinga Saga* indicates that what he received was 'the authority pertaining to his birthright', while the saga of Magnus' sons implies that, as the kings' candidate, he received both what his father, Earl Paul, and uncle, Erlend, had held, and that when he returned to Orkney he sought to establish his control over the whole earldom, excluding his kinsmen.[55] Shortly afterwards, however, Magnus Erlendsson arrived in Orkney to claim his birthright, enjoying strong backing from the king of Scots, the men of Caithness and his father's former allies in Orkney. There was, however, no show-down between the cousins but rather a mediated settlement which received royal approval in Norway and which seemed to provide a good basis for co-existence between the two earls.[56] The arrangement lasted for nearly a decade before it began to break down, and conflict between Hákon and Magnus was only avoided at Easter 1115 through mediation and an agreement to hold a final settlement discussion on the island of Egilsay.[57] No discussion took place, for Hákon and his men seized Magnus and, after a show of due judicial process, condemned him to death and killed him.[58] The problem of split rule had been solved by the simple expedient of killing one of the partners. Hákon now ruled alone and held the earldom until his death c. 1123. There are indications that he was spiritually troubled by the circumstances of what was in reality the murder

---

[53] Anderson, *Early Sources of Scottish History*, Vol. II, pp. 133, 135–36.
[54] Ibid., p. 138.
[55] *Orkneyinga Saga*, Chapter 88; Anderson, *Early Sources of Scottish History*, Vol. II, p. 138.
[56] *Orkneyinga Saga*, Chapter 44; Thomson, *History of Orkney*, pp. 57–58.
[57] *Orkneyinga Saga*, Chapters 46 and 47.   [58] Ibid., Chapters 48–50.

Figure 51 Round Church, Orphir, Orkney. Supposedly modelled on the Church of the Holy Sepulchre in Jerusalem, the church at Orphir was probably constructed by Earl Hákon Paulsson on returning from his penitential pilgrimage to Rome and Palestine, a journey undertaken after the killing of Earl Magnus Erlendsson.

of his cousin, and he was to travel on an extended pilgrimage to Rome and the Holy Land in search of absolution. On the latter journey he may have seen the Church of the Holy Sepulchre in Jerusalem, which formed the architectural inspiration for the round church built in the early twelfth century at Orphir on mainland Orkney, adjacent to one of his main residences (Figure 51).[59] These public displays of penance may have been designed to silence mutterings against him from former supporters of Magnus, and for a time they may have worked. By the time of his death, however, challenges were already emerging to his line's monopoly of power in the islands, and central to those challenges were suggestions that Magnus had died a martyr and was a saint, with reports of miracles occurring at his tomb in Christ Church at Birsay (Figure 52).[60]

Claims of sanctity for Magnus lay in the future, however, residing at the heart of efforts on behalf of the dead earl's nephew, Rognvald Kolsson, to secure his inheritance to the earldom. In the 1120s, however, Orkney was firmly in the hands of the Paulsson line, and on Hákon's death in c. 1123 control of the earldom passed unchallenged to his sons, Harald and Paul. As had happened so often in the past, there were tensions between these half-brothers, exacerbated by the ambitions of Harald's

[59] C. R. Wickham-Jones, *Orkney: A Historical Guide*. Edinburgh: Birlinn, 1998. pp. 138–39.
[60] *Orkneyinga Saga*, Chapters 50–52.

Figure 52 Brough of Birsay, Orkney, St Magnus' Church. Christianity was established in Orkney at the end of the tenth century, but it was only in the mid-eleventh century that a formal church structure was established in the earldom. St Magnus' Church was founded by Thorfinn the Mighty adjacent to his residence at Birsay and may later have become the seat of the first Orkney bishopric, which was moved to Kirkwall in the late twelfth century.

Caithness kin, headed by his aunt, Frakkok. Running like an undercurrent beneath the family tension was the by now familiar question of external political influences. These would surface spectacularly in the 1120s and 1130s. Relations between the rulers of Orkney and Caithness and the Scottish crown took a new turn in the first half of the twelfth century. From 1124 until the middle of the 1130s the Scottish king, David I, faced a succession of challenges to his position from rival segments of the royal family. Support for these pretenders was widespread in Scotland but was particularly strong in Moray and Ross, provinces with a long tradition of resistance to the intrusion of aggressive royal authority.[61] In the absence of strongly entrenched reserves of royal power in these regions, David depended heavily upon maintaining good personal relations with the principal regional rulers in northern Scotland. Orkney and Caithness figured significantly in his designs. A central strand in David's policies was the marriage c. 1134 of Margaret, daughter of Earl Hákon Paulsson, to Maddad, earl of Atholl.[62] This marriage forged a new political axis within northern Scotland, linking the principal noble family of the southern Highlands with the dominant force in the northern mainland. Between them, like the meat in a sandwich, lay Moray and Ross. According to *Orkneyinga Saga* the initiative for the marriage on the

---

[61] See, for example, R. Oram, *David I: The King Who Made Scotland*. Strond: Tempus, 2004. pp. 96–102.
[62] *Orkneyinga Saga*, Chapter 118.

Orkney side came from Frakkok, Margaret's aunt, a powerful woman in her own right who possessed extensive lands in south-east Sutherland and who had exercised great influence over her nephew, Harald Hákonsson.[63] Relations between this segment of the Orkney dynasty and the king of Scots may already have been strong, as saga tradition states that Earl Harald held his mainland territories as a Scottish vassal, and Frakkok appears to have seen in this relationship a means of strengthening her influence within the earldom. Her close association with Earl Harald, however, threw Frakkok into direct collision with Harald's brother and rival, Paul, and following Harald's suspicious death c. 1123,[64] soon after the half-brothers had succeeded their father to the earldom, Paul expelled her from Orkney on suspicion that she was plotting against him. His suspicions were justified, for Frakkok's household at Helmsdale in Sutherland formed something of a court-in-exile for Earl Paul's enemies.[65] It was at Helmsdale that Harald's son, Erlend, and Margaret, whose hatred of her brother Paul is attested in *Orkneyinga Saga*, found shelter.[66] For Frakkok, an alliance with the Earl of Atholl, who may have been a cousin of the Scottish king, would have immeasurably boosted the chances of Erlend succeeding to at least his father's lands and titles in Caithness and Sutherland, and may have held out the prospect of Scottish aid in securing even the earldom of Orkney itself. For David I, the Atholl-Orkney marriage offered the prospect of a strengthening of what had been in reality a rather nominal Scottish overlordship of Caithness and Sutherland in the time of Harald Hákonsson. Certainly, it bound Frakkok and her influential kin network to David's interest.[67] Traditional interpretations of the marriage have viewed it as being primarily of benefit to the Scots, increasing their influence in Caithness while neutralising Norwegian influence within the northern mainland from Orkney, but it may rather have been aimed at securing David I's interests in Moray and Ross.[68]

The dynastic strife in Orkney and Caithness took a new twist in 1135 when Rognvald Kolsson, grandson of Earl Erlend

[63] Ibid., Chapters 98 and 119.   [64] Ibid., Chapter 99.
[65] Ibid., Chapters 100–101.
[66] Ibid. Chapters 137–39; P. Topping, Harald Maddadson, earl of Orkney and Caithness, 1139–1206. *Scottish Historical Review*, Vol. 62, 1983, pp. 105–8.
[67] For Frakkok's kin, see *Orkneyinga Saga*, Chapters 97–98, 101.
[68] See Oram, *David I*, pp. 96–102.

Figure 53 Orphir, Orkney, the Earl's Bu. Orphir was one of the chief centres of the eleventh- and twelfth-century Orkney earldom. The excavated remains, adjacent to the ruins of the round church built in the 1120s, include a horizontal mill and the footings of a large hall, possibly the location of Earl Paul Hákonsson's great yule feast described in *Orkneyinga Saga*.

Thorfinsson, to whom the Norwegian king had granted half of Orkney, arrived in the islands to claim his share of the earldom. As early as 1129 he had received Norwegian confirmation of his rights, and in 1134 he had been given a fresh grant of half the earldom by King Harald Gilli.[69] Over the years various of his line's supporters had been working to secure his interest in the islands, and part of their work had seen the development of the cult of Magnus Erlendsson, Rognvald's uncle. Rognvald's first attempt in 1135 was defeated in Shetland and Caithness, but the following year, with backing from the Erlend party and the support of Frakkok and her kinsmen, and probably with the connivance of Earl Maddad of Atholl and his wife, Margaret, Rognvald captured and disposed of Earl Paul (Figure 53). At this point, however, agreement between the unfortunate Paul's rivals began to unravel, for Frakkok and her family were seeking a share in the earldom for Erlend Haraldsson, while Maddad and Margaret saw their son, Harald Maddadsson, as an alternative candidate.[70] King David I, who saw any further revival of Norwegian influence in the northern earldoms as a threat to his newly won control of northern Scotland, and who saw the Norwegian-appointed sole earl Rognvald Kolsson as that threat personified, presumably supported the Atholl plan. Erlend Haraldsson and his great-aunt Frakkok's kin network offered some counter-balance to Rognvald, but amenability to David's designs probably went no

---

[69] Thomson, *History of Orkney*, p. 61.　　[70] *Orkneyinga Saga*, Chapters 119, 138–39.

deeper than dynastic expediency dictated. For David the prospect of inserting the son of one of his own earls into Caithness was far more appealing, particularly since Harald Maddadsson was still a minor and would spend many years under the tutorship of guardians and councillors approved by the king.[71] David was hardly likely to pass up the opportunity of securing the closer integration of the northern mainland into his kingdom through the appointment of a half-Scottish earl.

David's support for Harald settled the issue in the child's favour. In 1139, aged five, he was admitted to a half-share in the Orkney earldom and the title of earl.[72] No record survives of a formal grant by David to Harald of the earldom of Caithness, but that had probably preceded the settlement with Rognvald Kolsson. This new arrangement was still vulnerable to challenge from Erlend Haraldsson's supporters, Frakkok in particular. Recognition of that danger by the Scots sealed Frakkok's fate, and she was soon afterwards burned to death in her own hall near Helmsdale by a force of men brought north from Atholl by Svein Asleifsson. Her slaying by Svein was ostensibly in revenge for her part in the murder of his father, but Svein Asleifsson was a notorious intriguer and violent mercenary who was associated closely with Maddad and Margaret. Indeed, *Orkneyinga Saga* presents him as their instrument for the removal of Earl Paul in 1136.[73] Family enmities amongst the Orkney dynasty were clearly being manipulated by the Scots in pursuit of strategic political interests. Harald Maddadsson's installation in Orkney and Caithness was a triumph for the Scots. Its main consequence was that through the 1140s Caithness and Sutherland were drawn increasingly into a Scottish orbit while Norwegian influence in Orkney was effectively neutralised. That being said, Harald was still a child, and Rognvald was to enjoy a long period as the dominant partner in the shared earldom by virtue of an agreed settlement brokered by the Scots.[74] Under his rule the position of the Erlend party in Orkney was considerably strengthened, not least through his forging of an alliance with the Church. The bishop, William the Old, who had sided with Hákon against Magnus, was won over with lavish promises and generous patronage, the most obvious manifestation of which was the

[71] Topping, Harald Maddadson, pp. 105–7.   [72] *Orkneyinga Saga*, Chapter 143.
[73] Ibid., Chapters 144–45.   [74] Thomson, *History of Orkney*, p. 69.

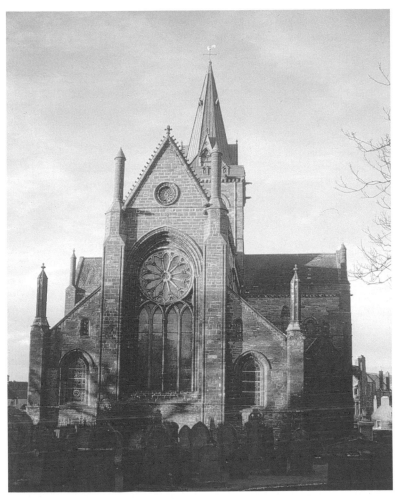

Figure 54 St Magnus Cathedral, Kirkwall, Orkney. Following his killing on the island of Egilsay, Earl Magnus was buried in Christchurch at Birsay. In 1135 his remains were moved into a shrine there, but in 1136–37 work began on a new cathedral at Kirkwall, to which his bones were eventually translated. The largest building erected in Orkney, employing masons from Durham, it is testimony to the wealth and power of the earldom in the mid-twelfth century.

establishment of a new cathedral at Kirkwall – in the heart of the Erlend line's main powerbase in east mainland Orkney – and its establishment as the shrine for the developing cult of Magnus Erlendsson (Figure 54).[75] The political deals between Rognvald and the supporters of Harald Maddadsson, together with Rognvald's sound working relationships with the other influential agents within the earldom, brought a long period of stability to the islands after the upheavals of the early twelfth century. Secure at home, Rognvald was able to depart on an extended pilgrimage to Jerusalem which took him through England and

[75] The best recent discussions of the development of St Magnus Cathedral and the cult are collected in B. E. Crawford, ed. St. Magnus Cathedral and Orkney's Twelfth-Century Renaissance. Aberdeen: Aberdeen University Press, 1988.

Figure 55 Castle of Old Wick, Wick, Caithness. Dating of the stark, cliff-top tower is uncertain, but its building is attributed to Earl Harald Maddadsson, in whose reign southern Scottish cultural influences – such as castle-building – penetrated the northern earldoms. The tower displays strong parallels with mid-twelfth and thirteenth-century stone castles elsewhere in Caithness and Orkney.

the Mediterranean lands, returning via Constantinople, Germany, Denmark and Norway.[76] His absence, however, was quickly to be capitalised on by his neighbours.

In 1151 King Eystein of Norway, with whom Harald Maddadsson had no formal political relationship, arrived in Orkney with a fleet. The teenage Harald, who had been left in nominal control of both Orkney and Caithness by Rognvald, was at Thurso in Caithness when Eystein arrived suddenly and captured him, forcing his submission to Norwegian overlordship as the price for his release (Figure 55).[77] At a stroke the Scottish domination of the earldom appeared to have been undone. Having achieved his primary objective, Eystein cruised rather aimlessly down the eastern coast of Scotland and England, raiding as he went, but apparently with no clear purpose other than to win plunder.[78] That same year, possibly in an attempt to counter this reverse, King David introduced a wild-card into the equation by advancing the claims of another member of the Orkney dynasty, Erlend Haraldsson, grandson of Earl Hákon and the son of the man disposed of by Harald Maddadsson's kin c. 1123. David granted him half of Caithness, re-emphasising the vassalic relationship between the rulers of Orkney and the Scottish crown in respect of their northern mainland earldom.

---

[76] *Orkneyinga Saga*, Chapters 86 to 89.
[77] Topping, Harald Maddadson, pp. 105–20; Thomson, *History of Orkney*, p. 70.
[78] *Orkneyinga Saga*, Chapter 91.

To further complicate matters, King Eystein granted Harald Maddadsson's half of Orkney to Erlend. The result was a three-cornered conflict between Erlend, Harald and Rognvald which ended in 1154 with the death of Erlend.[79] Four years later the murder of Rognvald – who was later to be venerated as a saint alongside his uncle, Magnus – left Harald in sole possession of the earldoms of Caithness and Orkney. With the undivided resources of the earldoms behind him, and with neither the Scots nor the Norwegians in a position to interfere in their government, Harald's ambitions were given free rein.

The career of Harald Maddadsson represented a final flourish in the long, turbulent history of the Norse earldom. Dynastic connections saw him enmeshed in the tortuous politics of Canmore Scotland, and his support for the meic Máel Coluim and meic Uilleim claimants to the Scottish throne contributed to the prolonging of the rebellions staged by those families against Kings Malcolm IV and William the Lion. The importance of Harald in these rebellions cannot be overstated, for his second wife, Hvarfloð, is said to have been a daughter of Máel Coluim, the illegitimate son of David I's elder brother, Alexander I. Their eldest son, Thorfinn, was therefore the successor to the meic Máel Coluim claims and, in the eyes of the kings of Scots, an enemy to be neutralised or eliminated. Down to the 1190s William the Lion undertook a series of campaigns into the far north of Scotland which brought the effective reach of Scottish royal power ever closer to Harald's powerbase in Caithness. The importance placed on Thorfinn can be seen in Scottish demands that he be handed over to them as a hostage for his father's good behaviour in various attempts to secure a settlement after Harald's capture in 1197, although he was neither Harald's eldest son nor his heir.[80] Clearly, the most important objective for William was to eliminate the threat to his position from this rival lineage rather than to control Earl Harald. The unfortunate Thorfinn was handed over as security and, following Harald's renewal of hostilities in 1198, suffered blinding and castration in his prison, dying shortly thereafter.[81]

[79]   Ibid., Chapters 92–94.
[80]   *The Chronicle of Melrose*, ed. A. O. Anderson, M. O. Anderson and W. C. Dickinson. London: P. Lund, Humphries & Co. Ltd, 1936. *sub anno* 1197.
[81]   W. F. Skene, ed. and F. J. H. Skene, trans. *The Historians of Scotland*. Vol. IV, *John of Fordun's Chronicle of the Scottish Nation*. Edinburgh: Edmonston and Douglas, 1872. *sub anno* 1196.

By the 1190s Harald's ambitions were being checked on all fronts. In the Isles and Ireland, where he had attempted to rebuild the empire controlled by his ancestor, Thorfinn the Mighty, and where he had forged an alliance with Somhairlidh mac Gilla Brighte in the late 1150s and early 1160s, his schemes had begun to unravel by 1171. To what extent Svein Asleifsson's final, fatal assault on Dublin represented a revival of Orkney designs on control of this still important city, rather than a private Viking enterprise, is a matter of conjecture, but it does emphasise the extent to which Harald and his men sought to capitalise on the political disturbances in the west that had followed on from the death of Somhairlidh in 1164, and to participate in the final death throes of Dublin's existence as an independent kingdom.[82] The impact of these northern raiders in mid-twelfth-century Ireland should not be downplayed: in 1170 an Orkney fleet had established a base in Ulster and had defeated and killed one of the northern Uí Néill king's leading warlords there.[83] Svein's death at Dublin in 1171[84] is usually seen as marking the end of Orkney activity down the western sea-lanes, but Harald himself clearly maintained an active interest in the Isles throughout his career, although that interest was never converted into effective action. Indeed, the main difficulty that Harald experienced in his career was his inability to focus his energies on one enterprise at a time, where he could bring the still formidable resources of his earldom to bear. Instead, he attempted opportunistically to exploit any opening that came his way, very much in the mould of his forebears but in a world where old-style Viking freedom of manoeuvre was becoming increasingly difficult to perform.

It was keenness to exert Orkney influence in Scandinavia whilst still embroiled in his wars in Scotland that proved almost to be Harald's undoing. In the early 1190s he threw his support behind a rebellion aimed at overthrowing the Norwegian king, Sverrir. Harald's immediate motive may have been to nip in the bud Norwegian support for another dynastic rival, Harald Ingiridsson, or Harald the Younger, the grandson of St Magnus, but he also saw a chance to establish an influential place in the councils of the

---

[82] See, for example, S. Duffy, Irishmen and Islesmen in the kingdoms of Dublin and Man, 1052–1171. Eriu, Vol. 43, 1992, pp. 132–33. For the possibility of Harald's interest in Ulster, see Topping, Harald Maddadson, pp. 109–11.

[83] Annals of Ulster, sub anno 1170.   [84] Orkneyinga Saga, Chapters 107–8.

Figure 56 Housa Voe, Papa Stour, Shetland. Norse colonisation of Shetland may have begun in the ninth century, and by the eleventh century its scattered community of wealthy farmers and traders formed part of the Orkney earldom. The Orkney earls lost control of Shetland to the Norwegian crown early in the thirteenth century, and their possessions in the islands, including farms on Papa Stour, became prized components of the royal estate.

young pretender to the Norwegian throne, Sigurd Magnusson. A large contingent of Orkney and Shetland warriors provided the backbone for the invasion of Norway, which at first enjoyed success and succeeded in defeating Sverrir and proclaiming Sigurd king. In early 1194, however, Sverrir struck back and defeated and slew his rival, killing also most of Harald's men. Faced with the prospect of a retaliatory attack by Sverrir, Harald travelled to Bergen and threw himself on the king's mercy. Sverrir imposed humiliating terms, which saw Shetland brought under the direct control of the Norwegian crown and heavy financial burdens placed on Orkney (Figure 56). Norwegian influence in Orkney now stood at a level higher than that ever exercised by Sverrir's predecessors, and crown authority there was set to grow stronger yet through the thirteenth century.[85]

[85] Thomson, *History of Orkney*, pp. 73–74.

Still reeling from this crisis, Harald was sucked into yet another round of the conflict in Scotland, which resulted in defeat and submission, and eventually in the death of his son, Thorfinn (see above). When Harald gained his release from Scottish captivity he returned to his earldom to face Harald the Younger, who had invaded Orkney. As Rognvald Kolsson had used the spiritual reputation of his uncle, Magnus, as a means of building support in the islands, so Harald the Younger used his grandfather, Rognvald, whose cult was advanced aggressively: 'God made manifest the worthiness of the Earl with a number of wondrous miracles.'[86] Support for the Erlend line had evidently remained strong in the earldom and, if the well-informed English royal clerk and chronicler, Roger of Howden, can be relied upon, Harald Maddadsson was driven out of Orkney to seek refuge and military support in the Western Isles.[87] There, presumably amongst the sons of his old ally, Somhairlidh, he raised a fleet and launched a surprise attack on Orkney, pursued Harald the Young to Caithness and killed him in a battle near Wick.[88] Recognising the probable consequences of his actions, Harald Maddadsson sought to come to terms with King William, but no settlement was reached and the king ordered the mutilation of the captive Thorfinn. William also formally deprived Harald of the Scottish earldom of Caithness and sold it to Rognvald Godredsson, king of Man, a great-grandson of Earl Hákon Paulsson, a man of pro-Scottish rather than pro-Norwegian leanings and a bitter enemy of Harald Maddadsson's meic Somhairlidh allies in the Hebrides.[89]

[86] *Orkneyinga Saga*, Chapter 104.
[87] *Chronica Magistri Rogeri de Houedene*, ed. W. Stubbs. Vol. IV. Rerum Britannicarum medii aevi scriptores, 51 . London: Longmans, Green, Reader, and Dyer, 1868. *sub anno* 1196. Howden is a fairly trustworthy source for the politics of late twelfth-century Scotland, holding a prebend of Glasgow and being present in Scotland on several occasions between 1187 and 1201 on both church affairs and also in the service of Henry II of England: A. Duncan, Roger of Howden and Scotland, 1187–1201. In *Church, Chronicle and Learning in Medieval and Early Renaissance Scotland. Essays Presented to Donald Watt on the Occasion of the Completion of the Publication of Bower's Scotichronicon*, ed. B. E. Crawford. Edinburgh: Mercat Press, 1999. pp. 135–60.
[88] *Chronica Magistri Rogeri*, *sub anno* 1196; *Orkneyinga Saga*, Chapter 109. *Orkneyinga Saga* suggests that there may have been an attempt to build up another saint's cult around Harald the Young: 'People in Caithness think him a true saint and a church stands where he was killed.'
[89] *Chronica Magistri Rogeri*, *sub anno* 1196; *Orkneyinga Saga*, trans. and introd. by H. Pálsson and P. Edwards. Penguin Classics. Harmondsworth: Penguin Books, 1981. Chapter 110.

It was a good plan, but Rognvald was unable to secure his grip on the northern earldom and, when he disbanded his warriors in the winter of 1201, Harald simply crossed from Orkney to Caithness, killed the Islesman's representatives and resumed control.[90] Although he had regained sole control of his two earldoms Harald was now more isolated than ever, for he knew that he could not depend upon Norwegian aid, and his defiance of King William and repeated breaches of faith with the Scottish king made a settlement from that quarter other than on the harshest of terms unlikely. Instead he turned to the one power capable of exerting pressure that would perhaps make William agree to a negotiated peace: King John of England. William's relationship with John was not good (William supported the claims of John's nephew, Arthur of Brittany, to the English throne), and the Scottish king could not risk concentrating his attention on the remote north of his kingdom whilst there was any threat of war in the south. Nevertheless, William did lead an army into the north but, mindful of the dangers to his rear, agreed a settlement with Harald without coming to battle.[91] Like the earlier settlement with King Sverrir in respect of Orkney, the deal with the Scots saw Harald make heavy financial concessions which bit deeply into his resources, and while it conceded him undisputed title to the earldom of Caithness, he was obliged to make explicit acknowledgement of Scottish overlordship of the earldom. The dream of an independent Orkney-Caithness sea-kingdom had finally dissolved, and when Harald died in 1206 Orkney's Viking Age died with him.

What the career of Harald Maddadsson revealed tellingly was how much the northern world had changed since the early eleventh century. The change was not simply a result of Scandinavian Orkney's fuller integration into the political and cultural mainstream of Europe, it was also a matter of how radically the political structures of the British Isles and Scandinavia had been redrawn in the course of the twelfth century. The fluidity of the eleventh and early twelfth centuries, which had seen the rapid rise and fall of personal empires, had given way to the emergence of fewer and more stable powers. In 1000 there had been many kings and kingdoms within the

---

[90] *Orkneyinga Saga*, Chapter 111.   [91] Thomson, *History of Orkney*, p. 77.

British Isles, but by 1200, although there were still many men who called themselves kings, only two viable kingdoms remained.[92] Royal power in mainland Britain and in Scandinavia had grown immeasurably, and that power had extended both in range and effectiveness. Harald's main successes had occurred generally at times when his Scottish or Norwegian overlords were otherwise distracted and when he had been able to capitalise on domestic challenges to their authority, but once their focus was turned fully upon him even the geographical remoteness from the centres of power that had once shielded Orkney from all but the most determined opponent could no longer protect him. Harald may have wished to act in the tradition of Thorfinn the Mighty and Sigurd the Stout, and certainly that is how *Orkneyinga Saga* portrayed him,[93] but in so doing he was functioning as a relic of a bygone age kicking against the march of the new.

What Harald and his successors had to contend with was not just kings who could draw upon superior military resources but rulers who had the will and the means to intervene directly in the affairs of Caithness and Orkney. Kings of Norway had sought to intrude their servants into the northern earldom since the early 1000s, meeting with variable and usually short-lived degrees of success. To be the Norwegian king's agent in the islands was frequently a passport to an early, and usually violent, death. Indeed in 1202 Harald had King Sverrir's representative, or sysselman (Old Norse *sýslumaðr*), Arne Lørja, murdered almost as soon as word of the king's death reached Orkney,[94] but the fact that he survived until after his master's death shows how limited Harald's freedom of action had become: Thorfinn and Hákon Paulsson had slain royal agents with virtual impunity. Harald's disposal of Arne Lørja, moreover, should not obscure the fact that the earl or his successors were unable to regain control of Shetland or the lands within Orkney that the crown had taken into its own hands in the 1150s and 1190s. Although Harald had died in a state of rebellion against the Norwegian crown in 1206, his sons, the earls John and David, had soon recognised the

[92] For the causes and consequences of this trend, see R. Frame, *The Political Development of the British Isles, 1100–1400*. Oxford: Oxford University Press, 1995; and R. R. Davies, *Domination and Conquest: The Experience of Ireland, Scotland and Wales, 1100–1300*. Cambridge: Cambridge University Press, 1990.

[93] *Orkneyinga Saga*, Chapter 112.   [94] Thomson, *History of Orkney*, p. 77.

futility of their father's stance and made a submission to the
Norwegian king, Ingi, 'which seems to have been as abject as
Harald Maddadsson's surrender' in 1194.[95] Ingi installed a new
sysselman and kept the earls on a tight rein thereafter, requiring
regular public acknowledgement of their submission and formal
displays of their vassal status. After Earl David's death in 1214
Earl John was acknowledged as sole earl but was obliged to
recognise his dependence on the Norwegian crown and to perform military service on demand, as in 1230 when he provided
ships for the Norwegian expedition to the Hebrides (see above,
p. 250). At no time in the past had the earls of Orkney so publicly
and explicitly accepted the bonds of dependence imposed upon
them by the crown of Norway.

The tightening of the Norwegian noose on Orkney coincided
with a strengthening of the Scottish grip on Caithness. The
somewhat anachronistic references in *Orkneyinga Saga* to elev-
enth- and early twelfth-century earls holding Caithness as a
vassal of the Scottish crown projects into the past the political
reality of the later twelfth and thirteenth centuries. What may
have started as a grudging acknowledgement of superior lordship
which had little substance behind it, or a convenient device to be
used against Norwegian pretensions, clearly acquired an uncomfortable reality once the Canmore kings began to flex their muscles in the northern mainland of Scotland. By the 1130s the
personal relationships with the earls upon which the Scots had
based their domination of the far north began to be replaced by
new mechanisms for control.[96] For much of the twelfth century
the Scottish crown was unable to establish secular agents to the
north of Ross in Sutherland or Caithness, but David I began a
policy of using clerics as his representatives there. There was a
double purpose behind this move, for not only was the Scottish
king introducing a dependable servant into a key position in the
regional power structure, he was also curtailing the influence
within his kingdom of a foreign bishop – the bishop of Orkney –
who was a suffragan of a foreign metropolitan. On one level this
was simply part of David's policy of excluding any foreign metropolitan influence from Scottish territory and establishing a

---

[95] Ibid., pp. 78–79.
[96] Oram, David I and the Scottish conquest and colonisation of moray, *Northern Scotland*, Vol. 19, 1999, pp. 12–15.

unitary *ecclesia Scoticana* coterminous with his kingdom. On another, however, it provided Scottish kings with an equivalent in Caithness of the Norwegian sysselmen in Orkney.

Like the sysselmen, to be the Scottish bishop of Caithness exposed the incumbent to a considerable degree of hostility and danger. How considerable that hostility and danger could be was revealed in 1201, when Bishop John of Caithness was targeted by Harald Maddadsson. John, who may have betrayed the earl's treasonable dealings with England to William the Lion, was captured in his castle at Scrabster and, according to tradition, blinded and had his tongue cut out.[97] In addition to acting as the Scottish king's informer, Bishop John may also have been impeding Harald's revenue-collecting in Caithness at a critical point in the earl's efforts to regain control of his domain. Harald, mindful of the dangers of creating another saintly martyr and of killing a bishop into the bargain, opted for mutilation instead and was prepared to pay the long-term financial consequences to reap the short-term political benefits. Twenty years later Harald's son, Earl John, found himself in a similar position with Bishop John's successor, Bishop Adam. Adam's attempts to re-organise his see and exercise his full spiritual and fiscal rights as bishop had brought him into conflict with the people of his diocese and, when they rose against him, Earl John saw an opportunity to remove a man who was identified closely with the interests of the Scottish king, Alexander II. When the bishop was murdered in his manor house at Halkirk in Caithness in the summer of 1222 Earl John almost literally stood by and watched. It was a gross miscalculation, for the young and aggressive Alexander II, benefiting from the recent Scottish colonisation of south-east Sutherland, led an army into Caithness and forced John's grovelling submission.[98] It was not quite the final fling for Caithness's resistance to the inexorable spread of Scottish power, but Alexander cannot but have left its earl and people with no question in their mind of the unshakeable grip over them now exercised by the Scottish crown.[99]

[97] Anderson, *Early Sources of Scottish History*, Vol. II, p. 355.
[98] *Chronicle of Melrose, sub anno* 1222.
[99] For a discussion of the role of the bishops of Caithness, see B. E. Crawford, Norse earls and Scottish bishops in Caithness: a clash of cultures. In *The Viking Age in Caithness, Orkney and the North Atlantic. Select papers from the Proceedings of the Eleventh*

The regular humiliation of John by his Norwegian and Scottish overlords probably contributed significantly to his downfall. There were still men in the northern earldoms who looked to the now distantly related representatives of the Erlend line to restore them to their former freedoms. The family claims had fallen to Snaekoll Gunisson, great-grandson of Rognvald Kolsson, who demanded restoration of his ancestral estates and who may have aspired to a share in the earldom title itself. Allied with the Norwegian sysselman, Hanef Ungi, Snaekoll built up a substantial following in the islands, and in 1230 Hanef and his men murdered Earl John at Thurso in Caithness. Pursued back to Orkney by John's vengeful kin, Hanef and Snaekoll took refuge in Cubbie Roo's Castle on the island of Wyre and successfully resisted all attempts to dislodge them. The stand-off on Wyre was only ended by an agreement by both sides to submit themselves to the judgement of King Hákon IV in Norway, but Hanef used his Norwegian connections to escape justice (Figure 57). Further disaster followed, for the vessel carrying the leading members of the murdered earl's kin and the principal land-holding families of Orkney sank on the return voyage, removing at a stroke the political leadership of the earldom. It was a cataclysm that later Orkney tradition saw as the source of all the islands' subsequent misfortunes.[100] John's death was in many ways the sunset of the old Scandinavian earldom. Although the line of earls continued, evidently represented by the heirs of one of John's sisters or daughters, they were from a family with almost purely Scottish perspectives and appear to have paid little more than lip-service to their Norwegian overlord. While Earl Magnus III (1256–73) accompanied Hákon IV on his westward voyage in the summer of 1263, displaying public enthusiasm for the great royal expedition against the Scots, when the king sailed south in August the earl remained in Orkney.[101] He took no further part in the campaign, and it is evident that the Scottish king, Alexander III, had used his domination of Caithness and the kinship ties between Magnus and the Scottish nobility to neutralise the earl. The former powerbroker

Viking Congress, Thurso and Kirkwall, 22 August–1 September 1989, ed. C. E. Botey, J. Jesch and C. D. Morris. Edinburgh: Edinburgh University Press, 1993, pp. 129–47.

[100] Thomson, *History of Orkney*, pp. 81–82.

[101] Anderson, *Early Sources of Scottish History*, Vol. II, p. 616.

Figure 57 Cubbie Roo's Castle, Wyre, Orkney. *Orkneyinga Saga* records that Kolbein Hruga (the name Cubbie Roo is a modern corruption of his proper name), owner of the island of Wyre, built 'a fine stone castle, which was a strong defence' c. 1145–50. The 7-metre square tower, now reduced to its lowest courses of stone, is the only surviving example of a new type of lordly building that appeared in Orkney in the mid-twelfth century. In 1231 it provided safe refuge to the murderers of Earl John Haraldsson against a siege by the earl's kinsmen and supporters.

had become the pawn: Orkney, far from shaping and directing the destinies of kingdoms, had become a staging post in a contest between greater powers. The dragon that had clawed and roared its bloody path through the epic struggles that spawned the medieval kingdoms of Norway, Scotland and England slunk from the political stage with barely a whimper.

CHAPTER 11

Crossing the North Atlantic

Dominating the popular perception of the people who flowed out of Scandinavia in the Viking Age is the image of the blood-thirsty warrior bent on slaughter, rape and pillage. It is a powerful image, ingrained by centuries of lurid tales from early chronicles, reworked and embellished to titillate the fantasies of later generations and re-emphasised in more recent times through literary and film depictions of Nordic psychopaths unleashed on the unsuspecting people of more civilised parts of Europe.[1] Although there was something of a reaction among scholars in the 1960s and 1970s against the standard portrayal of the Vikings in history as uniformly bloody-handed barbarians, with greater emphasis placed upon their mercantile and agricultural traditions, few would now seek to deny the negative aspect of the Viking impact on Europe. The re-ordering of the political map in the British Isles and the near-collapse of the rich religious culture of Anglo-Saxon England[2] were the consequences of bloody and protracted raiding and warfare in which the brief, roman candle-like brilliance of the Scandinavian colonies in York or Dublin and the ruthless warlords who contended for control over them dominate the traditional histories. Concentration on the violence of the Viking Age, however, means neglecting the colonial and mercantile aspect that drove Scandinavians in other directions: eastwards into what became European Russia and along the trade

---

[1] For an assessment of the 'memory of the Vikings' and the traditional image of the Scandinavians of the Viking Age, see K. Eldjárn, The Viking Myth. In *The Vikings*, ed. R. T. Farrell. London: Phillimore, 1982. pp. 262–73.

[2] A. P. Smyth, Effect of Scandinavian raiders on the English and Irish churches: a preliminary reassessment. In *Britain and Ireland 900–1300. Insular Responses to Medieval European Change*, ed. A. P. Smyth and B. Smith. Cambridge: Cambridge University Press, 1998. pp. 1–38; P. Cavill, *Vikings: Fear and Faith in Anglo-Saxon England*. London: HarperCollins, 2001.

routes to the Black Sea and Constantinople, and westwards into
the waters of the North Atlantic, where they followed the island
stepping-stones that lead from northern Scotland to the eastern
seaboard of what is now Canada. It is on these North Atlantic
colonies that this present chapter will focus.

The discovery and settlement of the islands of the North
Atlantic was a maritime enterpise that involved consideration
not only of the worth of these islands as new homelands, but
also the logistics of maintaining communication with the rest of
the Scandinavian world. Economic calculations depended in part
upon their suitability for maintaining the raiding tradition of
their new inhabitants, but more importantly upon ecological or
environmental suitability to permit agriculture and fishing.
Distance too was an issue. Contact between the islands and the
expanded world of Scandinavian Europe required vessels of a
kind suited to the transportation of people, stock, and both
exports and imports. The discovery of the islands of the North
Atlantic archipelago was discussed earlier. This chapter will first
consider the nature of colonisation and the settlements that were
established before turning to look at how this was achieved and
sustained as a maritime enterprise.

Settlements

At what point the raiders into the west began to put down roots
and establish settlements is one of the great unanswered – and
probably unanswerable – questions of the Viking Age. Most sagas
that purport to record the early stages of the process offer a
hopelessly garbled chronology, and their one regular theme –
an attribution of the incentive to migrate from Scandinavia to
hostility towards the state-building ambitions of Harald Hárfagri –
is bedevilled by the internal contradictions of the same sagas.
King Harald's rise to more than regional dominance may have
been one of several factors that encouraged many Norwegian
families to make the westward voyage, but archaeological evidence suggests that their predecessors had been making that
same voyage for at least a generation before them. Indeed, if
the identification of a grave partly eroded away by the sea at
Machrins on Colonsay in the Western Isles of Scotland as a

female burial is correct, then the dating of the interment to AD 780 ± 70 years could suggest that the earliest raiders were accompanied by their womenfolk.[3] Whether or not their presence on raiding voyages can be taken as a sign of an intention to settle remains open to question, but the possibility must be considered. As has been commented of settlement archaeology in the Western Isles, 'one or two sites can dramatically change a received picture',[4] and so it is with our understanding of the chronology of the colonisation of the North Atlantic islands. Dependence on the shaky calendar offered by the sagas is giving way to firmer chronologies based on the dating of excavated evidence, but the problem remains of the vagaries of chance in locating an early site or in securing material from it that can offer more secure dates.

Orkney and Shetland

It is likely that the first stage in the Scandinavian colonisation of the North Atlantic occurred in Shetland or in Orkney, island groups located strategically as staging posts along the routes from Norway to the most profitable raiding and trading areas in Ireland and northern England.[5] The exact chronology of Viking raids on the Northern Isles is a complete unknown, but it can be conjectured from the dating of recorded attacks on the British mainland and the Western Isles that Orkney and Shetland had been targeted in the second half of the eighth century. It has been pointed out that the sailing time from western Norway to Shetland is roughly twenty-four hours and that Orkney and mainland Britain lay only a few hours further to the south. Raids on the British Isles, therefore, may have been made in single voyages leaving direct from Scandinavia and returning to the home fjords in a single season.[6] There was no reason, then, for the eighth-century raiders to establish a base in the Northern Isles, but at some stage a decision was taken to move from raid to land-take.

---

[3] J. Ritchie, *Excavations at Machrins, Colonsay*. Proceedings of the Society of Antiquaries of Scotland, 111. Edinburgh: Society of Antiquaries of Scotland, 1991.

[4] C. D. Morris, The Vikings in the British Isles: some aspects of their settlement and economy. In *The Vikings*, see note 1 above, p. 73.

[5] E. Roesdahl, *The Vikings*. London: Penguin Books, 1998 [1987]. pp. 211–13.

[6] Roesdahl, *Vikings*, pp. 210–11.

At what point seasonal raiding parties did make that shift in policy and begin to establish temporary bases in the islands remains unknown, but it was a momentous decision, the shock-waves from which were to reverberate throughout north-west Europe down to the mid-thirteenth century.

The historical processes beneath this development are almost impossible to untangle from the mass of later mythology, no surviving Scottish source recording the narrative, and later saga tradition – none older than the late twelfth century – offering hopelessly contradictory scenarios. The wealth of prehistoric and early historic era archaeology in both Shetland and Orkney, much of it still strikingly visible in the islands' landscape, proclaims the presence there of a rich and sophisticated culture with roots reaching back to the early Neolithic.[7] From the sixth to the eighth centuries AD the islands had formed part of the culturally Pictish zone of northern Scotland and supported a vibrant society of warriors and craftsmen who left their mark in superb sculpture, such as the slabs from Bressay, Cunningsburgh or Papil in Shetland and from Birsay and Gurness in Orkney, and in fine metalwork such as the silverware discovered in the St Ninian's Isle hoard from Shetland.[8] There are hints, too, of sophisticated territorial organisation: a 'king of Orcc' is recorded as being present at the court of the Pictish king, Bridei mac Maelchu, near Inverness in the 560s.[9] Such evidence alone is sufficient to cause later Norwegian traditions of the first Scandinavian settlers in Orkney and Shetland arriving in a people-less landscape to be dismissed out of hand, but it is a striking feature of the sagas that the native islanders figure nowhere in accounts of the land-taking.

Embedded into most accounts of the origins of Scandinavian Orkney and Shetland is a tradition of the islands serving as a base for raiders who preyed on the lands to the south. How those raiders secured their bases has been a subject of endless

---

[7] A. Ritchie, *Prehistoric Orkney*. London: Batsford and Historic Scotland, 1995; this offers a superb overview of the islands' archaeological heritage from the Neolithic to the Iron Age.

[8] Ritchie, *Prehistoric Orkney*, pp. 117–18; S. Foster, *Picts, Gaels and Scots. Early Historic Scotland*. London: B.T. Batsford Ltd/Historic Scotland, 1996. pp. 30, 41, 43–44, 49, 66–67.

[9] *Adomnán's Life of Columba*, ed. and trans. M. O. Anderson. Oxford Medieval Texts. Oxford: Clarendon Press, 1991. Book II, Chapter 42.

conjecture, proposals ranging from lurid narratives of massacre and enslavement to late twentieth-century politically correct notions of peaceful integration and intermarriage.[10] The latter is a hopelessly naïve and utopian view, given what we know about the impact of the Scandinavians more widely in Britain and Europe. Integration and intermarriage formed part of the process of settlement, but it came at the end of long phases of predation and conquest. The burial of hoards of native goods, such as that from St Ninian's Isle,[11] points to instability and social disloca- tion, whilst the sharp changes in the cultural record on excavated sites, such as at Jarlshof in Shetland or Birsay in Orkney,[12] possibly indicate a process of dispossession and appropriation by incomers (Figures 58, 59). The very fact that Norse settlement and topographic names utterly dominate the place-name map of the Northern Isles must surely indicate that native populations and native naming traditions were swamped beneath a wave of colonists, and that the process occurred too rapidly for native traditions to be accommodated within those of the newcomers.[13] Although continuing archaeological work is allowing us con- stantly to refine the picture and permit us to identify instances of what appears to be native survival alongside Scandinavian

Figure 58
Brough of Birsay, Orkney, Viking long houses. The island site at Brough of Birsay appears to have been a centre of power even in pre-Norse times. Norse occupation at the site developed through the tenth century, to which period these houses belong, when it became one of the chief seats of the Orkney earls.

[10] Roesdahl, Vikings, p. 212.   [11] Foster, Picts, pp. 66–67.   [12] Ibid., p. 49.
[13] B. E. Crawford, Scandinavian Settlement in Northern Britain: Thirteen Studies of Place-Names in Their Historical Context. Studies in the Early History of Britain. London, New York: Leicester University Press, 1995.

Figure 59
Brough of Birsay, Orkney, Norse bath-house. Part of the late tenth- and early eleventh-century complex has been identified traditionally as the main residence of Sigurd the Stout and his son, Thorfinn the Mighty. The buildings include a hall with a raised dais, a network of drains and heating ducts, and a bath-house, all of which bear testimony to the sophistication of the earls' court.

colonisation,[14] the island society that emerged in the course of the tenth century was almost wholly Scandinavian in material culture and social organisation.

Occupation of Orkney and Shetland by the Norse provided them with a springboard for future expansion, of both their raiding activities and their colonial ventures. Orkney in particular became the hub from which Viking sea-lords extended their tentacles of power into the rest of the British Isles. From the beginning of the tenth century that importance had increased as the islands came to form a vital nexus in a series of sea-ways that stretched from the western shores of the European mainland, north through the Irish Sea and east to Scandinavia or on northwards to the Faroes, Iceland and Greenland.

The Faroes

As with the Northern Isles of Scotland we are reliant upon much later saga accounts for any non-archaeological evidence of the processes of colonisation in the Faeroe Islands. In common with the main tradition underlying the narrative of settlement in the Norse western colonies, the occupation of the Faroes is assigned to the reign of Harald Hárfagri (c. 880–c. 930) and to colonists

[14] Roesdahl, *Vikings*, p. 212.

seeking to escape from his tyranny in Norway. There are, however, problems with that tradition. If the Faroes are the islands mentioned in the early ninth century by the Irish monk Dicuil as having once been occupied by Irish hermits but abandoned by them owing to the unwelcome attentions of Scandinavian pirates, Norse settlement may have begun much earlier than the saga sources would indicate. The main source, *Færeyinga Saga*, which focusses on events in the late tenth and early eleventh centuries but was not composed until the early thirteenth century,[15] provides us with a first colonist – Grim Kamban – and assigns him a *floruit* in Harald's reign. Grim's by-name, however, raises some problems, for it is of Gaelic derivation, which implies that he had spent a considerable period, or had been born, in a region where there was already significant cultural interaction between Norse and Gaels, possibly in the Hebrides. Grim, then, may be part of that re-migration northwards from the Western Isles and northern mainland Scotland to Iceland that followed the collapse of Ketil Flatnef or Ketil Find's domain towards the close of the ninth century. How can these divergent pieces of evidence be reconciled, if at all? The answer may be that a similar process to what occurred in the Northern Isles took place in the Faroes. In the late eighth and early ninth centuries the islands were subject to periodic visits by Norwegian Vikings but, given the islands' proximity to northern Britain and Scandinavia which allowed raiders to sail there and return to their home bases in a single season, they were not at first settled permanently. Once Iceland had been discovered and its colonisation begun, the islands became an important staging point in the voyage between the Scandinavian homeland and colonies in the British Isles and the new settlements in Iceland.

The Faroes had much to attract them to colonists. Despite their northern latitude they benefit from a maritime climate tempered by the warmer waters of the Gulf Stream (Figures 60, 61). That same warm current brings a rich diversity of marine life, and the whales, fish shoals and sea-birds that feed on them. These exploitable marine resources provide a basis for subsistence. The islands themselves are generally precipitous, climbing steeply from the waters of the North Atlantic, but their slopes are

[15] Ibid., p. 270.

Figure 60
Mykines, Faeroe Islands. A mild climate, coupled with the rich pasture and abundant marine resources of the islands, attracted Norse colonists to Faeroe in the mid-ninth century.

Figure 61
Mykines, Faeroe Islands. Warmed by the Gulf Stream, the Faeroe Islands enjoy a richer environment than their northern latitude would otherwise permit. The lush grazing supported a largely pastoral economy, supplemented by the abundant fish and wildlife of the surrounding seas.

clothed with pasture capable of sustaining good-sized flocks and herds – the name Faeroe means 'Sheep Island' – although there is little cultivable land. Pollen evidence and saga tradition indicate that the pre-settlement landscape was clothed in extensive scrubland vegetation but no true woodland. The sagas, however, claim that the shores provided a rich supply of driftwood, carried to the islands from North America on the Atlantic currents. Timber suitable for building had to be imported from Norway, as had iron necessary for tools, weapons and rivets for ship-building, and grain to supplement the meagre supply of barley the islanders could grow for themselves.

A combination of marine erosion and the limited supply of suitable areas for development of settlement has meant that few archaeological remains have been identified that can be dated to the earliest phases of colonisation (Figure 62). One important, if damaged, site is at Kvívík, where erosion has removed most of what appears to have been a large farm complex comprising at least two long houses. The more complete site at Toftanes, datable to the late ninth or early tenth centuries, has produced evidence for a lifestyle very similar to that of Scandinavian Shetland.[16] As in Iceland (see below), the colony in the Faroes appears to have been dominated by a few wealthy,

Figure 62 Faeroe Islands. The mountainous landscape of Faeroe conceals a rich environment capable of supporting a substantial Norse colony. Settlement, the best pasture and arable were limited mainly to a narrow strip between the mountains and the sea, nowadays made to seem even more slender by coastal erosion and rising sea-levels, with rough pasture on the lower slopes of the steeply rising interior.

[16] S. S. Hansen, The Norse landnam in the Faroe Islands in the light of recent excavations at Toftanes, Leirvík. *Northern Studies*, Vol. 25, 1988, pp. 58–84.

Figure 63
Kirkjubøur,
Faeroe Islands.
The first church
on this site was
built c. 1060, over
half a century
after the
acceptance of
Christianity by
the Faeroese.
Around 1100
Kirkjubøur
became the seat
of a Faeroese
bishopric, which
in 1152 was made
subject to the
Norwegian
archdiocese of
Niðaros. There
are several
churches
clustered on the
site, including
the remains of
the original mid-
eleventh-century
building, but the
main ruin,
known as
Mururin, appears
to date to the
fourteenth or
fifteenth
centuries.

aristocratic families, and these came to control the political and legal life of the islands. Their control was formalised in the annual thing which met at Tinganes, now within the modern Faroese capital, Torshavn. This island elite was able to keep the claims of Norwegian kings to the overlordship of their colony at bay into the twelfth century, but c. 1180 the Norwegian crown succeeded in imposing its power on Faeroe. One agency that had contributed significantly to the build-up of Norwegian influence was the Church. Faeroe had converted to Christianity probably early in the eleventh century, and in the early 1100s a bishopric for the islands was established at Kirkjubøur,[17] where the ruins of the large medieval church that served as the cathedral survive (Figure 63). When the archdiocese of Niðaros (Trondheim) was established in 1152 the Faeroese bishopric was one of the sees included under its metropolitan jurisdiction. Within three decades, that ecclesiastical overlordship had been extended into political dominance.[18]

Iceland

In common with the colonisation of Orkney, Shetland, the Hebrides and the Faroes, medieval traditions relating to the

---

[17] I. Keillar, Kirkjubøur. *Northern Studies*, Vol. 20, 1983, pp. 38–44.
[18] J. Haywood, *Encyclopaedia of the Viking Age*. London: Thames & Hudson, 2000. p. 69.

Scandinavian settlement of Iceland attribute the beginnings of the movement to the reign of Harald Hárfagri and his extension of royal power in Norway in the 880s and 890s. Ari Thorgilsson, writing in the first quarter of the twelfth century, framed the basic narrative. He asserted that:

Iceland was first settled from Norway in the days of Harald Finehair [Hárfagri], son of Halfdan the Black, at the time ... when Ivar, son of Ragnar Lodbrok, had St Edmund, king of the Angles, killed. And that was 870 years after the birth of Christ, as is written in his biography.

There was a Norwegian called Ingolf, of whom it is said in truth that he first made his way from Norway to Iceland when Harald Finehair was 16 years old; and a second time a few years later. He settled in the south of Iceland, in Reykjavik. The place where he first landed is called Ingolfshofdi, to the east of Minhakseyr; and Ingolfsfell, to the west of the River Olfosa where he later took over the land.

At that time Iceland was overgrown with scrub between fell and foreshore. There were Christian men here then whom the Northmen call papar. But afterwards they went away because they did not want to stay here side by side with heathens. And they left behind them Irish books, bells and crosiers; from which one might deduce they were Irishmen.

After that a great emigration took place to Iceland from Norway, to the extent that King Harald had to forbid it because he was afraid it would lead to the depopulation of his country. The final agreement was that every man who was not exempt from it and who wanted to travel here from Norway had to pay the king five aurar ... Moreover men who know have said that Iceland was fully settled in sixty years, so that there was no more settlement after that.[19]

According to this account the first settlers were local chieftains with their families and followers who were fleeing the tyranny of the king and who established a society in the colony that preserved the traditional lifestyle that Harald's aggressive new style of kingship was destroying at home.[20] Personal animus and antipathy towards the king's policies became something of a motif in most Icelandic family sagas as the explanation for ancestral emigration to the island.

Ingimund met Saemund soon after the battle of Havsfjord and said to him that his prophecy about the conflict had turned out to be not far off the mark: 'I know also because of the words of the king, that it is not your lot to live in peace, and I think it would be a good idea for you to go away, because the king will carry out this threat, but I would like to spare you from a

---

[19] Ari Thorgilsson, Íslendingabók. In R. I. Page, Chronicles of the Vikings: Records, Memorials, and Myths. Toronto: University of Toronto Press, 1995. p. 59.
[20] Roesdahl, Vikings, p. 266.

harsher fate because of our friendship. It seems to me not a bad idea for you to head for Iceland, as many worthy men do these days who cannot be sure of defending themselves against the power of King Harald.'[21]

Unfortunately, attractively convenient though such a scenario is, it is generally unsustainable as an explanation in most cases, and the colonisation process may already have been underway by the 860s before Harald began to tighten his grip over Norway, although his activities may have provided an added stimulus for emigration towards the end of the ninth century.

The discovery of the island is attributed to Gardar Svavarsson, a Swede who was said to have been blown off course whilst sailing from Norway to the Hebrides c. 860. He spent a year exploring his discovery, which he modestly named Gardarsholm after himself, circumnavigating the island and over-wintering there.[22] Gardar did not return to colonise the new land; that appears to have been first attempted later in the 860s by Flóki Vilgerdarson. According to *Landnámabók*, the late eleventh- and early twelfth-century account of the settlement of Iceland, he:

was a great adventurer by sea. He set out for Gardarsholm, sailing from a place called Flokavardi. That is where Hordaland and Rogaland meet. First he went to the Shetlands and lay up in Flokavag there ...

Floki and his company sailed over Breidafiord to the west of Iceland, and reached land at the place that is now called Vatnsfiord, by Bardastrond. The fiord was well stocked with fish, and because of the plentiful catch they did not bother about hay-making, so all their cattle died that winter. The spring was pretty chill. Then Floki climbed up to a high fell and saw, to the north beyond the fells, a fiord full of drift-ice. So they called the land Iceland, and that has been its name ever since.

That summer Floki and his comrades planned a move and were ready for sea just before winter. They could not round Reykianes, and the ship's boat was torn away from them: Heriolf was on it. He came ashore at the place now called Heriolfshofn. Floki stayed that winter in Borgarfiord, and there he and Heriolf were re-united. Next summer they sailed back to Norway. When they were asked about the land, Floki spoke unflatteringly about it, but Heriolf told everything about the land, both good and bad. In his turn Thorolf said that butter dripped from every blade of grass in the land they had discovered. So he was known as Butter-Thorolf.[23]

---

[21] *The Saga of the People of Vatnsdal*, trans. A. Wawn. In *The Sagas of Icelanders*, ed. Ö. Thorsson. London: Penguin, 2001. p. 203. The same sentiment is expressed later in the saga (p. 205).

[22] Haywood, *Encyclopaedia*, p. 79.

[23] *Landnámabók*. In *Chronicles of the Vikings*, see note 19 above, p. 61.

Despite this initial failure Flóki eventually returned to Iceland and established a farm at Flokadalur in the north of the island.[24]

The successful colonisation of Iceland began c. 870 and was followed – according to Ari Thorgilsson's account and as presented in *Landnámabók* – by a period of some sixty years of fairly intensive settlement which saw most of the best land taken up by c. 930. Most, but by no means all, of the colonists came from western Norway, a substantial contingent also arriving from older colonies in the Hebrides and Ireland.[25] *Landnámabók*, which may have been intended to provide some kind of register for land-holding through which the leading families of early twelfth-century Iceland could legitimise their property claims and rights through providing evidence of descent or possession, lists around 430 leaders of settlements and the names of over 1,500 farms.[26] What the first colonists found was a land that seemed ideal for the direct implantation of their traditional Scandinavian lifestyle and that was overwhelmingly rural-based and agricultural or, more particularly, pastoral (Figure 64). All the sagas narrating the initial phase of settlement comment on the quality and abundance of the natural resources to be found there.

Grim said ... 'and I am off to Iceland this summer along with my brother, and many consider this no shame even though they are of noble birth. I have heard good things about the land – that livestock feed themselves during the winters, that there are fish in every river and lake, and great forests, and that men are free from the assaults of kings and criminals.'[27]

It was a decidedly rosy picture that was painted, but not everyone was convinced of the superiority of Iceland over the attractions of other areas.

Then they decided to leave the country [Norway], since Ketil's sons were greatly in favour of the idea and no one opposed it. Bjorn and Helgi wanted to go to Iceland, as they claimed they had heard many favourable reports of the country; there was good land available, they said, without having to pay for it. There were reported to be plenty of beached whales and salmon fishing, and good fishing every season.

[24] Haywood, *Encyclopaedia*, p. 73.
[25] P. Urbánczyk, Ethnic aspects of the settlement of Iceland. In *Papa Stour and 1299: Commemorating the 700th Anniversary of Shetland's First Document*, ed. B. E. Crawford and J. G. Jorgensen. Lerwick: Shetland Times, 2002. pp. 155–66.
[26] Haywood, *Encyclopaedia*, p. 114.
[27] *The Saga of the People of Vatnsdal*. In *The Sagas of Icelanders*, see note 21 above, p. 205.

Figure 64
Godfoss, Iceland.

To this Ketil answered, 'I do not intend to spend my old age in that fishing camp.'

Ketil said he preferred to travel to the west; there, he said, they seemed to have a good life. He knew the country well, for he had gone raiding through much of the area.[28]

Iceland did, however, offer an abundance of good pasture and had rich maritime and marine resources to exploit both to supplement the diets of the settlers and to provide trading commodities. It did not, however, have any abundance of natural forest, despite the claims made by some of the sagas. There was extensive scrublands and birch woods which provided fuel[29] and materials – especially bark – for use in construction and in manufacturing containers and the like, and in the early years of the colony there were substantial reserves of driftwood to be found on the beaches.[30] Once those reserves had been used up, however, the colonists became increasingly dependent on supplies of timber from Norway. Some of the more important members of the community

---

[28] *The Saga of the People of Laxardal*, trans. K. Kunz. Ibid., p. 277.
[29] I. Simpson, O. Vésteinsson, W. Adderley and T. McGovern, Fuel resource utilisation in landscapes of settlement. *Journal of Archaeological Science*, Vol. 30, 2003, pp. 1401–20.
[30] Roesdahl, *Vikings*, p. 266.

were able to use their kin and political connections in Scandinavia to secure the timber that they needed for building:

When Ingimund had lived for some time at Hof, he announced that he was going abroad to collect building-wood for himself, because he said that he wanted to live in fine style there, and that he expected King Harald to greet him warmly. Vigdis said that good was to be expected from the king. He appointed men to look after his estate, along with Vigdis. Ingimund took the bears [which he had captured] along with him.

The journey went well for him and he arrived in Norway. He asked where King Harald was; the country was then at peace. And when he found King Harald he was warmly welcomed. The king invited him to stay with him and Ingimund accepted. Throughout the winter he was entertained with great honour by the king. The king asked what the good points were about the new land. He spoke well of it, 'and it is my main object now to get some building timber'.

The king said, 'Good for you. I grant you permission to have whatever timber you want cut from our forests, and I will have it moved to the ship, and you need have no concerns on that score.'[31]

The search for more convenient supplies of timber, however, was one of the many factors that encouraged further exploration to the west of Iceland in the tenth century. The chief determining factor, however, appears to have been the impact that the attempt to pursue a Norwegian-style rural exploitation system had had on the Icelandic environment.

Despite the size of the island the area of settleable land in Iceland was comparatively limited. Most settlement was restricted to the coastal districts, the southern plains and the more sheltered valleys, for the centre of the island was barren and ice-bound or scarred by lava flows. As a result intense pressure was placed on the available reserves of good land, and by the later twelfth century Iceland was supporting a population of around 40,000. By that time, however, although the settlers appear to have understood the fragility of the system into which they had entered, environmental degradation brought about by the felling of the woodland, over-cropping of the soils and over-intensification of grazing had brought the colony to crisis (Figure 65).[32] Basic commodities such as fuel were in critical shortage, and all available alternatives, such as cattle dung, were

[31] *The Saga of the People of Vatnsdal.* In *The Sagas of Icelanders*, see note 21 above, pp. 212–13.
[32] I. Simpson, A. Dugmore, A. Thomson and O. Vésteinsson, Crossing the thresholds: human ecology and historical patterns of landscape degradation. *Catena*, Vol. 41, 2001, pp. 175–92.

Figure 65 Lake Myvatn, Iceland. The volcanic soils of Iceland supported scrub woodland and seemingly lush grasslands at the time of the first colonisation of the island. Over-grazing and exploitation of the natural resources led quickly to degradation of the landscape, pushing the Icelanders into economic and, ultimately, political crisis in the twelfth century.

used to the maximum.[33] The situation was exacerbated by the fall-out from volcanic eruptions in the early twelfth century and by a deterioration in the climate in the thirteenth century.

The early settlement also faced potential crisis arising from its lack of social organisation. From the outset the colonisation had been a venture undertaken by private initiative and free from the

[33] Simpson *et al.*, Fuel resource utilisation, pp. 1401–20.

interference of any higher authority who could impose unity and order. The consequence was the establishment of a scattered series of communities with few bonds to bring them together in any meaningful way. Within the individual communities, however, kin relationships and ties formed through dependence on the chieftain who may have founded the settlement provided a degree of local stability. In such circumstances there was a risk of conflict over disputed rights, and feud between kindred groups arising from such cases brought regular and often protracted upheaval. To ameliorate the situation the leading figures in the settlements adopted the practice used in Norway of holding local assemblies. In the course of the late ninth century the *goðar* class of wealthy chieftains offered leadership to local society and protection to lesser landowners (who became their clients in return) and came to preside over these assemblies at which conflicts could be resolved. The earliest of these assemblies – or *thing* – was supposedly that developed at Kjalarnes under the leadership of Thorstein Ingolfsson c. 900 as a meeting place of the free men of the district. Other regional things were established, until in 930 the *goðar* instituted an annual assembly for the entire colony, the *Althing*, which gathered at Thingvellir (Assembly Plains) in the Öxará valley, 48 kilometers east of Reykjavík (Figures 66a, 66b, 66c). This came to function as the venue for the settlement of major legal disputes and for the

Figure 66a
Thingvellir,
Iceland.

Figure 66b
Thingvellir,
Iceland.

Figure 66c
Thingvellir,
Iceland. The
'Parliament Plain'
in the Öxará
valley, east of
Reykjavík, was
the meeting place
of the Icelandic
Althing down to
1799. The
summer
meetings were
open-air events,
those attending
the Althing living
in tents or
temporary
shelters for the
duration.
Business was
conducted at the
Lögberg (Law
Rock) and the
Lögrétta (Law
Court).

promulgation of common laws for the whole colony. Under its
umbrella the colony emerged as a quasi-state, the so-called (in
modern terminology) Icelandic Commonwealth or Icelandic Free
State. The establishment of the Althing did not mean the wither-
ing away of the district things, and subsequently the island was
divided into quarters, each of which contained three or four local
assemblies. These were intended to act as venues at which local
disputes could be resolved, and only cases of great complexity or
importance would be referred up the hierarchy to the Althing.
The local things, like the Althing, were controlled by the *goðar*
class and became highly effective means for consolidating their
social and economic dominance of their districts.[34] That link
between control of the law and control of society was to be one

---

[34] J. L. Byock, *Medieval Iceland. Society, Sagas, and Power.* Berkeley: University of
California Press, 1988. pp. 55–71.

factor in the political crises that tore Icelandic society apart in the later twelfth and thirteenth centuries.

One of the first major crises to face Icelandic society came towards the end of the tenth century as Christianity began to make headway in the colony. There had been some Christians present in Iceland from fairly early in the colonial movement, mainly amongst the settlers arriving from Ireland and the Hebrides. They were not a significant presence, however, until the 990s, when Olaf Tryggvason, himself a recent convert to the new faith, took active measures to secure the conversion of Iceland. Soon after his accession to the Norwegian throne in 995 he is said to have sent a Christian Icelander, Stefnir Thorgilsson, back to Iceland to convert his fellow countrymen. Stefnir's methods were confrontational and divisive in the extreme, involving the violent destruction of pagan images and sanctuaries, and led to his outlawing and banishment from Iceland. His behaviour also produced a backlash against Christianity, the Althing passing a decree that instructed families to take action against Christians among them if they attacked the pagan religion in any way.[35] King Olaf did not give up after this initial setback, sending a second mission c. 997 headed by a German (or Flemish) priest called Thangbrand. His methods were as confrontational as Stefnir's had been, and in 999 he returned to Norway without having secured the conversion of Iceland. At this point the king decided to increase the pressure on the Icelanders, taking hostage members of important Icelandic families who were in Norway and threatening to kill them unless the island converted. Iceland's need to maintain good relations with Norway, particularly in view of the colony's continuing kinship ties with Scandinavia and dependence on the Norse homeland for its trade, meant that opinion in Iceland began to incline towards the Christians. At first this movement provoked even sharper divisions within the Icelandic state, for the Christians began to work to end all pagan practices that they found offensive and to bring about the conversion of the entire colony. Friction between the most active elements on both sides led to skirmishing and deaths. In summer 1000 the hostilities came to a head at the Althing, and there was a genuine prospect of civil war. Faced

---

[35] Ibid., p. 140.

with this stark possibility the two parties agreed to arbitration, and the mediator, himself a pagan, settled in favour of Christianity. Despite the fact that Norway itself partly reverted to paganism after the overthrow of Olaf in 1000, Iceland stood by the Althing settlement.[36]

The stratification of Icelandic society into an elite *goðar* class over a free peasant *bændr* class intensified in the course of the twelfth century. In comparison with the chieftain class in Norway, the influence of the Icelandic *goðar* was at first fairly small-scale and localised. Individual goðar competed with their class rivals for influence over and a following amongst the *bændr*, and their personal status within their own class could vary widely, depending upon the scale of their following and the range of its network of relationships. In the tenth century it had still been relatively easy for a successful farmer of the *bændr* class to migrate upwards into the ranks of the *goðar* through acquisition of territorial wealth and local political influence. The barriers between the classes, however, became more rigidly defined in the twelfth century, and fresh layers of social stratification began to emerge. In the early thirteenth century this stratification saw the division of the *goðar* into a general chieftain class and a new top level referred to in modern studies as *stórgoðar* ('great goðar').[37] By c. 1200 most of the early chieftainships had been consolidated into the control of just six families. The *goðar* as a broad class effectively disappeared, to be replaced by a new *bændr* elite, referred to as *stórbændr* ('big farmers'), who occupied the middle ground between the *stórgoðar* and the *bændr*.[38]

With the new hierarchy came new tensions. While the *stórgoðar* occupied the apex of the social and political system of Iceland, they did not necessarily dominate the economic system. Indeed, their aspirations towards establishing themselves as quasi-princely rulers controlling defined territorial lordships lacked the economic infrastructure necessary to support such status. The decentralised nature of Iceland's economy and the control exercised over its foreign trade by Norwegian merchants ensured

[36] Ibid., pp. 141–43. A formal ecclesiastical structure had been developed by the end of the first quarter of the eleventh century, but it was only in 1056 that the first Icelander was consecrated bishop. For a detailed discussion of the Icelandic conversion, the eleventh-century Church and later developments, see J. L. Byock, *Viking Age Iceland*. London: Penguin, 2001. pp. 324–40.

[37] Byock, *Viking Age Iceland*, pp. 66–69.   [38] Ibid., pp. 341–47.

that none of the *stórgoðar* were able to achieve the economic domination required to turn their social dominance into something approaching the status of the political elites of mainland Europe. The ambitions of the *stórgoðar* to consolidate a hold over the social, political and economic life of Iceland led to increasing competition between individual *stórgoðar* and a degeneration into feud and violence between them. This feuding was to produce one of the final crises of the old Icelandic state. Most of our information for this period comes from the so-called *Sturlunga saga* collection, a compilation that 'dwells on the violence and the greed for political power which characterized the lives of thirteenth-century leaders',[39] produced by members of the *stórgoðar* class and focussing upon the activities and aspirations of that group. *Íslendinga saga*, written in the late thirteenth century by Sturla Thordarson, a member of the Sturlung *stórgoðar* kin group,[40] reveals the complex power-play in all its gory horror. Its concentration on the interests and actions of this elite group, however, probably over-states the degree of political and social destabilisation that occurred during the peak of the feuding between the *stórgoðar* in the period 1220–50.

Watching closely the developments in Iceland was the Norwegian king, Hákon IV (1217–63), a ruler always looking for opportunities to strengthen and extend his power and kingdom. Various of the *stórgoðar* had turned to Norway for support in furthering their ambitions, but the king had played a careful political game, allowing the class to weaken itself progressively through its cycle of feud and murder. Hákon had played on the aspirations of several men such as Snorri Sturluson, a leading member of the Sturlung family, to whom he awarded noble titles as a sign of his support for that family's ambition. In 1258, however, it was not to the Sturlungs but to a rival, Gizur Thorvaldsson, a man who had actively courted the king's support since the 1230s, that he awarded the title of jarl ('earl'). Gizur was a bitter enemy of the Sturlungs and had taken the lead in blocking that family's bid to secure total domination of Iceland in the late 1230s, killing most of its leadership between 1238 and 1241. Although the king encouraged Gizur in his actions and ensured that he gained political domination over most of Iceland, Hákon

---

[39] Ibid., p. 347.   [40] Ibid., pp. 348–49.

was also careful to limit his powers and ensure that the earl did not supplant Norwegian royal influence with his own.[41] By the early 1260s Hákon was able to move directly to secure his sought-after political domination of Iceland. He sent his own representatives to deal directly with the *stórbændr* and *bændr* classes, offering them the prospect of stability and security under his rule through the removal of the *stórgoðar*.

Between 1262 and 1264 Norwegian royal authority was accepted as a means of ending the decades of feuding, and the *stórgoðar* class was effectively eliminated through the abolition of the *goðorð* upon which their power had been based. Four centuries of political independence ended in a series of covenants by which the Icelanders accepted the lordship of the king of Norway, but the remoteness of the king from his new subjects ensured that Iceland remained a semi-autonomous region within the Norwegian kingdom. The transition to Norwegian rule was comparatively smooth – there was no social dislocation caused by conquest and re-ordering – and the death of the abrasive Hákon IV in 1263 and the accession of his politically astute and conciliatory son, Magnus Law-Mender, helped to ease the transition. Before the end of the thirteenth century Iceland had been integrated successfully into the territories of the Norwegian crown.[42]

Greenland and the Americas

Towards the end of the tenth century, as the Icelandic landscape began to fill with colonists and experience significant environmental degradation through over-exploitation, Norse exploration began again to push west looking for new lands to settle.[43] In the 980s the Icelander Eirik the Red undertook a thorough investigation of the Greenland coast, which at that time was benefiting from a slightly warmer climate that may have made the land seem more attractive to settlers. Even with the better climatic conditions of the time, however, much of the north and interior of the island was covered with permanent fields of snow and ice. The southern tip of Greenland, however, lies on the same latitude as the Shetland Islands, and in the

---

[41] Ibid., pp. 350–51.   [42] Ibid., pp. 351–53.
[43] K. J. Krogh, *Viking Greenland*. Copenhagen: The National Museum, 1967.

sheltered fjords of its south-west coast there are areas of good pasture that would support a Scandinavian style of rural economy.[44] Indeed, Greenland was probably considerably more attractive then than now, for rising sea-levels and coastal erosion have stripped it of what was once a fertile, low-lying coastal fringe. It was here that the settlers were to establish the Greenland colony.

Unlike the colonisation of the islands around Scotland and the Faroes, the settlement of Greenland has a substantial saga tradition to illustrate it. The principal source is *Íslendingabók*,[45] whose composer was able to draw on contemporary oral observations by a man who had accompanied Eric's expedition, and there are two thirteenth-century sagas, *Grænlendinga Saga* and *Eiríks saga Rauða*, but these give accounts primarily of further voyages of exploration, including that which discovered 'Vinland'.[46] The limited development of the Greenland colony before its later medieval extinction has meant, however, that the settlements named in the sagas can be identified with a fair degree of confidence, and the equally limited modern development of the landscape has meant that significant archaeological remains have survived and been excavated.

Eirik's settlement of Greenland started c. 985 after his reconnaissance of the island. Tradition reports that he gave the island its name as a marketing strategy designed to disguise its harsh environment and make it attractive to would-be colonists, but in comparison with late tenth-century Iceland it was probably a very apt description. These colonists provided the core of two settlements – the Eastern Settlement and the Western Settlement – comprising several farms dispersed around the better pastureland in the sheltered fjords. Eirik settled at Brattahlíð in the Eastern Settlement, taking for himself one of the best locations in Greenland in the midst of one of the largest tracts of fertile plain. The site has been excavated, revealing the remains of

[44] Roesdahl, *Vikings*, p. 271.
[45] *The Book of the Icelanders by Ari Thorgilsson: Edited and Translated with an Introductory Essay and Notes by Halldor Hermannsson*, ed. and trans. H. Hermannsson. Ithaca: Cornell University Library, 1930.
[46] *Eyrbyggja Saga: Brands þáttr Orva. Eiríks Saga Rauða. Grænlendinga Saga. Grælendinga þáttr*, ed. Einar Ólafur Sveinsson and Matthías Þórðarson. Íslenzk fornrit IV. Reykjavík: Hið íslenzka fornritafélag, 1935; G. Jones, *Eirik the Red and Other Icelandic Sagas*. London: Oxford University Press, 1961.

several phases of a house, a small church of probably very early eleventh-century date, and a cemetery containing 155 inhumations that have provided invaluable information about the demographic make-up of the Scandinavian population and their physical state.[47] The condition of their skeletons and estimated age at death does not indicate that the lifestyle of the Greenlanders was significantly different from that of the other Scandinavian colonies in the North Atlantic.

Rich pasture, which would have supported the same kind of agricultural regime that the Norse had imported to Iceland from their Scandinavian homeland, was not the only attraction offered to the colonists. There were other sources of food, principally from abundant game, sea-birds, whales, seals and fish, with which to supplement their diet. The first settlers probably would have found abundant driftwood on the shores, sufficient to provide for their initial building and fuel needs. By the late tenth century the house-building tradition in Iceland had shifted towards a largely turf-built form in response to the environmental conditions and to the changing availability of the necessary resources for construction,[48] but timber was still needed for supporting beams and the major roof members. There were other natural resources, however, which would have given the Greenlanders the means with which to trade and secure materials that could not be obtained at home, such as iron, substantial timbers and grain. Greenland provided a range of exotic items that were much in demand in Europe, principally skins, furs and ivory, but also live falcons (for hunting with) and even polar bears.[49] In the eleventh and twelfth centuries most of this trade was channelled through the hands of Norwegian merchants, and Norway, rather than Iceland, exercised a growing influence on the life of the colony, formalised in 1261 when the Greenlanders acknowledged the overlordship of Hákon IV of Norway.[50]

Another important dimension of the colonists' life that was influenced from Norway was their religion. Eirik himself was, according to the sagas, antipathetic to the spread of Christianity in Iceland and had maintained his paganism at first

[47] Roesdahl, *Vikings*, p. 273.   [48] Byock, *Viking Age Iceland*, pp. 34–42.
[49] Roesdahl, *Vikings*, p. 272.
[50] Byock, *Viking Age Iceland*, pp. 265–66; Roesdahl, *Vikings*, p. 261.

when he settled at Brattahlíð. That being said, the only evidence for pagan religion that has been found in the excavated remains from Greenland is a tiny incised Thor's hammer on a piece of soapstone from Eirik's farm. It was at Brattahlíð, however, that the first church was erected in Greenland, by Eirik or his wife, Thjodhild, around 1000.[51] When the Norwegian archdiocese of Niðaros (Trondheim) was established in 1153 Greenland was one of the territories placed under its metropolitan jurisdiction.[52] A bishopric had already been established in 1125 at Garðar, to the south of Brattahlíð and a small church constructed to serve as a cathedral. Scandinavian Greenland was advancing well down the avenue of medieval European social development, its consolidation influenced by the economic, ecclesiastical and political dependence of the colony on distant Norway.

Remote though Greenland was from the Norse homeland, it was not the westernmost limit of Scandinavian exploration and colonisation. Bjarni Herjolfsson, who sighted the coast of part of North America but did not go ashore, reported this when he reached Greenland. That report prompted Eirik's son, Leif, to undertake an expedition, and he is usually credited with the discovery c. 1000 of the new land, which we now know to have been part of North America. Modern usage normally applies the name *Vinland* (for Old Norse Vinland, 'Wineland') to the whole of Leif Eiriksson's discovery, but the sagas also refer to *Markland* and *Helluland*. These three territories have not been identified with certainty but are usually thought to have been Newfoundland, Labrador and Baffin Island, although the area around the Gulf of St Lawrence, the northernmost limit of naturally occurring wild vine, has also been suggested as Vinland.[53] No permanent colony was established in these new lands, but it does not seem to have been for want of trying.

In comparison with Greenland and Iceland, the eastern seaboard of what is now Canada must have seemed ideal for colonisation by the Greenlanders. The climate was significantly milder, with longer summers, which meant that the fertile land could be cultivated as well as exploited for pasture. There was, moreover, rich hunting and fishing to be had. Still more attractive was the availability of iron, which could be smelted from

[51] Jones, *Eirik the Red*.   [52] Byock, *Viking Age Iceland*, p. 302.
[53] Roesdahl, *Vikings*, pp. 274–75.

bog-iron, and seemingly unlimited forest for timber, two commodities for which Greenland depended on the Norwegian-dominated trade with Europe. Colonisation was, therefore, attempted, and at L'Anse aux Meadows in Newfoundland the remains of a Norse settlement with turf-walled structures has been excavated (Figures 67a, 67b, 67c, 67d).[54] The excavated remains and the sagas, however, both indicate that the settlement was short-lived, the colonists probably withdrawing in the face of hostility from the native Americans who already exploited that land.[55] Whilst it can never be proven that it is the site in question, the temporary occupation of L'Anse aux Meadows parallels the events in the saga of Eirik the Red, which tells of the abortive attempt of his former daughter-in-law, Gudrid, and her husband, Thorfinn Karlsefni, to settle in Vinland c. 1010.[56] Despite the

Figure 67a
L'Anse aux
Meadows,
Newfoundland,
Canada.

[54] B. L. Wallace, L'Anse aux Meadows. Gateway to Vinland. *Acta Archaeologica*, Vol. 61, 1990, pp. 166–97.
[55] G. Jones, The Vikings and North America. In *The Vikings*, ed. R. T. Farrell. London: Phillimore, 1982. pp. 223–30.
[56] Byock, *Viking Age Iceland*, p. 372.

Figure 67b
L'Anse aux
Meadows,
Newfoundland,
Canada.

Figure 67c
L'Anse aux
Meadows,
Newfoundland,
Canada.

failure of their efforts to establish a permanent presence in North America, the Greenlanders did make later visits to Vinland to secure materials, and stray Norse finds have turned up in the excavation of native American sites, including a late eleventh-century Norwegian coin.[57]

The hunt for resources that may have driven these later expeditions underscores the basic weakness of the Greenland

[57] A useful select bibliography containing titles published between 1950 and 1980 can be found in L. Pitchmann, compiler. The Norsemen in America. In *The Vikings*, see note 55 above, pp. 231–35.

Figure 67d
L'Anse aux Meadows, Newfoundland, Canada. Discovered and excavated in the 1960s, L'Anse aux Meadows provided the first tangible proof that Europeans had reached North America before Columbus, and established the veracity of the *Vinland Sagas*. The remains comprised of a cluster of turf houses and workshops of similar style to eleventh-century examples from Norse settlements in Greenland and Iceland, located at the head of a sheltered beach. A reconstruction of the probable appearance of the settlement has been built nearby and furnished with replica equipment based on evidence from the excavated remains and from other Norse settlements of the period.

colony: availability of supply. By the time the Greenlanders acknowledged Hákon's overlordship in 1261 the colony may already have been in serious difficulties. The introduction of an identical style of rural economy as had destroyed the environment of Iceland in the tenth century had begun to wreak similar damage in Greenland, although the less intensive settlement of the island may have slowed the process of degradation. Further problems came as the climate deteriorated sharply after 1300, communications between the colony and Iceland and Norway becoming more limited by the shorter period during which the seas around Greenland were free of pack ice. Climatic deterioration would also have had a serious impact upon the pastoral regime of the colonists, and failure to adopt a lifestyle better suited to exploiting the natural resources of the Arctic contributed to the decline in population.[58] There is no agreement as to when and how the Greenland colonies eventually died out, theories ranging from epidemic to mass starvation in the grip of a prolonged phase of severe climatic deterioration to massacre by Inuits.[59] All that can be said with confidence is that contact with the dwindling colony became less frequent in the fourteenth century, intermittent through the fifteenth century and probably

[58] L. Barlow, J. Sadler *et al.* Interdisciplinary investigations of the end of the Norse Western Settlement in Greenland. *The Holocene*, Vol. 7 No. 4, 1997, pp. 489–99.
[59] Jones, The Vikings and North America. In *The Vikings*, see note 55 above, pp. 223–26.

ceased before 1500. In 1540 a ship reaching the Eastern Settlement found it abandoned. In 1712 the king of Denmark-Norway, as nominal overlord of Greenland, sent an expedition there to re-establish contact with his subjects – but none (at least of wholly Scandinavian descent) were found.[60]

[60] Haywood, *Encyclopaedia*, p. 86; Roesdahl, *The Vikings*, p. 276.

CHAPTER 12

Sailing the North Atlantic

Sailing the North Atlantic on a regular basis in what is, essentially, an open boat is quite an undertaking; and there can be no doubt that it must have exacted its toll in ships and lives. These voyages prompt many questions. How long did they last? What weather and sea conditions might be encountered? How did a vessel handle on the ocean? How were ships navigated? Our guides to answering these questions, or rather attempting to answer them, are the texts and the experience gained by sailing reconstructions of the merchant ships. With regard to the texts, their value lies not so much in the character, personality or exploits of men like Bjarni Herjolfsson, who may be credited with being the first man to sight and sail along part of the coast of North America, or Leif Eiriksson, his rival for that honour, or with Leif's father, Eirik the Red, but rather in the proper context-ualisation of what the sagas say about what happened to these men when at sea, or about the weather conditions and dangers that they faced. We should not ask ourselves the question, 'Did Bjarni (or anyone else) really do this or that aboard his vessel?' Rather we should ask, 'Is the type of behaviour described believable in the context in which it is said to have occurred?' An excellent example of the point made here is the description in *Laxdæla Saga* of an incident that occurs during the voyage of Olaf Peacock from Norway to Ireland. Storm-tossed and enveloped in dense fog, the crew lose their bearings and are in a state of 'sea-bewilderment'.[1] What happens next is that most natural reaction to a crisis – complete panic. The crew fall to bickering amongst themselves. They are even disinclined to believe that Ireland lies in the direction suggested by Orn, an experienced skipper in

---

[1] 'Sea-bewilderment' or Old Norse *hafvilla* is dealt with below, p. 348.

whose vessel Olaf had come to Norway from Iceland. Ultimately, common sense prevails and Orn's advice is taken and the helm entrusted to him. However, subsequently finding themselves in shoal waters close to land, disagreement flares up again. This time it is Olaf who questions Orn's command to the crew to sail about and who countermands this with an order to lower sail and put out anchors. The scene concludes with a gloomy discussion of what will happen in the morning when the Irish discover a Norwegian vessel apparently stranded on the shore.[2] The saga presents a convincing contextual narrative and illustrates the fact that sailing the waters of the North Atlantic was far from plain.

If, however, one should avoid the danger of underestimating the texts, one should be equally careful to avoid overestimating the value of experimental archaeology. There is no doubt that this has taught us a great deal about how to sail vessels of the Viking Age, but it cannot tell us exactly how the men of that time sailed those ships. Every item of modern nautical technology incorporated in a reconstruction (usually in order to satisfy safety requirements under modern maritime law) – an engine, charts, radar, satellite navigation, radio, life-rafts, etc. – takes us further away from the original craft and how their crews behaved. Consequently we may speculate, but we can never be certain. As long as we keep this in mind, however, there is nothing wrong in advancing hypotheses and, equally, nothing wrong in disagreeing with them.

Atlantic vessels

According to *Egil's Saga*, when Kveldulf left Norway for Iceland during the reign of Harald Hárfagri he and his retainers, with their womenfolk, children and possessions, sailed in *tvá knörru mikla* – 'two large knörrs'.[3] The perception of the author of this saga (very probably Snorri Sturluson) clearly was that these

---

[2] *The Saga of the People of Laxardal*, trans. K. Kunz. In *The Sagas of Icelanders*, ed. Ö. Thorsson. London: Penguin, 2001. pp. 306–7. *The Laxdale Saga*, trans. M. Press, introd. P. Foote. Everyman's Library, 597. London: Dent, 1964. pp. 58–59.

[3] *Egil's Saga*, trans. B. Scudder. In *The Sagas of Icelanders*, see note 2 above, p. 43.

vessels were cargo rather than fighting ships. The vessels found at Klåstad in western Norway and Äskekärr in Sweden provide clear proof that such specialised vessels were definitely in use in the ninth and tenth centuries.[4] By the eleventh century, however, larger merchant ships, represented by Skuldelev 1 and Hedeby 3, were being employed. The former, with an overall length of 16 metres, although certainly capable of crossing the North Atlantic, was more probably used on the Baltic and North Sea routes. The latter, with an overall length of 25 metres, was certainly better suited to plying the sea-lanes to Iceland and Greenland.

Distances and sailing rates

From Stad (which lies north of Bergen) to Horn in south-east Iceland is a voyage of approximately 530 nautical miles. From Snæfellsnes in west Iceland to Hvitserk (near present-day Ammassalik) in east Greenland is 277 nautical miles The distance from Reykjanes in south-west Iceland to Malin Head in Northern Ireland is 660 nautical miles. These are the distances involved in making the voyages described in Landnámabók:

Learned men state that from Stad in Norway it is seven days' sail (dægr sigling) west to Horn in the east of Iceland; and from Snæfellsnes, where the distance is shortest, it is four days' sea (dægr haf) west to Greenland... From Reykjanes in the south of Iceland there is five days sea (dægr haf) to Jolduhlaup in Ireland.[5]

From Reykjanes to the south-east coast of Greenland involves a voyage of 570 nautical miles. A direct voyage from Hernar in west Norway to Hvarf on the east coast of Greenland is

---

4 O. Crumlin-Pedersen, Cargo ships of northern Europe AD 800–1300. In Conference on Waterfront Technology in Northern European Towns, ed. A. Herteig. Bergen: Historisk Museum, 1985. pp. 83–93; O. Crumlin-Pederson, Ship types and sizes AD 800–1400. In Aspects of Maritime Scandinavia AD 200–1200. Proceedings of the Nordic seminar on maritime aspects of archaeology, Roskilde, 13–15 March 1989, ed. O. Crumlin-Pedersen. Roskilde: Vikingeskibshallen, 1991. pp. 69–82; A. Christopherson, Ports and trade in Norway during the transition to historical time. In Aspects of Maritime Scandinavia, see note above, pp. 159–70.

5 G. Jones, The Norse Atlantic Saga, Being the Norse Voyages of Discovery and Settlement to Iceland, Greenland, and North America. Oxford, New York: Oxford University Press, 1986 [1964]. p. 115. The passage quoted is taken from Sturlubók.

1,360 nautical miles.[6] It will be apparent that while we today measure distance in units known as nautical miles, *Landnámabók* measured it by the *dœgr* or day. It is likely that before the introduction of the sail distances were measured in terms of a day's rowing.[7] Subsequently, however, the terms *dœgr sigling*[8] and *dœgr haf* came to represent precise distances. Although the issue is not free from controversy, a convincing argument has recently been advanced that suggests the *dœgr haf* represented 144 nautical miles, the estimated distance a vessel might travel in a day,[9] and the *dœgr sigling* a distance of 72 nautical miles.[10] So if Horn was seven *dœgr sigling* sailing from Stad, this did not mean that it took seven days (it could well have taken longer) to sail between the two points; rather this represents the distance between them, which was considered to be 504 nautical miles. Likewise, if Reykjanes was five *dœgr haf* from Malin Head (Jolduhlaup?), the distance between the two points was thought to be 720 nautical miles. Neither of these, admittedly, correlate with the exact chart distance that can be plotted today, but both are close enough, bearing in mind that measurement of distance at sea throughout the medieval period was never an exact science.[11]

---

[6] This reference to a direct route from Norway to Greenland is mentioned in *Hauksbók*.

[7] R. Morcken, Norse nautical units and distance measurements. *Mariner's Mirror*, Vol. 54, 1968, p. 399.

[8] Ohthere uses the concept of a day's sailing in his voyage to the White Sea, which was rendered in Old English as *dagum gesiglan*: *Two Voyagers at the Court of King Alfred: The Ventures of Ohthere and Wulfstan, Together with the Description of Northern Europe from the Old English Orosius*, ed. N. Lund, trans. C. E. Fell. York: Sessions, 1984. pp. 18–19.

[9] M. Vinner, Unnasigling – the seaworthiness of the merchant vessel. In *Viking Voyages to North America*, ed. B. Clausen. Roskilde: Vikingeskibshallen, 1993. pp. 100–101.

[10] S. Fløttum, The Norse *vika sjovar* and the nautical mile. *Mariner's Mirror*, Vol. 87, 2001, pp. 390–405. Fløttum challenges Morcken's concept of the half *dœgr*, which, the latter conceded, is not found in the texts.

[11] A mid- to late thirteenth-century treatise on geography composed in Iceland and known as *Rim II* is very precise on the measurement of distances. One should, however, hesitate before assuming that sea-farers possessed or required such exact details: Fløttum, The Norse *vika sjovar*, pp. 393–94. On medieval navigation generally, see J. B. Hewson, *A History of the Practice of Navigation*. Glasgow: Brown, Son & Ferguson, 1983; E. G. R. Taylor, *The Haven-Finding Art: A History of Navigation from Odysseus to Captain Cook*. London: Hollis and Carter for the Institute of Navigation, 1971.

Climate and winds

In *Konungs Skuggsjá*, the thirteenth-century voyager west to Greenland and the settlements there is told to beware drifting ice.[12] Ice, however, presented few problems for vessels sailing the North Atlantic during the period now known as the 'medieval climatic optimum', roughly 800–1150. In the North Atlantic the sea temperature was warmer than it is today and, consequently, the chances of encountering serious amounts of drift ice south of latitude 70° N. would have been fairly small.[13] Furthermore, the location of the circumpolar vortex, an air stream that influences the strength and direction of winds in the North Atlantic region, produced predominantly westerly winds which, during the summer months, were not particularly strong.[14] This ties in with the description in *Konungs Skuggsjá* of sailing seasons when voyages might be undertaken. In the case of 'small seas' (e.g. the North Sea) the season ran from April to mid-October at the latest. Indeed, even a winter voyage is condoned, provided the distance is short: that is, no more than two days' sailing. However, the perils of sailing, even on a short voyage from Norway to Orkney, may be illustrated by a voyage taken by Earl Rognald in winter. What should have been a few days' sail at most turned into something much longer and more eventful. *Orkneyinga Saga* paints a portrait of a merchant ship, driven off course, forced by stress of weather to make for land well to the south of Orkney at Tarbat Ness, near the entrance to the Dornoch Firth. The earl just made it home for Christmas.[15] Vessels intending to cross the 'largest' seas (e.g. the North Atlantic) were advised that an April

---

[12] *The King's Mirror (Speculum Regale [or] Konungs Skuggsjá) Translated from the Old Norwegian*, ed. and trans. L. M. Larson. New York: The American-Scandinavian Foundation, 1917. pp. 138–39.

[13] Jones, *The Norse Atlantic Saga*, p. 57, also suggests that the area of permanent ice was to the north of latitude 80° N. For other studies of the medieval climatic optimum, see K. Frydendahl, The summer climate in the North Atlantic about the year 1000. In *Viking Voyages*, see note 9 above, pp. 90–94; I. Whyte, Climatic change and the North Atlantic seaways during the Norse expansion. *Northern Studies*, Vol. 21, 1984, pp. 22–33. Note also H. H. Lamb, *Climate, History and the Modern World*. London, New York: Routledge, 1995 [1982].

[14] Whyte, Climatic change, pp. 22–23.

[15] *Orkneyinga Saga*, trans. and introd. H. Pálsson and P. Edwards. Penguin Classics. Harmondsworth: Penguin Books, 1981. p. 183. This saga also refers to raiding the Western Isles in winter: ibid., p. 195.

start was unwise, and that the return trip should not be attempted later than early October.[16]

The point has already been made that the saga accounts of the 'discovery' of Iceland, the Faroes, Greenland and North America share a common element, namely that their discoverers saw them by chance, having been blown off course en route to their intended destinations. In the two redactions of *Landnámabók* (*Sturlubók* and *Hauksbók*) the first persons who claimed to have sighted Iceland were Naddod and Gardar. The former was bound for the Faroes, the latter for the Hebrides, but weather conditions pushed them westwards beyond their intended destinations. Later, when Iceland was settled, Gunnbjorn Ulf-Krakasson (according to both *Grænlendinga Saga* and *Eiriks saga Rauða*) was blown past it and sighted eastern Greenland. In *Grænlendinga Saga* it is Bjarni Herjolfsson who, shaping a course for Greenland, was blown further to the south and west, duly sighting some part of the North American coastline. In *Eiriks saga Rauða* it is Eric's son Leif who first sights North America, but again this sighting is accidental and due to his having been blown off his course from Norway to Greenland. Stripped of their heroic characters, but with due regard paid to the possibility that the original discoverers of the Faroes and Iceland may have been *papar*, these stories indicate that even during the spring/summer sailing season the prevailing wind direction might abruptly change, and fierce easterly gales push westward-bound vessels past their intended landfalls. Such changes in wind direction might have been caused by areas of high pressure over Iceland colliding with areas of low pressure over the British Isles.[17]

Sailing and seamanship

The prevailing winds a thousand and more years ago were from the west, a fact that has implications for our understanding of the sailing capabilities of the vessels that crossed the North Atlantic then. As we have seen, Viking Age vessels carried only a single,

---

[16] *The King's Mirror*, pp. 156–58. *Egil's Saga* talks of a trading voyage from Norway to England which leaves in spring and returns in autumn: see *Egil's Saga*, trans. B. Scudder. In *The Sagas of Icelanders*, see note 2 above, p. 28, and summer raiding voyages to the Baltic are also described in this saga: ibid., pp. 71, 79.

[17] Whyte, Climatic change, pp. 25–26.

square sail, and it was supposed at one time that this particular configuration would permit a vessel to sail only with the wind behind her.[18] Even today one encounters statements such as this:

Viking boats sailed well only when the wind blew from behind ... If the Vikings wanted to go against the wind, they lowered the sail and let the rowers use their oars to move the boat.[19]

This statement, only partly true in the case of a long ship (it does not factor in wave height and the distance between waves), is wholly inaccurate in the case of large merchant vessels. While vessels on the outward voyage might wait for a favourable easterly wind, and those homeward bound for a westerly blow, once underway conditions might quickly change.[20] If, therefore, a square-rigged vessel could sail only before the wind, Scandinavians would rarely have ventured out of their fjords, let alone sailed about the Atlantic archipelago. It is true that a merchant ship bound for Iceland or Greenland would have sailed best on a broad reach, i.e. with the wind astern or on either of her stern quarters. But if the wind shifted so that the vessel was almost broadside to it, this did not mean that the sail had to be lowered and the crew do their best with the oars. Instead, the yard could be slewed round by using the braces and the sail presented at an oblique angle to the wind; today we would term this 'sailing on a beam reach' (see Figure 68). It is, again, true that a square-rigger would not have been able to sail directly into a headwind. However, if the crew braced the yard sharp, so that it was aligned with the fore- and after-stem, the vessel, now with her sail close-hauled, could tack at about 60° off the wind.[21] Although tacking does increase the overall distance to be sailed, it nevertheless permits a vessel to make forward progress

---

[18] G. J. Marcus, The navigation of the Norsemen. *Mariner's Mirror*, Vol. 29, 1953, pp. 112–31. In fairness, however, Marcus only asserts that this was true for the 'earlier Viking period', which certainly included the ninth century. He concedes that when new technology was introduced even a square-rigger might be sailed close-hauled. Cf. Fløttum, The Norse vika sjøvar, p. 404, note 6.

[19] http://www.scottforesman.com/resources/ya/hissoil. With increasing use of Internet resources, this statement is doubly unfortunate.

[20] *Eirik the Red's Saga*, trans. K. Kunz. In *The Sagas of Icelanders*, see note 2 above, p. 657.

[21] This account of the sailing a square-rigger is based partly on personal experience aboard Skuldelev 5. Formal accounts of sailing a merchant ship based on Skuldelev 1, *Saga Siglar*, are found in Vinner, *Unnasigling* – the seaworthiness of the merchant vessel. In *Viking Voyages*, see note 9 above, pp. 100–108. M. Vinner, A Viking ship off Cape Farewell. In *Shipshape: Essays for Ole Crumlin-Pedersen*, ed. O. Olsen, J. Skamby Madsen and F. Rieck. Roskilde: The Viking Ship Museum, 1995. pp. 289–304. Note also M. Vinner, *Viking Ship Museum Boats*. Roskilde: The Viking Ship Museum, 2002. pp. 14–21.

Figure 68 Sailing *Helge Ask* on Roskilde Fjord, Sjælland. This vessel is a reconstruction of Skuldelev 5. The vessel is sailing on a beam reach, hence the angle of the sail. On this occasion (26 April 2003) the vessel reached an estimated speed of 12 knots.

towards her intended destination. We should not, therefore, assume when we read that a vessel had 'favourable' winds that these were following winds.[22]

The preceding paragraph may appear to ask readers to take what is said about the sailing capabilities of a Viking Age vessel on trust. How can we possibly know that these vessels could tack and sail close-hauled without capsizing? How can we know how they coped with large Atlantic swells and in storms? The sagas, skaldic poetry and texts such as *Konungs Skuggsjá* are replete with accounts of weather conditions, storms, hazards and shipwreck. We are not, however, wholly reliant on what the literature tells us, since experimental archaeology, in the form of the reconstructed vessels, allows us to bench-test what we read about.

In a passage from *Grænlendinga Saga* we are told that as he approached Greenland one of the crew asked Leif why he was sailing 'so close to the wind'.[23] In order to sail close-hauled (even on a modern Bermuda-rigged vessel with triangular fore and aft sail configuration) it is important to keep the leading edge of the sail as taut as possible. In this respect, the elasticity of a woollen

[22] *The Saga of the Greenlanders*, trans. K. Kunz. In *The Sagas of Icelanders*, see note 2 above, p. 651; *Eirik the Red's Saga*, trans. K. Kunz, ibid., p. 660; *Njal's Saga*, ed. and trans. M. Magnusson and H. Pálsson. Penguin Classics. London: Penguin Books, 1960. p. 49; *Egil's Saga* trans. B. Scudder. In *The Sagas of Icelanders*, see note 2 above, p. 54, where a 'strong headwind' is used to describe 'unfavourable sailing weather'.

[23] *The Saga of the Greenlanders*, trans. K. Kunz. In *The Sagas of Icelanders*, see note 2 above, p. 641.

sail, which was mentioned earlier, may have presented something of a problem. Although a heavy coating of animal fat mixed with ochre not only coloured and weatherproofed the sail but also stiffened it,[24] by itself this application was not enough to keep the leading edge sufficiently taut to maintain the vessel's head to the wind. This is where the *beitiáss* played its role. A line in a mid-twelfth-century poem reads: *út berum ás at beita* – 'we bear out the spar to sail close-hauled'.[25] A wooden block to which one end of this spar was attached was recovered from the remains of Skuldelev 1;[26] the other end was attached to the foot of the leading edge of the sail. This simple device provided the sail with a very tight edge and allowed the vessel to tack to and fro, beating into the wind.

In 1984 a reconstructed version of Skuldelev 1, *Saga Siglar*, crossing the North Atlantic from Norway to Greenland, and sailing before the wind and with the wind abeam, recorded a top speed of 13 knots. How could such a vessel be sailed on a beam reach without capsizing? Here the answer lies in the configuration of the hull of Skuldelev 1 and other vessels of her type. Mention was made earlier of the *meginhúfr*: an extra-thick plank fitted just below the waterline on both sides of the hull. The effect of these strakes has been described as follows:

The purpose of the two bilge keels must certainly have been to reduce leeway without increasing the draught of the ship with a keel, while the circular currents of air and water that develop along these bilge keels at high speeds tend to stabilise the course, almost as though the ship is running on rails. Without the bilge keels the ship would probably be inefficient at tacking against the wind.[27]

---

[24] On the effect of treating sails with such a mixture, see R. T. Johansen, Fra *Ottars* logbog. *Marinarkæologisk Nyhedsbrev fra Roskilde*, Vol. 18, 2002, p. 30. Sailing trials with *Ottar*, the most recent reconstruction of Skuldelev 1, showed that a horsehair bolt-rope shrank too much when wet. This badly affected the sailing capability of the vessel. Replacement with a bolt-rope of tarred hemp solved the problem; Johansen, Fra *Ottars* logbog, ibid., p. 32.

[25] P. G. Foote, Wrecks and rhymes. In *Aurvandilstá: Norse Studies*. Viking Collection, 2. Odense: Odense University Press, 1984. p. 230. Note also W. Sayers, A Norse etymology for luff 'weather-edge of a sail'. *American Neptune*, Vol. 61, 2001, pp. 25–38.

[26] O. Crumlin-Pedersen, Description and analysis of the ships as found. In *Ships and Boats of the North*, ed. O. Crumlin-Pedersen and O. Olsen. The *Skuldelev Ships*. Roskilde: Viking Ship Museum, 2002, p. 119.

[27] M. Vinner, *Unnasigling* – the seaworthiness of the merchant vessel. In *Viking Voyages*, see note 9 above, pp. 96–97.

In short, the hull shape below the waterline helped a vessel to 'grip' the sea and reduced the risk of the vessel being pushed over on her beam end, shipping water, and then sinking. We should, however, keep in mind that a large, ocean-going merchant vessel of the type described as a *skip mikil* ('big ship') or *kaupskip mikil* ('big merchant ship') was a very different craft from the doubt-lessly more elegant vessels represented by the Oseberg find, a reconstruction of which capsized in a flat sea when sailing on a tack as the result of being struck by a somewhat 'fresher breeze'.[28] There are numerous literary references to tacking, but the most richly evocative is surely that in *Orkneyinga Saga*. It may be poetry, and it may not have been written in Orkney, but the composer of the following verse certainly captures the feel-ings experienced as one watches a grey dawn break over a cold, grey sea:[29]

High the wave heaves
while we tack off Humber,
the mast sways, in the swell
sink Veslu Sands:
sea-spray never soaks
the warrior at assembly,
nor stings the sight
of the sleepy citizen.

In heavy seas and high winds a large square sail has to be reefed in order to prevent undue strain on the mast. This involves short-ening the foot of the sail by rolling it up and making this secure by tying the reef points along its length. If this is not done, there is a danger that the vessel will begin, as *Flateyarbók* puts it, to *sigla lausum kili*, 'to sail itself keelless',[30] i.e. it will start to plane and be in danger of being rolled into a wave trough and capsizing. As no complete sails have survived, there is no empirical evidence that they had reef-points. *Orkneyinga Saga* does, however, make

[28] M. Carver, On – and – off the Edda. In *Shipshape*, see note 21 above, p. 309. This may have been due to factors such as sail size and mast height. But it does little to dispel the belief that the Oseberg vessel was never intended for the open sea and that oar, not sail, power was the normal method of propulsion.

[29] *Orkneyinga Saga*, p. 165. Tacking is mentioned elsewhere in this saga: pp. 172, 191. Note also *Egil's Saga*, p. 109.

[30] Vinner, *Unnasigling* – the seaworthiness of the merchant vessel. In *Viking Voyages*, see note 9 above, p. 104.

reference to reefing sails in order to reduce speed.[31] In worsening sea conditions the yard itself might be lowered and the sail reefed further. In the worst of conditions, when the boat could make no headway against wind and waves, it is highly probable that the crew turned her (a risky manoeuvre in high seas, since there is the danger of broaching) and tried to run before the sea with the yard lowered and the sail area reduced to just enough to provide steerage.[32]

Sea conditions

When, towards the end of the tenth century and the beginning of the eleventh[33] Eirik the Red sailed from Iceland to Greenland with settlers, according to *Grænlendinga Saga* only fourteen of the twenty-five ships in his fleet completed the voyage. Of the others we are told that some perished.[34] If Eirik followed the course that he set several years earlier when he sailed to rediscover the land that Gunnbjorn Ulf-Krakasson had sighted years before, then he sailed a course from Snæfellsnes to a point on Greenland's east coast which came to be known as Bláserk before turning south and coasting down to and round Cape Farewell to what would become the Eastern and Western Settlements. This easterly crossing is only about 277 nautical miles and would not have taken more than a few days in good weather to accomplish. Yet, if the narrative is to be believed, it must have been on this relatively short passage that the foul weather was encountered. Describing a direct voyage from Norway to Greenland *Óláfs saga Helga* also tells of the heavy weather encountered by Thorarin Nefjolfsson in the Greenland Sea. Ultimately, Thorarin was forced back and made land in Iceland. Thorbjorn Laugarbrekka, sailing from

---

[31] *Orkneyinga Saga*, p. 191: 'Since Svein had the faster ship, he had to reef his sail and wait in turn for Anakol.'

[32] M. Vinner, A Viking ship off Cape Farewell. In *Shipshape*, see note 21 above, p. 299. In this instance the crew of Saga Siglar resorted to two luxuries denied the vessels in this situation a thousand years ago: they deployed a reserve stern rudder (the side rudder had been disabled) and switched on the auxiliary engine!

[33] Dating the time of settling Greenland and the first voyage to Vinland is problematic: see H. Pálsson, Vinland revisited. *Northern Studies*, Vol. 35, 2000, pp. 12–13; Jones, *The Norse Atlantic Saga*, pp. 43–47.

[34] *Grænlendinga Saga*, ibid. pp. 144.

Iceland, had better luck, although high seas ensured that the voyage was not a swift one and, in view of the fact that his vessel 'took on much water', it was certainly a hazardous one.[35] It is interesting to note that on the North Atlantic crossing made by *Saga Siglar*, the vessel shipped 200 litres of water when struck by a large wave; and in the Denmark Strait she encountered steep seas with an average wave height of more than 4 metres.[36] Several years later even this fine reconstruction met her end at the hands of the sea, foundering in a storm where wave heights were in the region of 14 to 15 metres.[37] It is to the subject of waves that we now turn.

Hafgerðingadrápa is the title of a poem of which two fragments survive.[38] The poem was probably composed in the twelfth century (and almost certainly cannot be dated earlier than the mid-eleventh) and appears to be connected with the colonisation of Greenland.[39] The title may be translated as the 'Lay of the Towering Waves',[40] and *hafgerðingar* themselves are often rendered as 'sea-hedges'.[41] *Konungs Skuggsjá*, the only text to explore this phenomenon, has this to say:[42]

Now there is still another marvel in the seas of Greenland, the facts of which I do not know precisely. It is called 'sea-hedges', and it has the appearance as if all the waves and tempests of the ocean had been collected into three heaps, out of which three billows are formed. These hedge in the entire sea, so that no opening can be seen anywhere; they are higher than lofty mountains and resemble steep, over-hanging cliffs. In a few cases only have the men been known to escape who were upon the seas when such a thing occurred.

---

[35] *Eirik the Red's Saga*, trans. K. Kunz. In *The Sagas of Icelanders*, see note 2 above, p. 657. This would have involved the crew in bailing out the vessel.

[36] Vinner, A Viking ship off Cape Farewell. In *Shipshape*, see note 21 above, pp. 293–95.

[37] Ibid., pp. 303–4. A reconstruction of the Oseberg ship, which Vinner describes as 'certainly not an offshore-going vessel', went down in the same storm three hours earlier.

[38] The fragments are to be found in *Landnámabók* and *Grœnlendinga Saga* and are discussed by J. Benediktson, *Hafgerðingadrápa*. In *Speculum Norroenum: Norse Studies in Memory of Gabriel Turville-Petre*, ed. U. Dronke, G. Helgadóttir, G. Weber and H. Becker-Nielsen. Odense: Odense University Press, 1981. pp. 27–32.

[39] *Hafgerðingadrápa*. In *Speculum Norroenum*, see note 38 above, p. 31.

[40] Jones, *The Norse Atlantic Saga*, p. 146.

[41] *The King's Mirror*, p. 137; G. J. Marcus, The course for Greenland. *Saga-Book*, Vol. 14, 1953–57, p. 16; G. J. Marcus, *The Conquest of the North Atlantic*. Woodbridge, Suffolk: Boydell Press, 1980. pp. 60, 94.

[42] *The King's Mirror*, p. 137.

This account of *hafgerðingar* has been dismissed as 'rather improbable' and in any case suspect since it was based on hearsay.[43] In short, we are asked to believe that seamen exaggerate and that waves which resemble cliffs and come at a ship from all directions are tall tales and not to be trusted. A more scientific approach to the subject, and one that appears to have some currency still, is that these waves were caused by seismic upheavals or sea-quakes in a volcanically active area.[44] However, there is another possible interpretation of what *hafgerðingar* may have been intended to describe.

On 28 September 2000 the cruise liner *Oriana*, at sea in the North Atlantic in Force 10 conditions (with wind speeds in excess of 52 knots and waves exceeding 9 metres in height),[45] had some of her side windows smashed in by a wave of almost 13 metres. Other recorded incidents of huge waves striking vessels in the North Atlantic include one in 1995, when the QE2 faced into a wave of 29 metres, and in 1998, when a floating production rig was struck by a wave of more than 18 metres. Laser measurement of the wave that struck a drilling rig in the North Sea on 1 January 1995 showed a height of 26 metres from trough to crest.[46] When this exceptional wave struck it, the rig was already experiencing what is classified as a violent storm, wave heights of around 12 metres buffeting the platform. In February 2001 the *Caledonian Star* was cruising in the Antarctic Ocean when she too ran into a violent storm and was struck and badly damaged by a wave whose height was estimated to be 30 metres. A European remote sensing satellite has also detected waves of this same height.

In the fairly recent past oceanographers dismissed the 'rogue' or 'episodic' wave as a myth. It was as inconceivable to them as the *hafgerðingar* were to the study-bound scholars of the texts. The linear model used to calculate wave height indicated that a 30-metre wave was a scientific impossibility. Now, however, an explanation for such monster waves is a matter of relatively

[43] *Hafgerðingadrápa*. In *Speculum Norroenum*, see note 38 above, p. 27.

[44] J. Steenstrup, Hvad er kongespeilets havgjerdinger? *Aarbøger for nordisk oldkyndighed og historie* (1871). Cited by Jones, *The Norse Atlantic Saga*, p. 146; Marcus, *The course for Greenland*, p. 16, footnote 9.

[45] On the Beaufort Scale used to describe weather conditions at sea, the *Oriana* was weathering a 'storm'.

[46] G. Lawton Monsters of the deep. *Scientific American*, Vol. 2297, 2001, pp. 28–32.

simple physics. Imagine three waves in a queue, as it were. If the last wave catches up with the middle one, and the middle one catches up with the leader, then the middle wave will increase in size and pile on top of the one in front. The result will be a wave – a rogue wave – that has absorbed the energy of two other waves. These waves need not come singly, and they may also come at a vessel from more than one direction.

A wooden vessel rises to the sea better than a steel one; and the fact that a wave is 6 or 7 metres high is not in itself a problem. What is critical in these conditions is not so much the height of each wave as the steepness of its face and reverse side. The vessel will sail up an incline with relative ease. Where, however, the face of the wave is vertical and cresting, the vessel heading into it is in real danger. This will also be the case if, having sailed up the face of a wave, the ship finds that the wave behind the first one is a rogue. Her descent will be steep and, moreover, it will be straight into the trough between the first wave and the rogue. The vessel will, in short, face a wall of water which looks rather like a steep cliff. If such waves can sink modern bulk carriers, merchant ships on the North Atlantic a thousand years ago would have stood little or no chance, although other vessels in the vicinity not struck would survive to tell the tale. This interpretation of what *hafgerðingar* may have been is speculation. But it is preferable to lofty dismissal and more probable than erupting sub-sea volcanoes.

Another sea condition described in *Orkneyinga Saga* is also worth at least a brief mention. The passage reads as follows:

[Earl Magnus] had two ships . . . he went to Egilsay. As they were rowing away upon a calm, smooth sea, a breaker suddenly rose high over the ship . . . His men were astonished to see such a breaker rise up from a calm sea . . . and there was deep water beneath them.[47]

This is a perfect description of what Scottish fishermen today term a 'lump' of water. The Pentland Firth, on whose waters the event is said to have occurred, and the adjacent sea have a particular reputation for generating such lumps.

---

[47] *Orkneyinga Saga*, p. 92. This passage may be contrasted with that in *Njal's Saga*, p. 340, where Flosi and the burners are struck by breakers as they near land (Orkney) in fog.

Navigating the North Atlantic[48]

It is said if one sails from Bergen due west to Hvarf in Greenland that one's course will lie some seventy or more miles south of Iceland.[49]

From Hernar in Norway one must sail a direct course west to Hvarf in Greenland, in which case one sails north of Shetland so that one sights land in clear weather only, then south of the Faroes so that the sea looks half-way up the mountainsides, then south of Iceland so that one gets sight of birds and whales from there.[50]

Bergen lies on latitude 60° 4′ N.; and Cape Farewell in Greenland lies on latitude 59° 45′ N. Add to this that the meaning of 'Hvarf' (Cape Wrath, the extreme north-west point on the Scottish mainland, is derived from Old Norse *hvarf*)[51] is 'turning point', and two rather neat conclusions present themselves. The first is that the merchant ship making the long run to Greenland could sail along an exact parallel of latitude which would take her there. The second is that by following that exact parallel she would strike Cape Farewell and then turn north-west towards the settlements.[52] There is a further extrapolation that can be made from these sailing directions. If a Scandinavian vessel could sail along an exact parallel of latitude, then the crew must have possessed something that allowed them to keep to that parallel and correct any deviations from it. Does this mean, therefore, that they had some form of compass? But before we embark on the vexed topic of the compass, one simple fact must be kept in mind. A single degree of latitude comprises 60 minutes; and each minute represents 1 nautical mile. If, therefore, a turning point is missed by 1 degree, it is missed by 60 miles; if one is 2 degrees out, the

---

[48] On navigation generally, see G. J. Marcus, The navigation of the Norsemen. *Mariner's Mirror*, Vol. 29, 1953, pp. 112–31; Marcus, *Conquest*, pp. 100–118; J. Bill, Ships and seamanship. In *The Oxford Illustrated History of the Vikings*, ed. P. H. Sawyer. Oxford: Oxford University Press, 1997. pp. 197–99; S. Thirslund, Navigation by the Vikings on the open sea. In *Viking Voyages*, see note 9 above, pp. 109–17; S. Thirslund, *Viking Navigation* [Sun-Compass Guided Norsemen First to America]. Humblebæk, Denmark: S. Thirslund, 1996; U. Schnall, Early shiphandling and navigation in northern Europe. In *The Earliest Ships. The Evolution of Boats into Ships*, ed. R. Gardiner and A. E. Christensen. Conway's History of the Ship. London: Conway Maritime Press, 1996. pp. 120–28.

[49] *Sturlubók*, in Jones, *The Norse Atlantic Saga*, p. 115.

[50] *Hauksbók*, ibid., p. 115.

[51] A. Room, *Brewer's Dictionary of Names*. London, New York: Cassell, 1992.

[52] E.g. Bill, Ships and seamanship. In *The Oxford Illustrated History of the Vikings*, see note 48 above, p. 198; B. Cunliffe, *Facing the Ocean: The Atlantic and Its Peoples* Oxford: Oxford University Press. 2001. p. 504 also equates Hvarf precisely with Cape Farewell.

turning point is missed by 120 miles. At the very outset, therefore, this has implications for any interpretation of 'Hvarf' as referring to Cape Farewell. No competent navigator a thousand years ago would have risked a course intended to strike that particular promontory. If, however, they were following a parallel of latitude, a due course west along latitude 61° N. from Hernar would take the vessel to Cape Discord on Greenland's east coast, roughly 60 nautical miles to the north of Cape Farewell.[53] At this point the vessel could turn south and coast down to Cape Farewell, keeping land to starboard before rounding the Cape. With this understood, we can now return to the question – did these vessels navigate by compass?

A fragment of a wooden disk dating to around 1000 was found in present-day Uunartoq during the course of excavations in the Eastern Settlement of Greenland (Figure 69). The half-disk was notched to provide fourteen points, and various lines appear to be inscribed across its face. It has been argued from the overall appearance of this find that it is part of a compass and that the incisions represent gnomic lines indicating the sun's trajectory throughout the day.[54] The theory of the sun-compass was thus born. It must be said that the instrument is simplicity itself. First, a disk must be cut to shape. Then a gnomon, such as a thin stick or nail, is inserted at the centre of the disk. As the sun rises and strikes the gnomon it casts a shadow which moves around the disk as the day progresses. If the tip of the shadow cast is marked at regular intervals, at the end of the day these points can be connected by incising a line touching each so as to produce a curve. The point on this curve where it is closest to the gnomon then represents the point at which the shadow cast was shortest and, therefore, where the sun was at its zenith, which, in the northern hemisphere, will be north. Knowing where north lies then enables the user to establish where the other points of the compass should be. Two further points should, however, be noted. First, the gnomon curve needs to be redrawn every few days, and, second, accuracy can only be guaranteed to within a few degrees.

---

[53] Vinner, A Viking ship off Cape Farewell. In *Shipshape*, see note 21 above, pp. 297–98.
[54] Thirslund, *Viking Navigation*, pp. 12–15.

Figure 69 Sun-compass? This wooden disk was found during excavations at Uunartoq, Greenland. The find has been the subject of much speculation. The notches around the perimeter and the scratch marks have been taken to indicate that this is a 'sun-compass' used by Scandinavian sea-farers crossing the North Atlantic. This is highly unlikely, since the compass would have to be recalibrated frequently, and in any event was not pin-point accurate. There are no references to such a compass in any of the written sources.

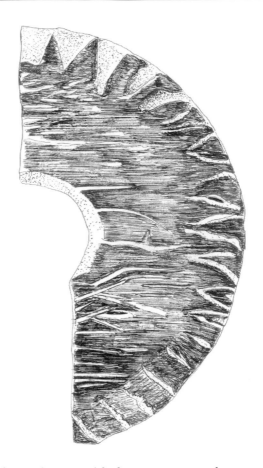

Practical experiments with the sun-compass have generally produced a positive reaction from those who have used them.[55] Most scholars, however, remain sceptical,[56] and there are certainly serious difficulties associated with the view that sun-compasses were used. The first is that although there is a superficial similarity between the Uunartoq half-disk and a compass, without the entire disk we cannot be sure that it was indeed a sun-compass. A second problem is that the premise upon which the argument for a sun-compass is based is flawed. One cannot predicate the argument that the Scandinavian sea-farer of the eleventh century navigated by this means on the fact that we are able to construct a working sun-compass in the twentieth century. A third problem is the rather

[55] Ibid. pp. 18–19, 29–30; Vinner, A Viking ship off Cape Farewell. In *Shipshape*, see note 21 above, p. 297.

[56] Bill, Ships and seamanship. In *The Oxford Illustrated History of the Vikings*, see note 48 above, p. 198; Schnall, Early shiphandling and navigation in northern Europe. In *The Earliest Ships*, see note 48 above, pp. 120–28.

obvious one that a sun-compass only works when there is sun. It will not function in fog or on cloudy days; and in the North Atlantic, even during summer, overcast skies and banks of fog are quite normal.[57] Finally, it is the seeming precision with which the passage in *Hauksbók* gives sailing directions to Greenland, and the fact that latitude 61° N. lies just to the north of Shetland and just to the south of the Faeroes, that predisposes some to conclude that a vessel could hold to this course along an exact parallel of latitude. If, however, the directions are interpreted as providing points to fix one's bearings, and not thought of as exact plots on a continuous line, a very different picture emerges. The Shetland Isles measure approximately 110 kilometres along their north–south axis. A vessel bound for Greenland, bearing in mind that it might have to tack or alter course to take advantage of the wind, needed only to sight the eastern littoral of these islands at any spot and then sail north until the northernmost tip of Unst was just visible before making for the Faroes. Sighting the eastern coast of this island group, again about 110 kilometres along its north–south axis, the vessel would bear south until the sea appeared to be half-way up the cliffs of Syderö (it is easier to reckon the height of a cliff having seen both its base and top than if only the top is visible) before bearing west again in the general direction of Iceland. It is quite noticeable in *Egil's Saga* that vessels did not aim to make land at their point of destination. Rather they headed for where they knew that land ought to be and, on sighting it, got their bearings and sailed along the coast until they reached their destination. The Atlantic coast of Norway is some 700 kilometres long, and we are told of a ship bound for Sognefjord sighting Hordaland to the south and then turning north towards the fjord.[58] Without further contemporary evidence for its existence, and it is nowhere mentioned in the texts, we should treat the argument for the use of a sun-compass as being far from satisfactorily proved.

Discounting the sun-compass does not disparage in any way, however, the navigational skills of the crews who made the voyages to Greenland and the other islands of the North

---

[57] Vinner, A Viking ship off Cape Farewell. In *Shipshape*, see note 21 above, p. 297. Vinner confirms that the sun-compass he used depended on clear skies.

[58] *Egil's Saga*, trans. B. Scudder. In *The Sagas of Icelanders*, see note 2 above, p. 64: 'Thorolf [Skallagrimsson] set off that summer and had a smooth passage, making land at Hordaland and heading north to Sognefjord.'

Atlantic archipelago. Nor does its use, if that was the case, diminish their accomplishment, since it was not a precision instrument. Navigation in the tenth and eleventh centuries was an art rather than a science, and it consisted in making use of a range of features observable by sea-farers in the North Atlantic.[59]

At the outset one has to accept that sea-farers in a less technologically reliant culture will make use of the sea itself as a navigational tool. Wave quality, direction and colour all provide information to the navigator.[60] For example, to the south-west of the Faroes there are several banks that rise up from the deeper waters around them. In a relatively flat sea a perceptible swell builds up over these banks which would have been noted as a general pointer to the direction in which the islands lay. The sea-bed to the west of the Faroes Bank also drops away to around 2,000 metres before rising again sharply to form the Reykjanes Ridge, and then, equally sharply, it descends to a depth of 3,000 metres to form the Irminger Basin to the east of Greenland. Although these depths are too great to sound with a lead and line, since the lead will not sink to the bottom quickly enough to give a vertical reading as the vessel continues to sail on,[61] there is an intriguing line in *Konungs Skuggsjá* which refers to the 'deepest part of the [Greenland] ocean'.[62] That the lead and line was used in the Viking Age has tended to be assumed, largely on the basis of one scene from the Bayeux Tapestry which may depict a lead and line. However, if this passage is to be believed, it carries with it the implication that this part of the North Atlantic was too deep for effective use of the lead. However, the fact that one is out of sounding depth is, in itself, an important indication of relative

[59] Many of these are noted by Marcus, *Conquest*, pp. 100–118.
[60] Navigation by wave quality and direction was practised by Polynesians on their inter-island voyages across the wide expanse of the southern Pacific. See A. Sharp, *Ancient Voyagers in the Pacific*. Harmondsworth: Penguin Books, 1957; J. Golson, *Polynesian Navigation*. Wellington: Polynesian Society, 1963. Some Polynesian navigators say that wave rhythms can be detected by the swing of their testicles: D. Lewis, *The Voyaging Stars: Secrets of the Pacific Island Navigators*. London: Fontana, 1978; D. Lewis, *We, the Navigators: The Ancient Art of Landfinding in the Pacific*. Honolulu: University Press of Hawaii, 1972. We must discount this possible means in more northerly climes.
[61] The problem of drift was noted by William Scoresby during voyages he made to Greenland and the Arctic between 1810 and 1822. Note also G. Hutchinson, *Medieval Ships and Shipping*. The Archaeology of Medieval Britain. London: Leicester University Press, 1997 [1994]. pp. 175–76.
[62] *The King's Mirror*, p. 138.

position, particularly if that area is between two natural features (such as the Faroes Bank and crest of the Reykjanes Ridge) where soundings are possible.[63]

Even without the sounding lead there was still a great store of observable data for the navigator to deploy. The crest of the Reykjanes Ridge lies some 500 metres below the surface to the south-east of Iceland. Plankton is abundant here, as are the fish that feed on it, and the whales that feed on the fish, and the birds that take the fish and what is left after the larger predators have finished. This is the area to which *Hauksbók* refers as the place 'that one gets sight of birds and whales', and *Konungs Skuggsjá* also refers to the many kinds of 'toothed whales' (i.e. the kind that eat fish) in the seas around Iceland. As for the birds, apart from the fact that bird migration routes between the British Isles and the Faroes and Iceland could be used as a means of fixing the position of those islands,[64] the type of bird encountered at sea would indicate roughly how near or far the vessel was from them. Puffins and small auks, for example, do not fish far from land. Gannets and guillemots fish farther out to sea. Both groups would therefore provide a rough indication of the proximity of land, and their flight lines would point the direction in which land lay.[65] It has also been noted that the birds from Iceland, which *Hauksbók* mentions, are first encountered roughly 240 kilometres to the south of the island – which would locate them along the course that *Hauksbók* says should be sailed. [66]

In *Grænlendinga Saga*, when Bjarni Herjolfsson left Iceland for Greenland to join his father he had three days' sailing before land 'disappeared below the horizon'. But how could Bjarni still have sight of land at a distance of 216 nautical miles? Obviously he would be below the rim of the horizon and so land itself could not be visible. On the other hand it should be understood that in the unpolluted Arctic sky, including that over Iceland, refraction would project a vertical image of land which was actually below

[63] Cf. B. Gelsinger, Lodestone and sunstone in medieval Iceland. *Mariner's Mirror*, Vol. 56, 1970, pp. 219–26.

[64] J. Hornell, The role of birds in early navigation. *Antiquity*, Vol. 20, 1946, p. 146.

[65] On bird navigation, see G. Matthews, Recent developments in the study of bird navigation. *Journal of the Institute of Navigation*, Vol. 6, 1972, pp. 264–70; P. Fenton, The navigator as natural historian. *Mariner's Mirror*, Vol. 79, 1993, pp. 44–57.

[66] Marcus, *Conquest*, p. 115. Reference to birds as an indication of the direction in which land lies is to be found in *Færeyinga Saga* and *Eirik the Red's Saga*.

the visible horizon seen from the deck or mast-head of a ship. In some cases refraction has even been known to produce two vertical images, the second superimposed upon the first.[67] Bjarni may, therefore, have seen what was in effect a mirage, in which 'objects are seen from far greater distances than in the ordinary state of the atmosphere'.[68] Sailing more or less due west from Snæfellsnes in Iceland to Bláserk in Greenland, which was the course we are told that Eirik took on his first voyage there, the distance is about 277 nautical miles. On a clear day the refracted images of both Snæfellsjökull and Bláserk would be visible. Indeed, even without refraction, high ground such as Öræfajökull (2,199 metres) in south-east Iceland is visible up to 145 kilometres offshore. However, although terrestrial refraction may have helped vessels sailing to Greenland, its occurrence could be something of a mixed blessing, as the story of Bjarni Herjolfsson indicates. Immediately after land disappeared, the following sequence of events is narrated:[69]

Then the wind dropped and they were beset by winds from the north and fog; for many days they did not know where they were sailing. After that they saw the sun and could take their bearings.

In Grænlendinga Saga this combination of fog and wind is termed hafvilla;[70] and we now know that when conditions are such as to cause refraction the mirage produced is often followed by fog.[71] The saga then paints a plausible picture of what anyone blown off course and with no instruments to guide them would do – look to the sun's position. If the zenith was higher in the sky than it was in Iceland, Bjarni would conclude that he was much too far south to be in the area of Greenland. Had Bjarni[72] possessed a sun-compass, or rather had the composer of the saga known about them, it is unlikely that he would have been portrayed as relying on dead-reckoning to sail out of a tight spot. There is also no possibility that Bjarni, or anyone else lost in fog at sea for that

---

[67] Arctic Pilot, 4th ed. (1933–46), Vol. II, p. 18. London: H.M.S.O.
[68] Ibid. Note also Marcus, Conquest, pp. 26, 55.
[69] The Saga of the Greenlanders, trans. K. Kunz. In The Sagas of Icelanders, see note 2 above, p. 637.
[70] G. J. Marcus, Hafvilla: a note on Norse navigation. Speculum, Vol. 30, 1955, pp. 601–5; Marcus, Conquest, pp. 59–62, 106–7. Other instances of hafvilla are encountered in Landnámabók and Njál's Saga.
[71] Arctic Pilot, p. 18.
[72] Or, for that matter, Olaf Peacock or Orn, when they too suffered 'sea-bewilderment' in the episode described above, p. 328.

matter, used a *sólarsteinn* or sunstone. It has been argued that this entirely fictional contrivance acted as a prism allowing polarised light to filter through, thereby indicating the sun's position.[73] However, experiments with Icelandic felspar have proved that this does not work. Moreover, literary scholars agree that references to *sólarsteinar* only appear after 1200 and probably refer to a 'burning-glass' and not a navigational instrument.[74] Even attempts to calculate approximate latitude by reference to the sun's elevation above the rim of the horizon, using such simple tools as a notched stick or even one's hand, knuckles or thumb, might result in mishap where the true horizon was obscured by fog and one's position estimated on the basis of a false sighting.

Not even navigation by reference to the stars is free from problems. Polaris, the Pole Star, is part of the constellation known as Ursa Minor. Sighting this star, therefore, indicates where north lies.[75] Identifying Polaris is also relatively easy if one traces a line through the stars at the end of Ursa Major. In the higher latitudes of the northern hemisphere Polaris and the lower stars in Ursa Minor will appear high in the night sky. The further south a vessel is (although it must still be in the northern hemisphere), the lower Polaris and its 'guardian' stars will appear in the night sky. It is, however, more likely that the observer will notice the guardians dropping closer to the horizon, or below it, before it is realised that Polaris too is getting lower. To the seafarers of our period Polaris was the *leiðarstjarna* – the guiding star.[76] On the North Atlantic crossing, the lower Polaris or the guardians were, the further south the ship was and the course would need to be altered to bring her back on line. However, just as a sun-compass needs sun, to use Polaris and the other stars as guides on the North Atlantic it must be dark. At the height of summer, when the sun never sets above latitude 60° N., the stars cannot help one navigate. This has prompted the rather weak suggestion that vessels made the crossing in spring and autumn.[77] If they did, it was contrary to the advice given in *Konungs Skuggsjá*.

[73] T. Ramskou, Solstenen. *Skalk*, 2, 1967, pp. 16–17.

[74] P. Foote, Icelandic sólarsteinn and the medieval background. In *Aurvandilstá*, see note 25 above, pp. 140–54.

[75] Polaris is actually about 1° from the North Pole.

[76] Marcus, The course for Greenland, pp. 110–12.

[77] Marcus, *Conquest*, p. 112.

When one considers all of the evidence, it can be argued that during the tenth and eleventh centuries the voyages west from Norway were conducted along what may be thought of as a sailing corridor lying between latitude 60° N. and latitude 65° N. That corridor was definable in terms of bird and marine life, sea conditions, winds, and the position of the sun and (at times) the stars. The objective of the crew was to sail the boat within the parameters of the corridor, which would take them to fairly close to their destination. That done, the vessel could then coast to her intended port of call. The information needed to accomplish this was the product of experience,[78] experience that would be passed down the generations. Where a skipper was completely unfamiliar with a route, however, it is probable that he tried to take someone with him who had sailed it before as leiðsagnarmaðr ('guide' or 'pilot').[79]

The Scandinavians successfully spread across northern Europe and the North Atlantic. Over a remarkably long period they maintained a common culture and regular contact in the face of long distances and difficult conditions, from the Northern Isles to the Faroes, Iceland and Greenland. Only one settlement must be called a failure – Vinland. It was not the distances involved, however, that brought the Vinland experiment to an unsatisfactory conclusion, but rather the exposure of a very small number of Europeans to a densely populated region of North America in which peaceful co-existence with the original inhabitants proved to be impossible.

Iceland and Greeenland, on the other hand, must be accounted relatively successful settlements. Both soon developed their own laws and institutions and acquired their own bishops, initially under the authority of the archdiocese of Lund and later that of Niðaros (Trondheim). The Catholic Church was keenly aware of the unusual nature of these far-flung outposts of Christianity, and allowed them access to its institutions through their Scandinavian ecclesiastical superiors, who spoke for them in the larger European forum. Both settlements sent young men to

---

[78] On the mental maps that seamen can create and transmit, see C. Frake, Cognitive maps of time and tide among medieval seafarers. *Man*, (New Series) Vol. 20, 1985, pp. 254–70; K. Oatley, Mental maps for navigation. *New Scientist*, 1974, pp. 863–66;.

[79] As Bjarni Herjolfsson failed to do: *The Saga of the Greenlanders*, trans. K. Kunz. In *The Sagas of Icelanders*, see note 2 above, p. 637.

be educated at universities on the continent and celebrated the Mass according to the prescripts of the Western Church. Both settlements were on the geographical and environmental margins of Europe. In 1261 the Greenland settlements bowed to the inevitable and submitted to the Norwegian king. Following their example, two years later the Icelanders were forced to concede defeat to both internal and external political pressure and submitted to the Norwegian king, Hákon IV, in return for peace, regular contact and access to essential supplies. Iceland remained a part of Europe, but Europe gradually lost sight of the Greenland settlements during the later Middle Ages. It is ironic that as the Age of Reconnaisance dawned, and Europeans crossed the Atlantic to the Americas once more, the continent's original Viking discoverers lay dying in Greenland.

CHAPTER 13

Scandinavia and European integration: reform and rebirth

Although it took its name from Pope Gregory VII (1073–85), the movement that became known as the 'Gregorian reform' had its beginnings in the reign of Pope Leo IX (1048–54). When Leo IX ascended the apostolic throne, he did so in the year that followed the coronation of King Svein Estridsøn (1047–74). The Danish North Sea empire had started to collapse almost immediately following Canute the Great's death in 1035. His son by Emma, Hardacanute, only maintained control over parts of the empire, and when he died seven years later the Danes had to accept a Norwegian, Magnus 'the Good', as their king. Magnus' father, St Olaf of Norway, had been killed in battle against Canute the Great at Sticklestad in 1030 when he had mounted a threat to the Danish hegemony in the Baltic, and his son ruled over Denmark for only five years. His pedigree as the son of one of the enemies of the Danish kingdom meant that he had to focus on politics in Scandinavia, and thus he was not able to maintain Scandinavian control over England. Instead, as we have seen, this passed on to the Anglo-Saxon line and the English Godwinsons, and eventually to William of Normandy in 1066. During his time as king of Denmark Magnus also had to deal with the serious rebellion of Svein Estridsøn, who eventually assumed the Danish crown after Magnus' death in 1047. Svein faced a new enemy in Harald Harðráði, who took control of Norway, helped in no small part by the fortune he had amassed as a commander of the Varangian guard in Byzantium. Svein may have ruled over a much-diminished Danish kingdom, but he maintained peace there for twenty-seven years, and during his time as king Europe changed beyond recognition.

Reform movements had influenced the Western Church and society for around a century and a half by the time of the accesion of Svein. The urge for reform was sparked by a new-found freedom for parts of the Church, starting with the foundation in 910 of a monastery at Cluny in Burgundy. Cluny had been endowed with lands in such a way that they were beyond the control of secular rulers. The original founders, the duke and duchess of Aquitaine, hit upon the idea of making their donation to Saints Paul and Peter. They therefore designated the pope, the successor to these saints, as the protector of the worldly interests of the monastery, and Cluny was thus 'free' of worldly influence and soon became a spiritual centre for medieval Christianity.[1] Out of Cluny rose a movement, later known as the 'Cluniac reform', for the implementation of 'the peace of God' which emphasised the primacy of the word of the Bible against the concerns of secular rulers.[2] The spiritual leadership demonstrated in this programme and in the magnificent and elaborate celebrations of the Christian mysteries that took place in the monastery attracted even more foundations, and rulers, bishops, rich landowners and even serfs rushed to demonstrate their support in the form of donations to the monastery. Cluny thus became richer and even more influential. Powerful men and women joined together to call on Cluniac abbots to reform the practice of Christianity in their geographical areas as well. Cluny picked up the challenge and focussed on the salvation of souls, lay and clerical. Perhaps uniquely at the time, Cluny spoke out not only against the excesses of the rich laity but also against clerical marriage and ecclesiastical dynasties.

In its opposition to the twin evils of nicolaitism (the appointment of family to offices in the Church) and simony (the purchase of ecclesiastiacal offices) the monastery of Cluny struck a deep chord in the European psyche. In certain areas of southern and Mediterranean Europe it was becoming increasingly clear that the institution of married clergy allowed the development of ecclesiastical dynasties and that a married bishop would want to pass on both the secular and ecclesiastical part of his estate to a son. The laity was understandably concerned about this. One reason was that this practice concentrated land and wealth in

---

[1] The foundation charter is translated in E. F. Henderson, ed. and trans. *Select Historical Documents of the Middle Ages*. London: George Bell and Sons, 1910. pp. 329–33.

[2] Two examples of the proclamation of the peace of God are translated in B. Tierney, ed. *The Middle Ages*. Vol. I, *Sources of Medieval History*. 5 ed. New York: McGraw-Hill, 1992 [1983]. pp. 136–38.

the hands of members of the Church; another was that the laity came to see the ecclesiastical hierarchy as simply just another noble family, but one with the unfair advantage of having added influence granted by their close association with the authority of the papacy. A faction of the ecclesiastical hierarchy was also concerned, but for less practical reasons. This concern was more high-minded and focussed on the smooth functioning of the Church, the authority of the Church and the purity of the practitioners of the Church. The flagrant venality of ecclesiastical dynasties inspired members of this faction to seek out rules in canon law that circumscribed and eventually prohibited the two main evils, as they saw it: the transfer of spiritual power for money and the sordidness of sexually active priests handling the sacraments of the Church.

Initially these reformers received the backing of the Holy Roman Emperor, who saw in them a useful weapon in his battle to control the power of the Church. The emperor, Henry III (1039–56), knew that he had been anointed by God through his representative on earth, the pope. Like most of his predecessors, he saw himself as the protector of the Church and wished to safeguard ecclesiastical interests. Demonstrating how seriously he took his role (and incidentally also showing how one could interpret canon law slightly differently from the reformers), he refused to accept money or gifts for appointing bishops to their posts. It was clear to Henry that reform and a drive towards purity within the Church were sorely needed. Despite his best efforts, however, by the mid-eleventh century elevations to the papal throne had taken on an undeniably venal aspect that to the modern eye can appear almost comical. Benedict IX, for example, became pope three times. He became pope in 1032, having bought the office from the previous holder, his uncle, John XIX (1024–32). In 1045 Benedict sold the office to his successor, Gregory VI (1045–46). Benedict may be an extreme example, but he does embody the general moral tone of the papacy during these years. This scandal saw a climax of some kind in 1046. In this year, as protector of the Church, Emperor Henry III presided over a synod in Sutri and deposed no fewer than three rival popes (Benedict IX, Gregory VI and Sylvester III) and appointed a fourth – Suidger, the bishop of Bamberg – who took the name Clement II. It is a measure of the degradation of the office of pope that the archbishop of Hamburg-Bremen, Adalbert (who would have had a special concern for the Scandinavian mission), refused the appointment.[3] Clement II did not last long, however, dying after less than a year in office. He was followed by two further popes who reigned simultaneously. The first of these schismatic popes took the name Damasius II and reigned briefly from July 1047 to December 1048. The other was Benedict IX, who returned for a third and final brief spell as pope from November 1047 to July 1048. Taken together, these three papal reigns lasted only twenty-four months, from December 1046 to December 1048. In the latter year Henry's cousin, Bruno, bishop of Toul, was appointed pope and took the name Leo IX. The Gregorian reform, as it is now known, took its shape with that election. When Emperor Henry III appointed Leo IX, whose programme of reform was superficially similar to imperial policy, he set the papacy on its path to regain control over the Western Church and to liberate it from the control of the empire. Henry should have realised that trouble was coming when Leo insisted on being elected not only by the emperor but also 'by the clergy and people of Rome', and when he spent most of his time as pope travelling across Europe. Despite his ostentatious concern with the proper procedure for his election, Leo spent only six months of his papacy in the city of Rome. He crossed the Alps three times to go to France and Germany, where he presided over numerous synods, issuing decree after decree against simony, clerical marriage, violence and moral laxity. He also attracted some of the best legal minds of his generation, such as Peter Damian, Hildebrand (later Pope Gregory VII) and Humbert de Silva Candida, to the curia. In this way he gave the papacy a much higher profile and made its incumbent both more visible and more approachable to the laity.

This new high profile of the pope changed the direction of the Cluniac reform. Under the influence of Mediterranean canon lawyers the French reformers, who had previously focussed on reform by example, now began to support a reform programme that emphasised the authority, indeed the supremacy, of the papacy over lay powers. The schism with Byzantium, which was brought to a head when Humbert de Silva Candida

[3] J. P. Whitney, The reform of the Church. In *The Cambridge Medieval History*. Vol. V, *Contest of Empire and Papacy*. Cambridge: Cambridge University Press, 1926. p. 22.

excommunicated the patriarch of Constantinople in 1054, was one example of the new-found emphasis on apostolic supremacy. Another, and for our purposes more important, aspect of the ascendancy of the papacy was the increasing papal attack on the authority of the emperor himself.

It would take too long here to trace the history of the Gregorian reform and the conflict that culminated with Emperor Henry IV standing barefoot for three days in the snow as a penitent before Pope Gregory VII at the castle of Canossa in the Alps in the month of January 1077. However, some details are important for a proper understanding of the interaction of the Scandinavian kingdoms and the German empire. When Emperor Henry III died in 1056 he left an underage son to succeed him. During the boy's minority the empire was ruled by his mother and Archbishops Anno of Cologne and Adalbert of Hamburg-Bremen, the archdiocese that claimed supremacy over the Scandinavians by virtue of the mission to the area that had been initiated by St Anskar. When Henry IV reached his majority he found that events in the nine-year gap between his own and his father's reign had seriously undermined his imperial authority. Local lords, who were nominally under imperial authority whether they lived in the north or the south of the empire, had become noticeably more independent and had no intention of relinquishing their power, and the papacy had gained valuable support from the lords of Lorraine and Tuscany and from the Norman dukes of southern Italy. The new balance of power resulted in a clash between pope and emperor when Henry insisted on participating in the investiture of the new archbishop of Milan.

At a synod in 1075 in Rome Gregory VII forbade investiture by laymen. Bishops were to cease being dependent on the crown and instead become the dependants of the papacy. Bishops had been the most important officials of the empire, and their 'imperial' church domains were also the chief source of income for the emperor. Henry realised that it would spell the end for the empire if he allowed control of church domains to slip out of his hands, and thus a bitter conflict between the two powers began. At a synod at Worms (1076), convened by Henry, German and Italian bishops withdrew their allegiance to Rome and deposed Gregory, denouncing him in a letter addressed to 'Hildebrand, no longer pope, but false monk'.[4] Gregory's answer to Henry's action was to excommunicate him at a synod in early 1076, and, like Henry, he did not mince his words:

I withdraw . . . from Henry the king, son of Henry the emperor, who has risen against thy Church with unheard-of insolence, the rule over the whole kingdom of the Germans and over Italy. And I absolve all Christians from the bonds of the oath which they have made or shall make to him, and I forbid anyone to serve him as king.[5]

In effect Gregory was calling for the Christian kings and nobles of the empire to rebel against Henry. The emperor was not slow to grasp the significance of this and embarked on a damage-limitation exercise. He travelled to the fortress of Canossa, high in the Italian Alps, and there presented himself to Gregory – in a gesture as astute as it was striking – as a penitent sinner. He knew that Gregory would eventually have to accept him back into the Church: the pope, who was supposed to be the model of Christian mercy, could not refuse a penitent without appearing petty and the opposite of what the father of the Christian Church should be. Henry's gesture had the desired effect, but despite this spectacular success for the papacy, Gregory's programme of reform was ultimately not successful, at least not in its most radical form, although it did inspire a new spirit of local freedom among the Christian kings in the northern reaches of the empire, who tried to use the reform to re-assert their independence from the empire.

Ecclesiastical reform in Scandinavia

The Gregorian reform took on a less dramatic aspect in Scandinavia. Unlike much of the rest of Europe, here simony was perceived to be less of a problem. At the beginning of the reform in the 1050s Denmark may have been the oldest Christian Scandinavian kingdom, but Christianity was still relatively new, and the Church had not seen the development of ruling dynasties, as some of the Italian sees had. It was Harald Bluetooth who claimed to 'have made the Danes Christian', but he had died only two generations earlier. Organisationally the Danish church was also in its infancy: German clerics were appointed to the Danish

[4] Tierney, *The Middle Ages*, Vol. I, pp. 146–47.   [5] Ibid., p. 148.

dioceses of Schleswig, Ribe and Århus, which were first mentioned in 948, and also to the diocese of Odense, which appears
in the following century. It is uncertain whether these men
actually ever set foot in the country. Indeed it is possible to
argue that they were not welcome. The first Scandinavian ruler
to be born a Christian, Svein Forkbeard, had emphasised the
independence of the Danish church through his endowment of
churches. The two church buildings that Anskar had consecrated
in Denmark in the ninth century were dedicated to the Virgin
Mary, thus imitating the dedication of the archbishopric's main
church in Hamburg. However, during the reign of Svein, new
churches at Roskilde and Lund were dedicated to the Holy Trinity,
in imitation of the royal church in Winchester.[6]

We are perhaps on firmer ground for believing that Canute the
Great wanted to emphasise the sovereignty of the English church
over that of the German imperial archdiocese in Hamburg-
Bremen. He did so by appointing Englishmen to the sees of
Lund and Roskilde in the early eleventh century. In contrast to
their German counterparts, these English bishops were certainly
active in Denmark, as was Bishop Odinkar, a Dane, in Ribe.
Although Canute's appointment of English clerics caused conster-
nation in Hamburg-Bremen, towards the end of his reign he
agreed a compromise with Emperor Conrad II: the Danish sees
should be under the supremacy of the Hamburg-Bremen archdiocese, but keep their English clerics. Their legality was thus
acknowledged and condoned by Conrad II, with whose son
Canute negotiated a marriage for his daughter during his visit to
the pope in Rome in Easter 1027. The toll reductions for English
and Danish clergy travelling to Rome which Conrad II conceded at
the same time emphasise that the relations between Canute and
the empire were cordial, as did the fact that Canute walked in the
imperial procession next to Rudolph of Burgundy and the emperor himself after the emperor's coronation on 26 March 1027.[7]

[6] E. Jørgensen, *Fremmed indflydelse under den danske kirkes tidligste udvikling*. Det
kongelige danske videnskabernes selskabs skrifter, 7 Række. Historisk og filosofisk afdeling Vol. I: 2. Copenhagen: Bianco Luno, 1908. p. 126.; H. Andersen,
Martyr? *Skalk*, 1, 2004, pp. 18–19.

[7] D. Whitelock, ed. *English Historical Documents*. Vol. I, *English Historical Documents, c.
500–1042*, gen. ed. D. C. Douglas. London: Eyre and Spottiswode, 1955. p. 416;
E. Arup, *Danmarks historie*. Vol. I, *Land og folk til 1282*. Copenhagen: H. Hagerup,
1925. p. 136.

Despite the conflicts over supremacy, however, there is no doubting the ordinary Dane's enthusiasm for the new religion. Writing at the end of the eleventh century, Adam of Bremen informs us that there were 300 churches in Skåne, 150 on Sjælland (Zealand) and 100 on Fyn. He does not mention the number of churches in Jylland (Jutland) but we know that there were more churches on the peninsula than in other Danish provinces.[8]

In 1043, when Adalbert became archbishop of Hamburg-Bremen, German bishops were littered across the Danish sees, and this time we can say for certain that they were active in the country. The German cleric Rudolph, who had been translated from Cologne to Schleswig, presided over a peace treaty between Adalbert's predecessor, Bescelin Alebrand, and the Norwegian/ Danish King Magnus the Good. In northern Jylland there was a Bremen cleric called Vale and, in the eastern Danish area, Avoco (who may possibly have been a Dane) had been appointed by the bishop of Hamburg-Bremen. The situation as it looked in 1060 was a clear improvement for Hamburg-Bremen compared with the situation just after Harald Bluetooth's death in 986. There were more dioceses, and the offices were filled by men not only present in the country but also actively involved in the politics of the realm.[9]

THE REFORMS OF SVEIN ESTRIDSØN (1047–1074)

The death of Vale around 1060 gave the Danish king Svein Estridsøn the opportunity to re-organise the diocese of Ribe. He divided it into four: Ribe, Viborg, Århus and 'the island Wendila', i.e. northern Jylland. When Avoco died soon afterwards Svein divided his diocese in southern Scandinavia into three: Roskilde, Dalby and Lund. An English cleric called Henry was the first incumbent of the diocese of Lund. He was appointed despite the wishes of the archbishop of Hamburg-Bremen, whose candidate, Egino, was passed over. Instead Egino was

---

[8] I. Skovgaard-Petersen, Oldtid og vikingetid. In *Danmarks historie*. Vol. I, *Tiden indtil 1340*, exec. ed. A. E. Christensen, H. P. Clausen, Svend Ellehøj and Søren Mørch. Copenhagen: Gyldendal, 1980. p. 201.

[9] A. E. Christensen, Tiden 1042–1241. In *Danmarks historie*, Vol. I, see note 8 above, pp. 229–30.

given the diocese of Dalby. Henry had been the treasurer of Canute the Great and came to Lund after a time as bishop of Orkney.[10] Adam of Bremen was not impressed by Henry, whom he called a drunk and man of wanton living: according to Adam, Henry met his death on 21 August 1060 as a consequence of his overeating. Soon afterwards Svein Estridsøn agreed to combine Dalby and Lund, and Egino was called to the episcopacy, where he served until 1072. Being the man chosen for the job by Archbishop Adalbert of Hamburg-Bremen, it is not surprising that Egino gets a glowing reference from Adam of Bremen as a man of honest devotion to his office who died after a pilgrimage to Rome.[11]

Egino's successor, Ricwald, was a controversial choice. At the time of his appointment Ricwald had been excommunicated by Bishop Imad of Paderborn, the excommunication having been confirmed by Archbishop Liemar of Hamburg-Bremen. On the other hand Ricwald was commemorated as the founder of the Church in Lund by the *Necrologium Lundense*.[12] The year of his appointment, 1072, was a time of conflict between the empire and the Church, and Ricwald's excommunication may not have been confirmed by Pope Gregory VII. This suggests that Ricwald may have been one of the earliest supporters of the Gregorian reform movement in Denmark. The anti-imperial slant of Danish policies is confirmed by the fact that King Canute IV sheltered several prominent opponents of the empire in the country, among them the bishops of Magdeburg and Halberstadt, both of whom were avid supporters of the Gregorian reform.[13] The consequences of this ecclesiastical re-orientation were not difficult to predict. Inevitably the proliferation of dioceses in Denmark meant increased friction between the German-dominated see of Hamburg-Bremen and the Danish kings, from Svein Estridsøn to Canute IV.

Danish kings maintained good relationships with the papacy. Svein was particularly close to Popes Alexander II (1061–73) and

[10] Christensen, ibid., pp. 229–30.
[11] A. Nissen, *Danske bisperækker*. Ansgariusforeningens skrifter. Copenhagen: Ansgariusforeningen, 1935. pp. 13–14.
[12] L. Weibull, *Necrologium Lundense. Lunds Domkyrkas Nekrologium*. Lund: Berlingska Boktryckeriet, 1923.
[13] Skovgaard-Petersen, Oldtid og vikingetid. In *Danmarks historie*, Vol. I, see note 8 above, pp. 244–45.

Gregory VII (1073–85).[14] Archbishop Adalbert lost influence in the area as a consequence of the re-organisation of 1060, and in an effort to reverse this setback Adalbert 'by power of a papal legation and in the hope of Danish royal assistance' called a synod in Hamburg to bring the practices of the Scandinavian church into line with the rest of Europe.[15] In particular he wished to introduce the payment of tithes so that bishops did not 'sell' their blessings.[16] However, Adam informs his readers that the 'trans-marine' bishops did not show up, and therefore the hoped-for royal support must also have not been forthcoming, for it is difficult to conceive of a bishop wilfully ignoring a call to synod from his superior.[17] Adalbert's position weakened further when he abandoned a planned mission to Scandinavia following 'the advice of the wise Danish king who informed him that the barbarian peoples were more easily turned to the Faith by people speaking their own language and sharing their customs'.[18] Papal letters confirm that a synod was called but also display a certain sympathy towards the Danish cause. All in all it appears that Svein succeeded in establishing a national Danish church under royal control.

An indicator of Svein's success, and of the way in which Gregory VII was aware of Denmark's wish to maintain a church independent from the imperially dominated see of Hamburg-Bremen, is a letter dated 25 January 1075 in which the pope deplored the fact that, although he had often received letters and emissaries from Svein when he was a cardinal, Svein stopped writing to him once he became pope. The letter went on to praise Svein in general terms for the interest he took in the Church and urged him to send legates to Rome so that the two could decide

---

[14] A. E. Christensen, Tiden 1042–1241. In *Danmarks historie*, Vol. I, see note 8 above, pp. 230–31.

[15] The phrase is Adam of Bremen's, but the events are attested in two letters from Pope Alexander II from the period 1061–72. L. Weibull, ed. *Diplomatarium danicum*, 1. Række, Vol. II, *Diplomatarium danicum 1053–1169*, in collaboration with N. Skyum-Nielsen. Det danske sprog- og litteraturselskab. Copenhagen: Ejnar Munksgaards Forlag, 1963. pp. 11–14.

[16] A. E. Christensen, Tiden 1042–1241. In *Danmarks historie*, Vol. I, see note 8 above, pp. 230–32.

[17] Adamus Bremensis, *Hamburgische Kirchengeschichte*. 3rd ed, ed. B. Schmeidler. *Monumenta Germaniae historica*: Scriptores rerum Germanicarum in usum scholarum separatim editi. Vol. XVII. Hanover: Hahn, 1977 [1917]. Book III, Chapter 72.

[18] Ibid.

what to do concerning 'the metropolitan see'.[19] In fact the pope
had a falling-out with the new bishop of Hamburg-Bremen,
Liemar, and was trying to forge an alliance, both spiritual and
military, with King Svein. For this reason he was prepared to
consider the elevation of a Danish diocese into an archdiocese. In
the event the letter did not have much effect: it almost certainly
did not reach Svein. In fact he was probably already dead by the
time of its composition. However, like the Romans a millennium
earlier, Gregory VII saw and understood that the Scandinavian
kingdoms could be valuable allies in Roman attempts to control
the German empire.

Harald III Hen (1074–1080)

In the sixty years following Svein's death in 1074, Denmark was
ruled by five of his sons. Four of them ruled during the first thirty
years and the last, King Nicholas, ruled for thirty years, from 1104
to 1134. We know comparatively little about these kings, and
certainly the connections between Denmark and the papacy
seem less intense in this period. Svein was succeeded to the
Danish throne by Harald Hen, who ruled from 1074 until 1080.
A papal letter to Norway in 1078 indicates that Harald's succession was not uncontested. In it, the pope warned the Norwegian
king, Olaf Kyrre, that he should not support the sons of Svein
militarily to force a division of the kingdom of Denmark. Instead
the pope encouraged Olaf to work towards a peaceful solution
that provided the sons of Svein with an honourable living and
good possessions so that they could live in royal style.[20] It is clear
that the pope was out of touch with the political and cultural
conditions in Denmark, and we must presume that the very
feudal, hierarchical social structure that is implied in his letter
is not a reflection of the reality of the situation in Denmark.

King Harald inadvertently presented the chroniclers with a
problem: he was succeeded by King Canute IV, who was made a
saint in 1103. This ought to imply that Harald had been a bad
king. But even the early twelfth-century chonicler Ælnoth, who
was a great fan of Canute, tells how Harald was the *elected* king of

---

[19] Weibull, *Diplomatarium danicum*, pp. 21–24.   [20] Ibid., pp. 37–39.

the people, who preferred him to the irascible Canute (1080–86). In fact Harald seems to have been a reasonable king. Ælnoth informs us that when he had been elected:

> he strove to meet the wishes of the people, not only by giving them the laws and rights they desired, but also by ratifying by his royal will the rules of law for the successors they had chosen.[21]

In other words he gave the Danish equivalent to the English Magna Carta, and it is significant that Ælnoth continues:

> Whenever a king is elected, the Danes have demanded that he observe the laws that Harald ratified. [For this reason] he is still reputed to be the prescient beginning of peace and common freedoms.[22]

Harald was an elected king who had negotiated the terms and conditions of his kingship with the magnates of the realm (i.e. 'the people' in the quote above). It was not until three generations later that Valdemar I managed to change the order of succession into a succession of the bloodline rather than popular acclamation. Harald was criticised for being a weak king by Saxo, writing in the late twelfth to early thirteenth centuries, but Saxo's slightly older colleague, the author of the so-called Roskilde Chronicle, who wrote around 1139–43, called him *vir optimus et rector justissimus* and adds that he gave back to the people the forests that the magnates had appropriated for themselves.[23] Ælnoth calls him 'a lawgiver beloved by his people'.[24]

Harald's reign is not well documented by the narrative sources, but we can see that he continued his father's policy of detaching the Danish church from German supremacy in the shape of the archdiocese of Hamburg-Bremen. Papal letters from 1077 to 1080 indicate a growing sympathy for the Danish cause, but Gregory VII stopped short of appointing an archbishop for Scandinavia.[25] Two reasons for the lack of Danish success have been suggested: it was either impossible to find a suitable candidate or Gregory was uncomfortable with the

---

[21] Aelnoth, *Gesta Swenonimagni regis et filiorum eius et passio gloriosissimi Canuti regis et martyris*, ed. M. C. Geertz. In *Vitae sanctorum danorum: novam editionem criticam*. Copenhagen: Selskabet for Udgivelse af Kilder til dansk Historie, 1908–12.

[22] Ibid.

[23] *Roskildekrøniken*, trans. and ed. M. Gelting. Copenhagen: Wormanium, 1979. pp. 20–21.

[24] Skovgaard-Petersen, Oldtid og vikingetid. In *Danmarks historie*, Vol. I, see note 8 above, p. 241.

[25] Weibull, *Diplomatarium danicum*, pp. 35–43.

generally low quality of the Scandinavian church.[26] It is indicative of this conflict that (as mentioned above) the bishop of
Lund at the time, Ricwald, had been excommunicated by Bishop
Imad of Paderborn and the excommunication had been confirmed by Archbishop Liemar of Hamburg-Bremen. Saxo claims
that the bishop of Roskilde, Svein the Norwegian, was a former
member of the personal guard of the king and poorly educated,
although the Roskilde Chronicle (c. 1140) praises his sober
living, his endowment of fifteen prebends and the building of
a monastery 'in stone'. He was also behind the dedication of the
cathedral in Roskilde to the Holy Trinity, a fact that signals that,
if nothing else, he was willing to snub Hamburg-Bremen by
refusing to dedicate his church to the dedicatee of the cathedral
in Hamburg, the Virgin Mary.[27] We should also not forget that
the pope was involved in a major struggle with the German
emperor over investiture, that the interests of the Scandinavian
church had to be subordinated to the wider reform of the
European church, and that Scandinavia was but one player in
the politics of the Gregorian reform. For this reason the relations between the papacy and the Danish king remained cordial,
even warm, until Harald's death in 1080.[28]

Canute IV (1080/1081–1086)

Harald was succeeded by his younger brother, Canute IV, who
was later to become St Canute. We know nothing about the
circumstances of his election to the kingship. It is likely that he
was one of the sons of Svein referred to in the papal letter to Olaf
Kyrre, and if that is so, he had tried for years to become king of
Denmark.[29] It is also likely that his military prowess helped his
ambitions. This conjecture is based on the thirteenth-century
Knytlingesaga, which mentions a now lost poem by Kalf
Mánason in which Canute is praised as the conqueror of ten

[26] K. Hørby, Denmark. In *Medieval Scandinavia: An Encyclopedia*, ed. P. Pulsiano,
assisted by K. Wolf. Garland Encyclopedias of the Middle Ages, 1. New York,
London: Garland Publishing, 1993. p. 128.
[27] *Roskildekrøniken*, p. 20.
[28] See e.g. Gregory VII's letter of 19 April 1080 which praises Harald's 'recent
triumph and glory'. Weibull, *Diplomatarium danicum*, p. 41.
[29] Ibid., pp. 37–39.

kings in the east.[30] Canute's six-year reign is more controversial than Harald's. The events of his reign eclipse the sources for the reign of his brother; they are even more difficult to interpret than the sparse documentation of Harald's reign. The reason for this is two-fold: first, owing to the circumstances of his death, Canute was canonised soon after being murdered before the altar of St Alban's church in Odense in 1086; and, second, letters to and from the papacy dried up during his reign and only two records of his actions as king survive that are roughly contemporary – his donation letter to the church in Lund and a notice in Ælnoth's *Historia sancti Kanuti regis et martyris*.[31] There is no doubt, however, that Canute was a devout Christian king and a supporter of the reforms: in the first surviving Danish charter, he richly endowed the diocese of Lund in 1085[32] and did the same for the Augustinian canons of Dalby, the chapter of Roskilde and the church of St Alban in Odense, who all remember him in their *necrologia*. Canute's concern for the Church is underlined by the witness list to the donation to the church in Lund: in accordance with the new European custom, clerics were listed before magnates and nobles, indicating the king's respect for them.

Despite the hagiographical sheen of the narrative sources for his reign, it is possible to discern that Canute was interested in the programme of the Gregorian reform: the most likely explanation for Canute's rich gifts to the Church is that he sought and received the support of the Church for his internal policies. Prominent among his supporters appears to have been Ricwald of Lund, the excommunicated cleric who had been appointed bishop of Lund by Canute's father, Svein Estridsøn. According to the *Necrologium Lundense* (second third of the twelfth century) Canute's re-organisation of the Church followed 'the advice of his faithful bishops and in particular of master Ricwald in Lund'.[33] He rejected the he authority of Pope Clement III (1080–1100) – despite that fact that Clement had the support of the archbishop of Hamburg-Bremen, Liemar. Canute sheltered

[30] *Knytlingesaga, Knud den Store, Knud den Hellige, deres Mænd, deres Slægt*, trans. J. P. Ægidius, introd. by H. Bekker-Nielsen and O. Widding. Copenhagen: G. E. C. Gad, 1977. p. 41.

[31] Aelnoth, *Gesta*, p. 545.

[32] Weibull, *Diplomatarium danicum*, pp. 43–52.

[33] L. Weibull, *Necrologium Lundense. Lunds Domkyrkas Nekrologium*. Lund: Berlingska Boktryckeriet, 1923.

the bishops of Halberstadt and Magdeburg, both supporters of the papal party of Gregory VII against the German emperor.[34]

Canute's avid support for ecclesiastical reform did not impede his interest in the reconquest of England. He had already participated in raids on England in the sailing season of 1069–70, during the reign of his father, and in 1075 he joined his men to those of the fleet of Earl Hákon to support the 'Revolt of the Earls' in William of Normandy's recently conquered England. This was an uprising planned by the Norman Earls Roger of Hereford and Ralph de Gael of Norfolk. The revolt was a disaster and quickly over: Ralph fled from Norfolk castle to Brittany and Earl Roger was stopped in Herefordshire by a force led by two English bishops. Thus the revolt was over before Canute and Hákon arrived, and Canute limited his activity to general pillage along the coasts of the Danelaw before heading off to pick up his bride, Ethel, the daughter of Count Robert of Flanders. The lost poem by Kalf Mánason that mentioned Canute's exploits in the east has already been mentioned. If Kalf is right, Canute was the last of the Scandinavian kings to be militarily active in the entire Scandinavian sphere of influence from the Bay of Bothnia to the English Channel.[35]

Canute was not a popular king, but the manner of his death made him the first Danish saint and provided Pope Paschal II with the excuse he needed to elevate the diocese of Lund to become the first Scandinavian archdiocese.[36] The sources must therefore be approached with caution. All authorities agree the main outline of Canute's reign: his actions caused dissatisfaction among the people and in the end he was assassinated in front of the altar in St Alban's church in Odense. The authorities do not agree on the cause of the dissatisfaction. The hagiographical literature assigns it to Canute's ecclesiastical reforms, which had strengthened the position of the Church at the expense of the nobility. The *Passio sancti Canuti*, written in Odense in the first half of the twelfth century, links Canute's passion to his introduction of church tithes, while the chronicler Ælnoth emphasises

[34] Christensen, Tiden 1042–1241. In *Danmarks historie*, Vol. I, see note 8 above, pp. 244–45.

[35] Arup, *Land og folk*, pp. 171–72.

[36] M. Skeggjason, *Eriksdrápa*. In *Den Norsk-Islandske Skjaldedigtning*, ed. Finnur Jónsson. Vol. I. København og Kristiania: Gyldendal, Nordisk Forlag, 1912. pp. 417–21.

the way in which the people wanted the king to adhere to the old rules (presumably the concord between Harald Hen and 'the people') and claimed that the people rose against Canute because of his ecclesiastical reforms.[37] However, the Roskilde Chronicle claims that Canute introduced an 'unheard-of' new tax called *nefgiald*, and Svein Aggesøn, another chronicler (writing in the 1180s), links Canute's murder to dissatisfaction with his aborted invasion of England in 1085.[38] *Knytlingesaga* may be closer to the truth, as it links the assassination to well-known later conflicts over regal rights, in particular the king's right to all land not previously claimed by others, forestry rights in Halland and Skåne, the rights to the Skåne fisheries and the king's visitation rights.[39] The gift to the archdiocese of Lund demonstrates that Canute was acquainted with and tried to implement the rights of the most advanced feudal kings of his time, William the Conqueror and Count Robert of Flanders.

At the end of the day it is certain that Canute's death came about in connection with the aborted invasion of England in 1085, for which a navy of more than a thousand ships was said to have been mustered off the coast of Jylland. The plans were abandoned after a long wait because Canute did not appear at the muster in person: he was busy with the defence of the southern border against Germany and spent the summer in Schleswig. As a consequence the magnates of Jylland approached the king's brother Olaf and through him informed the king of their intention to leave the fleet and go home to tend to their harvests. In an attempt to rob the magnates of their ring-leader, Canute banished his brother Olaf to Flanders. The situation went from bad to worse as Canute began to collect fines from the rebellious magnates for their desertion. As a result Canute soon faced a full-scale rebellion and beat a hasty retreat from the town of Schleswig to Odense, where he first sought refuge in his royal manor. When that no longer offered enough protection, he retreated to the church of St Alban's. On 10 July 1086 he was killed in front of the altar, together with his brother Benedict and

---

[37] Christensen, *Tiden* 1042–1241. In *Danmarks historie*, Vol. I, see note 8 above, p. 245.

[38] S. Aggesøn, *Sven Aggesøns historiske skrifter oversatte efter den på grundlag af Codex Arnæmagnæanus 33, 4to restaurerede nye Text*, ed. M. C. Gertz, Selskabet for historiske kilders oversættelse. Copenhagen: Schønberg, 1917. pp. 68–69.

[39] *Knytlingesaga*, pp. 71–80.

seventeen other members of his personal guard.[40] The rebels subsequently made contact with Count Robert of Flanders, who agreed to release Olaf in return for his younger brother Nicholas and the return of his daughter Adela and grandchild, Charles. Charles succeeded as count of Flanders in 1119 and died in 1127 under similar circumstances to his father, while Adela married the Norman Duke Roger of Apulia and ended her days in Italy.

Olaf Hunger (1086–1095)

We know next to nothing about the reign of Canute's brother Olaf. What we do know is that he reigned from 1086 to 1095 and that he gained the unlovely epithet 'Hunger' because the country was plagued by a series of poor harvests in that decade. Denmark was not unusual in this: most other European countries saw famine as well. But in Denmark the famines came to be seen as God's punishment of the country for the reckless murder of its true monarch. However, contrary to most narrative sources' dismissal of Olaf as the lowest of the low for his treachery against his brother, or just as plain incompetent, Olaf seems to have managed to keep Denmark out of the dangerous schism originally initiated by the German emperor in 1061, which saw two popes vying for the support of the European magnates until Emperor Henry IV failed to find a new candidate for the papacy in 1100. Olaf's reign also saw the succession in 1088 of the former royal chaplain Arnold to the see of Roskilde and the alleged Canute supporter Asser Thrugotsøn to the see of Lund.[41]

Throughout Olaf's reign, the cult of his brother grew: Canute's bones were exposed to a number of tests and were declared to be possessed of magical properties. In the spring of 1095 the bones were transferred to a stone sarcophagus in the unfinished crypt of the new cathedral church of Odense, which Canute himself had endowed. Olaf died in September the same year and was succeeded by his brother, Eirik I Ejegod.

---

[40] O. Fenger, *Gyldendal og Politikens Danmarkshistorie*. Vol. IV, '*Kirker rejses alle vegne*' 1050–1250, exec. ed. O. Olsen. Copenhagen: Gyldendal & Politiken, 2002 [1989]. pp. 67–68.

[41] Ibid., pp. 253–59.

Eirik I Ejegod (1095–1104)

Eirik was another son of Svein Estridsøn, and his reign was also characterised by a strong interest in ecclesiastical matters. He had an interest in the liturgy and structure of the English church and with his queen, Bodil, appears in the memorial book of Durham Cathedral.[42] Upon ascending the throne Eirik almost immediately invited a group of monks from Evesham to found a monastery in Denmark.[43] They were intended to observe the rites of the increasingly popular cult of Eirik's murdered brother, Canute. Based near the cathedral in Odense they came to form the nucleus of the dean and chapter of the cathedral. Eirik also elevated an English monk called Hubald, who had been a chaplain in Lund, to be the new bishop of Odense, and he re-established Danish connections with the papacy when he visited Bari in Italy in 1098. He managed to persuade Pope Urban II to authorise Canute's translation to the sainthood, although it was another two years before the actual translation took place, on 19 April 1100/1101.[44] The ceremony, in which Canute's remains were moved from the crypt of the cathedral to the main altar of the church, was attended by all the Danish bishops and 'the entire people'; the remains were swathed in Italian silk brocade and deposited in a golden reliquary, both items donated by the former queen, Adela, now Duchess Adela of Apulia. This event marked a turning point for the Danish kingdom.

Eirik consolidated his family's claim to royal power by a string of successes. Through his successful pleas to have his brother elevated to the sainthood he created the foundation for the elevation of the diocese of Lund to an archdiocese. Markus Skeggjason, in his Eriksdrápa, confirms a Lund tradition that it was because of Eirik's intervention that the pope granted the new status to Lund. Eriksdrápa also mentions how the king waged war against the Wends south of the country, praises him as the paragon of Christian kingship who built five stone churches, and mentions how it was during Eirik's reign that the noble Skjalm Hvide conquered the island of Rügen.[45] The Roskilde Chronicle, on the other hand, slated him for being the originator

[42] Ibid., pp. 70–71.   [43] Weibull, Diplomatarium danicum, pp. 55–56.
[44] Ibid., pp. 58–61.
[45] Skeggjason, Eriksdrápa. In Den Norsk-Islandske Skjaldedigtning, see note 36 above.

of 'many unreasonable and unjust laws'.[46] Eirik was thus not seen by contemporaries as material for the sainthood. Instead his reign coincided with the earliest calls for the crusades, and this clarion call to the European nobility struck a deep chord in the Scandinavian kingdoms.

The crusades

The call for the first crusade went out at the church council that met at Clermont outside Paris on 18 November 1095. The council was attended mainly by bishops of southern France, but there was also a scattering of representatives from the north and elsewhere. After the transaction of many important items of ecclesiastical business, which resulted in a series of canons, the council enacted a canon that granted a plenary indulgence to those who undertook to come to the aid of the Christians in the east. At an outdoor assembly Pope Urban II addressed a large crowd. Precisely what the pope said will never be known, since the only surviving accounts of his speech were written years later. But there is no doubt that his words hit a nerve with his audience. He probably painted a picture of the eastern Christian community in dire need of support. He would have mentioned the plight of eastern Christians, the molestation of pilgrims to the holy city of Jerusalem and the desecration of holy places. He urged those of his hearers who were guilty of disturbing the peace to turn their warlike energies towards a holy cause. He emphasised the need for penance, for the acceptance of suffering. No one should undertake this pilgrimage for any but the most exalted of motives.[47] The appeal of the call to arms was truly international: Fulcher of Chartres, a participant in the crusade, wrote that people 'of any and every occupation' took the cross:

Whoever heard of such a mixture of languages in one army, since there were French, Flemings, Frisians, Gauls, Savoyards, Lotharingians, Allemani, Bavarians, Normans, English, Scots, Aquitainians, Italians, Danes, Apulians, Iberians, Bretons, Greeks and Armenians?

[46] *Roskildekrøniken*, p. 24.
[47] *Gesta francorum et aliorum Hierosolymitanorum: The Deeds of the Franks*, ed. and trans. Rosalind M. Hill. London: Nelson, 1962. pp. 28–30.

Everyone, high and low, was affected by the idea of liberating the Holy Land, and most Europeans either left their estates and farms to go on the crusades or left bequests for this, the new exalted goal of Western Christianity in their wills. The duke of Normandy and the count of Flanders were amongst the most prominent participants in the first crusade, but they were not alone among the nobles of Europe. The chronicler Albert of Aachen (writing between 1095 and 1121) describes how Svein Estridsøn's son, also Svein, met his heroic death in a hail of arrows in the plains of Anatolia[48] and that a group of Danes were in an Anglo-Flemish fleet that landed at Jaffa in 1106.[49] The call for participation in the first crusade was heard as far away as Iceland and persuaded numerous people from Iceland and Orkney.[50] The Norwegians are first mentioned in this context about 1102, when Skopte Ogmundsson and his three sons left Norway with five ships. Like many Scandinavians, they died before they arrived in the Holy Land: Skopte died at Rome in the autumn of 1102, and the last of his sons died in Sicily later that year.[51] But by far the most illustrious of these Nordic crusaders is Sigurd the Crusader, who left Norway with sixty ships in the autumn of 1108. Following a route via England, France, Spain, Sicily and Palestine, he was said to have assisted King Baldwin of Jerusalem in the siege of Sidon. On the way back to Norway he waited two weeks for a following wind to take him past Cyprus:

Although every day it blew a breeze for going before the wind to the north; but Sigurd would wait for a side wind, so that the sails might stretch fore and aft in the ship; for in all his sails there was silk joined in, before and behind in the sail, and neither those before nor those behind the ships could see the slightest appearance of this, if the vessel was before the wind; so they would rather wait for a side wind.[52]

---

[48] Fenger, *Gyldendal og Politikens Danmarkshistorie*, p. 71.

[49] J. Gallén, Korståg. In *Kulturhistorisk leksikon for nordisk middelalder*, ed. O. Olsen, P. Skautrup, N. Skyum-Nielsen and A. Steensberg. Copenhagen: Rosenkilde og Bagger, 1959–77.

[50] G. Storm, ed. *Islandske Annaler indtil 1578*. Christiania: Grøndahl & søns Bogtrykkeri, 1888. p. 110; A. Bøe, Korståg: vestnordiske. In *Kulturhistorisk leksikon*, see note 49 above.

[51] *Magnus Barefoot's Saga*. In *Heimskringla: History of the Kings of Norway*, trans. L. M. Hollander. Austin: Published for the American-Scandinavian Foundation by the University of Texas Press, 1964. Chapter 22.

[52] *Saga of Sigurd the Crusader and his Brothers Eystein and Olaf*. In *Heimskringla*, see note 51 above, Chapter 11.

Apart from Svein's heroic, legendary death and Sigurd's inter-vention in the siege of Sidon, the Scandinavians were never militarily significant in the crusades to the Holy land. Many set out from Scandinavia and many died en route to Palestine, and that was ultimately also to be the fate of King Eirik. He died on Cyprus, and his queen, Bodil, died when she arrived in Jerusalem in 1103.[53]

The first archdiocese

In 1103 or 1104 Asser accepted the pallium from the papal legate Alberich and became the first archbishop of Lund. Asser was an experienced man of the Church: he had been bishop of Lund since 1089 and came from an aristocratic background in the magnate family, the Thrugots in Jylland. Lund was not just a national archdiocese but the primate of all three Scandinavian countries, including the North Atlantic islands, Iceland and Greenland. For this purpose Lund was eminently suited (Figure 70). The church was centrally placed, it had been well endowed by the now sainted King Canute, and in its first arch-bishop it possessed a man well suited to the job: high-born, a nephew of the queen and an experienced church leader. King Eirik further endowed the church with enough income to make it the richest of the Scandinavian dioceses and probably also insti-tuted the payment of tithes to provide the church with a steady income. The success of the Danish church was even noticed by Archbishop Anselm of Canterbury, who sent a congratulatory letter to Asser in 1104 that also warned him against dangerous schismatics and their attempts to infiltrate the Danish church (probably an oblique reference to German clerics who were unwilling to pay homage to the pope in Rome).[54]

The election of a new Danish king was by acclamation at the three public *things* in Jylland, Sjælland and Skåne, and the sons of Estrid provided an unbroken line of five kings in the period from the death of the successor to Canute the Great, the Norwegian Magnus the Good, in 1047, to the reign of Niels, with a fairly smooth transfer. The close collaboration between the Church and

---

[53] Fenger, *Gyldendal og Politikens Danmarkshistorie*, p. 71.
[54] Weibull, *Diplomatarium danicum*, pp. 65–66.

Figure 70 Lund Cathedral, Skåne, Sweden. The cathedral was 'brought back to its medieval state' in the nineteenth century. The east façade gives the best impression of what the original church would have looked like when the church was consecrated in 1145. Like other Scandinavian churches, the cathedral was built in stone and followed the same architectural layout and style as churches in mainland Europe.

King Eirik, and the king's many travels are two aspects of the slow process of Europeanisation that affected the Viking kingdoms in the eleventh and early twelfth centuries. The years that followed Eirik's death in Cyprus in 1103 saw his successor, Niels (1104–34), add to the prerogatives of the Danish kings in accordance with new European ideals of kingship. We find this exemplified by the royal deed of King Niels recording a gift to the church of St Canute in Odense. In it the king reserves the right to levy fines for outlawry and for refusals to appear at naval musters, and the right to flotsam and jetsam, and also limits the Church's rights to inheritance, extending meanwhile the king's right to take inheritance after any man who dies intestate and without any blood relatives.[55]

Overall the reign of King Niels was a success, but it was to have a disastrous end. Niels saw the Church as an ally in his struggle to maintain power. The increasing power of and demands for privileges by the European church made it possible for the king to counter-balance the demands of the aristocracy. In return King Niels granted the Church the right to raise tithes – a tax of one-tenth of all agricultural produce throughout the land, which was used to finance the building of many hundreds of stone churches across the land over the next century.[56]

[55] Ibid., pp. 73–77.
[56] Fenger, *Gyldendal og Politikens Danmarkshistorie*, pp. 103–7; Weibull, *Diplomatarium danicum*, pp. 66–67.

However, as King Niels grew old, it became clear in the late 1120s to early 1130s that there would be two claimants to the throne: Niels' son Magnus and Niels' nephew, Eirik I's son, Duke Canute Lavard (the Breadgiver). In 1131 Magnus took the standard approach to this problem: he and his men ambushed Canute in a forest outside Roskilde and murdered him. However, this murder of the popular duke seriously backfired, ultimately providing Denmark with its second saint and Canute Lavard's son, Valdemar, with the justification for his branch of the family's claim to the Danish throne. But the immediate effect in 1131 was that the people rose up against Magnus' father, Niels, and in 1134 his troops were defeated at the Battle of Fotevig in Skåne by the combined troops of Duke Canute's brother, Eirik (Emune, 'the Memorable'), and Archbishop Asser, who had changed his allegiance to the new King Eirik just before the battle.[57] Magnus, and five rebel bishops who did not follow Archbishop Asser when he changed sides, died in the battle. King Niels fled to Urnehoved, where he appointed as his co-regent the bastard son of Eirik I Ejegod, Harald Kesja, a previous claimant to the throne who had been rejected as king because of his outlawry thirty years earlier. In an attempt to raise a larger army Niels then left the country to go to Germany but was murdered in 1134 in Schleswig.[58]

King Niels' death heralded the beginning of a period of national unrest and rebellion which was to last twenty-three years. Towards the end of the period Denmark even saw three kings – Svein, Canute and Valdemar – rule over different regions. But in 1157 it was clear that the son of Canute Lavard, Valdemar, was the victor in the civil war, and he was crowned king by acclamation at separate meetings of the three *things*.

Svein III, Canute V and Valdemar I (1146–1157)

After a period of relative peace under King Eirik II Emune 1134–37 and his successor Eirik III Lamb (1137–46) Denmark was once again thrown into turmoil. The crisis was a direct result of the new crusading fever that swept Europe. In 1144 Christian Edessa

---

[57] Fenger, *Gyldendal og Politikens Danmarkshistorie*, pp. 73–76.
[58] Christensen, Tiden 1042–1241. In *Danmarks historie*, Vol. I, see note 8 above, pp. 282–87.

had fallen to the Muslim ruler Zenghi. When news reached the pope in Rome measures were taken to launch another crusade. This time the crusaders were sent against a variety of targets, not only those in the Middle East. Delegates from Emperor Alfonso VII of Spain, king of Castille-Léon, managed to procure an extension of the crusading bull granting indulgence to those fighting the Muslims in Spain. With this authority Alfonso conquered the Ebro basin, with important cities such as Tortosa, between 1144 and 1158. In addition King Alfonso Henriques of Portugal succeeded in taking Lisbon from the Muslims in 1147 with the help of Flemish and English crusaders on their way to the Holy Land. At the same time a northern crusade was launched against the pagan Slavs. Some German princes had argued that they could not leave their frontiers undefended in order to go to the Holy Land, and in March 1147 they were granted permission by Bernard of Clairvaux to fulfil their crusading obligation by fighting the Slavs east of the Elbe. The duke of Saxony, Henry the Lion, and the count of Brandenburg, Albert the Bear, together with other German princes attacked the Slavs at Dobin and further eastwards at Steczin.

Crusading fever also hit Denmark. In 1146 a papal legate preached the crusade to the court of King Eirik. Paradoxically, although the call was to take up arms against the pagans, the result was that King Eirik abdicated, entered a monastery and died soon afterwards.[59] At the time of his abdication the succession to the throne was not clear. Two kings were elected in the country: King Svein III was elected king by the populace of Skåne and Sjælland in 1146, but the thing in Jylland refused to confirm his election as king of that area. Instead, the grandson of King Niels, Canute V, was elected.[60] The result was that the kingdom was split in two. There was no love lost between the two kings, but Archbishop Eskil of Lund managed to reconcile them in 1147. It is perhaps a reflection of their continued animosity that the crusade they organised against the Wends the following year was not successful.[61] It did not take long before the two kings were quarrelling again, and two years later (in 1149) Svein defeated

[59] Ibid., p. 291; K. V. Jensen, Denmark and the Second Crusade: the formation of a crusader state? In *The Second Crusade: Scope and Consequences*, ed. J. Phillips and M. Hoch. Manchester: Manchester University Press, 2001. p. 164.
[60] Ibid., p. 165.   [61] Ibid., pp. 167–68.

Canute in a battle at Høje Taastrup outside present-day Copenhagen, and again outside Viborg the same year. As a result of this unrest Emperor Frederik I Barbarossa called the two kings before him in Merseburg.[62] The emperor granted the kingdom to Svein in return for Svein granting Sjælland to Canute as a fiefdom. However, Svein only sullenly filled his part of the bargain and thereby insulted Valdemar, who was one of the guarantors of the settlement. Valdemar, the son of Duke Canute Lavard, was to be the first of several kings of that name in Denmark, all of them characterised by clear-headedness, extreme political ambition and an ability to see their aims through to the end. Valdemar I (the Great) reigned from 1157 to 1182, Valdemar II (the Victorious) from 1202 to 1241 and the last great Valdemar, Valdemar IV (New Day), from 1340 to 1375. The latter will not concern us here, but the reign of Valdemar I is one of the great periods of Danish medieval history.[63] He was born on 14 January 1131 in Schleswig, the son of Canute Lavard and a Russian princess called Ingeborg. He was given the name Valdemar, which he shared with his grandfather, Grand Duke Vladimir of Russia, and grew up in the *familia* of Skjalm Hvide, one of the most influential magnates of the realm. During this time he became friends with Absalon – the crusading hero of Rügen (see below) and Skjalm Hvide's son – who was to be one of the great reformers and warrior bishops of the country. Valdemar's first entry onto the national political stage was in 1148, when King Svein III made Valdemar duke of southern Jylland. To begin with Valdemar supported Svein against Canute V, but he soon changed sides and joined Canute, even though Canute's father was Duke Magnus, the man who had killed Valdemar's father, Canute Lavard. As a token of his fidelity to Canute's cause Valdemar was engaged to Sophie, the daughter of Vladimir

---

[62] Christensen, Tiden 1042–1241. In *Danmarks historie*, Vol. I, see note 8 above, p. 293.

[63] Numerous studies of the period of the Valdemars are available in the Scandinavian languages. See K. Erslev, *Den senere middelalder. Danmarks riges historie*, ed. K. Erslev, J. Steenstrup, A. Helse, V. Mollerup, J. Fridericia, E. Holm, and A. Jørgensen. Vol. I. Copenhagen: Det Nordiske Forlag, 1898–1905. pp. 593–849; Arup, *Land og folk*, pp. 286–311; C. H. J. Weibull, *Saxo: kritiska undersökningar i Danmarks historia från Sven Estridsens död till Knut VI.* Lund: Berlingska Boktryckeriet, 1915; A. E. Christensen, *Kongemagt og aristokrati: epoker i middelalderlig dansk statsopfattelse indtil unionstiden.* Københavns Universitets Fond til Tilvejebringelse af Læremidler. Copenhagen: Ejnar Munksgaards Forlag, 1968. pp. 40–67.

Rurik, duke of Novgorod, and Canute's half-sister.[64] As a consequence Canute and Valdemar joined forces and forced Svein to enter a new treaty on the island of Lolland on 6 August 1157. According to this treaty Denmark was divided into three parts, Svein, Canute and Valdemar each receiving one-third of the kingdom. Following tradition, the treaty was celebrated in Roskilde three days later. Reneging on all his promises, Svein had his men attack his two co-regents. Canute was murdered, but Valdemar escaped with his foster-brother Absalon, and together they fled to Jylland. Having mustered his forces, Valdemar married Princess Sophie on 23 October in Viborg and then rode out to meet Svein in pitched battle on Grathe Moore south of the town.[65] In this battle Svein's army was definitively defeated and King Svein himself was murdered by a freeman after the battle.[66] The kingdom of Denmark was once again united, and Valdemar brought an end to twenty-three years of civil war.

During those years of civil war the Wends to the south of the country had become a growing problem. Exploiting the weakness of the Danish kings they had increased their attacks on the kingdom. In 1135 they had even attacked the southern point of Norway, which was clearly unacceptable given that control of the narrow straits of Denmark was the *raison d'être* of any Danish king. The end to the civil war also brought an end to this state of affairs. Valdemar initiated a programme to strengthen the navy and army and, as a consequence of the joint talents of Absalon and the revitalised kingdom, the Wends soon saw some of their main towns ransacked by the Danes.[67] In 1169 the Danes succeeded in conquering the fort of Arkona and imposing Danish supremacy on the Wends, at least for a short while. However, before this success, in 1162 Valdemar had to accept the German emperor, Frederik I Barbarossa, as his liege lord, although it is clear that Valdemar regarded this as mere form, for he strengthened the Danish borders with Germany.[68]

[64] Fenger, *Gyldendal og Politikens Danmarkshistorie*, p. 141.
[65] Erslev, *Den senere middelalder*, pp. 586–89.
[66] Fenger, *Gyldendal og Politikens Danmarkshistorie*, p. 141.
[67] Ibid., pp. 141–43.   [68] Ibid.

Valdemar, Canute and Absalon (1157–1182)

The reigns of Valdemar I (1157–82) and of his son Canute VI (1182–1202) were characterised once again by close ties with the Church, especially between the foster-brothers Valdemar and Absalon, the bishop of Roskilde (1158–77) and later archbishop of Lund (1177–1201). Perhaps the fact that Absalon was a man of the Church obscures the fact that the personal friendship between him and Valdemar was also an alliance between the king and the most powerful family of magnates in the realm, the Hvide family, which included Valdemar's foster-father, Skjalm Hvide, the hero of the Rügen crusade (see below), Absalon's brother, Esbern Snare, who became chancellor of the realm, and their cousin Sune Ebbesøn. Their collaboration was seen by nineteenth- and early twentieth-century historians as a golden time in Denmark's past, mainly because of the persuasive and linguistically brilliant chronicle of Absalon's clerk, Saxo Grammaticus.[69] Central to Saxo's narrative is Absalon's importance in the fight against the pagan Wends south of the Baltic, which culminated in the conquest and sacking of the island of Rügen in 1168 or 1169 and the victory over the Wendish/German Duke Bugislav of Pomerania in 1185.[70] These military conquests were no doubt important, but in the final analysis they mattered little, for it was the Germans who colonised and controlled the Wend lands in the thirteenth century. These victories had limited international impact but were crucial to the construction of the Scandinavian medieval state: through them the Scandinavian peasantry became used to the idea of the king as their military commander and the magnates,

[69] Erslev, Den senere middelalder, pp. 593–849; Arup, Land og folk.

[70] Saxo's narrative formed the basis of most Scandinavian historians' work until the shift of paradigm brought about by the Swedish historians Laurits and Curt Weibull who, in a series of brilliant studies, showed that Saxo, despite his statement that he wrote almost at the dictation of Absalon, in fact rewrote already existing written documents and histories but changed them in such a way that they reflected the dynastic and social programme of Absalon and Valdemar. L. Weibull, Kritiska undersökningar i Nordens historia omkring år 1000. Lund: C. W. K. Gleerup, 1911. Their results were first reflected in two major Danish historical works: Arup, Land og folk; and H. Koch, Den danske kirkes historie. Vol. I, Den ældre middelalder indtil 1241, ed. H. Koch and B. Kornerup. København: Gyldendalsk Boghandel Nordisk Forlag, 1950; and in A. E. Christensen, Mellem vikingetid og Valdemarstid: et forsøg på en syntese. (Danish) Historisk Tidsskrift, Vol. 12 No. 2, 1966, pp. 31–56 (English translation in A. E. Christensen, From the Viking Age to the age of the Valdemars. An attempt at a synthesis. Medieval Scandinavia, Vol. 1, 1969, pp. 28–50).

both Danish and those from other Scandinavian countries, rallied around the king and his crusade to christianise the pagans.

The leader of the Danish church for the early part of this period was the archbishop of Lund, Eskild (fl. 1137–77). He represented an ecclesiastical policy that did not always agree with royal policy. Eskild was an ardent supporter of the Gregorian reform. The main focal point in this movement, in Scandinavia as well as in the rest of Europe, became Eskild's insistence that the election of bishops should be free, i.e. that elections were to be conducted by members of the Church. As we have seen, such a programme of reform did not sit well with magnates throughout Europe. Secular powers, from the Holy Roman Emperor to local kings and magnates, reacted against such a display of ecclesiastical independence because the Church had large financial incomes and because bishops were the close allies of the magnates.[71] In 1122 the Church and the emperor reached an agreement known as the Concordat of Worms. According to this a bishop should be elected by the diocesan chapter and receive confirmation of the election from representatives of the pope and the king. The emperor's representative could be present at the elections but could not vote.

The Concordat of Worms combined with internal politics to produce a unique hybrid in Denmark. In 1137 a new archbishop of Lund was appointed. Not only was the successful candidate, Eskil, from a long line of clerics and a well-educated man but he was also the nephew of the previous archbishop, Asser and of Bishop Sven of Viborg (d. 1153). His great-grandmother's brother, Svein, had been one of the knights martyred with King Canute IV in Odense in 1086. Eskil's nephew, Svein Aggesøn (d. 1185), wrote the first medieval history of Denmark.[72] Eskil was born around 1100 and studied at the school in Hildesheim in Saxony, one of the European centres

---

[71] There are many brilliant studies of the Gregorian reform, but currently the best introduction for the general reader to the main issues is B. H. Rosenwein, *A Short History of the Middle Ages*. Peterborough, Ontario: Broadview Press, 2002. pp. 117–21.

[72] S. Aggesøn, *Scriptores minores historiæ danicæ medii ævi*. Vol. I, *Suenonis Aggonis filii opuscula historica: I. Lex Catrensis; II. Brevis historia regum Dacie; III. Series et geneaologia regum danorum*. Copenhagen: Selskabet for Udgivelse af Kilder til dansk Historie, n.d. pp. 55–156.; Sven Aggesen, *The Works of Sven Aggesen, Twelfth-Century Danish Historian*, trans. E. Christiansen. London: Viking Society for Northern Research, 1992.

of ecclesiastical reform. There he familiarised himself with the latest developments in the law of the Church. Later in life he became a personal friend of St Bernard of Clairvaux. Eskil can be seen as one of the beneficiaries of the political turmoil in the Danish kingdom after the murder of Canute Lavard. In 1134, after the Battle of Fotevig (where five bishops died in the revolt against King Niels), Eskil was appointed bishop of Roskilde. However, according to Saxo Grammaticus, this was not enough to fulfil his political ambitions. He soon joined the magnate Peter Bodilsøn in a revolt against King Eirik II. Bodilsøn was a Sjælland magnate who came to be centrally involved in ecclesiastical reform; he had founded the monastery of Næstved at around this time.[73]

Eirik's army was defeated on Sjælland, but he returned with another army, this time recruited in Jylland, which defeated the Sjælland revolt. It is a measure of the relative weakness of the royal party after the revolt that its ring-leaders, Eskil and Peter Bodilsøn, were let off lightly. Following an intercession by the archbishop of Lund, his uncle Asser, Eskil was fined only 20 marks. Eskil's luck did not abandon him when it came to be time to elect a new archbishop of Lund on his uncle's death in May 1137. The chapter initially elected the bishop of Schleswig, Rike, but when King Eirik died that September Peter Bodilsøn managed to persuade the chapter of the archdiocese of Lund to reject the royal candidate and instead grant the pallium to Eskil. His political skills were probably also behind the fact that Rike seems to have accepted the apparent demotion with little opposition. Instead he became bishop of Roskilde. Although this election showed some irregularities and interference from magnates, the main principle of the reform – that the election of the archbishop should be made by the cathedral chapter – stood.

Eskil pursued a clear policy of integration of the Scandinavian church into Europe. In 1140 he founded the first Scandinavian Cistercian monastery, at Herrevad in Skåne.[74] This was followed by foundations in Alvastra and Nydala, and all three were populated by monks from the monastery in Clairvaux. Other monastic

---

[73] Fenger, *Gyldendal og Politikens Danmarkshistorie*, p. 145.

[74] B. P. McGuire, *The Cistercians in Denmark: Their Attitudes, Roles, and Functions in Medieval Society*. Cistercian Studies Series. Kalamazoo: Cistercian Publications, 1982. p. 10.

foundations, Praemonstratensian, Carthusian and Benedictine, followed soon afterwards.[75] The latter order was even endowed by Eskil with a monastery that provided the first opportunity for nuns to take the veil in Scandinavia.[76] In 1143 Eskil received donations from King Eirik III (Lamb) for his part in the quelling of a revolt in Skåne lasting from 1137 to 1143, which was headed by Oluf, the son of Harald Kesja (who had briefly reigned as king of Denmark 1103–4),[77] and these donations provided the foundation for another Cistercian monastery, Esrum on Sjælland, which, like Herrevad, was populated with monks from Clairvaux. In 1145 Eskil officiated at the consecration of the new cathedral church in Lund, an ambitious building of European importance, dedicated to St Lawrence in an almost defiant refusal to follow the tradition of the former archdiocese of Scandinavia, Hamburg-Bremen, which was dedicated to the Virgin Mary.[78]

Eskil took pride in the political role of the Church. During the civil wars 1147–57 Eskil was instrumental in negotiating a short-lived peace between Kings Svein and Canute. He admonished the two kings to seal the peace by embarking on a crusade against the only partially christianised Obodrites south of the country. Svein and Canute, together with a force of Danish and German magnates and kings, were easily defeated by the Obodrites and, as a consequence, the two pretenders turned away from the arbitration of the Church and sought the help of the German emperor, Frederik I Barbarossa, at his diet in Merseburg in 1152. There King Svein repeated the oath of fealty that King Magnus had made in 1134 and promised to give the island of Sjælland to Canute as his fief. By his actions Svein seriously jeopardised not only the position of Eskil but also the freedom of the Scandinavian church. This danger had already materialised in 1151 when Archbishop Hartwig of Hamburg-Bremen, supported by Conrad III, petitioned Pope Eugenius III to acknowledge the supremacy of the German archdiocese over the Scandinavian bishops.[79] These events coincided with the arrival of a French cleric called William, who was the designated abbot of the new Cistercian monastery at Esrom. William was not only a cleric of

[75] Arup, Land og Folk, p. 225.   [76] Ibid., p. 226.
[77] Ibid., p. 209.
[78] Fenger, Gyldendal og Politikens Danmarkshistorie, p. 149.
[79] Weibull, Diplomatarium danicum, pp. 190–92.

outstanding learning (he had been abbot of St Geniviéve, one of the early centres of learning in Paris) but also a friend of Bernard of Clairvaux. William probably informed Eskil of the poor health of Bernard, and in 1153 Eskil left Denmark for France, where he managed to meet Bernard before the latter's death in that year.[80] He was therefore not in Scandinavia when the papal legate, Nicholas Breakspear (later Pope Hadrian IV), visited Scandinavia and decided against the wishes of Hamburg-Bremen that the area in fact needed a further two archdioceses, at Uppsala and Niðaros.

In 1158 the time had come, following the election of Eskil, to elect a new Danish bishop, the bishop of Roskilde having died. King Valdemar appeared in person and, in accordance with the principles of the Concordat of Worms, informed the assembled clergy that he was not there to influence the election. For that reason, he suggested, it would be better to proceed to a closed ballot. Absalon's po-faced pro-Valdemar chronicler, Saxo Grammaticus, reports: 'Then it happened that all votes were cast on Absalon.'[81]

For Archbishop Eskil the most important part of his mission was to ensure that the Danish bishops supported the international Gregorian reform movement. This meant that he supported the Church against the German Emperor Conrad III, who caused a schism by sponsoring the election of a number of anti-popes from 1159 to 1180. Conrad was not of a mind to support the duly elected Pope Alexander III, who insisted that even the emperor held his power from the Church, and his supporters apppointed instead Victor IV. Eskil was a strong supporter of the Roman pontiff, but his king, Valdemar, sent the bishop of Ribe to Pavia in 1160 to indicate the support of the Danish king for the newly elected imperial candidate and for a synod in Lodi in 1161. In other words, Valdemar committed himself and the kingdom to the cause of Victor IV. The following year Valdemar paid fealty to Conrad at Dôle in France Comté in the presence of Bishop Absalon and his chaplain, Radulf.

---

[80] Fenger, *Gyldendal og Politikens Danmarkshistorie*, p. 149.
[81] Saxo Grammaticus, *Danorum regum herorumque historia. Books X–XVI. The text of the first edition with translation and commentary in three volumes*, ed. and trans. E. Chistiansen. Oxford: B.A.R., 1980. Vol LXXXIV, Book XIV; Saxo Grammaticus, *Danmarks riges krønike*, trans. F. W. Horn. Copenhagen: Gyledendalske Boghandel, 1980. p. 123.

Acknowledging their support, Victor IV consecrated a certain Livo, whom Valdemar had already appointed bishop of Odense.[82] Eskil chose exile. He set out for France in 1160 and travelled to Rome and Jerusalem rather than compromise his principles. However, this dispute between the Danish king and the archbishop resolved itself with the death of Victor IV in 1164 and Valdemar's subsequent submission to Alexander III. In 1170 Eskil and Valdemar publicly demonstrated their reconciliation when Eskil presided over the simultaneous beatification of Valdemar's father, who became St Canute Lavard, and the coronation of Valdemar's six-year-old son, Canute VI. Thus the branch of the royal line that traced its ancestry through Canute Lavard had won the definitive victory in its attempt to claim the crown of the Danish kingdom. From now on Canute Lavard's heirs had a privileged claim over other claimants – be they royal, magnate or freemen – sanctioned by the grace of God and His Church.

During the long period of civil unrest it was clear the kingdom was a disparate collection of regions. Although the political skill of Valdemar was evident in the years of his reign, he still made some bad calls. When his foster-brother Absalon was elected archbishop of Lund in 1177, Valdemar was again present at the election, as he had been at Absalon's election to the see of Roskilde in 1158. Afterwards Absalon tried to strengthen his power in Skåne by packing his administration with relatives and dependants from the island of Sjælland. As a result of this action he faced a powerful rebellion directed against his brother Esbern and his cousin Sune Ebbesøn in 1180, which was checked only when the king himself intervened – at first with persuasion, later with force – to rally the Skåne magnates behind him. Valdemar only managed this feat with great difficulty by giving the Skåne magnates a number of concessions, *inter alia* the suspension of the payment of tithes to the bishop.[83] The Skåne rebellion marks a pronounced change in the cohesion of the country. King Valdemar had asserted his authority over the three regions of the country and brought the rebellious population to book.

[82] Arup, *Land og folk*, p. 236; Nissen, *Danske bisperækker*, p. 47.
[83] Arup, *Land og folk*, pp. 255–57; Christensen, *Kongemagt*, pp. 350–52.

The crusades and the north

There were three theatres of war for the crusades in the twelfth century: the Baltic, the Iberian Peninsula and the Middle East. They were seen by contemporaries as three fronts of the same war against the enemies of the Church. The renewed focus on the northern frontier was welcome to the Scandinavians. It was clear from earlier encounters that a high proportion of those who travelled to the southern theatres succumbed to disease en route, and added to this danger was the fact that crusading took time. The Norwegian Sigurd the Crusader, for example, spent three years abroad.[84] To fight against the Slavs was therefore a welcome option, and still helped to support Jerusalem. The main aim of the Scandinavians was to eradicate the last pockets of paganism on the southern and eastern shores of the Baltic, and the most important enemies there were the Wendish or West Slav people to the south of Denmark. Since 1108 crusades had been launched against this group, and in 1147 these crusades even became part of Eskil's peace-making efforts. The Swedes organised a crusade against the Finns in 1157, and soon afterwards the Danes began their series of Wendish crusades.[85] Apart from the obvious religious purpose of the crusade, the effect in Denmark was to unite the kingdom, which had suffered a decade of unrest under the Christian banner – one that was remarkably similar to that of the knights of St John, namely a white cross on a red background.[86] These initial Wendish crusades culminated in the capture of Arkona, a fortified pagan temple, on St Vitus' Day (15 June) 1168.

But the capture of Arkona was not the end of crusading in the Baltic. Indeed, it became the beginning of a new push to the east. Following the success of 1168, Pope Alexander III wrote a letter to Absalon as the bishop of Roskilde in which he acknowledged the conquest of Arkona, and soon afterwards he followed this letter with another two exhorting the Danes to join a crusade to convert the Estonians.[87] In them he exhorts the

---

[84] *The Saga of Sigurd the Crusader and his Brothers Eystein and Olaf.* In *Heimskringla*, see note 51 above, Chapter 14.

[85] Gallén, Korståg. In *Kulturhistorisk leksikon*, see note 49 above.

[86] Christensen, Tiden 1042–1241. In *Danmarks historie*, Vol. I, see note 8 above, p. 136.

[87] Weibull, *Diplomatarium danicum*, p. 345.

Danes to take up arms in a more radical attempt to convert the people of Estonia, who 'with unheard audacity' rejected the authority of the Church. Alexander III promised the same crusader privileges to those engaged in this Estonian crusade as the Church granted to those going to the Holy Land: the penitent crusader would receive the partial or full remission of his sins.[88] In fact, one side-effect of the nearness of Estonia was that the Baltic crusaders got off relatively lightly, as they gained their remission of sins after serving the Church for just one year, while those going to Palestine could expect to serve at least three years.[89] Doubtless the crusaders were concerned about their souls, but other privileges, such as exemption from royal taxes and the right to claim benefit of clergy (i.e. the right to be tried by the church courts), would have been additional attractions for these pious warriors.

The Danes were not the only Scandinavians that went crusading in the Baltic. The Swedes and Norwegians also participated, and German clergy had been on mission work in the area now known as Livonia (roughly, modern Latvia and Estonia) for some years. The German cleric Meinhard was appointed the first bishop of Livonia in 1186, and his successor, Bertold, was killed in the first regular battle with the Livonians in 1198. He was succeeded in the see by Albert, a man of considerable organisational and strategic skills.[90] Not only did Albert step up the crusading activity, but he abandoned his predecessors' fortified church in Üxküll and founded Riga in Latvia as a commercial and ecclesiastical centre in 1201. Riga soon developed into a powerful hub of activity, and the town provided a fortified and safe beachhead for incoming crusaders, who arrived twice a year to celebrate the vigils of two important crusading saints. Bishop Albert's foresight was not matched by the Danes until 1219, when they founded Reval in Estonia (present-day Tallinn).

The Danish crusading focus was on present-day Estonia. Although there was little co-ordinated crusading there before the first decades of the thirteenth century, Pope Alexander III's

[88] Ibid., pp. 343–45.
[89] The mention of the three years in *The Saga of Sigurd the Crusader* was clearly intended by Snorri to impress the listener with the uniqueness and speed of Sigurd's success.
[90] Fenger, *Gyldendal og Politikens Danmarkshistorie*, pp. 239–40.

letters demonstrate that the Danes were showing a strong interest in the area from at least the 1170s. We know that King Canute VI, Valdemar II's elder brother, attacked Estonia on several occasions, but he was unsuccessful in his attempts to establish a permanent presence there.[91] He founded some monasteries, but even the hardy Cistercians he put there found Estonia too much for them.

The Estonians did not willingly suffer these incursions. In 1203, the year after Valdemar II acceded to the Danish throne (left vacant the previous year by his brother Canute VI, who died at the relatively young age of thirty-eight), Estonians from the island of Øsel landed a small force in Listerby in south-east Sweden (then a part of Denmark). This very real military threat focussed Valdemar's mind. In 1206 a Danish fleet commanded either by the king himself or by the archbishop of Lund, Anders Sunesøn (successor to Absalon, who died on 21 May 1201), and his brothers set sail towards Øsel. Anders Suneson had received papal authorisation to appoint a bishop in Livonia.[92] This attack was not particularly successful, however, for none of the Danish crusaders was willing to stay on the island in their hastily constructed wooden fortification, and most returned home the same winter, having first dismantled the fort. As a consequence, the inhabitants of Øsel continued their raids into Denmark for decades to come.

However, Anders Sunesøn had not returned home with his army. Instead, he and King Valdemar's chancellor, Bishop Nicholas of Schleswig. stayed for the next two years in Riga, where Anders frequently lectured the cathedral chapter, exhorting them to complete the mission to Livonia.[93] What Bishop Albert of Riga, supported by the German Hohenstaufen King Philip of Swabia, may have thought about this we do not know, and anyway he was absent in Germany preaching the crusade.[94] But Anders Suneøn was a papal legate and thus had the authority in any case to overrule the bishop.

---

[91] Ibid., p. 240.

[92] N. Skyum-Nielsen, ed. *Diplomatarium danicum*, 1. Række, Vol. IV, *Diplomatarium danicum 1200–1210*. Det danske sprog- og litteraturselskab. Copenhagen: Ejnar Munksgaard Forlag, 1958. pp. 214–15.

[93] Fenger, *Gyldendal og Politikens Danmarkshistorie*, p. 240.

[94] Christensen, Tiden 1042–1241. In *Danmarks historie*, Vol. I, see note 8 above, p. 376.

Anders must have been a talented diplomat as well as being able to invoke his papal authority: in 1208 Danish crusaders joined an attack on the Estonian fortification in Fellinn on the border between Estonia and Livonia. The Danes and the Germans had realised that they shared military goals and strategies, and Anders remained in Riga in control of the Danish forces from the south. Bishop Albert in Germany at last turned his attention towards Estonia and initiated a campaign to gain control of its northern areas after successfully converting the Livonians and Lithuanians, who then joined the crusade against the Estonians. The motivations of the Germans and Danes on the one hand and the Lithuanians and Livonians on the other were probably very different: the Germans and Danes were mostly there on a mission for Christ, while the Livonians and Lithuanians saw an opportunity to settle old scores. The campaign lasted for the next ten years. The joint army was led by the Grand Master of the Knights of the Sword, a newly founded (1202) Lithuanian crusading order.[95]

Again, the Estonians fought back. In 1218 they allied themselves with the duchy of Novgorod and attacked the diocese of Riga and Bishop Albert's army with renewed vigour. Bishop Albert had gradually fallen out with the Knights of the Sword, and the discord between them severely hampered his efficiency, which meant that his resources were stretched to the utmost. It was in this context that he turned to King Valdemar of Denmark for help in 1218. Why Valdemar rather than the German emperor? Probably because he needed the legitimacy of an unimpeachable Christian king: his superior, Emperor Frederik II, was under interdict for heresy. It is also likely that the Danes had been preparing for another attack on the Estonians for some time, for they raised an army surprisingly swiftly and initiated their crusade towards the end of the summer. The papacy supported the venture at relatively short notice as well. A letter from the beginning of the campaign, dated 18 October, from Pope Honorius III granted Valdemar the right to rule over all the land that he might conquer in Estonia as a consequence of the crusade.[96]

---

[95] Ibid., pp. 376–77.
[96] Skyum-Nielsen, *Diplomatarium danicum*, pp. 196–97.

In spring 1218, one of Valdemar's German vassals – his nephew, Count Albert of Holstein and Orlamünde – was planning his own crusade against the heathen of Livonia. Inspired by previous experience of crusading in the Baltic with Valdemar, Count Albert had given his crusading vow on returning from his adventures with his uncle, and this rash action had created friction with some of Albert's own vassals. They, in their turn, had promised to go to the Holy Land, and their master's vow to go crusading in Livonia left them with a conflict of loyalties. There was, however, a loop-hole in the shape of a papal dispensation to Albert's men. This had been dispatched from the Lateran on 25 January 1217. Pope Honorius III, having heard that Albert was a 'God-fearing man devoted to the Apostolic See' who had demonstrated 'his willingness to serve our lord Jesus Christ', granted the conversion of ten crusaders' vows to go to the Holy Land into an obligation to fight for Christ in the Baltic. The naming of the ten was left to Albert and Bishop Nicholas of Schleswig by the pope.[97] Albert left in spring 1218 for Livonia to fight the Estonians. He even planned to attack the island of Øsel over the frozen ice – a plan he had to abandon when a sudden thaw set in.

King Valdemar himself joined the crusade in 1219 and probably reached Estonia's northernmost province, Revele, in the beginning of June that year. With him he brought a large fleet, a number of Danish nobles who had taken up the cross and a contingent of high-ranking Danish ecclesiastics, including the archbishop of Lund, Anders Sunesøn, and Bishop Theoderic of Estonia, a close ally of Bishop Albert of Riga. The army also included some of Valdemars' German vassals and a Wendish contingent under the leadership of their own Count Witslaw of Rügen, the son of Jaroslaw I. Witslaw had converted to Christianity and become a Danish vassal following the capture of Arkona in 1168. The chronicler Henry of Livonia tells how the Danish army set up camp near Lyndanise, an Estonian fortification, which they immediately proceeded to dismantle to make place for the *Castrum Danorum*.[98] During its construction some Estonian leaders came to the Danish king to parley, according to Henry 'in order to gain time'. Valdemar did not suspect any foul play and showed them around and showered them with gifts.

---

[97] Ibid., pp. 147–49.
[98] Later Tallinn: 'the fort of the Danes' in Estonian.

Some of them even accepted a Christian baptism and at the end of the day the leaders returned to their people with promises of peace from Valdemar. He may have been a little bit too naïve, however, for only three days later the Estonian leaders returned, this time bringing their armies. Thus, on the evening of 15 June 1219, fifty-one years after the capture of Arkona, just as the crusaders sat down to supper, their camp was attacked from five sides simultaneously. In the mêlée that followed, Bishop Theoderic was killed, apparently because the Estonians believed his tent to be that of the Danish king. However, the day was not lost for the Danes, for unbeknown to the Estonians, Duke Witslaw's forces were encamped in a valley nearby, and his counter-charge allowed the Danish and German forces to regroup, and together the crusading armies regained the field before night fell.[99]

Although decisive, this victory did not augur the end of Estonian resistance. Henry of Livonia explains how Valdemar quickly finished the castle and stationed a garrison there, who were to consolidate the Danish beachhead and, if possible, extend Danish possession of the area. With them the garrison had a number of missionaries, and in the aftermath of the battle Archbishop Anders Sunesøn consecrated the cleric Wescelin bishop of Estonia. It was this insistence of the Danish archbishop that he was primate of the new territories that eventually created major friction between the Germans and the Danes. Anders Sunesøn insisted on his papal authority and that the newly converted Estonians were the subjects of the archdiocese of Lund (and hence of the Danish king). The conflict eventually got to be so intense that the Danes were even accused of having executed a number of Estonians because they had not been converted by them but by German crusaders.[100]

Meanwhile Bishop Albert of Riga appointed a new (German) bishop of Estonia. The new bishop, Hermann, also happened to be Albert's brother. In the absence of the Scandinavian primate, the archbishop of Lund, the consecration took place in the presence of the German archbishop of Magdeburg. This challenge to Scandinavian supremacy enraged King Valdemar when the news reached Denmark. Valdemar decided to show his strength:

---

[99] Henry of Livonia, *The Chronicle of Henry of Livonia*, ed. and trans. J. A. Brundage. Madison: University of Wisconsin Press, 1961. pp. 173–74.
[100] Ibid., pp. 186–87.

Archbishop Albert was dependent upon the arrival of a steady stream of crusading knights in order to maintain control of the country, and most of these left for Riga from the city of Lübeck, arriving via the island of Gotland. In the absence of a strong German emperor, Lübeck had acknowledged Valdemar as its lord early on in his reign, and Valdemar now used his position to blockade the harbour of Lübeck and thus stifle Albert's lifeline. Valdemar's was a high-risk strategy, though, and could not last for long. By his actions he alienated a large number of devout and influential crusaders who had left their homes to achieve the Christianisation of Lithuania, and who were not impressed by being treated as pawns in local power struggles.[101] On 29 October 1219 Pope Honorius III wrote to Valdemar from Viterbo commanding him to end the blockade.[102] Valdemar paid no heed, and on 19 April 1220 Honorius sharpened his tone and once again demanded that Valdemar lift the blockade. Valdemar, he advised, needed to abandon his vainglorious attempt to increase his worldly power and consider his salvation. By his actions, Honorius concluded, Valdemar was impeding the work to save the souls of the newly converted in Livonia.[103] However, by this time Valdemar had already reached an understanding with Albert, and in return for his acknowledgement of Danish supremacy over the newly converted areas, he had raised the blockade. Further negotiations over the control of the area took place in 1222, after Valdemar led a new raid on Øsel to rid the Baltic of the threat of Estonian pirates. To maintain control of the island the Danes built another, stone, castle. During its construction Bishop Albert and the Grand Master of the Knights of the Sword visited the building works. They seem to have engaged in negotiations with the Danes at this time, and an uneasy truce was made concerning the supremacy of the area.

However, the next year saw the end of Danish imperial designs there. During a hunt on the island of Lyø, Valdemar was captured by a small and otherwise insignificant German count called Henry of Schwerin, who held him for ransom for four years.[104]

---

[101] Christensen, Tiden 1042–1241. In *Danmarks historie*, Vol. I, see note 8 above, pp. 376–77.

[102] Skyum-Nielsen, *Diplomatarium danicum*, pp. 211–12.

[103] Ibid., pp. 222–24.

[104] G. Jacobsen, Wicked Count Henry: the capture of Valdemar II (1223) and Danish influence in the Baltic. *Journal of Baltic Studies*, Vol. 9 No. 4, 1978, pp. 326–38.

The Estonians took this as the signal for revolt, and around the end of 1223 the inhabitants of Øsel rebelled against the Danes. This revolt quickly spread to the mainland and a massacre of the new rulers was only averted by concerted military actions by the Danes, Livonians, Lithuanians and the German crusaders. Five years later Estonia accepted the supremacy of Pope Honorius III, who honoured the country with the appointment of a special envoy, William of Modena, whose remit was to sort out under whose supremacy the country belonged.[105]

Conclusion

By the time of Valdemar II's capture on Lyø in 1223 Scandinavia had been fully integrated into the world of medieval Christendom. The Scandinavian church had found its final administrative form, and the bishops, headed by the archbishops of Lund, had a profound influence on events in the region. Five rebel bishops may have died participating in the Battle of Fotevig, but by the early thirteenth century the Scandinavian church had gained in stature internationally and was able to take on a role as a significant regional leader. The spiritual authority of the imposing figures of the archbishops of Lund – Asser, Eskil, Absalon and Anders Sunesøn – all in their own way secured the autonomy of the Church unquestioned and unassailable. Their styles and concerns were very different. Asser secured the independence of the Scandinavian church from Hamburg-Bremen; Eskil brought in talent and knowledge from European centres of learning and nurtured the talents of later great ecclesiastics such as Absalon and Anders Sunesøn. In his advocacy of the Gregorian reform Eskil, like Pope Leo IX, rose above the questions that could be asked about his election, and he provided a crucial continuity in office and impressive international contacts with the centres of ecclesiastical power in the early years of the Scandinavian church. In his later years he provided equally crucial stability for the royal line of the Valdemars by presiding over the simultaneous

---

[105] N. Skyum-Nielsen, Estonia under Danish rule. In *Danish Medieval History: New Currents. A Symposium held in celebration of the 500th anniversary of the University of Copenhagen*, ed. N. Skyum-Nielsen and N. Lund. Copenhagen: Museum Tusculanum Press, 1981. pp. 112–35.

canonisation of Duke Canute Lavard and the coronation of the
six-year-old King Canute VI. The Danish kingdom – and by
extension all of Scandinavia – was fortunate in the personal
chemistry between Eskil's sucessor, Archbishop Absalon, and
King Valdemar I. The spiritual gains of Eskil and the military
gains of Valdemar were consolidated in the elevation of Absalon
to the archbishopric of Lund, where he and his sucessor, Anders
Sunesøn, were granted both the authority of a papal legate and
the primacy of the Scandinavian church. The latter had once
again become an important part of European politics, and
together the kingdom and the Church were able to withstand
the Holy Roman Emperor, influence events in continental Europe
and attract such scholars as St William of Æbelholt, a former
master of one of the major schools in Paris, to the area. The
Viking Empire of the Norwegians maintained much of its western
focus but was soon to run out of steam. The Viking Empire of
Canute the Great, which also faced towards the west, had been
transformed into the Danish Baltic Empire, with a focus towards
the east. The capture of Valdemar II during his hunting expedition on Lyø introduced a new theme that was to become a
constant in the power politics of the region: the Scandinavian
kingdoms were strong, but they faced almost unanimous opposition, whose single goal was to prevent one country from dominating the waters of the Baltic. The kings and magnates who had
ruled the Baltic, the North Sea and the Atlantic Ocean had been
integrated into the the larger European enterprise of converting
the heathen. In doing so their horizons had narrowed to such an
extent that their conquests and influence were forgotten for
centuries, only to be resurrected when nationalism and romanti-
cism made Europe search for its roots once again.

CHAPTER 14

Conclusions

A constant theme in this book has been the integration and involvement of Scandinavia in a wider northern and ultimately European context. We have encouraged the reader to travel along a different path from that traditionally taken by studies of 'the Vikings'. We began our journey when the Roman Empire was at its height and some parts of Scandinavia broke away from its involvement in the Celtic world. The failure of Roman expansion north of the Rhine opened up new possibilities for the emerging dynasties of Scandinavia.

From the earliest times the Scandinavians were a part of the larger European community. They reacted and interacted not only with their immediate neighbours but even participated in the distant wars of the Roman Empire. The emerging aristocracies of Scandinavia imported military hardware and ordinary merchandise from the Romans and their successors, and through the period traditionally called the Viking Age they continued their involvement in the development of an emerging Europe. From the second century AD they were active from northern Europe to the Black Sea and continued that involvement until the cut-off date for this study: around the time of the Fifth Crusade (1228). Their religion and their ideologies may have changed, as did their horizons, but a constant theme has been their involvement far beyond the confines of the Scandinavian homelands in the spheres of war, trade and politics. Scandinavian involvement in Europe was multi-faceted: it included outright military conquest, political interference and settlement. In some cases they drove out the indigenous population, in others they settled in previously unpopulated regions. Traditionally, raiding and settlement have been described as discrete events separated by a considerable time span. But often – as in the case of Francia and the Western Isles of Scotland – settlement followed soon after initial military contact. A crucial aspect of this development was the adaptability of the Scandinavian settlers, who accepted the mores and often the religion of the areas in which they settled. Theirs was indeed one of the first multi-cultural societies in Europe, and the relative ease of their integration provided an important strand of tolerance in the European psyche.

The easy integration of the Scandinavians into mainstream European society is perhaps a concept that many brought up on a traditional narrative of blood-soaked Viking barbarism in violent collision with that same European mainstream may find difficult to accept. Certainly, it would be a revisionist step too far to attempt to dismiss the historical record of the impact of the late eighth- and ninth-century raids on Britain, Ireland and the Frankish Empire as fantastical or overblown. There can be no questioning the negative impact of the raids and invasions of the First Viking Age, which saw the destruction of the old political order amongst Anglo-Saxons and Picts, the radical redrawing of the political landscape of Ireland and the collapse of the established dynastic power structure of the western portion of the Carolingian state. The elimination of native dynasties in Pictland, Northumbria and East Anglia, the overthrow of the native ruling elites of Mercia and Brittany, and the systematic targeting of the spiritual centres that symbolised the Christian cultures of these societies from Iona in the far north-west to Fiesole in the south cannot be written off as monastic propaganda and hyperbole. First contact was bloodily traumatic for those visited by the raids, and the spectacular successes of the attackers convinced many who were looking for the approach of the Apocalypse that resistance was futile. In the Vikings, Christians saw the hordes of Gog and Magog descending from the ends of the earth, burning and slaughtering their way to the final conflict at Armageddon.

But Armageddon did not come. While the Christian west reeled before the onslaught, the raiders were already settling down to capitalise on the business opportunities offered in the territories through which they had rampaged. Within a generation the Danes, who had all but destroyed the Christian kingdoms and culture of Anglo-Saxon England and built their own kingdoms and colonies on the ruins, had embraced the religion of their erstwhile victims and were forging new alliances with the Church. The power of Anglo-Danish York was built on an alliance of commercial, religious and political interests which united against the common threat of spreading West Saxon power in the late ninth and tenth centuries. Dublin and its rival colonies in Ireland grew fat on the plunder from raids and the profits from slave-taking, but more important for these port communities was the two-way flow of merchandise in more conventional commodities which quickly developed through these new conduits into the wider world beyond Britain and Ireland. New bonds of mutual interest between colonists and conquered served to speed the integration of the two into a dynamic new hybrid. And similar patterns can be seen elsewhere in the zones of Scandinavian colonisation, from Normandy, where the settlers re-invented themselves as patrons and protectors of the Church, to the Hebrides, where the descendants of the men who had plundered Iona and slaughtered its monks came to end their days in religious seclusion.

Even where the Vikings retained their paganism until the close of the tenth century they had ceased to be treated as pariahs by their Christian neighbours. From Orkney to Dublin, intermarriage and integration into the wider framework of power in the Christian West was underway a century before the final conversion of the ruling elites of the Scandinavian western colonies. Irish and Scottish kings could either compete against or collaborate with the Viking interlopers, and most chose the latter option, which gave them access to the mercantile wealth and military muscle of the predator-cum-parasite communities planted in their midst. Vikings, who had once preyed indiscriminately upon the peoples they encountered, became powerbrokers in the internecine conflicts of the Christian powers in the British Isles. But entry into and involvement in the political alliances of the host society changed the relationship forever. The outsider, whatever label was applied to distinguish him from the native – Gentile, Foreigner, Gall-Gaedhil, Ostman, Dane – had become part of the established order of things, and no amount of labelling could disguise the fact that with this acceptance of political realities came a whole raft of other changes that had commenced as soon as the raider settled down to become a colonist. The distinction afforded by these labels was a porous shell through which flowed a two-way cultural traffic. Intermarriage brought linguistic exchange, and contact at all levels and of all forms – including violent encounters – brought technological and artistic influences. Christianity was simply one of the most visible means through which encounter was turned into assimilation.

The adoption of Christianity in Scandinavia marks a turning point in the history of the Viking Empires. The Danes, quickly followed by the Norwegians, accepted the new religion with relatively little friction. The archaeological evidence of the Jelling stones erected by the Danish king, Harald Bluetooth, and the many jewellery moulds in which the emblem of the god Thor is flanked by the cross of the Christian redeemer emphasise the Scandinavians' wish for a smooth transition from paganism to Christianity. In their emphasis on Harald's sovereignty over Norway, the Jelling stones introduce a crucial new theme in the history of Scandinavia. There is a seamless fit between the spiritual values of the Christian religion and the political struggles for sovereignty between the Scandinavians themselves, and between the Holy Roman Emperors and the Scandinavian kings. Svein Forkbeard, the second Christian king of Denmark, signalled his independence of the German archdiocese of Hamburg-Bremen through his refusal to dedicate new churches in Denmark to the patron saint of the minster of the archdiocese, the Blessed Virgin Mary, and it was not until well into the reign of his son, Canute the Great, that the matter resolved itself in 1027, when Canute came to an agreement with Emperor Conrad II during an Easter pilgrimage to Rome.

The success of the Viking Empires was short-lived. This was not only because England found itself taken over in 1066 by a new strongman – himself laying claim to the English throne partly by virtue of his Scandinavian ancestry – but also because the death of the Norwegian king, Harald Harðráði, at Stamford Bridge the same year, opened the path to a show-down in England between Harold Godwinson and William the Bastard of Normandy. Moreover, Harald Harðráði's death afforded the opportunity for the sons of the Danish king, Svein Estridsøn – himself the child of the Englishman Ulf (who had been assassinated at Roskilde on the order of King Canute the Great some time before 1027) – to attempt the Scandinavian reconquest of England in 1069–70. Svein Estridsøn's death in 1074 and the short-lived reigns of his two sons, Harald III Hen and St Canute (IV), marked the end of Danish interest in the reconquest of England. This did not mean that the Danes lost their interest in military exploits, but Canute's disastrous, aborted attempt at an English reconquest, when he faced the rebellion of the Danish fleet in 1085, resulted in the re-orientation of Denmark towards conquest in the east as part of the larger European crusading movement of the eleventh and twelfth centuries.

While Denmark's focus may have shifted eastwards in the later eleventh century, we have seen that Norway's interests – when not turned inwards through its protracted periods of civil warfare – remained rooted firmly in the west. Here, however, the Norwegians faced competition from other upstart and ambitious powers, most notably the Scots, who saw themselves increasingly as the rightful lords of all of northern mainland Britain and its satellite islands. Powerful Norwegian kings, such as Magnus Barelegs, had stopped the Scottish advance in its tracks in the late 1090s and re-asserted Norwegian lordship over the old Norse colonies in Orkney and Caithness, and in the hybridised society of the kingdom of Man and the Isles. Magnus stood on the brink of re-imposing a Norse hegemony over the British Isles when he died in a pointless skirmish with one of his nominal allies in Ireland, and the empire that he had built was revealed as a brittle phantasm held together only by his force of will. It was a personal empire, and without his guiding hand it collapsed.

Evanescent though Magnus Barelegs' empire had been, it had stopped the spread of Scottish power for a generation. By the time the Scots resumed the military offensive in the 1130s under David I (1124–53) the progressive integration of the Norse regions of the north and west into the orbit of power of the Scottish kings had already advanced to the limits of the mainland. Marriage ties, far more than military pressure, were used to draw the rulers of Orkney and the Isles into the Scottish nexus. But intermarriage can also be seen to have created a new crisis for the rulers of the old Norse colonies and their people, for whereas once it had established them as a bridge between the two cultures, brokers who held the balance of power in the complex interplay of politics and trade in the maritime west, now it was a source of division and weakness. Through the twelfth century, although the kings of Man and the petty princes of the

Norse-Gaelic world bid fair to play off their nominal Scottish or Norwegian overlords against each other, it became increasingly clear that the future lay in one direction or the other, not in both. It was a new reality driven by seismic shifts in the wider political, commercial and cultural patterns of Britain and Ireland, as Scotland became increasingly drawn into a Frankish and mainland European orientation, and the formerly Scandinavian colonies in Ireland became rooted first in Gaelic Irish society and then fixed their focus decisively on England. The trade that had been the lifeblood of the western sea-lanes was turned into new channels, reducing the power of the north–south pull of Norway and the North Atlantic colonies.

But even declining empires can still strike back, and Norway was not prepared to relinquish its hold without a struggle. Traditional Scottish historiography has tended to focus on the long struggle for survival against England, but this perspective neglects the far longer struggle with Norway for the mastery of northern Britain. It was a struggle largely fought out in the personal feuds and marriage beds of the rulers of Orkney and the Isles, as rivals for power in these petty kingdoms courted the support of Scotland and Norway to advance their ambitions. All the while, what had once been largely nominal overlordship was being redefined and tightened, as the price of such support steadily grew. Kings as ruthless as Alexander II (1214–49) were not prepared to tolerate any ambivalence in the relationship between the Scottish crown and the lords of the Norse-Gaelic west. In his hands the Scottish kingdom bid fair to swallow up the last vestiges of the Scandinavian colonies around its northern and western peripheries. Yet even at this late date Norway still looked to extend its power, and kinglets and warlords, fearful of a future that was entirely Scottish, saw an appeal to Norway under its aggressive ruler, Hákon IV, as a means of staving off the inevitable. In the twelfth and earlier thirteenth centuries this had worked, Norwegian kings giving their blessing to individual rulers and sending naval forces to re-inforce their nominee's authority, but never travelling west in person to give substance to their own claims. In Hákon the Islesmen found an empire-builder as ruthless and ambitious as Alexander II, determined to convert nominal lordship into something more real. The ambitions of Alexander and Hákon collided in 1230–31, but the resulting war was brief and inconclusive, and the long-anticipated final onslaught launched against the Isles by Alexander in 1249 fizzled out with the king's unexpected death from illness.

Hákon's power grew steadily through the 1250s, until in the early 1260s he had brought the once independent colonies in the Faroes, Iceland and Greenland under his authority. Shetland and Orkney, too, recognised his lordship. After the death of Alexander II there had not been much threat from Scotland, but the coming-of-age of his equally ambitious son, Alexander III (1249–86), revealed that the decade's respite had been but the calm before the storm. Alexander III was determined to end once and for all the ambiguity in the relationship of the Hebrideans with the Scottish crown: there could be no more dual allegiances. Pressure on the Isles by Alexander's vassals produced the familiar response of an appeal for aid from Norway, but on this occasion the Islesmen had misjudged their man. Expecting to receive the traditional nomination of one of their number as the chosen deputy of the Norwegian king and the dispatch of a force of galleys to provide backbone for their defence, they found instead Hákon sailing west at the head of a fleet. Faced now with a choice between Scotland and Norway, most found that the Norwegians were an alien culture with which they had little in common. Their main political, familial, commercial, cultural and religious bonds were with the Scots: integration into one culture had resulted in alienation from the other. Hákon's military successes could not conceal the fact that his active intervention was resented bitterly by those who had called for his aid. Nor could his conquests be made secure without either an overwhelming victory over Alexander or the wholehearted support of the Islesmen. He gained neither, and he can have been under no illusion as to the hollowness of his achievement as he withdrew northwards to the comfortably Scandinavian shelter of Orkney. His death in December 1263 brought down the final curtain on this last act in the Norwegian imperial age. Long before his successor negotiated the formal cession of the Western Isles in 1266, the people of the islands had seen the future, and it was Scottish.

As for the Scandinavians, they had also seen the future, and for them it was to be at the heart of Europe and to participate fully in the new Europe of the Middle Ages. The change was palpable and was well under way at the time when Adam of Bremen wrote his history of the bishops of Hamburg:

Behold the cruel Danish, Norwegian, and Swedish races who in the word of the holy Gregory 'did not know except how to grind their teeth like barbarians, but who can now already intone a Halleluja to the praise of God'. Behold that race of pirates who used to raid the coasts of Gaul and Germany, like we have read, but who are now satisfied with their own lands and who say with the Apostle 'Here we cannot have a permanant city, but we seek the one to come.' Their ferocity has gone, the prophets of the truth are gaining everywhere, churches are raised everywhere and the name of Christ is praised by everyone in unison.

Bibliography

Adamus Bremensis, *History of the Archbishops of Hamburg-Bremen*, trans. F. J. Tschan. Records of Civilization: Sources and Studies. New York: Columbia University Press, 1959.

Monumenta Germaniae historica. Vol. XVII, *Hamburgische Kirchengeschichte*, 3rd ed., ed. B. Schmeidler. Scriptores rerum germanicarum in usum scholarum separatim editi. Hanover: Hahn, 1977 [1917].

Adomnán of Iona, *Life of St. Columba*, trans. R. Sharpe. Penguin Classics. London: Penguin, 1995.

Adomnán's *Life of Columba*, ed. and trans. M. O. Anderson. Oxford Medieval Texts. Oxford: Clarendon Press, 1991.

Aelnoth, *Gesta Swenonimagni regis et filiorum eius et passio gloriosissimi Canuti regis et martyris*, ed. M. C. Geertz. In *Vitae sanctorum danorum: novam editionem criticam*. København: Selskabet for Udgivelse af Kilder til dansk Historie, 1908–12.

Aggesen, Sven. *The Works of Sven Aggesen, Twelfth-Century Danish Historian*, trans. E. Christiansen. London: Viking Society for Northern Research, 1992.

Aggesøn, S. *Sven Aggesøns historiske skrifter oversatte efter den på grundlag af Codex Arnæmagnæanus 33, 4to restaurerede nye text*, ed. M. C. Gertz. Selskabet for historiske kilders oversættelse. København: Schønberg, 1917.

Scriptores minores historiæ danicæ medii ævi. Vol. I, *Suenonis Aggonis filii opuscula historica: I. Lex Castrensis; II. Brevis historia regum Dacie; III. Series et geneaologia regum danorum*. København: Selskabet for Udgivelse af Kilder til Dansk Historie, n.d. pp. 55–156.

Ahronson, K. Testing the evidence for Northern North Atlantic Papar: a cave site in southern Iceland. In *The Papar in the North Atlantic Environment and History. Proceedings of a day conference, 24 Februrary 2001*. ed. B. E. Crawford. Vol. I, The Papar Project. St Andrews: University of St Andrews, 2002, pp. 107–20.

One North Atlantic cave settlement: preliminary archaeological, environmental investigations at Seljaland, southern Iceland. *Northern Studies*, Vol. 37, 2003, pp. 53–70.

Alcuin, *Willibrord, Apostel der Friesen: Seine Vita nach Alkuin und Thiofrid: Lateinisch-Deutsch*, trans. and ed. H.-J. Reischmann. Sigmaringendorf: Glock und Lutz, 1989.

Alexander, D., Neighbour, T. and Oram, R. Glorious victory? The Battle of Largs, 2 October 1263. *History Scotland*, Vol. 2, No. 2, 2002, pp. 17–22.

Allen, A. The boat. In *Scar: A Viking Boat Burial on Sanday, Orkney*, ed. O. Owen, A. Allen and M. Dalland. East Linton: Historic Scotland in association with Tuckwell Press, 1999. pp. 39–51.

Andersen, E. Square sails of wool. In *Shipshape: Essays for Ole Crumlin-Pedersen*, ed. O. Olsen, J. Skamby Madsen and F. Rieck. Roskilde: The Viking Ship Museum, 1995. pp. 249–70.

Andersen, H. Martyr? *Skalk*, 2004, 1, pp. 18–19.

Andersen, H. C. H. New investigations in Ejsbøl bog. In *The Spoils of Victory: The North in the Shadow of the Roman Empire*, ed. L. Jørgensen, B. Storgaard and L. G. Thomsen. København: Nationalmuseet, 2003. pp. 246–57.

Andersen, H. H. Et bolværk af træ. *Skalk*, 1973, 6, pp. 3–11.

Anderson, A. O., ed. *Early Sources of Scottish History, A.D. 500 to 1286*. Vol. I. Edinburgh and London: Oliver and Boyd, 1922.

Anderson, P. *Passages from Antiquity to Feudalism*. London: Verso Editions, 1978.

The Anglo-Saxon Chronicles, ed. and trans. M. J. Swanton. London: Phoenix, 2000.

Annales Cambriae, ed. J. Williams. London: Longman, Green, Longman, and Roberts, 1860.

The Annals of Clonmacnoise, ed. D. Murphy. Dublin, 1896.

The Annals of Fulda, ed. T. Reuter. Ninth-Century Histories, 2. Manchester: Manchester University Press.

Annals of Furness. In *Chronicles of the Reigns of Stephen, Henry II, and Richard I. Vol. II, The Fifth Book of the 'Historia Rerum Anglicarum' of William of Newburgh. A Continuation of William of Newburgh's History to A.D. 1298. The 'Draco Normannicus' of Etienne de Rouen*, ed. Richard Howlett. London: Longman, 1884.

The Annals of Inisfallen (MS Rawlinson B.503), ed. and trans. S. Mac Airt. Dublin: Dublin Institute for Advanced Studies, 1951.

The Annals of Loch Cé: A Chronicle of Irish Affairs from A.D. 1014 to A.D. 1590, ed. and trans. W. M. Hennessy. Rerum britannicarum medii ævi scriptores, 54. London: Stationery Office, 1871.

The Annals of St. Bertin, ed and annotated Janet L. Nelson. Ninth-Century Histories, 1. Manchester: Manchester University Press, 1991.

The Annals of Tigernach, Being Annals of Ireland, 807 B.C. to A.D. 1178, ed. W. Stokes. *Revue Celtique*, pp. 16, 17, 18, 342. Paris: Librairie Emile Bouillon (Off-prints), 1895–97.

The Annals of Ulster (to A.D. 1131), ed. and trans. S. Mac Airt and G. Mac Niocaill. Dublin: Dublin Institute for Advanced Studies, 1983.

Arctic Pilot, 4th ed. (1933–46), Vol. II. London: H.M.S.O.

Arup, E. *Danmarks historie*. Vol. I, *Land og folk til 1282*. København: H. Hogerup, 1925.

Augustus (AD 14) Res gestae divi Augusti. Ankara (Online) (http://www.csun.edu/~hcfll004/resgest.html).

Bailey, R. N. Aspects of Viking-Age sculpture in Cumbria. In *Scandinavians in Cumbria*, ed. J. Baldwin and I. Whyte. Collins Archaeology. Edinburgh: Scottish Society for Northern Studies, 1980. pp. 53–63.

Barlow, F. *William Rufus*. London: Methuen, 1983.

Edward the Confessor. Kings and Queens of Medieval England. Stroud: Tempus, 2000.

Barlow, L., Sadler, J. *et al.* Interdisciplinary investigations of the end of the Norse Western Settlement in Greenland. *The Holocene*, Vol. 7 No. 4, 1997, pp. 489–99.

Barrow, G. W. S., ed. *Regesta regum scottorum, 1153–1424*. Vol. I, *The Acts of Malcolm IV*. Edinburgh: Edinburgh University Press, 1960.

Kingship and Unity: Scotland, 1000–1306. Edinburgh: Edinburgh University Press, 1989.

The army of Alexander III's Scotland. In *Scotland in the Reign of Alexander III*, ed. N. Reid. Edinburgh: John Donald, 1990. pp. 132–47.

Bartlett, R. *The Making of Europe: Conquest, Colonization, and Cultural Change, 950–1350*. London: Penguin, 1994.

England under the Norman and Angevin Kings, 1075–1225. The New Oxford History of England. Oxford: Clarendon Press, Oxford University Press, 2000.

Bates, D. C. *William the Conqueror*. Kings and Queens of Medieval England. Stroud: Tempus, 2000.

Benediktson, J. *Hafgerðingadrápa*. In *Speculum Norroenum: Norse Studies in Memory of Gabriel Turville-Petre*, ed. U. Dronke, G. Helgadóttir, G. Weber and H. Becker-Nielsen. Odense: Odense University Press, 1981. pp. 27–32.

Bernard, J. Trade and finance in the Middle Ages, 900–1500. In *The Fontana Economic History of Europe*. Vol. I, *The Middle Ages*, ed. C. M. Cipolla. London: Collins/Fontana Books, 1972. pp. 274–338.

Bill, J. Iron nails in Iron Age and medieval shipbuilding. In *Crossroads in Ancient Shipbuilding. Proceedings of the Sixth International Symposium on Boat and Ship Archaeology, Roskilde, 1991*, ed. C. Westerdahl. Vol. XL. Oxbow Monograph. Oxford: Oxbow Books, 1994. pp. 55–63.

Ship construction: tools and techniques. In *Cogs, Caravels, and Galleons: The Sailing Ship, 1000–1650*, ed. R. Gardiner and R. W. Unger. Conway's History of the Ship. London: Conway Maritime Press, 1994. pp. 151–59.

Ships and seamanship. In *The Oxford Illustrated History of the Vikings*, ed. P. H. Sawyer. Oxford: Oxford University Press, 1997. pp. 182–201.

Binns, A. Ships and shipbuilding. In *Medieval Scandinavia: An Encyclopedia*, ed. P. Pulsiano and K. Wolf. Garland Encyclopedias of the Middle Ages, 1. New York: Garland, 1993. pp. 578–80.

Birch, W. d. G., ed. *Cartularium Saxonicum: A Collection of Charters Relating to Anglo-Saxon History.* Vol. I, A.D. 430–839. London: Whiting & Company, 1885.

Blom, G. A. Gilde (Norge). In *Kulturhistorisk leksikon for nordisk middelalder,* ed. O. Olsen, P. Skautrup, N. Skyum-Nielsen and A. Steensberg. København: Rosenkilde og Bagger, 1959–77.

Stad (Norge). In *Kulturhistorisk leksikon for nordisk middelalder,* ed. O. Olsen, P. Skautrup, N. Skyum-Nielsen and A. Steensberg. København: Rosenkilde og Bagger, 1959–77.

Stadsprivilegier (Norge). In *Kulturhistorisk leksikon for nordisk middelalder,* ed. O. Olsen, P. Skautrup, N. Skyum-Nielsen and A. Steensberg. København: Rosenkilde og Bagger, 1959–77.

Blomqvist, R. Stadsbebyggelse och stadsplan (Sverige och Skåne). In *Kulturhistorisk leksikon for nordisk middelalder,* ed. O. Olsen, P. Skautrup, N. Skyum-Nielsen and A. Steensberg. København: Rosenkilde og Bagger, 1959–77.

Bøe, A. Korståg: vestnordiske korståg. In *Kulturhistorisk leksikon for nordisk middelalder,* ed. O. Olsen, P. Skautrup, N. Skyum-Nielsen and A. Steensberg. København: Rosenkilde og Bagger, 1959–77.

The Book of the Icelanders by Ari Thorgilsson: Edited and Translated with an Introductory Essay and Notes by Halldor Hermannsson, ed. and trans. H. Hermannsson. Ithaca: Cornell University Library, 1930.

Bower, W. *Scotichronicon in Latin and English,* ed. D. E. R. Watt. Vol. V. Aberdeen: Aberdeen University Press, 1987.

Bradley, S. A. J. *Anglo-Saxon Poetry.* London: Dent, 1982 (http://www.wwnorton.com/nael/middleages/topic4/widsith.htm).

Brøgger, A. W. and Shetelig, H. *The Viking Ships: Their Ancestry and Evolution.* Oslo: Dreyer, 1971.

Brooke, D. *Wild Men and Holy Places: St. Ninian, Whithorn and the Medieval Realm of Galloway.* Edinburgh: Canongate Press, 1994.

Bruce-Mitford, R. L. S. *The Sutton Hoo Ship-Burial.* London: Published for the Trustees of the British Museum by British Museum Publications, 1975.

Byock, J. L. *Medieval Iceland. Society, Sagas, and Power.* Berkeley: University of California Press, 1988.

Viking Age Iceland. London: Penguin, 2001.

Byrne, F. J. *Irish Kings and High-Kings.* London: Batsford, 1973.

Campbell, E. A cross-marked quern from Dunadd and other evidence for relations between Dunadd and Iona. In *Proceedings of the Society of Antiquaries of Scotland.* Vol. 117. Edinburgh: Society of Antiquaries, 1987. pp. 105–17.

Campbell, J. *The Anglo-Saxon State.* London: Hambledon and London, 2000.

Carnap-Bornstein, C. v. The ornamental belts from Ejsbøl bog and Neudorf-Bornstein. In *The Spoils of Victory: The North in the Shadow of the Roman Empire,* ed. L. Jørgensen, B. Storgaard and L. G. Thomsen. København: Nationalmuseet, 2003. pp. 240–45.

Carolingian Chronicles: Royal Frankish Annals and Nithard's Histories, ed. and trans. B. W. Scholz and B. Rogers. Ann Arbor: University of Michigan Press, 1970.

Carver, M. On – and – off the Edda. In *Shipshape: Essays for Ole Crumlin-Pedersen*, ed. O. Olsen, J. Skamby Madsen and F. Rieck. Roskilde: The Viking Ship Museum, 1995. pp. 303–12.

Cavill, P. *Vikings: Fear and Faith in Anglo-Saxon England*. London: HarperCollins, 2001.

Christensen, A. E. Mellem vikingetid og Valdemarstid: et forsøg på en syntese. (Danish) *Historisk Tidsskrift*, Vol. 12 No. 2, 1966. pp. 31–56. (English translation in A. E. Christensen, from the Viking Age to the age of the Valdemars. An attempt at a synthesis. *Medieval Scandinavia*, Vol. 1, 1969, pp. 28–50.)

Kongemagt og aristokrati: epoker i middelalderlig dansk statsopfattelse indtil unionstiden. Københavns Universitets Fond til Tilvejebringelse af Læremidler. København: Ejnar Munksgaards Forlag, 1968.

Vikingetidens Denmark paa oldhistorisk baggrund. København: Københavns Universitets Fond til Tilvejebringelse af Læremidler i kommission hos Gyldendals forlag, 1969.

Tiden 1042–1241. In *Danmarks historie*. Vol. I, *Tiden indtil 1340*, exec. ed. A. E. Christensen, H. P. Clausen, Svend Ellehøj and Søren Mørch. København: Gyldendal, 1980. pp. 211–399.

Ship graffiti and models. In *Medieval Dublin Excavations, 1962–81*. Vol. II, *Miscellanea 1*, ed. P. F. Wallace. Series B. Dublin: Royal Irish Academy, 1988. pp. 13–26.

Ship graffiti. In *The Ship as Symbol in Prehistoric and Medieval Scandinavia. Papers from an international research seminar at the Danish National Museum, Copenhagen, 5–7 May 1994*, ed. O. Crumlin-Pedersen, and B. Munch Thye. Vol. I. Publications from the National Museum. København: Nationalmuseet, 1995. pp. 181–85.

Proto-Viking, Viking and Norse craft. In *The Earliest Ships: The Evolution of Boats into Ships*, ed. R. Gardiner and A. E. Christensen. Conway's History of the Ship. London: Conway Maritime Press, 1996. pp. 78–88.

Christensen, C. and Nielsen, H., eds. *Diplomatarium danicum, 1. Række*, Vol. I, *Diplomatarium danicum: Regester 789–1052*. Det danske sprog- og litteraturselskab. København: C. A. Reitzels Forlag, 1975.

Christensen, T. Sagntidens Kongsgård. *Skalk*, 5, 1996, pp. 5–10.

Christopherson, A. Ports and trade in Norway during the transition to historical time. In *Aspects of Maritime Scandinavia AD 200–1200. Proceedings of the Nordic seminar on maritime aspects of archaeology, Roskilde, 13–15 March 1989*, ed. O. Crumlin-Pedersen. Roskilde: Vikingeskibshallen, 1991. pp. 159–70.

Chronica Magistri Rogeri de Houedene, ed. W. Stubbs. Vol. IV. Rerum britannicarum medii aevi scriptores, 51. London: Longmans, Green, Reader, and Dyer, 1868.

Chronica regum Manniae et Insularum: The Chronicle of Man and the Isles: A Facsimile of the Manuscript Codex Julius A. VII in the British Museum, ed. P. A. Munch. Douglas: Published at the Museum, 1924.

The Chronicle of Aethelweard, ed. A. Campbell, Medieval Texts. London: Nelson, 1962.

The Chronicle of Melrose, ed. A. O. Anderson, M. O. Anderson and W. C. Dickinson. London: P. Lund, Humphries & Co. Ltd, 1936.

Chronicles of the Scots, ed. W. M. Hennessy. *Chronicon Scotorum*. Rolls Series No. 46, p. 8.

Church, A. J. and Brodribb, W. J., trans. *The Annals*. London: W. Heinemann, 1925 (http://classics.mit.edu//Tacitus/annals.html).

Coghadh Gaedhel re Gallaibh: The War of the Gaedhil with the Gaill: Or the Invasions of Ireland by the Danes and Other Norsemen: The Original Irish Text, ed. and trans. J. H. Todd. Rerum britannicarum medii aevi scriptores, 48. Vaduz, Liechtenstein: Kraus Reprint, 1965 [1867].

Cohat, Y. *The Vikings: Lords of the Seas*. New York: Harry N. Abrams, 1992.

Coull, J. R. *The Sea Fisheries of Scotland: A Historical Geography*. Edinburgh: John Donald Publishers, 1996.

Cowan, E. Norwegian sunset – Scottish dawn: Hakon IV and Alexander III. In *Scotland in the Reign of Alexander III*, ed. N. Reid. Edinburgh, 1990. pp. 103–31.

Crawford, B. E. *Scandinavian Scotland. Scotland in the Early Middle Ages*. Leicester: Leicester University Press, 1987.

ed. *St. Magnus Cathedral and Orkney's Twelfth-Century Renaissance*. Aberdeen: Aberdeen University Press, 1988.

Norse earls and Scottish bishops in Caithness: a clash of cultures. In *The Viking Age in Caithness, Orkney and the North Atlantic. Select papers from the Proceedings of the Eleventh Viking Congress, Thurso and Kirkwall, 22 August–1 September 1989*, ed. C. E. Batey, J. Jesch and C. D. Morris. Edinburgh: Edinburgh University Press, 1993. pp. 129–47.

Scandinavian Settlement in Northern Britain: Thirteen Studies of Place-Names in Their Historical Context. Studies in the Early History of Britain. London, New York: Leicester University Press, 1995.

The dedication to St Clement and Rodil, Harris. In *Church, Chronicle and Learning in Medieval and Early Renaissance Scotland. Essays Presented to Donald Watt on the Occasion of the Completion of the Publication of Bower's Scotichronicon*, ed. B. E. Crawford. Edinburgh: Mercat Press, 1999. pp. 109–22.

Crouch, D. *The Normans: The History of a Dynasty*. London: Hambledon and London, 2002.

Crumlin-Pedersen, O. Two Danish side rudders. *Mariner's Mirror*, Vol. 52, 1966. pp. 251–61.

Ships, navigation and routes in the reports of Ohthere and Wulfstan. In *Two Voyagers at the Court of King Alfred: The Ventures of Ohthere and Wulfstan, Together with the Description of Northern Europe from the Old*

English Orosius, ed. N. Lund, trans. C. E. Fell. York: Sessions, 1984. pp. 30–42.

Cargo ships of northern Europe AD 800–1300. In *Conference on Waterfront Technology in Northern European Towns*, ed. A. Herteig. Bergen: Historisk Museum, 1985. pp. 83–93.

ed. *Aspects of Maritime Scandinavia AD 200–1200*. Roskilde: Viking Ship Museum, 1991.

Ship types and sizes AD 800–1400. In *Aspects of Maritime Scandinavia AD 200–1200. Proceedings of the Nordic seminar on maritime aspects of archaeology, Roskilde, 13–15 March 1989*, ed. O. Crumlin-Pedersen. Roskilde: Vikingeskibshallen, 1991. pp. 69–82.

Problems of reconstruction and the estimation of performance. In *The Earliest Ships: The Evolution of Boats into Ships*, ed. R. Gardiner and A. E. Christensen. Conway's History of the Ship. London: Conway Maritime Press, 1996. pp. 110–19.

Dendro-dating and analysis: dating and provenance of timber. In *Ships and Boats of the North*, ed. O. Crumlin-Pedersen and O. Olsen. Vol. IV.1, *The Skuldelev Ships 1, Topography, Archaeology, History, Conservation and Display*. Roskilde: Viking Ship Museum, 2002. pp. 64–68.

Description and analysis of the ships as found. In *Ships and Boats of the North*, ed. O. Crumlin-Pedersen and O. Olsen. Vol. IV.1, *The Skuldelev Ships 1, Topography, Archaeology, History, Conservation and Display*. Roskilde: Viking Ship Museum, 2002. pp. 101–19.

Crumlin-Pedersen, O. and Olsen, O., eds. *Ships and Boats of the North. Vol. IV.1, The Skuldelev Ships I, Topography, Archaeology, History, Conservation and Display*, by O. Crumlin-Pedersen, with contributions from E. Bondesen, P. Jensen, O. Olsen, A. Petersen and K. Strætkvern. Roskilde: Viking Ship Museum, 2002.

Wood technology. In *Ships and Boats of the North*, ed. O. Crumlin-Pedersen and O. Olsen. Vol. IV.1, *The Skuldelev Ships 1, Topography, Archaeology, History, Conservation and Display*. Roskilde: Viking Ship Museum, 2002. p. 57.

Cunliffe, B. *Facing the Ocean: The Atlantic and Its Peoples*. Oxford: Oxford University Press, 2001.

Davies, R. R. *Domination and Conquest: The Experience of Ireland, Scotland and Wales, 1100–1300*. Cambridge: Cambridge University Press, 1990.

Davies, W. *Wales in the Early Middle Ages*. Studies in the Early History of Britain. Leicester: Leicester University Press, 1982.

Davis, H. W. C. *Medieval Europe*. Home University Library of Modern Knowledge. London, New York: Oxford University Press, 1960.

Davis, R. H. C. *A History of Medieval Europe from Constantine to Saint Louis*. London, New York: Longmans, Green, 1957.

Dennison, E. Burghs and burgesses: a time of consolidation? In *Scotland in the Reign of Alexander II*, ed. R. Oram. Leiden: Brill, 2005.

Dollinger, P. *The German Hanse*. London: Macmillan, 1980.

Douglas, D. C. *William the Conqueror: The Norman Impact on England*. English Monarchs Series. London: Eyre & Spottiswode, 1966.

Dudo of St. Quentin, *History of the Normans*, ed. and trans. E. Christiansen. Woodbridge: Boydell Press, 1998.

Dudo of St. Quentin's Gesta Normannorum: An English Translation, ed. and trans. F. Lipschitz, 1998 (Online) (http://www.the-orb.net/orb_done/dudo/chapter02.html).

Duffy, S. Irishmen and Islesmen in the kingdoms of Dublin and Man, 1052–1171. Eriu, Vol. 43, 1992, pp. 93–133.

Ireland in the Middle Ages. British History in Perspective. New York: St. Martin's Press, 1997.

Dumville, D. The North Atlantic monastic thalassocracy: sailing to the desert in early medieval insular spirituality. In *The Papar in the North Atlantic Environment and History. The proceedings of a day conference held on 24 Februrary 2001*, ed. B. E. Crawford. Vol. V: 1, The Papar Project. St Andrews: University of St Andrews, 2002.

Duncan, A. A. M. *Scotland: The Making of the Kingdom*. Vol. I, Edinburgh History of Scotland. Edinburgh: Oliver and Boyd, 1975.

Roger of Howden and Scotland, 1187–1201. In *Church, Chronicle and Learning in Medieval and Early Renaissance Scotland. Essays Presented to Donald Watt on the Occasion of the Completion of the Publication of Bower's Scotichronicon*, ed. B. E. Crawford. Edinburgh: Mercat Press, 1999. pp. 135–60.

Duncan, A. A. M. and Brown, A. L. Argyll and the Isles in the earlier Middle Ages. *Proceedings of the Society of Antiquaries of Scotland*, Vol. 90, 1956–57. pp. 192–220.

Duncan, A. A. M. and Dunbar, J. Tarbert Castle: a contribution to the history of Argyll. *Scottish Historical Review*, Vol. 50 No. 1, 1971. pp. 1–17.

Egil's Saga. In *The Sagas of Icelanders*, ed. Ö. Thorsson, trans. B. Scudder. London: Penguin, 2001. pp. 8–184.

Eirik the Red's Saga. In *The Sagas of Icelanders*, ed. Ö. Thorsson, trans. K. Kunz. London: Penguin, 2001. pp. 653–76.

Eirspennill's Hakon Hakon's Son's Saga. In A. O. Anderson, ed. and trans. *Early Sources of Scottish History, A.D. 500 to 1286*. Vol. II. Edinburgh and London: Oliver and Boyd, 1922. pp. 473–78.

Eldjárn, K. The Viking Myth. In *The Vikings*, ed. R. T. Farrell. London: Phillimore, 1982. pp. 262–73.

Ellmers, D. Valhalla and the Gotland stones. In *The Ship as Symbol in Prehistoric and Medieval Scandinavia. Papers from an international research seminar at the Danish National Museum, Copenhagen, 5–7 May 1994*, ed. O. Crumlin-Pedersen and B. Munch Thye. Vol. I. Publications from the National Museum. København: Nationalmuseet, 1995. pp. 165–70.

Celtic plank boats and ships, 500 BC–AD 1000. In *The Earliest Ships: The Evolution of Boats into Ships*, ed. R. Gardiner and

A. E. Christensen. Conway's History of the Ship. London: Conway Maritime Press, 1996. pp. 52–71.

Encomium Emmae Reginae, ed. A. Campbell. Camden Third Series, 72. London: Offices of the Royal Historical Society, 1949.

Engelhardt, C. Om Vimosefundet. In Aarbøger for nordisk oldkyndighed og historie. København: Gyldendal, 1867. pp. 233–57.

Fynske Mosefund. Vol. II, Vimose-Fundet. København. 1869.

Erslev, K. Den senere middelalder. In Danmarks riges historie, ed. J. Steenstrup, K. Erslev, A. Heise, V. Mollerup, J. A. Fridericia, E. Holm and A. D. Jørgensen. København: Nordiske forlag, E. Bojesen, 1898–1905.

Eyrbyggja Saga: Brands Þáttr Orva. Eiríks Saga Rauða. Grænlendinga Saga. Grænlendinga Þáttr, ed. Einar Ólafur Sveinsson and Matthías Þórðarson. Íslenzk fornrit IV. Reykjavík: Hið íslenzka fornritafélag, 1935.

Falk, H. Altnordisches Seewesen. Wörter und Sachen, Vol. 5, 1912, pp. 1–122.

Fellows-Jensen, G. Viking settlements in the Northern and Western Isles – the place-name evidence as seen from Denmark and the Danelaw. In The Northern and Western Isles in the Viking World, ed. A. Fenton and H. Pálsson. Edinburgh: John Donald, 1984. pp. 148–68.

Scandinavians in southern Scotland? Nomina: A Journal of Name Studies Relating to Great Britain and Ireland, Vol. 13 (1989–90), 1991, pp. 41–60.

Fenger, O. Gyldendal og Politikens Danmarkshistorie. Vol. IV, 'Kirker rejses alle vegne' 1050–1250, exec. ed. O. Olsen. København: Gyldendal & Politiken, 2002 [1989].

Fenton, A. and Pálsson, H., eds. The Northern and Western Isles in the Viking World. Edinburgh: John Donald, 1984.

Fenton, P. The navigator as natural historian. Mariner's Mirror, Vol. 79, 1993, pp. 44–57.

Fenwick, V. and Morley, A., eds. British Archaeological Reports, Vol. LIII, The Graveney Boat: A Tenth Century Find: Excavation and Recording; Interpretation of the Boat Remains and the Environment; Reconstruction and Other Research, Conservation and Display. BAR British Series. Oxford, 1978.

Fletcher, R. Bloodfeud: Murder and Revenge in Anglo-Saxon England. London: Penguin, 2002.

Fløttum, S. The Norse vika sjovar and the nautical mile. Mariner's Mirror, Vol. 87, 2001, pp. 390–405.

Foote, P. G. Icelandic sólarsteinn and the medieval background. In Aurvandilstá: Norse Studies, ed. M. Barnes, H. Bekker-Nielsen and G. W. Weber. Odense: Odense University Press, 1984. pp. 140–54.

Wrecks and rhymes. In Aurvandilstá: Norse Studies, ed. M. Barnes, H. Bekker-Nielsen and G. W. Weber. Odense: University Press, 1984. pp. 222–35.

Foote, P. G. and Wilson, D. M. *The Viking Achievement: The Society and Culture of Early Medieval Scandinavia*. London: St. Martin's Press, 1990.

Foster, S. *Picts, Gaels and Scots: Early Historic Scotland*. London: B. T. Batsford Ltd/Historic Scotland, 1996.

Frake, C. Cognitive maps of time and tide among medieval seafarers. *Man*, (New Series) Vol. 20, 1985, pp. 254–70.

Frame, R. *The Political Development of the British Isles, 1100–1400*. Oxford: Oxford University Press, 1995.

Frandsen, L. B. and Jensen, S. Kongen bød. *Skalk*, 4, 1988, pp. 3–8.

Friel, I. *The Good Ship: Ships, Shipbuilding and Technology in England 1200–1520*. London: British Museum, 1995.

Fritz, B. Stad. In *Kulturhistorisk leksikon for nordisk middelalder*, ed. O. Olsen, P. Skautrup, N. Skyum-Nielsen and A. Steensberg. København: Rosenkilde og Bagger, 1959–77.

Frydendahl, K. The summer climate in the North Atlantic about the year 1000. In *Viking Voyages to North America*, ed. B. Clausen. Roskilde: Vikingeskibshallen, 1993. pp. 90–94.

Gallén, J. Korståg. In *Kulturhistorisk leksikon for nordisk middelalder*, ed. O. Olsen, P. Skautrup, N. Skyum-Nielsen and A. Steensberg. København: Rosenkilde og Bagger, 1959–77.

Gelsinger, B. Lodestone and sunstone in medieval Iceland. *Mariner's Mirror*, Vol. 56, 1970, pp. 219–26.

Gesta francorum et aliorum Hierosolymitanorum: The Deeds of the Franks, ed. and trans. Rosalind M. Hill. London: Nelson, 1962.

Gísli Sigurðson. *Gaelic Influence in Iceland: Historical and Literary Contacts: A Survey of Research*. Studia Islandica 46. Reykjavík: Bókaútgáfa Menningarsjóð, 1988.

Godal, J. B. The use of wood in boatbuilding. In *Shipshape: Essays for Ole Crumlin-Pedersen*, ed. O. Olsen, J. Skamby Madsen and F. Rieck. Roskilde: Viking Ship Museum, 1995. pp. 271–82.

Golson, J. *Polynesian Navigation*. Wellington: Polynesian Society, 1963.

The Gothic History of Jordanes in English Version, trans. C. C. Mierow. Cambridge and New York: Barnes & Noble, 1960.

Graham-Campbell, J. *The Viking World*. New Haven: Ticknor & Fields, 1989 [1980].

Graham-Campbell, J. and Batey, C. E. *Vikings in Scotland: An Archaeological Survey*. Edinburgh: Edinburgh University Press, 1998.

Gregory of Tours, *Libri Historiarum X*, ed. B. Krusch. Monumenta Germaniae historica: scriptores rerum Merovingicarum. Hanover: Hahn, 1965.

   The History of the Franks, ed. and trans. L. Thorpe. Penguin Classics. London: Penguin, 1974.

Grettir's Saga, ed. and trans. Denton Fox and Hermann Pálsson. Toronto: University of Toronto Press, 1974.

Hakon Broad-shoulder. In *Heimskringla: History of the Kings of Norway*, trans. L. M. Hollander. Austin: Published for the American-Scandinavian Foundation by the University of Texas Press, 1964.

Hakon the Good's Saga. In *Heimskringla: History of the Kings of Norway*, trans. L. M. Hollander. Austin: Published for the American-Scandinavian Foundation by the University of Texas Press, 1964.

Hald, K. Daner. In *Kulturhistorisk leksikon for nordisk middelalder*, ed. O. Olsen, P. Skautrup, N. Skyum-Nielsen and A. Steensberg. København: Rosenkilde og Bagger, 1959–77.

Hale, J. R. The Viking longship. *Scientific American*, Vol. 2245, 1998, pp. 46–53.

Hansen, S. S. The Norse landnam in the Faroe Islands in the light of recent excavations at Toftanes, Leirvík. *Northern Studies*, Vol. 25, 1988, pp. 58–84.

Hansen, U. L. Hobyfundet. In *Arkæologileksikon*, ed. L. Hedeager and K. Kristiansen. København: Politiken, 1986. pp. 125–26.

Hansen, U. L., Alexandersen, V. and Hatting, T., eds. *Himlingøje, Seeland, Europa: ein Gräberfeld der jüngeren römischen Kaiserzeit auf Seeland, seine Bedeutung und internationalen Beziehungen*. Nordiske fortidsminder. Serie B. Bd. XIII. København: Kongelige Nordiske Oldskriftselskab, 1995.

Harmer, F. E. *Anglo-Saxon Writs*. Manchester: Manchester University Press, 1952.

Harold Fairhair's Saga. In *Heimskringla: History of the Kings of Norway*, ed. L. M. Hollander. Austin: Published for the American-Scandinavian Foundation by the University of Texas Press, 1964.

Haywood, J. *Encyclopaedia of the Viking Age*. London: Thames & Hudson, 2000.

Heaney, S., trans. and ed. *Beowulf*. London: Faber and Faber, 1999.

Hedeager, L. Danmarkshistorien. Vol. II, *Danernes land: fra ca. 200 f.kr. til ca. 700 e.kr.*, 2. ed., exec. ed. O. Olsen. København: Gyldendal & Politiken, 2002 [1988].

Hedeager, L. and Kristiansen, K. Bendstrup: en fyrstegrav fra den romerske jernalder, dens sociale og historiske miljø. *KUML*, 1981, pp. 84–149.

eds. *Arkæologileksikon*. København: Politiken, 1986.

Hedeager, L. and Tvarnø, H. *Tusen års europahistorie: Romere, germanere og nordboere*. Oslo: Pax, 2001.

Heimskringla: History of the Kings of Norway, trans. L. M. Hollander. Austin: Published for the American-Scandinavian Foundation by the University of Texas Press, 1964.

Henderson, E. F., ed. and trans. *Select Historical Documents of the Middle Ages*. London: George Bell and Sons, 1910.

Henry of Livonia, *The Chronicle of Henry of Livonia*, ed. and trans. J. A. Brundage. Madison: University of Wisconsin Press, 1961.

Hewson, J. B. *A History of the Practice of Navigation*. Glasgow: Brown, Son & Ferguson, 1983.

Higham, N. J. The Scandinavians in north Cumbria: raids and settlement in the later ninth to mid-tenth centuries. In *The Scandinavians in Cumbria*, ed. J. R. Baldwin and I. D. Whyte. Edinburgh: Scottish Society for Northern Studies, 1985. pp. 37–51.

Historia Norvegiæ, ed. G. Storm. *Monumenta historica Norvegiæ: latinske kildeskrifter til Norges historie i middelalderen*. Kristiania: A. W. Brøger, 1880.

Hødnebo, F. Viking. In *Kulturhistorisk leksikon for nordisk middelalder*, ed. O. Olsen, P. Skautrup, N. Skyum-Nielsen and A. Steensberg. København: Rosenkilde og Bagger, 1959–77.

Hooper. N. Some observations on the navy in late Anglo-Saxon England. In *Studies in Medieval History Presented to R. Allen Brown*, ed. C. Harper-Bill, C. J. Holdsworth and J. L. Nelson. Wolfeboro: Boydell Press, 1989. pp. 203–13.

Hørby, K. Denmark. In *Medieval Scandinavia: An Encyclopedia*, ed. P. Pulsiano, assisted by K. Wolf. Garland Encyclopedias of the Middle Ages, 1. New York, London: Garland Publishing, 1993. pp. 127–30.

Hornell, J. The role of birds in early navigation. *Antiquity*, Vol. 20, 1946, pp. 142–49.

Howard, I. *Swein Forkbeard's Invasions and the Danish Conquest of England, 991–1017*. Warfare in History. Woodbridge: Boydell Press, 2003.

Hudson, B. T. Elech and the Scots in Strathclyde. *Scottish Gaelic Studies*, Vol. 15, 1988, pp. 145–49.

Knútr and Viking Dublin. *Scandinavian Studies*, Vol. 66 No. 3, 1994, pp. 319–35.

Hunter, J., ed. *The Pipe Rolls of 2–3–4 Henry II*. London: HMSO, 1930.

Hutchinson, G. The Southwold side rudders. *Antiquity*, Vol. 60, 1986, pp. 219–21.

Two English side-rudders. In *Shipshape: Essays for Ole Crumlin-Pedersen*, ed. O. Olsen, J. Skamby Madsen and F. Rieck. Roskilde: The Viking Ship Museum, 1995. pp. 97–102.

Medieval Ships and Shipping. The Archaeology of Medieval Britain. London: Leicester University Press, 1997 [1994].

Hvass, S. Vorbasse. The Viking-Age settlement at Vorbasse, central Jutland. *Acta Archaeologica*, Vol. 50 (for 1979), 1980, pp. 137–72.

Årtusinders landsby. *Skalk*, 3, 1984, pp. 20–30.

Vorbasse. The development of a settlement through the first millennium A.D. *Journal of Danish Archaeology*, Vol. 2, 1992, pp. 127–36.

Vorbasse, 190604–295. Digitale udgravningsarkiver. Kulturarvsstyre lsen (English summary) (http://udgravningsarkiver.ancher.kulturhotel.dk/vorbasse_summary.htm).

Vorbasse, 190604–295. Kulturarvsstyrelsen (Danish-language full excavation report) (Website) (http://udgravningsarkiver.ancher.kulturhotel.dk/vorbasse.htm).

Ilkjær, J. *Illerup Ådal.* Vols. III–IV, *Die Gürtel: Bestandteile und Zubehör.* Aarhus: Jutland Archaeological Society Publications, 25, 1993.

Fjender og forbundsfæller i romertidens Nordeuropa. In *Fiender og forbundsfeller: regional kontakt gjennom historien*, Karmøyseminaret, 1999 (http://www.illerup.dk/documents/illerup_78.pdf).

Illerup Ådal – et arkælogisk tryllespejl. Aarhus: Moesgård, 2000.

Centres of power in Scandinavia before the medieval kingdoms. In *Kingdoms and Regionality. Proceedings from the 49th Sahsensymposium 1998 in Uppsala.* Stockholm: Archaeological Research Laboratory Stockholm University, 2001 (http://www.illerup.dk/documents/illerup_75.pdf).

Illerup Ådal. Vols. IX–X, *Die Schilde.* Aarhus: Jutland Archaeological Society Publications, 25, 2001.

Danish war booty sacrifices. In *The Spoils of Victory: The North in the Shadow of the Roman Empire*, ed. L. Jørgensen, B. Storgaard and L. G. Thomsen. København: Nationalmuseet, 2003. pp. 44–65.

Illerup Ådal: Archaeology as a Magic Mirror. Aarhus: Moesgård, 2003.

Ilkjær, J. and Carnap-Bornheim, C. v. *Illerup Ådal.* Vols. I–II, *Die Lansen und Speere.* Aarhus: Jutland Archaeological Society Publications, 25, 1990.

Illerup Ådal. Vols. V–VIII, *Die Prachtausrüstungen.* Aarhus: Jutland Archaeological Society Publications, 25, 1996.

Import af romersk militærudstyr til Norge i yngre romertid. In *I et hus med mange rum: Vennebok til Bjørn Myhre på 60-årsdagen*, Bind A, AmS-rapport 11A, ed. I. Fuglestvedt, T. Gansum and A. Opedal (Online).

Ingi's Saga. In *Heimskringla: History of the Kings of Norway*, trans. L. M. Hollander. Austin: Published for the American-Scandinavian Foundation by the University of Texas Press, 1964.

Inncs, C., ed. *Registrum episcopatus Glasguensis munimenta ecclesie metropolitane Glasguensis a sede restaurata seculo ineunte XII ad reformatam religionem.* Edinburgh: Maitland Club Publications, 1843.

Iordanis Romana et Getica, ed. T. Mommsen. Gesellschaft für Ältere Deutsche Geschichtskunde. Berlin: Weidmann, 1882.

Iversen, J. The development of Denmark's nature since the last glacial. In *Danmarks geologiske undersøgelser*, V. Række, No. 7-C, 1973.

Jacobsen, G. Wicked Count Henry: the capture of Valdemar II (1223) and Danish influence in the Baltic. *Journal of Baltic Studies*, Vol. 9 No. 4, 1978, pp. 326–38.

Jensen, K. V. Denmark and the Second Crusade: the formation of a crusader state? In *The Second Crusade: Scope and Consequences*, ed. J. Phillips and M. Hoch. Manchester: Manchester University Press, 2001. pp. 164–79.

Jensen, S. *The Vikings of Ribe.* Ribe: Den Antikvariske Samling, 1991.

Jensen, X. P. The Vimose find. In *The Spoils of Victory: The North in the Shadow of the Roman Empire*, ed. L. Jørgensen, B. Storgaard and L. G. Thomsen. København: Nationalmuseet, 2003. pp. 224–39.

Johannson, A. Die erste Westrwiking. *Acta Philologica Scandinavica*, 1934, pp. 1–67.

Johansen, K. F. *Nordiske fortidsminder*. Vol. II.3, *Hoby-Fundet*. København: Gyldendalske Boghandel, 1923.

Johansen, R. T. Fra Ottars logbog. *Marinarkæologisk Nyhedsbrev fra Roskilde*, Vol. 18, 2002, pp. 28–33.

Jones, G. *Eirik the Red and Other Icelandic Sagas*. London: Oxford University Press, 1961.

The Vikings and North America. In *The Vikings*, ed. R. T. Farrell. London: Phillimore, 1982. pp. 219–30.

A History of the Vikings. Oxford, New York: Oxford University Press, 1984 [1968].

The Norse Atlantic Saga, Being the Norse Voyages of Discovery and Settlement to Iceland, Greenland, and North America. Oxford, New York: Oxford University Press, 1986 [1964].

Jørgensen, A. N. Fortifications and the control of land and sea traffic in the pre-Roman and Roman Iron Age. In *The Spoils of Victory: The North in the Shadow of the Roman Empire*, ed. L. Jørgensen, B. Storgaard and L. G. Thomsen. København: Nationalmuseet, 2003. pp. 194–210.

Jørgensen, E. *Fremmed indflydelse under den danske kirkes tidligste udvikling*. Det kongelige danske videnskabernes selskabs skrifter, 7 Række, Historisk og filosofisk afdeling I: 2. København: Bianco Luno, 1908.

Jørgensen, E. and Petersen, P. V. Nydam Bog: new finds and observations. In *The Spoils of Victory: The North in the Shadow of the Roman Empire*, ed. L. Jørgensen, B. Storgaard and L. G. Thomsen. København: Nationalmuseet, 2003. pp. 258–85.

Jørgensen, L. B. *North European Textiles until AD 1000*. Aarhus: Aarhus University Press, 1992.

Jørgensen, M. S. Vej, vejstrøg og vejspærringer: jernalderens landfærdsel. In *Fra stamme til stat i Danmark*. Vol. I, *Jernalderens stammesamfund*, ed. P. Mortensen and B. Rasmussen Århus: Jysk Arkæologisk Selskab i Kommission hos Aarhus Universitetsforlag, 1988. pp. 101–16.

Julius Caesar, *The Conquest of Gaul*. Harmondsworth: Penguin Books, 1963.

The Gallic War, ed. and trans. H. Edwards. London: William Heinemann Ltd, 1986 [1917].

Kapelle, W. E. *The Norman Conquest of the North: The Region and its Transformation, 1000–1135*. Chapel Hill: University of North Carolina Press, 1979.

Kaul, F. The Hjortspring find: the oldest of the large Nordic war booty sacrifices. In *The Spoils of Victory: The North in the Shadow of the Roman Empire*, ed. L. Jørgensen, B. Storgaard and L. G. Thomsen. København: Nationalmuseet, 2003, pp. 212–23.

Keillar, I. Kirkjubøur. *Northern Studies*, Vol. 20, 1983, pp. 38–44.

Keynes, S. Cnut's earls. In *The Reign of Cnut King of England, Denmark and Norway*, ed. A. Rumble. Studies in the Early History of Britain: Makers of England. Leicester: Leicester University Press, 1993. pp. 43–88.

The Vikings in England c. 790–716. In *The Oxford Illustrated History of the Vikings*, ed. P. H. Sawyer. Oxford: Oxford University Press, 1997. pp. 48–82.

King Harald's Saga. In *Heimskringla: History of the Kings of Norway*, trans. L. M. Hollander. Austin: Published for the American-Scandinavian Foundation by the University of Texas Press, 1964.

The King's Mirror (Speculum Regale [or] Konungs Skuggsjá) Translated from the Old Norwegian, ed. and trans. L. M. Larson. New York: The American-Scandinavian Foundation, 1917.

Klindt-Jensen, O. and Wilson, D. M. *Viking Art*. The Nordic Series, 6. Minneapolis: University of Minnesota Press, 1980.

Knytlingesaga, Knud den Store, Knud den Hellige, deres Mænd, deres Slægt, trans. J. P. Ægidius, introd. by H. Bekker-Nielsen and O. Widding. København: G. E. C. Gad, 1977.

Koch, H. *Den danske kirkes historie*. Vol. I, *Den ældre middelalder indtil 1241*, ed. H. Koch and B. Kornerup. København: Gyldendalsk Boghandel Nordisk Forlag, 1950.

Kokowski, A. Ein sogenanntes 'Fürstengrab' von Rudka in Wolhynien. Seine Bedeutung für die Rekonstruktion des Bildes der germanischen Eliten im späten Altertum. In *Military Aspects of the Aristocracy in Barbaricum in the Roman and Early Migration Period. Papers presented at an international research seminar at the Danish National Museum, Copenhagen, 10–11 December 1999*. Studies in archaeology and history, ed. B. Storgaard. Vol. V. København: The National Museum, 2001. pp. 41 – 53.

Krogh, K. J. *Viking Greenland*. København: The National Museum, 1967.

Kroman, E. Stadsprivilegier (Danmark). In *Kulturhistorisk leksikon for nordisk middelalder*, ed. O. Olsen, P. Skautrup, N. Skyum-Nielsen and A. Steensberg. København: Rosenkilde og Bagger, 1959–77.

Lamb, H. H. *Climate, History and the Modern World*. London, New York: Routledge, 1995 [1982].

Landnámabók. In *Origines Islandicae: A Collection of the more Important Sagas and other Native Writings relating to the Settlement and Early History of Iceland*, ed. and trans. G. Vigfusson and F. Y. Powell. Oxford: Clarendon Press, 1905.

Larson, L. M., ed. and trans. *The Earliest Norwegian Laws, Being the Gulathing Law and Frostathing Law*. New York: Columbia University Press, 1935.

Lavelle, R. *Aethelred II King of the English, 978–1016*. Kings and Queens of Medieval England. Stroud: Tempus, 2002.

Lawrie, A. C. *Early Scottish Charters prior to A.D. 1153*. Glasgow: J. MacLehose and Sons, 1905.

Lawson, M. K. Archbishop Wulfstan and the homiletic element in the laws of Athelred II and Cnut. In *The Reign of Cnut King of England, Denmark and Norway*, ed. A. Rumble. Studies in the Early History of Britain: Makers of England. Leicester: Leicester University Press, 1993, pp. 141–64.

Lawton, G. Monsters of the deep. *Scientific American*, Vol. 2297, 2001, pp. 28–32.

The Laxdale Saga, trans. M. Press, introd. P. Foote. Everyman's Library, 597. London: Dent, 1964.

Le Bon, L. Ancient ship graffiti: symbol and context. In *The Ship as Symbol in Prehistoric and Medieval Scandinavia. Papers from an international research seminar at the Danish National Museum, Copenhagen, 5–7 May 1994*, ed. O. Crumlin-Pedersen, and B. Munch Thye. Vol. I. Publications from the National Museum. København: Nationalmuseet, 1995. pp. 172–79.

Lewis, D. *We, the Navigators: The Ancient Art of Landfinding in the Pacific.* Honolulu: University Press of Hawaii, 1972.

   The Voyaging Stars: Secrets of the Pacific Island Navigators. London: Fontana, 1978.

Lidén, H.-E. Stadsbebyggelse och stadsplan (Norge). In *Kulturhistorisk leksikon for nordisk middelalder*, ed. O. Olsen, P. Skautrup, N. Skyum-Nielsen and A. Steensberg. København: Rosenkilde og Bagger, 1959–77.

Ljung, S. Gilde (Sverige). In *Kulturhistorisk leksikon for nordisk middelalder*, ed. O. Olsen, P. Skautrup, N. Skyum-Nielsen and A. Steensberg. København: Rosenkilde og Bagger, 1959–77.

Lönroth, L. The Vikings in history and legend. In *The Oxford Illustrated History of the Vikings*, ed. P. H. Sawyer. Oxford: Oxford University Press, 1997. pp. 225–49.

Lund, N. Cnut's Danish kingdom. In *The Reign of Cnut King of England, Denmark and Norway*, ed. A. R. Rumble. Studies in the Early History of Britain. Leicester: Leicester University Press, 1994. pp. 27–42.

   The Danish empire and the end of the Viking Age. In *The Oxford Illustrated History of the Vikings*, ed. P. H. Sawyer. Oxford: Oxford University Press, 1997. pp. 156–81.

Mac Airt, S., ed. and trans. *The Annals of Innis fallen.* Dublin: Dublin Institute for Advanced Studies, 1951.

MacCarthy, B. *The Codex Palatino-Vaticanus.* No. 830, *Texts, Translations and Indices by B. MacCarthy.* Todd lecture series, 3. Dublin: Royal Irish Academy, 1892.

MacFirbis, D. *Annals of Ireland. Three fragments, copied from ancient sources by Dubhaltach MacFirbisigh; and edited, with a translation and notes, from a manuscript preserved in the Burgundian Library at Brussels*, ed. J. O'Donovan. Dublin: Irish Archaeological and Celtic Society, 1860.

MacQuarrie, A. The Kings of Strathclyde, c. 400–1018. In *Medieval Scotland, Crown, Lordship and Community: Essays Presented to*

G.W.S Barrow, ed. A. Grant and K. Stringer. Edinburgh: Edinburgh University Press, 1993. pp. 5–11.

MacQueen, J. Picts in Galloway. *Transactions of the Dumfriesshire and Galloway Natural History and Antiquarian Society*, Vol. 39, 1960–61, pp. 137–43.

Magnus, B. En liten gylden ring. In *Drik – og du vil leve skønt: Festskrift til Ulla Lund Hansen på 60-årsdagen 18 august 2002*, ed. J. Pind, A. N. Jørgensen, B. Storgaard, P. Rindel and J. Ilkjær. Vol. VII. Publications from the National Museum, Studies in archaeology and history. København: Nationalmuseet, 2002. pp. 255–62.

Magnus Barefoot's Saga. In *Heimskringla: History of the Kings of Norway*, trans. L. M. Hollander. Austin: Published for the American-Scandinavian Foundation by the University of Texas Press, 1964.

Malmros, R. Leding og skjaldekvad. Det elvte århundredes nordiske krigsflåder, deres teknologi og organisation og deres placering i samfundet, belyst gennem den samtidige fyrstedigtning. *Aarbøger for nordisk oldkyndighed og historie*, 1985, pp. 89–139.

Marcus, G. J. The course for Greenland. *Saga-Book*, Vol. 14, 1953–57, pp. 12–35.

The navigation of the Norsemen. *Mariner's Mirror*, Vol. 29, 1953, pp. 112–31.

Hafvilla: a note on Norse navigation. *Speculum*, Vol. 30, 1955, pp. 601–5.

The Conquest of the North Atlantic. Woodbridge, Suffolk: Boydell Press, 1980.

Marcus, J. G. The Conquest of the North Atlantic. Woodbridge: Boydell, 1998 [1990]. pp. 16–32.

Marsden, J. *Somerled and the Emergence of Gaelic Scotland*. East Linton: Tuckwell Press, 2000.

Marsden, P. Early ships, boats and ports in Britain. In *Shipshape: Essays for Ole Crumlin-Pedersen*, ed. O. Olsen, J. Skamby Madsen and F. Rieck. Roskilde: The Viking Ship Museum, 1995. pp. 167–74.

Matthews, G. Recent developments in the study of bird navigation. *Journal of the Institute of Navigation*, Vol. 6, 1972, pp. 264–70.

McDonald, R. A. *The Kingdom of the Isles: Scotland's Western Seaboard in the Central Middle Ages, c. 1000–c. 1336*. Scottish Historical Review Monographs Series. East Lothian: Tuckwell Press, 1997.

McGrail, S. *Medieval Dublin Excavations, 1962–1981*. Vol. III, *Medieval Boat and Ship Timbers from Dublin*. Dublin: Royal Irish Academy, 1993.

Ancient Boats in NW Europe: The Archaeology of Water Transport to AD 1500. Longman Archaeology Series. London, New York: Longman 1997 [1987].

McGuire, B. P. *The Cistercians in Denmark: Their Attitudes, Roles, and Functions in Medieval Society*. Cistercian Studies Series. Kalamazoo: Cistercian Publications, 1982.

A Mediaeval Prince of Wales: The Life of Gruffudd Ap Cynan, ed. and trans. D. S. Evans. Felinfach: Llanerch, 1990.

Migne, J.-P. *Patrologiae Cursus Completus Series Latina*, Vol. CL, *Opera Alcuini*. Paris: Garnier, 1844–1905.

Monumenta Germaniae historica inde ab anno Christi quingentesimo usque ad annum millesimum et quingentesimum, ed. G. H. Pertz, G. Waitz, W. Wattenbach, R. Pauli, F. Liebermann, Finnur Jónsson, M. Perlbach, L. V. Heinemann, O. Holder-Egger and A. Hofmeister. Vol. V, *Annales ævi suevici*. Hanover: Hahn, 1826.

Monumenta Germaniae historica inde ab anno Christi quingentesimo usque ad annum millesimum et quingentesimum. Vol. XVIX, *Annales ævi suevici*. Hanover: Hahn.

Morcken, R. Norse nautical units and distance measurements. *Mariner's Mirror*, Vol. 54, 1968, pp. 393–401.

Morris, C. D. The Vikings in the British Isles: some aspects of their settlement and economy. In *The Vikings*, ed. R. T. Farrell. London: Phillimore, 1982. pp. 70–94.

Much, R., ed. and trans. *Die 'Germania' des Tacitus*, 3rd ed., ed. W. Lange, in collaboration with H. Jankuhn. Heidelburg: Winther, 1967 [1937].

Murray, N. Swerving from the path of justice: Alexander II's relations with Argyll and the Isles, 1214–49. In *Scotland in the Reign of Alexander II*, ed. R. Oram. Leiden: Brill, 2005.

Nadel-Klein, J. *Fishing for Heritage: Modernity and Loss along the Scottish Coast*. Oxford: Berg, 2003.

Näsman, U. Sea trade during the Scandinavian Iron Age: its character, commodities, and routes. In *Aspects of Maritime Scandinavia AD 200–1200. Proceedings of the Nordic seminar on maritime aspects of archaeology, Roskilde, 13–15 March 1989*, ed. O. Crumlin-Pedersen. Roskilde: Vikingeskibshallen, 1991. pp. 23–40.

Nelson, J. L. The Frankish Empire. In *The Oxford Illustrated History of the Vikings*, ed. P. H. Sawyer. Oxford: Oxford University Press, 1997. pp. 19–47.

Neumann, H. *Olgerdiget, et bidrag til Danmarks tidligste historie*. Skrifter fra museumsrådet for Sønderjyllands Amt. Haderslev: Haderslev Museum, 1982.

Nielsen, S. The bottom is formed. *Maritime Archaeology Newsletter from Roskilde*, No. 17, 2001.

Nissen, A. *Danske bisperækker*. Ansgariusforeningens skrifter. København: Ansgariusforeningen, 1935.

Njal's Saga, ed. and trans. M. Magnusson and H. Pálsson. Penguin Classics. London: Penguin Books, 1960.

Nørlund, P. *Trelleborg*. København: Nationalmuseet, 1945.

Oatley, K. Mental maps for navigation. *New Scientist*, 1974, pp. 863–66.

O'Corráin, D. *Ireland Before the Normans*. The Gill History of Ireland. Dublin: Gill and Macmillan, 1972.

O'Donovan, J., ed. and trans. *Annálaríoghachta Éireann: Annals of the Kingdom of Ireland by the Four Masters, from the Earliest Period to the*

Year 1616; Edited from MSS in the Library of the Royal Irish Academy and of Trinity College, Dublin, with a Translation, and Copious Notes, Dublin, 1851.

Olaf Tryggvi's Son's Saga. In *Heimskringla, History of the Kings of Norway*, ed. and trans. L. M. Hollander. Austin: University of Texas Press, 1964.

Olsen, O. and Crumlin-Pedersen, O. *Five Viking Ships from Roskilde Fjord*. København: National Museum of Denmark, 1990 [1978].

Oram, R. David I and the Scottish conquest and colonisation of Moray. *Northern Scotland*, Vol. 19, 1999, pp. 1–19.

   The Lordship of Galloway. Edinburgh: John Donald, 2000.

   Continuity, adaptation and integration: the earls and earldom of Mar, c. 1150–c. 1300. In *The Exercise of Power in Medieval Scotland c. 1200–1500*, ed. S. Boardman and A. Ross. Dublin: Four Courts Press, 2003. pp. 46–66.

   David I: The King Who Made Scotland. Stroud: Tempus, 2004.

The Orkneyinga Saga, ed. and trans. A. B. Taylor. Edinburgh: Oliver & Boyd, 1938.

Orkneyinga Saga, trans. and introd. by H. Pálsson and P. Edwards. Penguin Classics. Harmondsworth: Penguin Books, 1981.

Orkneyinga Saga: The History of the Earls of Orkney, trans. H. Pálsson and P. Edwards. London: Hogarth Press, 1978.

Ørsted, P. *Danmark før Danmark: Romerne og os*. København: Samleren, 1999.

Owen, O., Allen, A. and Dalland, M. *Scar. A Viking Boat Burial on Sanday, Orkney*. East Linton: Historic Scotland in association with Tuckwell Press, 1999.

Oxford Dictionary of English, ed. C. Soanes, A. Stevenson, J. Pearsall and P. Hanks. Oxford: Oxford University Press, 2003.

Page, R. I. *Chronicles of the Vikings: Records, Memorials, and Myths*. Toronto: University of Toronto Press, 1995.

Pálsson, H. *Keltar á Íslandi*. Reykjavík: Háskólaútgáfan, 1996.

   Vinland revisited. *Northern Studies*, Vol. 35, 2000, pp. 11–38.

Pedersen, F. The *fællig* and the family: the understanding of the family in Danish medieval law. *Continuity and Change*, Vol. 7 No. 1, 1992, pp. 1–12.

Pitchmann, L., comp. The Norsemen in America. In *The Vikings*, ed. R. T. Farrell. London: Phillimore, 1982, pp. 231–35.

Powers, R. Magnus Bareleg's expedition to the west. *Scottish Historical Review*, Vol. 65, 1986, pp. 107–32.

Procopius, with an English Translation, trans. H. B. Dewing. Loeb Classical Library. Cambridge, Mass.: Harvard University Press; London: W. Heinemann, 1953–62.

Pytheas, *Pytheas of Massilia on the Ocean*, trans. C. H. Roseman. Chicago: Ares, 1994.

Raine, J., ed. *The Historians of the Church of York and its Archbishops*. Rerum britannicarum medii aevi scriptores, 71. New York: Kraus Reprint, 1965 [1879–84].

Ramskou, T. Solstenen. *Skalk*, 2, 1967, pp. 16–17.

Randsborg, K. *The Viking Age in Denmark: The Formation of a State*. New York: St. Martin's Press, 1980.

Seafaring and society in south Scandinavian and European perspective. In *Aspects of Maritime Scandinavia AD 200–1200. Proceedings of the Nordic seminar on maritime aspects of archaeology, Roskilde, 13–15 March 1989*, ed. O. Crumlin-Pedersen. Roskilde: Vikingeskibshallen, 1991. pp. 11–22.

Rasmussen, B. B. The soldiers of the Roman Empire and the Roman army. In *The Spoils of Victory: The North in the Shadow of the Roman Empire*, ed. L. Jørgensen, B. Storgaard and L. G. Thomsen København: Nationalmuseet, 2003. pp. 149–64.

Rau, R. *Ausgewählte Quellen zur deutschen Geschichte des Mittelalters*. Vols. V–VII, *Quellen zur Karolingischen Reichsgeschichte I–III*. Unveränderter reprografischer Nachdruck der Ausg. von 1955–60, ed. Reinhold Rau. Berlin: Deutscher Verlag der Wissenschaften, 1966 [1955–60].

Registrum Monasterii de Passelet, ed. C. Innes. Edinburgh: Maitland Club, 1877.

Registrum S. Marie de Neubotle: Abbacie cisterciensis Beate Virginis de Neubotle chartarium vetus, 1140–1528, ed. C. Innes. Bannatyne Club Publications. Edinburgh: Bannatyne Club, 1849.

Rembert, Anskar, the Apostle of the North 801–965, trans. C. H. Robinson. Lives of Early and Mediaeval Missionaries. London: The Society for the Propagation of the Gospel in Foreign Parts, 1921.

Reuter, T., ed. *The Annals of Fulda*. Ninth-Century Histories, 2. Manchester: Manchester University Press, 1992.

Ridel, E. Viking maritime heritage in Normandy from a British Isles perspective. *Northern Studies*, Vol. 35, 2000, pp. 79–93.

Rieck, F. Aspects of coastal defence in Denmark. In *Aspects of Maritime Scandinavia AD 200–1200*. Roskilde: Viking Ship Museum, 1991. pp. 83–96.

The ships from Nydam Bog. In *The Spoils of Victory: The North in the Shadow of the Roman Empire*, ed. L. Jørgensen, B. Storgaard and L. G. Thomsen. København: Nationalmuseet, 2003. pp. 296–309.

Ritchie, A. *Prehistoric Orkney*. London: Batsford and Historic Scotland, 1995.

Ritchie, J. *Excavations at Machrins, Colonsay*. Proceedings of the Society of Antiquaries of Scotland, 111. Edinburgh: Society of Antiquaries of Scotland, 1991.

Rixson, D. *The West Highland Galley*. Edinburgh: Birlinn, 1998.

Rodger, N. *A Naval History of Britain*. Vol. I (660–1649), *The Safeguard of the Sea*. London: HarperCollins, 1997.

Roesdahl, E. *The Vikings*. London: Penguin Books, 1998 [1987].

Vikingetid og trosskifte (800–1050). In *Middelalderens Danmark*, ed. P. Ingesman, U. Kjær, P. K. Madsen and J. Vellev. København: Gads Forlag, 1999. pp. 16–27.

Roger of Wendover, *Liber qui dicitur Flores historiarum ab anno domini MCLIV. annoque Henrici anglorum regis secundi primo*, ed. H. G. Hewlett. London: Printed for H. M. Stationery Office by Eyre and Spottiswode, 1886.

Ronay, G. *The Lost King of England: The East European Adventures of Edward the Exile.* Wolfeboro: Boydell Press, 1989.

Room, A. *Brewer's Dictionary of Names.* London, New York: Cassell, 1992.

Rosenwein, B. H. *A Short History of the Middle Ages.* Peterborough, Ontario: Broadview Press, 2002.

Roskildekrøniken, trans. and ed. M. Gelting. København: Wormanium, 1979.

Royal Commission on the Ancient and Historical Monuments of Scotland, *Argyll: An Inventory of the Ancient Monuments.* Vol. IV, *Iona.* Edinburgh: Royal Commission on the Ancient and Historical Monuments of Scotland, 1982.

Rud, M. *The Bayeux Tapestry and the Battle of Hastings, 1066.* København: Christian Eilers, 1996 [1974].

The Saga of the Greenlanders, trans. K. Kunz. In *The Sagas of Icelanders*, ed. Ö. Thorsson. London: Penguin, 2001. pp. 636–52.

The Saga of the People of Laxardal, trans. K. Kunz. In *The Sagas of Icelanders*, ed. Ö. Thorsson. London: Penguin, 2001. pp. 270–421.

The Saga of the People of Vatnsdal, trans. A. Wawn. In *The Sagas of Icelanders*, ed. Ö. Thorsson. London: Penguin, 2001. pp. 185–269.

The Saga of Sigurd the Crusader and his Brothers Eystein and Olaf. In *Heimskringla: History of the Kings of Norway*, trans. L. M. Hollander. Austin: Published for the American-Scandinavian Foundation by the University of Texas Press, 1964.

St Olaf's Saga. In *Heimskringla, History of the Kings of Norway*, ed. and trans. L. M. Hollander. Austin: Published for the American-Scandinavian Association by the University of Texas Press, 1964.

Sawyer, P. II. *Kings and Vikings: Scandinavia and Europe, A.D. 700–1100.* London, New York: Methuen, 1982.

Cnut's Scandinavian empire. In *The Reign of Cnut King of England, Denmark and Norway*, ed. A. R. Rumble. Studies in the Early History of Britain. Leicester: Leicester University Press, 1994. pp. 10–26.

Gyldendal og Politikens Danmarkshistorie. Vol. III, *Da Danmark blev Danmark*, gen. ed. O. Olsen, trans. M. Hvidt. København: Gyldendal & Politiken, 2002 [1986].

Saxo Grammaticus, *Danmarks riges krønike*, trans. F. W. Horn. København: Gyldendalske Boghandel, 1980.

Danorum regum herorumque historia. Books X–XVI. The text of the first edition with translation and commentary in three volumes, ed. and trans. E. Chistiansen. Oxford: B.A.R., 1980. Vol. LXXXIV.

Sayers, W. The etymology and semantics of Old Norse knörr 'cargo ship'. The Irish and English evidence. *Scandinavian Studies*, Vol. 68, 1996, pp. 279–90.

A Norse etymology for luff 'weather-edge of a sail'. *American Neptune*, Vol. 61, 2001, pp. 25–38.

Schnall, U. Early shiphandling and navigation in northern Europe. In *The Earliest Ships: The Evolution of Boats into Ships*, ed. R. Gardiner and A. E. Christensen. Conway's History of the Ship. London: Conway Maritime Press, 1996. pp. 120–28.

Sharp, A. *Ancient Voyagers in the Pacific*. Harmondsworth: Penguin Books, 1957.

Shead, N. The origins of the medieval diocese of Glasgow. *Scottish Historical Review*, Vol. 48, 1969, pp. 220–25.

Simek, R. Old Norse ship names and ship terms. *Northern Studies*, Vol. 13, 1979, pp. 26–36.

Simpson, I., Dugmore, A., Thomson, A. and Vésteinsson, O. Crossing the thresholds: human ecology and historical patterns of landscape degradation. *Catena*, Vol. 41, 2001, pp. 175–92.

Simpson, I., Vésteinsson, O., Adderley, W. and McGovern, T. Fuel resource utilisation in landscapes of settlement. *Journal of Archaeological Science*, Vol. 30, 2003, pp. 1401–20.

Skeggjason, M. *Eiríksdrápa*. In *Den Norsk-Islandske Skjaldedigtning*, ed. Finnur Jónsson. Vol. I. København og Kristiania: Gyldendal, Nordisk Forlag, 1912.

Skene, W. F. *Chronicles of the Picts, Chronicles of the Scots, and Other Early Memorials of Scottish History*. Edinburgh: HM General Register House, 9, 1867.

Skene, W. F., ed. and Skene, F. J. H., trans. *The Historians of Scotland*. Vol. IV, *John of Fordun's Chronicle of the Scottish Nation*. Edinburgh: Edmonston and Douglas, 1872.

Skovgaard-Petersen, I. Oldtid og vikingetid. In *Danmarks historie*. Vol. I, *Tiden indtil 1340*, exec. ed. A. E. Christensen, H. P. Clausen, Svend Ellehøj and Søren Mørch. København: Gyldendal, 1980.

Skyum-Nielsen, N., ed. *Diplomatarium danicum*, 1. Række, Vol. IV, *Diplomatarium danicum 1200–1210*, Det danske sprog- og litteraturselskab. København: Ejnar Munksgaard Forlag, 1958.

Diplomatarium danicum, 1. Række, Vol. V, *Diplomatarium danicum 1211–1223*, Det danske sprog- og litteraturselskab. København: Ejnar Munksgaard Forlag, 1958.

Estonia under Danish rule. In *Danish Medieval History: New Currents. A Symposium held in celebration of the 500th anniversary of the University of Copenhagen*, ed. N. Skyum-Nielsen and N. Lund. København: Museum Tusculanum Press, 1981. pp. 112–35.

Smyth, A. P. *Scandinavian York and Dublin: The History and Archaeology of Two Related Viking Kingdoms*. Vol. II. Dublin: Humanities Press/ Templekieran Press, 1979.

New History of Scotland. Vol. I, *Warlords and Holy Men: Scotland, AD 80–1000*. London: Edward Arnold, 1984.

King Alfred the Great. Oxford: Oxford University Press, 1995.

Effect of Scandinavian raiders on the English and Irish churches: a preliminary reassessment. In *Britain and Ireland 900–1300. Insular Responses to Medieval European Change*, ed. A. P. Smyth and B. Smith. Cambridge: Cambridge University Press, 1998. pp. 1–38.

Snorri Sturluson, *King Harald's Saga: Harald Hardradi of Norway*, ed. and trans. M. Magnusson and H. Pálsson. Penguin Classics. Harmondsworth: Penguin, 1966.

Heimskringla, or The Lives of the Norse Kings, ed. E. Monsen, trans. A. H. Smith. New York: Dover, 1990.

Søgård, H. Gilde (Danmark). In *Kulturhistorisk leksikon for nordisk middelalder*, ed. O. Olsen, P. Skautrup, N. Skyum-Nielsen and A. Steensberg. København: Rosenkilde og Bagger, 1959–77.

Stadsbebyggelse och stadsplan (Danmark). In *Kulturhistorisk leksikon for nordisk middelalder*, ed. O. Olsen, P. Skautrup, N. Skyum-Nielsen and A. Steensberg. København: Rosenkilde og Bagger, 1959–77.

Sørensen, A. C. In *Ships and Boats of the North*, ed. O. Crumlin-Pedersen and O. Olsen. Vol. III, *Ladby: A Ship Grave from the Viking Age*, in collaboration with V. Bischoff, K. Jensen and H. Henrichsen. Roskilde: Viking Ship Museum, 2001.

Steenstrup, J. *Normannerne*. Vol. I, *Indledning i Normannertiden*. København: Rudolph Klein, 1876.

Steenstrup, J. C. H. R. Oldtiden og den ældre middelalder. In *Danmarks riges historie*, ed. J. Steenstrup, K. Erslev, A. Heise, V. Mollerup, J. A. Fridericia, E. Holm and A. D. Jørgensen. København: Nordiske forlag, E. Bojesen, 1897–1904.

Stenton, F. M. *The Oxford History of England*. Vol. II, *Anglo-Saxon England*. Oxford: Oxford University Press, 1947 [1943].

Storgaard, B. The Årslev grave and connections between Funen and the continent at the end of the later Roman Iron Age. In *The Archaeology of Gudme and Lundeborg. Papers presented at a conference at Svendborg, October 1991*. Akræologiske Studier, ed. P.O. Nielsen and K. Randsborg. Vol. X. København: Akademisk Forlag, 1994. pp. 160–68.

Cosmopolitan aristocrats. In *The Spoils of Victory: The North in the Shadow of the Roman Empire*, ed. L. Jørgensen, B. Storgaard and L. G. Thomsen. København: Nationalmuseet, 2003. pp. 106–25.

Storm, G., ed. *Islandske Annaler indtil 1578*. Christiania: Grøndahl & søns Bogtrykkeri, 1888.

Straume, E. The grave from Nordre Rør, Rygge, Østfold: The burial of a Danish woman from the 3rd century AD? In *Trade and Exchange in Prehistory. Studies in Honour of Berta Stjernquist*. Acta archaeologica lundensia. Lund: Lunds Universitets Historiske Museum, 1988. pp. 167–76.

Sveinbjarnardóttir, G. The question of *papar* in Iceland. In *The Papar in the North Atlantic Environment and History. The proceedings of a day conference* held on 24 February 2001, ed. B. E. Crawford. Vol. V: 1, *The Papar Project*. St Andrews: University of St Andrews, 2002. pp. 97–106.

Swanton, M. J. King Alfred's ships: text and context. *Anglo-Saxon England*, Vol. 28, 1999, pp. 1–22.

Symeonis monachi opera omnia, ed. T. Arnold. Rerum britannicarum medii aevi scriptores, 51, 75. New York: Kraus Reprint Ltd, 1965 [1885].

Tacitus, *Germania*, ed. and trans. N. W. Bruun and A. A. Lund. Vols. I–II. Århus: Wormanium, 1974.

Taylor, E. G. R. *The Haven-Finding Art: A History of Navigation from Odysseus to Captain Cook*. London: Hollis and Carter for the Institute of Navigation, 1971.

Theodoricus monachus Nidrosiensi, *De regibus vetustis Norvagicis.*, ed. B. C. Kirchmann and J. Kirchmann. Amsterdam: Apud Jansonio Waesbergios, 1684.

Thirslund, S. Navigation by the Vikings on the open sea. In *Viking Voyages to North America*, ed. B. L. Clausen. Roskilde: Vikingeskibsmuseet, 1993, pp. 109–17.

   Viking Navigation [Sun-Compass Guided Norsemen First to America]. Humblebæk, Denmark: S. Thirslund, 1996.

Thomson, W. P. L. *History of Orkney*. Edinburgh: Mercat Press, 1987.

Thrall, W. F. Clerical sea pilgrimages and the 'Imramma'. The *Manly Anniversary Studies*, 1923, pp. 278–83.

Tierney, B., ed. *The Middle Ages*. Vol. I, *Sources of Medieval History*, 5 ed. New York: McGraw-Hill, 1992 [1983].

Todd, M. and Fleming, A. *The South-West to AD 1000*. Regional History of England. London, New York: Longman, 1987.

Topping, P. Harald Maddadson, earl of Orkney and Caithness, 1139–1206. *Scottish Historical Review*, Vol. 62, 1983, pp. 105–20.

Trillmich, W. and Buchner, R. *Quellen des 9. und 11. Jahrhunderts zur Geschichte der hamburgischen Kirche und des Reiches*. Vol. XI, Rimbert, *Leben Ansgars*; Adam von Bremen, *Bischofsgeschichte der Hamburger Kirche*; Wipo, *Taten Kaiser Konrads II*. Neu übertragen, trans. K. Nobbe and R. Buchner. Ausgewählte Quellen zur deutschen Geschichte des Mittelalters. Berlin: Rütten & Loening, 1961.

Two Voyagers at the Court of King Alfred: The Ventures of Ohthere and Wulfstan, Together with the Description of Northern Europe from the Old English Orosius, ed. N. Lund, trans. C. E. Fell. York: Sessions, 1984.

Urbánczyk, P. Ethnic aspects of the settlement of Iceland. In *Papa Stour and 1299: Commemorating the 700th Anniversary of Shetland's First Document*, ed. B. E. Crawford and J. G. Jorgensen. Lerwick: Shetland Times, 2002. pp. 155–66.

Vinner, M. *Unnasigling* – the seaworthiness of the merchant vessel. In *Viking Voyages to North America*, ed. B. Clausen. Roskilde: Vikingeskibshallen, 1993. pp. 95–108.

A Viking ship off Cape Farewell. In *Shipshape: Essays for Ole Crumlin-Pedersen*, ed. O. Olsen, J. Skamby Madsen and F. Rieck. Roskilde: The Viking Ship Museum, 1995. pp. 289–304.

Viking Ship Museum Boats. Roskilde: The Viking Ship Museum, 2002.

Wallace, B. L. L'Anse aux Meadows. Gateway to Vinland. *Acta Archaeologica*, Vol. 61, 1990, pp. 166–97.

Ward, G. The Vikings came to Thanet. *Archaologia Cantiana*, 1950, pp. 57–62.

Weibull, C. H. J. *Saxo: kritiska undersökningar i Danmarks historia från Sven Estridsens död till Knut VI*. Lund: Berlingska Boktryckeriet, 1915.

Weibull, L. *Kritiska undersökningar i Nordens historia omkring år 1000*. Lund: C. W. K. Gleerup, 1911.

Necrologium Lundense. Lunds Domkyrkas Nekrologium. Lund: Berlingska Boktryckeriet, 1923.

ed. *Diplomatarium danicum*, 1. Række, Vol. II, *Diplomatarium danicum 1053–1169*, in collaboration with N. Skyum-Nielsen. Det danske sprog- og litteraturselskab. København: Ejnar Munksgaards Forlag, 1963.

Wenskus, R. *Stammesbildung und Verfassung*. Cologne: Böhlau, 1961.

White, L., Jr. The expansion of technology 500–1500. In *The Fontana Economic History of Europe*. Vol. I, *The Middle Ages*, ed. C. M. Cipolla. London: Collins/Fontana Books, 1972. pp. 143–74.

Whitelock, D., ed. *English Historical Documents*. Vol. I, *English Historical Documents, c. 500–1042*, gen. ed. D. C. Douglas. London: Eyre and Spottiswode, 1955.

Whitney, J. P. The reform of the Church. In *The Cambridge Medieval History*. Vol. V, *Contest of Empire and Papacy*. Cambridge: Cambridge University Press, 1926. pp. 1–51.

Whyte, I. Climatic change and the North Atlantic seaways during the Norse expansion. *Northern Studies*, Vol. 21, 1984, pp. 22–33.

Wickham-Jones, C. R. *Orkney: A Historical Guide*. Edinburgh: Birlinn, 1998.

Wikstrøm, L. Stadsprivilegier (Sverige). In *Kulturhistorisk leksikon for nordisk middelalder*, ed. O. Olsen, P. Skautrup, N. Skyum-Nielsen and A. Steensberg. København: Rosenkilde og Bagger, 1959–77.

William of Malmesbury, *Gesta regum Anglorum: The History of the English Kings*, ed. and trans. R. A. B. Mynors. Oxford Medieval Texts, 1. Oxford, New York: Clarendon Press, 1998.

Wilson, D. M., ed. *The Northern World: The History and Heritage of Northern Europe, AD 400–1100*. London: Thames and Hudson, 2003 [1980].

Index